DATE DUE

Unless Recalled Earlier

DEMCO, INC. 38-2931

The Coast Guard in World War I

The

COAST GUARD

in

WORLD WAR I

An Untold Story

Alex R. Larzelere

Naval Institute Press
Annapolis, Maryland

Naval Institute Press

291 Wood Road

Annapolis, MD 21402

Library of Congress Cataloging-in-Publication Data

Larzelere, Alex, 1936–

  The Coast Guard in World War I : an untold story / Alex R. Larzelere.

    p. cm.

  ISBN 1-55750-476-8 (hard: alk. paper)

  1. World War, 1914–1918—Naval operations, American. 2. United States. Coast Guard—History—World War, 1914–1918. I. Title: Coast Guard in World War One. II. Title: Coast Guard in World War 1. III. Title.

  D589.U6L37 2003

  940.4'5973—dc21

                                        2002153480

Printed in the United States of America on acid-free paper ∞

10 09 08 07 06 05 04 03   9 8 7 6 5 4 3 2

First printing

To my wife Rita, with appreciation for her patience and understanding.

CONTENTS

FOREWORD

The second decade of the twentieth century was an enormously crucial time for the U.S. Coast Guard. It was an even more ominous decade for the world as a whole as the first truly global conflict raged in the trenches of Europe in what was commonly referred to as the "War to End All Wars." Unfortunately, as we all know, this was a misnomer. Every one of us has personal references to the World War I period of time through our family and friends. I have four such points of reference. First, as a coast guard officer for thirty-eight years, I am keenly aware of the importance of 28 January 1915. On that day, Congress, after intense debate and with significant recommendations to the contrary, created the modern-day U.S. Coast Guard by combining the Revenue-Cutter Service and the Life-Saving Service. The direction then set by Captain Commandant Ellsworth P. Bertholf continued the service to America that had begun in 1790 and continues today. Second, on Coast Guard Hill at Arlington National Cemetery stands a monument to the lives lost on the cutters *Seneca* and *Tampa*, as brilliantly described in these pages. Four years ago an annual Armistice Day ceremony was initiated at the site to remind all coast guardmen and coast guardwomen that their legacy is a proud and enduring one. The ceremony grows in size every year. Third, I have always been fascinated not only by the war at sea but also by the diplomatic intrigue associated with World War I. I selected the end of U.S. neutrality in the war as my thesis topic for graduate studies at Wesleyan University in 1970. The role played by the infamous Zimmermann telegram is covered factually in these pages and is the subject of a book length treatment by gifted historian Barbara Tuchman. The calculated use of the content of the communiqué to the Mexican government was brilliantly timed by the British to influence American public opinion and the ongoing debate in Congress. The information completely disillusioned President Woodrow Wilson. Only a month after being re-elected because "he kept us out of war," the president sent his war message to Congress.

Mostly, however, I must simply admit to being deeply honored by my former commanding officer. I gratefully offer a foreword to his third significant contribution to the storied history of our beloved service. Our service together aboard coast guard cutter *Courageous* in 1974–1975 offered me a wonderful opportunity to learn about respect and professional excellence. His earlier treatments of our common experiences in Vietnam and in the 1980 Cuban boatlift are reflective of his meticulous research and objective storytelling ability. I remember like yesterday the conversations we had at the wardroom table. He had just come from an assignment as President Richard Nixon's military aide-de-camp. I had just finished a teaching tour at the Coast Guard Academy and had been deeply influenced by graduate work at a very liberal university in the late 1960s. We often clashed intellectually, sometimes so much so that the junior officers would disappear from the table! What was always part of those conversations was learning and appreciation for opinions that were not necessarily our own. Alex Larzelere's *The Coast Guard in World War I* is a treatise based on historical research rather than contemporary anecdotes. It is a story of organizational flexibility and individual heroism. It documents the contribution made by our small proud service in the many different venues that were important to the success of the American experience in World War I. This book should be read by all.

During my time as commandant, I tried to revive an interest in and appreciation for our history as America's guardian. Within these pages, Alex Larzelere reminds all us U.S. Coast Guard service members just how proud we have the right to be.

ADM. (RET.) JAMES M. LOY, USCG
COMMANDANT U.S. COAST GUARD, 1998–2002

PREFACE AND ACKNOWLEDGMENTS

The U.S. Coast Guard has always been a major influence in my life. I grew up in a coast guard family, where service traditions and a sense of history were always important. My father, a career enlisted man, retired the year I reported to the U.S. Coast Guard Academy. As I progressed through my twenty-nine-year career, my awareness of the importance of my service's heritage continued to increase. I came to realize that the U.S. Coast Guard's history and traditions were the foundation for its future. During my duty aboard seven cutters, five of which I commanded, I was constantly reminded of the continuous connection between today's cuttermen and those of earlier times. Rituals such as holding colors, rendering honors, making evening reports, and reporting the approach of noon were all links to the past. Ship's logs, written more than seventy-five years ago, contain the same standard entries being recorded today. Despite rapid transformations in technology, customs and traditions still provide a sense of continuity and order for today's U.S. Coast Guard.

World War I was an important time in U.S. Coast Guard history, but has received limited attention. After the merger of the Revenue-Cutter Service and the Life-Saving Service, the service was adapting to a new organization. It was a time of new innovations: communications were improved; aviation was introduced; and new missions, such as port security, were initiated. Service with the U.S. Navy during the war broadened the perspectives of the U.S. Coast Guard's relatively conservative personnel. When the service was transferred to the U.S. Navy on 6 April

1917, it was the beginning of a period of unprecedented integration. The small service was literally absorbed by the large naval establishment. Cutters and cuttermen did not just serve with the U.S. Navy, they became U.S. Navy. Coast guard personnel, particularly officers, were ordered to navy ships and units, just the same as navy personnel. Navy officers and enlisted men, primarily reserves, were similarly assigned to coast guard cutters for duty.

At the time of the war, the U.S. Coast Guard was a small service, with an authorization for less than 5,200 officers and men. It continued to remain small with only a modest increase in manpower to 6,500 by the time the war ended. During the same period, however, the navy experienced explosive growth. It increased from 69,000 men, at the war's beginning, to more than half a million officers and men. While the U.S. Coast Guard was a relatively insignificant force, in comparison to the U.S. Navy, its supply of experienced mariners proved to be an important asset. It was an asset the navy sorely needed to fill positions of responsibility in its rapidly expanded force. The success experienced by coast guardsmen, in serving with the U.S. Navy, instilled the service with confidence and strengthened its character for the future. The war was also a time of great sorrow for the U.S. Coast Guard. The cruising cutter USS *Tampa* was sunk by a German submarine near the end of the war. The loss of the cutter with all hands caused the U.S. Coast Guard to suffer the highest percentage of casualties of all the American armed forces.

The degree to which coast guard personnel and assets were integrated into the navy made research for this book difficult. The activities of coast guard cutters and personnel were buried in naval records. The National Archives had very few files that dealt separately with coast guard activities during the war. The most significant information available at the National Archives was found in cutter logs, including the logs of the six cutters deployed to the European war zone. When I first began work on the project, I went to the National Archives to see what materials were available. When an archivist asked if I would like to look at any of the cutter logs, I asked to see the wartime logs of the cutter *Tampa*. I went to the main reading room and, after a short wait, a box was put on the table in front of me. When I opened the container, there were *Tampa*'s original logs. They were complete up to the month before it was sunk. Before me were the handwritten entries and signatures of the young officers and petty officers who perished less than one month later in the cold waters of the Bristol Channel. I was overwhelmed; I just sat for a minute, staring at the pages.

The most important document I found, and one I used heavily in my research, was the unpublished "History of the Coast Guard in the World War." Work was begun on the manuscript by Cdr. Charles E. Johnston at Coast Guard Headquarters in October 1919. Working from official records, he documented the U.S. Coast Guard's participation during the war. His efforts continued until his death on 30 May 1920. A year later Cdr. Richard O. Crisp was ordered to special duty at headquarters, to complete the work. Crisp finished the manuscript in 1922, but it was never published. A copy of the manuscript was in the Coast Guard Historian's Office and portions of the original manuscript were at the Department of Transportation Library. Another document, which proved to be extremely valuable in researching the subject, was compiled by the assistant commandant of the U.S. Coast Guard in 1933: a bound book entitled *Record of the Movements, Vessels of the United States Coast Guard: 1790–December 31, 1933*. In addition to the assignment of cutters during the 143-year period, the book contains a 59-page section devoted to World War I. The section listed all the navy ships coast guardsmen served on during the war and detailed the wartime duty assignments of all the service's officers.

Correspondence and telephone interviews with relatives of coast guardsmen who served during the war were also very helpful in bringing the history of the era to life. Unfortunately, they were one of the few sources available for information about the activities of enlisted men during the period. Milton R. Daniels Jr. sent me a copy of a document his father brought back from Europe after the war. The 190-page "Supplement to the Monthly Navy List" contained excellent data. It showed the basing of all U.S. naval forces operating in European waters and where each officer was assigned. It provided confirmation on the assignment of coast guard officers to navy ships.

The U.S. Coast Guard historian Robert Browning and his assistant historian Scott Price were very helpful in providing coast guard documents for me to review. I am also grateful for the valuable assistance and access to primary source material provided by Cindee Herrick, curator of the Coast Guard Museum in New London, Connecticut; Glenn Helm, head of reference at the Navy Library in Washington, D.C.; Fielding Tyler, executive director of the Old Coast Guard Station at Virginia Beach, Virginia; and Gene Davis, director of the Coast Guard Museum Northwest in Seattle, Washington. The research assistance provided by the staffs of the National Archives, the Library of Congress, the Naval War College Library, the National Defense University Library, the New York Public Library, and the Mariners' Museum, was also appreciated.

Appendixes were compiled to give concise information for the various resources associated with the U.S. Coast Guard's contribution to the war effort. Coast guard cutters were transferred to the U.S. Navy when war was declared on 6 April 1917 (Appendix A). Appendix B lists navy ships commanded by coast guard officers. Coast guard officers were also assigned to other navy ships (Appendix C). Coast guard officers commanded and served aboard troop transports (Appendix D). The organization of coast guard coastal stations transferred to the navy at the outbreak of war is detailed in Appendix E. Numerous coast guardsmen, some posthumously, were honored for distinctive service during the war (Appendix F).

CHRONOLOGY

1914

28 June   Assassination of Archduke Franz Ferdinand, heir to the Austrian Empire, at Sarajevo, Bosnia, brings Europe to the brink of war.

28 July   Germany declares war on Serbia and bombards Belgrade. Russia mobilizes.

1 Aug.   Russia declares war on Germany. The war eventually pits the Allies (England, France, Russia, Belgium, Serbia, Montenegro, and Japan) against the Central Powers (Germany, Austria-Hungary, and the Ottoman Empire).

4 Aug.   President Wilson proclaims United States neutrality.

1915

7 May   German submarine torpedoes British passenger liner SS *Lusitania* without warning. Of the 1,198 people killed when the ship sinks, 128 are Americans.

23 May   Italy declares war on Austria.

1916

28 Jan.   Congress creates the U.S. Coast Guard by combining the Revenue-Cutter Service and the Life-Saving Service.

21 Mar.   Third Lt. Elmer F. Stone is the first officer ordered to flight training.

| 7–8 Oct. | German submarine anchors at Newport, Rhode Island. Its captain goes ashore to obtain information about ships leaving New York. The submarine gets under way and sinks five Allied ships. |
| 13 Nov. | Interdepartmental Board on Coastal Communications recommends U.S. Coast Guard be given the means to bring its coastal telephone communications system to a high state of readiness and extend the system to include all stations as well as lighthouses and other government coastal facilities. |

1917

31 Jan.	Germany declares unrestricted submarine warfare against all ships trading with its enemies.
3 Feb.	United States recalls its ambassador to Germany and severs diplomatic relations.
21 Feb.	German submarine sinks United States tanker SS *Healdton* without warning in a safe zone off the coast of Holland. American seamen are killed.
1 Mar.	German Foreign Minister Arthur Zimmermann sends secret communiqué to Mexico, proposing an alliance against the United States. When content of the intercepted message is revealed, Americans are outraged.
22 Mar.	Coast guard commandant issues Confidential Order No. 2, "Mobilization of the U.S. Coast Guard When Required to Operate as a Part of the Navy." Third Lieutenant Stone completes flight training and becomes the U.S. Coast Guard's first aviator.
2 Apr.	President Woodrow Wilson asks Congress for declaration of war.
6 Apr.	United States declares war on Germany. Armed forces mobilize and the U.S. Coast Guard transfers to the U.S. Navy. Cutters report to naval districts for

duty. Cutters provide armed parties to seize German ships interned in U.S. ports.

Engineers from the cutter *Itasca* prevent Germans from scuttling ship in San Juan Harbor.

16 Apr.   Harbor cutters *Hudson* and *Wissahickon* are outfitted for minesweeping and commence sweeping operations in New York's Ambrose Channel.

1 May   Capt. Harry G. Hamlet takes command of Bensonhurst Naval Training Camp and Section Base No. 6 in New York.

13 May   *Algonquin* is designated flagship for Patrol Squadron Three, operating out of Guantánamo Bay, Cuba.

8 June   *Manning* rescues passenger and crew from Portuguese ship *Ile de St. Hiago*, which foundered off Block Island, Rhode Island.

13 June   SS *Governor* collides with cruising cutter *McCulloch* in fog off the California coast. When cutter sinks, entire crew is rescued. One man later dies at hospital.

15 June   President Wilson signs Espionage Act of 1917. The act shifts responsibility for regulation of anchorages and movement of vessels from Army Corps of Engineers to the Treasury Department. Regulations are to be enforced by the U.S. Coast Guard.

21 June   Navy assigns 2d Lt. Paul H. Harrison as the first commanding officer of the naval training camp being built at Cape May, New Jersey.

3 Aug.   Cruising cutter *Yamacraw* is ordered to shipyard to be "outfitted for distant service."

9 Aug.   U.S. Coast Guard begins providing officers and men to man converted yachts, U.S. Coast and Geodetic Survey vessels, and Fish Commission vessels acquired by the U.S. Navy.

30 Aug.   *Ossipee* arrives at Gibraltar and reports for duty to the commander of Patrol Force, Atlantic Fleet.

11 Sept.	Sr. Capt. William E. Reynolds is designated chief of staff by the commandant of the Twelfth Naval District.
1 Oct.	*Mohawk* is struck by British tanker *Vennachar* while on patrol at entrance to New York harbor. All hands are rescued when the cutter sinks.
19 Oct.	*Seneca* sails as the first U.S. Coast Guard ocean escort, convoying eleven ships from Gibraltar to Wales.
27 Oct.	*Tampa* is last of six cruising cutters to reach Gibraltar.
10 Nov.	Navy begins assigning U.S. Coast Guard officers to six seized German and Austrian cruise liners that will be used as troop transports. Officers serve in billets as commanding officer, executive officer, chief engineer, and navigator.
6 Dec.	French SS *Mont Blanc*, loaded with explosives, blows up in Halifax harbor. Rescue party from *Morrill*, anchored in the harbor, is the first to reach the devastated city.
8 Dec.	Navy assigns coast guard officers to five navy cruisers operating from ports in the United States.
11 Dec.	First Lt. Stanley V. Parker is the first commanding officer of Naval Air Station Key West.
15 Dec.	Russia capitulates and Germany dictates a crushing and exorbitant peace in the terms of the armistice of Brest-Litovsk.
29 Dec.	Capt. John C. Cantwell takes command of the naval reserve training center in San Diego.

1918

21 Jan.	Capt. Bernard H. Camden takes command of the naval training camp at Bumpkin Island, Massachusetts.
20 Feb.	British steamship *Venturia* runs aground on Cape Hatteras in a dense fog. Cruising cutter *Onondaga* locates the ship and rescues entire crew of forty-six.

21 Feb.	U.S. Coast Guard officers begin taking command of converted yachts, and patrol in French waters.
14 Mar.	First Lt. (Eng.) Charles E. Sugden becomes first commanding officer of naval air station at Ile Tudy, France.
30 Mar.	Coast guard officers from cutters at Gibraltar and the United States are ordered to command converted yachts based at Gibraltar.
25 Apr.	*Seneca* successfully rescues entire crew of eighty-one from torpedoed British escort *Cowslip*.
1 May	*Morrill* is designated flagship for the Fourth Naval District's minesweeping squadron, with the cutter's commanding officer named squadron commander.
19 June	Second Lt. (Eng.) Philip B. Eaton takes command of naval air station at Chatham, Massachusetts.
28 June	Convoy flagship SS *Queen* is torpedoed and sinks in Biscay Bay. *Seneca* rescues twenty-seven of the fifty-one crewmembers.
1 July	U.S. Coast Guard is authorized to temporarily promote officers to higher grades. Enlistments for men are extended from one year to "period of the war, not to exceed three years."
21 July	German submarine shells tug and barges four miles off Cape Cod. Two planes from Naval Air Station Chatham, one flown by Eaton, attack U-boat.
6 Aug.	German submarine shells and sinks Diamond Shoals Lightship off Cape Hatteras. Captain Parker reports to naval air station at Rockaway, New York, as commanding officer.
8 Aug.	Capt. Randolph Ridgely Jr. is ordered from command of the cutter *Yamacraw* to command of navy gunboat *Castine*, escorting convoys in the Mediterranean Sea.
16 Aug.	Keeper John A. Midgett and the crew from Chicamicomico station in North Carolina rescue sur-

vivors from burning waters, after British tanker *Mirlo* strikes a mine planted by a German submarine.

31 Aug.   First Lt. Robert Donohue is first commanding officer of naval air station at North Sydney, Nova Scotia.

16 Sept.   *Rambler* rescues crew of British ship *Philomel*, torpedoed off the coast of France.

17 Sept.   Eleven men from the crew of the cutter *Seneca* are killed at sea during attempt to save torpedoed British collier SS *Wellington*.

26 Sept.   *Tampa* sinks with all hands after being torpedoed in Bristol Bay. Cutter's entire crew of 115 is killed, along with 16 British passengers.

4–7 Oct.   Companies from the U.S. Coast Guard's New York division respond to the explosions and fires at the Gillespie Shell Loading Plant in Morgan City, New Jersey.

30 Oct.   Turkey surrenders to Allies.

11 Nov.   Germany surrenders, signing armistice at 11 AM.

14 Dec.   Bill is prepared in Congress to permanently transfer the U.S. Coast Guard to the U.S. Navy.

1919

1–3 Jan.   Transport *Northern Pacific*, returning troops from Europe, runs aground in fog, off Fire Island, New York. Surfboats from coast guard stations help remove troops.

13 Jan.   House of Representatives Committee on Interstate and Foreign Commerce holds hearing on bill to permanently transfer the U.S. Coast Guard to the U.S. Navy.

6 Feb.   Committee holds second hearing on transfer bill.

26 Feb.   Interstate and Foreign Commerce Committee recommends approval of Joint Resolution 382, which calls for return of U.S. Coast Guard to the Treasury Department.

15 Mar.	First of the coast guard officers assigned to German ocean liners reports for duty. German liners were turned over to the United States after the armistice to bring troops home.
27–29 Apr.	Captain Hamlet, in command of gunboat *Marietta*, rescues crews from minesweepers caught in a storm off French coast.
27 May	First Lieutenant Stone is senior pilot of navy aircraft NC-4—the first plane to fly across the Atlantic Ocean.
27 June	Coast guard officers are assigned to six American passenger ships returning troops to the United States—two as commanding officers, two as executive officers, four as chief engineers, and one as watch officer.
28 Aug.	President Wilson issues Executive Order No. 3160, which returns the U.S. Coast Guard to the Treasury Department.

THE COAST GUARD IN WORLD WAR I

CHAPTER I

TRANSFER TO THE NAVY

President proclaims war; warns enemy aliens here; 91 german ships seized and spies put under arrest; navy mobilized at once; cuba and brazil may join us

—HEADLINE, NEW YORK TIMES,
   7 APRIL 1917

SS *HEALDTON*

The 4,488-ton tanker SS *Healdton* was making ten knots on a southwesterly course en route to Rotterdam, Holland, on the night of 21 February 1917. Icy winds blowing out of the northwest sent salt spray whipping across the decks. The U.S. ship, manned by a crew of forty-one including sixteen Americans, was riding low with 2,137,711 gallons of oil in its tanks. Passing heavy snow squalls obscured visibility. The tank ship was thirty-five miles inside the safe channel established by Germany for neutral ships in the North Sea. Welcoming flashes from the lightship at Terschelling Island, Holland, were just visible when a torpedo sliced through the icy waters and slammed into the tanker's port side; the detonation sent a shudder throughout the ship. The tanker's American captain, Charles Christopher, said, "At 8:15 o'clock Wednesday evening, I was in my cabin when aroused by a terrific concussion. All the lights went out and I rushed on deck in my shirt sleeves to stop the engines. I found that a torpedo had gone through amidships at the spot where the ship's name was illuminated brightly, wrecking the engine room. The light clearly served as a target. If we hadn't shown our lights we might have been saved."[1]

After the torpedo struck, Christopher said, "The lifeboats were made ready and equipped for lowering. I rushed back to the cabin in the dark and was just able to grab a coat and a sextant when a second explosion shook the ship." The second torpedo hit farther aft and exploded in the bunkers, setting the oil ablaze. "Burning oil was running in all directions," he said, "necessitating a quick getaway. I found that my boat, Number One, apparently having been cut from the tow line prematurely, had capsized near the ship. None of its occupants were seen again." *Healdton* was settling quickly, down by the stern and listing to port. The captain said, "One or two fellows in the bunkers never came up. I expect they were killed there by the explosion." Christopher managed to jump into the no. 2 boat just before it left the sinking ship. The captain and twelve men were in one open boat and the chief officer, Otto O. Willerup, and another seven men were in a second boat. The boats pulled clear of the burning ship and stopped. G. H. Krogh, American vice consul at Rotterdam, said in a cablegram to the State Department, "Captain saw submarine approaching when he was lying off *Healdton* watching vessel sink. Nationality submarine impossible to determine, because it possessed no distinguishing marks and was seen from a distance of 100 feet toward. No words were exchanged with the submarine. Captain and crew believed submarine undoubtedly German. No other vessels were present or in sight when *Healdton* torpedoed. Submarine made no effort to assist crew or officers to save their lives, but disappeared immediately after *Healdton* sunk. Ship's papers were not demanded."[2]

The ship sank in twenty minutes and the submarine slipped below the surface and disappeared. The men in the two boats were left to the mercy of the sea and the freezing weather. Christopher said, "Then came twelve hours in open boats, insufficiently clad, and exposed to bitter hail and snow storms." The survivors rigged the sails on the boats and sailed and rowed in the darkness toward Terschelling Lightship, twenty-three miles to the southwest. When the crew of the Dutch trawler *Java* saw a boat under sail the next morning, they stopped fishing and investigated. They reached the lifeboat carrying Captain Christopher and his men at 8:00 AM. The crewmen from *Healdton* were so exhausted and hypothermic they could not maneuver the boat alongside the trawler. The skipper of the trawler managed to get close enough to the lifeboat for Dutch fishermen to jump aboard. The fishermen brought the boat alongside and the survivors were taken on board. They were cared for, given dry clothes, and taken to Terschelling. The second boat with the first mate and seven men was later found by the Dutch torpedo boat G-13 near Terschelling; the men had been exposed to the freezing weather for seventeen hours.

Krogh reported, "Perils and hardships suffered by all survivors extraordinary. Some possess no clothes. Others had no shoes." Two stokers, Jose Jacinto and Jose Gonzales, had their clothes burned off in the fire and were naked. Jacinto died from exposure and burns in the first mate's boat. Gonzales died later at the hospital. None of the survivors were fully clothed. The first assistant engineer, G. W. Embry, had no clothes. Doctors said he would have died if he had been in the boat for another hour. The second assistant engineer wore only his underclothes and was barefoot. The third boat, which had capsized, was found by the Dutch steam trawler *Ocean*. Inside the boat, they found a Norwegian crewman from *Healdton*. His arms and legs were frozen, but he was still alive. Somehow, he had managed to right the boat and climb into it. The trawler took him into Ymulden, Holland, for medical treatment.[3]

PROVOCATION

On 31 January 1917, Germany announced that it would commence a campaign of unrestricted submarine warfare against all ships trading with its enemies, including neutrals. German submarines were already exacting a heavy toll on shipping vital to the war effort. Germany's foreign minister, Arthur Zimmermann, believed unrestricted submarine warfare would force Britain, which was at the limits of its financial resources, to sue for peace within a few months as long as the United States remained neutral. The German government established zones around Great

Britain, France, Italy, and in the eastern Mediterranean in which "all ships met within the zone will be sunk." President Woodrow Wilson's response to Germany's action came four days later when he addressed a joint session of Congress on 3 February 1917. He stated, "I have therefore directed the Secretary of State to announce to his Excellency the German Ambassador that all diplomatic relations between the United States and the German Empire are severed and that the American ambassador at Berlin will be immediately withdrawn; and, in accordance with this decision, to hand to his Excellency his passport."[4]

On the same day that diplomatic relations were broken, a German U-boat stopped the American steamship *Housatonic* in the Bay of Biscay. *Housatonic*'s master, Capt. Thomas A. Ensor, was taken aboard the submarine with the ship's papers. The German lieutenant in command of the U-boat examined the ship's cargo manifest and told Ensor to return to his ship immediately and have his crew take to the boats. He said he was going to sink the ship. While *Housatonic*'s crew of twenty-six were leaving the ship in three boats, German sailors placed explosive charges aboard the 2,022-ton cargo ship. Within minutes after the American crew pulled away from the ship, there was a large explosion and then a second explosion, farther aft. In less than twenty-five minutes, swirling eddies and floating debris were all that remained of *Housatonic*.[5]

When the Germans first boarded *Housatonic*, Captain Ensor reported that "while the officer was examining the (ship's) papers, I noticed the men had life preservers bearing 'U-53' stamped in black letters on the brown canvas." Ensor was familiar with U-53 because of what the submarine had done in 1916, when the commanding officer, Kapitänleutnant Hans Rose, took advantage of American neutrality. On 7 October 1916, Rose sailed U-53 past Brenton Point and into Rhode Island's Narragansett Bay. He anchored the submarine off Newport, Rhode Island, put over a small boat, and went ashore. Rose made a courtesy call on the U.S. Navy commander at Newport and bought a copy of that morning's *New York Times*. Fluent in English, he checked the shipping section to see which ships of Germany's enemies would be sailing from New York and where they were bound. Armed with the shipping information, he returned to his U-boat and got under way at noon.[6]

U-53 laid in wait near the Narragansett Shoal Lightship for the unsus-

Kapitänleutnant Hans Rose and his crew aboard German submarine U-53 in Narragansett Bay, Rhode Island. The U-boat anchored off Newport on 7 October 1916 before the United States and Germany were at war. After this picture was taken, U-53 sailed and, in the next two days, sank five allied merchant ships near Narragansett Lightship. *U.S. Naval Historical Center*

pecting ships leaving New York. Vessels sailing across the Atlantic Ocean used the lightship as a point of departure for their crossing. Anticipating the German's intentions, the U.S. Navy commander at Newport sent a flotilla of destroyers to sea to conduct maneuvers in the vicinity of the lightship, hoping to disrupt and discourage the submarine's planned ambush. At 10:30 the next morning, U-53 stopped the Norwegian tanker *Christian Knudsen* and ordered the crew to leave the ship. The U-boat fired several rounds of ammunition from the deck gun and used one torpedo to sink the ship. Rose next stopped the British ship *West Point* at 2:20 PM forty-five miles from the lightship. He ordered the ship's master to abandon ship. The submarine's crew attached explosives to the ship's dangling boat falls and detonated the charges at the water line. *West Point*'s master said, "They blew a hole in her side large enough to drive a cart through." U-53 towed the lifeboats from the two ships, with considerable difficulty, to within sight of the lightship and released them.[7]

The submarine then forced the crew of the Dutch ship *Blommersdyk* to abandon ship at 6:00 PM. Rose used two torpedoes to sink the nine-thousand-ton ship, which was bound for Liverpool with wheat and automobiles. The passengers and crew of the French ship *Stephano* were forced to take to the boats at 7:00 PM, and the ship was sunk with gunfire and one torpedo. U.S. destroyers, helpless to do more, rescued 216 survivors from the ill-fated ships—two British, one French, one Dutch, and one Norwegian. Four large passenger ships, scheduled to transit the same route past the lightship, never appeared. The United States, in violation of the Neutrality Act, warned the passenger ships of the presence of the submarine so they could take different routes to avoid U-53's ambush.[8]

In the month following Germany's declaration of unrestricted submarine warfare, U-boats sank seven U.S. merchant ships, killing thirty-six Americans. The loss of the ships and the deaths of American citizens pressed the United States to the brink of war. Anti-German sentiment in the United States had been building steadily ever since 128 Americans were killed when the British ocean liner *Lusitania* was torpedoed—without warning—by the German submarine U-20 off the Irish coast on 7 May 1915. As the war in Europe continued and Britain's battle fleet gained control over the seas, Germany resorted to even more drastic undersea warfare in an attempt to stem the flow of materials to its enemies. The animosity caused by submarine attacks was compounded by the revelation of the contents of an intercepted telegram from German Foreign Minister Zimmermann. When the contents of the secret communiqué, intercepted and decoded by British intelligence, were published in the United States, Americans were outraged. In the communication, sent to the German embassy in Mexico, Zimmermann proposed a Mexican-German alliance against the United States. In the telegram, Zimmermann said:

> We intend to begin unrestricted submarine warfare on the first of February.
> We shall endeavor in spite of this to keep the United States neutral. In the
> event of this not succeeding, we make Mexico a proposal of alliance on the
> following basis: make war together, make peace together, generous financial

support, and an understanding on our part that Mexico is to reconquer the lost territory in Texas, New Mexico, and Arizona.

The telegram further proposed that the Mexican president, Gen. Venustiano Carranza, act as an intermediary in getting Japan to switch sides and form an alliance with Germany. In return, Japan would be given lands in California. Zimmermann believed that alliances with Mexico and Japan would tie up American resources at home if the United States entered the war. With the United States engaged on the western side of the Atlantic, Germany could finish off the struggling Britain. The telegram left President Wilson no alternative but to declare war. In his war message to Congress on 2 April 1917, Wilson said, "Self-governing nations do not fill their neighbor states with spies or set the course of intrigue to bring about some critical posture of affairs which will give the opportunity to strike and make conquest."[9]

MOBILIZATION

At 3:12 AM on Friday, 6 April 1917, Congress voted to approve President Wilson's request for a declaration of war. The Senate and House of Representatives resolved, "That a state of war between the United States and the Imperial German Government which has been thrust upon the United States is hereby formally declared." After war was declared, Secretary of the Navy Josephus Daniels picked up his pen that afternoon at 4:05 PM and signed the order mobilizing the U.S. Navy. Within minutes, coded messages were dispatched from the office of Adm. W. S. Benson, chief of naval operations, placing all navy ships and shore stations on a wartime footing. The mobilization order also applied to the ships, stations, and personnel of the U.S. Coast Guard, which were transferred from the Treasury Department to the U.S. Navy upon the declaration of war.[10]

When the U.S. Coast Guard was created in 1915 by combining the Revenue-Cutter Service and the Life-Saving Service, Congress was already concerned about the prospects of war with Germany and the threat of German submarines. They anticipated the need for the coast guard–armed ships and trained crews. Revenue cutters had served with the

Ellsworth P. Bertholf was named captain commandant of the U.S. Coast Guard in 1915 when it was created by combining the Revenue-Cutter Service and the Life-Saving Service. He continued to serve as commandant throughout World War I. *U.S. Coast Guard Museum*

navy during the recent war with Spain and proved their military worth. While there had always been a close association and cooperation between the U.S. Navy and the Revenue-Cutter Service, during times of hostility Congress wanted a more formalized relationship. The 28 January 1915 act creating the U.S. Coast Guard included specific language about the military nature of the service. The act directed that the U.S. Coast Guard "shall constitute a part of the military forces of the United States and which shall operate under the Treasury Department in time of peace and operate as a part of the Navy, subject to the orders of the Secretary of the Navy, in time of war or when the President shall so direct."[11]

In response to the order to mobilize, U.S. Coast Guard Captain Commandant Ellsworth P. Bertholf released a prepared "Alcut" (all cutter) message for delivery to all coast guard cutters, stations, and facilities. The coded message was transmitted by wireless and telegraph from the U.S. Navy's Arlington radio station in Virginia and by messenger. The message read, "Plan One. Acknowledge." In anticipation of war with Germany, Bertholf had issued Confidential Order No. 2, a twelve-page booklet, on 22 March 1917. Copies of the order, entitled "Mobilization of the U.S. Coast Guard When Required to Operate as a Part of the Navy," were given to each commissioned officer of the U.S. Coast Guard. Instructions stated, "Each officer will consider himself personally responsible for the safe-keeping of this publication, will keep it in his possession, will not explain nor deliver its contents to any person not regularly connected to the Coast Guard or the naval service, and will be prepared to turn it in at once when called upon by headquarters."[12]

The first part of the confidential mobilization order was entitled Plan One and called for "combining the entire forces of the Coast Guard with the Navy in time of war." It assigned cutters to naval districts and directed commanding officers to "report by code telegram to the commandant of the naval district to which assigned, giving the vessel's position and then await orders from him for movement, if those have not previously been arranged for in connection with mobilization." Cutters assigned to commanders of sections within naval districts were told to report to their section commander and await orders. Plan One directed coast guard stations to "continue performing, 'wreck and rescue' duty, unless instructions were received from proper authority to suspend such operations, in specific instances." When the order to mobilize was received, commanding officers of cutters and keepers of stations reported to their U.S. Navy commanders. They then mustered their crews and read the mobilization orders, which transferred them from the U.S. Coast Guard to the U.S. Navy.[13]

When the order to mobilize was given, Secretary of the Treasury William G. McAdoo sent a letter to the Captain Commandant Bertholf. In the 6 April letter, he said, "In thus departing from your humanitarian status to engage in the sterner necessities of the hour, I take the occasion to extend to you, and through you to the officers and men under your command, my sincere felicitations, and to express the confidence I feel in the loyalty, integrity, and efficiency of the Coast Guard to perform with great credit, under the direction of the Secretary of the Navy, all the hazards and difficult duties which may come to it in defense of our beloved country."[14]

Administration

Secretary of the Navy Daniels also sent a communication to Bertholf on 6 April 1917, saying, in accordance with the law, the U.S. Coast Guard was now part of the U.S. Navy and subject to the orders of the secretary of the navy. Daniels gave Bertholf instructions concerning the administration of the U.S. Coast Guard: "Your office will be known as Coast Guard

Headquarters. Incoming correspondence affecting Coast Guard forces will be referred to Coast Guard Headquarters for recommendation as to action by the Navy Department. Outgoing correspondence affecting the Coast Guard will be sent to Coast Guard Headquarters for appropriate action, or when action is taken by the (Navy) Department, a copy of such correspondence will be furnished that office (Coast Guard)."[15]

In 1917, Coast Guard Headquarters was located one block from the Treasury Department in Washington, D.C. Its offices were in the Bond building, at New York Avenue and 14th Street, Northwest. Coast Guard Headquarters was organized into five separate divisions. The division of operations consisted of four sections: personnel and operations, ordnance and communications, law, and statistics. The materiel division had sections for supplies, accounts, and mail and files. The remaining three divisions were construction and repair, engineering, and inspection. Secretary Daniels told Bertholf, "You are directed to continue until further orders, the interior administration of the Coast Guard in all respects the same as when operating under the Treasury Department." When mobilized, most commissioned officers stationed at headquarters were detached and reassigned to more pressing duties with the navy. The small staff that remained in Washington was responsible for the routine operation of stations and for providing and administering pay and rations for coast guard personnel. Cutters continued to pick up pay for their crews from the collectors of customs and special disbursing agents at the various ports where they were "headquartered" or where they called. The navy was responsible for providing fuel, oil, supplies, and repairs for cutters.

Coast guard rescue stations continued to submit reports and correspondence just as they had before mobilization, with the exception of correspondence concerning operations specifically directed by navy section commanders. Coast guard superintendents, who were in charge of stations within their districts, continued to report directly to Coast Guard Headquarters. They only reported to the U.S. Navy for matters involving the distribution of naval funds from disbursing officers. Authority for imposing discipline at stations shifted from the superintendents to the commandants of naval districts. Personnel matters for all coast guardsmen—including enlistments, reenlistments, ratings, disratings, and discharges—remained the responsibility of the U.S. Coast Guard. The U.S.

Coast Guard Academy at New London, Connecticut, with twenty-four cadets and one civilian instructor, and the depot at Arundel Cove, Maryland, remained under the direct control of the commandant.[16]

FIELD ORGANIZATION

The U.S. Coast Guard was created by combining the Revenue-Cutter Service and the Life-Saving Service two years before the United States entered World War I. Both agencies were in the Treasury Department and had a history of cooperation. Revenue-Cutter Service officers served as inspectors for the Life-Saving Service and, at one time, the two services had been jointly administered within the department. While the services had common ties, there were also significant differences. Surfmen were not trained for shipboard duty and cuttermen lacked the skills for operating boats in the surf. There were cultural differences as well. Cuttermen traveled widely and were subject to frequent transfers, while surfmen were drawn from local communities. Surfmen often spent their entire career at a single station and were more likely to be family men. Of the cutter *Tampa*'s crew of 111 cuttermen, only 9 listed a wife as their next of kin. Transfers between the two service branches were infrequent. When a surfman did put in for a transfer to a cutter going to the war zone, he was reduced in rating because of his lack of shipboard skills. The 4 July 1917 entry in the cutter *Tampa*'s log reported, "Felix G. Poppel[l], surfman, reported aboard for duty, disrated to ordinary seaman in accordance with instructions contained in H/L [headquarters letter] of July 3, 1917." The two service components were still adjusting to their union when the U.S. Coast Guard was mobilized; they essentially remained separate entities throughout the conflict.[17]

CUTTERS

At the time of mobilization in 1917, the U.S. Coast Guard had a fleet of twenty-three active cruising cutters and twenty-one harbor cutters. A list of cutters, with descriptions, is given in Appendix A. Cruising cutters were seagoing vessels, capable of putting to sea in all kinds of weather to render assistance to vessels in distress. They had the capacity to carry large quantities of fuel, water, and supplies, enabling them to cruise for extended periods in search of derelicts or in distant waters such as Alaska. National defense was an essential mission of the U.S. Coast Guard and cutters were required to conform to navy requirements. The U.S. Navy's General Board established the characteristics for a gunboat as: a sustained speed of 12 knots, a displacement of between 1,000 and 1,400 tons, a medium draft, and as large a steaming radius as practical. Cruising cutters generally met these characteristics and the U.S. Coast Guard's policy was to design all new seagoing cutters to meet the standards adapted by the U.S. Navy for gunboat-class vessels. The U.S. Coast Guard's harbor cutters were primarily used for going alongside incoming vessels, for the purpose of boarding. They required sturdy construction, maneuverability for operating alongside ships, and medium speed. Tugboat-type vessels were found to be suitable for this class and duty. Fast motorboats were also being added to the fleet in 1917 for law enforcement work.[18]

Cutter operations were controlled and supported by senior captains assigned as commanders of the U.S. Coast Guard's four geographical divisions and by the captain commandant at headquarters. The commander of the eastern division was headquartered at Boston, Massachusetts. His division had five cutters under its command—four cruising cutters and one harbor cutter. *Ossipee*, operating out of Portland, Maine, patrolled coastal waters from Eastport, Maine, to Cape Ann, Massachusetts. *Androscoggin* and *Gresham* were homeported at Boston, Massachusetts. *Androscoggin* was assigned to the eastern fishing banks to render assistance and provided medical and surgical aid to American vessels of the deep-sea fishing fleet. *Gresham* covered the waters from Portsmouth, New Hampshire, to Nantucket Shoals Lightship. *Acushnet*, stationed at Woods Hole, Massachusetts, patrolled Buzzards Bay, Nantucket Shoals, and the adjacent waters. The harbor cutter *Winnisimmet* carried out boarding duties for customs at Boston, Massachusetts.

The New York division, with headquarters at New York City, had seven cutters, all homeported in New York City. The cruising cutter *Seneca* was a derelict destroyer. Congress had specifically directed that a cutter be "fitted for and adapted to service at sea and in bad weather, for the purpose of blowing up or otherwise destroying or towing into port wrecks, derelicts, and other floating dangers to navigation." *Seneca* operated along the entire

In 1906 Congress funded the construction of a "derelict destroyer" to remove floating and sunken hazards to navigation at sea. Construction of the 204-foot cutter
Seneca, which was designed for "keeping the seas for long periods in any kind of
weather," was completed in 1908. A green hull and stripes on the smokestack indicated *Seneca* was a derelict destroyer. *Mariners' Museum, Newport News, Virginia*

length of the Atlantic coast. *Mohawk* was a cruising cutter assigned to
patrol the Atlantic coast from Gay Head, Massachusetts, to the entrance
to the Delaware Bay. The harbor cutter *Hudson* was used for customs
boardings. The remaining four harbor cutters, *Manhattan, Guide, Patrol,*
and *Calumet*, were assigned to the New York division. The New York division was unique, because it had the additional responsibility of supervising anchorages for New York City and vicinity.[19]

The Pacific coast was divided into two divisions. The northern division was responsible for the coast north of Cape Blanco, Oregon, with
headquarters at Seattle, Washington. The division controlled the activities of three cruising cutters and three harbor cutters. Cruising cutters
Algonquin, stationed at Astoria, Oregon, and *Unalga*, stationed at Seattle,
patrolled in the Pacific Ocean. The cruising cutter *Snohomish* patrolled
waters in the vicinity of Cape Flattery, from its homeport at Neah Bay,

Washington. The division's three harbor cutters—*Arcata*, out of Port Townsend, Washington; *Guard*, out of Friday Harbor, Washington; and *Scout*, out of Seattle—patrolled Puget Sound. The commander of the southern division was stationed at San Francisco, California, and had two cruising cutters and two harbor cutters assigned. The cruising cutter *Bear*, headquartered at San Diego, patrolled the southern coast of California. The northern coast of California and the Oregon coast, south of Cape Blanco, were patrolled by the cruising cutter *McCulloch*, out of San Francisco. Harbor cutters *Golden Gate* and *Hartley* were assigned to customs boarding duty at San Francisco. Cutters from the northern and southern divisions were sent north to Alaska and detailed to the U.S. Coast Guard's Bering Sea Fleet from May to October of each year. The Bering Sea Fleet commander was stationed at Unalaska, Alaska.[20]

The U.S. Coast Guard's remaining twelve cruising cutters and ten harbor cutters were classified as independent vessels; their movements, support, and inspections were directed by Coast Guard Headquarters. Four cruising cutters—*Yamacraw*, *Seminole*, *Manning*, and *Tampa*—patrolled in the Atlantic Ocean from New Jersey south to the tip of Florida and in the Gulf of Mexico as far north as Tampa, Florida. The remaining Gulf coast, west to the border of Mexico, was the responsibility of cruising cutters *Tallapoosa* and *Comanche*. The cruising cutter *Apache* patrolled the inland waters of the Chesapeake Bay and its tributaries. Cutter *Pamlico* was responsible for North Carolina's Pamlico and Albermarle sounds. Three cutters were assigned to the Great Lakes. From its homeport in Detroit, Michigan, cruising cutter *Morrill* patrolled in Lakes Huron, Ontario, and Erie. The cruising cutter *Tuscarora*, out of Milwaukee, Wisconsin, was assigned to Lake Michigan and Lake Superior. The harbor cutter *Mackinac* and four launches were stationed at Sault Ste. Marie, Michigan, under an officer-in-charge. They enforced laws regulating the anchorage of vessels and the movement of traffic in the "Soo Canal" and St. Mary's River. The cruising cutter *Itasca* was homeported at San Juan, Puerto Rico, and patrolled the water of Puerto Rico and the Virgin Islands. During the summer months, *Itasca* was detailed to the U.S. Coast Guard Academy for the annual practice cruise for cadets. At the time of mobilization, the cruising cutter *Onondaga* was inactive, undergoing repairs at the coast guard depot, located at Arundel Cove in South Baltimore,

Maryland. The cutter *Colfax*, with its machinery removed, was moored at the depot and used as a station ship. The remaining nine harbor cutters assisted customs authorities with boarding incoming vessels at ports of entry. They also enforced navigation and anchorage regulations at the ports. The Arundel Cove depot was used to overhaul and repair cutters on the Atlantic coast. The U.S. Coast Guard also had facilities known as "stores" that served as storehouses for purchasing, storing, and issuing supplies. They were located at New York City, Grand Haven, Michigan, and San Francisco.[21]

STATIONS

When the United States declared war on Germany, the U.S. Coast Guard had 272 rescue stations distributed along the coasts of the Atlantic Ocean, Gulf of Mexico, Great Lakes, and Pacific Ocean. The stations were manned by crews of six to twelve men, with a warrant officer in charge of each station. A station consisted of living quarters, boat house, lookout tower, and outbuildings. Each station was equipped with two to six boats of varying types, depending on needs and location. By 1917, 60 percent of the stations on the Atlantic and Gulf coasts were equipped with power boats. Two thirds of the Atlantic and Gulf coast stations launched their boats over the beach. Power boats were assigned to all stations on the Great Lakes, except one, and to three fourths of the Pacific coast stations. The Great Lakes and Pacific stations had the larger thirty-four-foot and thirty-six-foot motorized lifeboats. The larger lifeboats were required, because of the extreme weather conditions and distances traveled on the lakes and because of coastal sea conditions in the Pacific. The large motorized lifeboats, too large and too heavy to launch through the surf, were kept at moorings or on launching ramps in protected waters.

The stations were divided into thirteen geographical districts, with a civilian superintendent in charge of each district. The largest number of stations were located in districts one through seven, along the coasts of the New England and the Mid-Atlantic states. Waters along these coasts had the largest amount of shipping activity and were subjected to severe weather, particularly in the winter months. One hundred and seventy-one stations dotted the coast from the northern tip of Maine south through North Carolina. The Great Lakes had the second largest concentration, with sixty-three stations divided into three districts. Nineteen stations spread along the Atlantic coast south of North Carolina and in the Gulf of Mexico to the Texas-Mexico border were divided into two districts. Nineteen stations were located on the Pacific Ocean. The districts, the number of stations in each district, and the areas each district covered before the war is given in Appendix E. When war was declared, the coast guard stations were transferred to the U.S. Navy, with each station reporting to the naval district outlined in Plan One instructions.[22]

PERSONNEL

In 1917, the U.S. Coast Guard was authorized 270 commissioned officers and 4,897 warrant officers, petty officers, and "men." According to the 1917 register of officers, there were actually only 225 commissioned officers on active duty. Forty-five officer billets, in the grades of third lieutenant and third lieutenant of engineers, were left vacant aboard cutters. Accurate accounting for enlisted personnel was difficult, because cutters and stations did their own recruiting and enlistments were for one year. Available records indicated that there were 257 warrant officers and 3,478 enlisted men on active duty in 1917, leaving more than a thousand billets vacant. The U.S. Navy's active duty strength was 4,376 officers and 64,686 enlisted men when the United States entered the war. There were another 22,000 men in the naval militia and reserve. When the war ended, the U.S. Navy had increased to 33,000 officers and 500,000 enlisted men while the U.S. Coast Guard authorization for officers remained at 270 and the enlisted force increased to about 6,000.[23]

The titles for officer ranks in the U.S. Coast Guard were carried over from the Revenue-Cutter Service (R-CS). Because of the military nature of the service, Congress had established military ranks for R-CS officers in a 2 March 1799 act. It authorized the use of the military ranks of "captain" and "lieutenant," rather than the titles of "master" and "mate," as were used on merchant ships. While the names of the coast guard ranks differed from those used by the navy and the army, the pay grades, as established by law, were equal. The following is a list of equivalent ranks:[24]

Officer Ranks

Coast Guard	Navy	Army
Captain Commandant	Captain	Colonel
Senior Captain and Engineer in Chief	Commander	Lieutenant Colonel
Captain and Captain of Engineers	Lieutenant Commander	Major
First Lieutenant and First Lieutenant of Engineers	Lieutenant (senior)	Captain
Second Lieutenant and Second Lieutenant of Engineers	Lieutenant (junior)	First Lieutenant
Third Lieutenant and Third Lieutenant of Engineers	Ensign	Second Lieutenant

The seniority for U.S. Coast Guard officers, with a few exceptions, was based on time in grade and time in service. The captain commandant of the U.S. Coast Guard and the service's engineer in chief were the two exceptions. Captain Commandant Ellsworth P. Bertholf had ten years less commissioned service than the senior captain listed next below him on the order of precedence of officers. Eng. in Chief Charles A. McAllister, selected from among the captains of engineers, was listed with the senior captains as the most junior. He had ten years less commissioned service than the captain below him on the list. In 1917, it took approximately thirty-five years to reach the rank of senior captain (O-5), nineteen years to achieve the grade of captain (O-4), eleven years to make first lieutenant (O-3), and four years for second lieutenant (O-2).

The 270 commissioned officer billets authorized by Congress were divided into six pay grades. There was only one billet in the highest pay grade—captain commandant. The remaining billets were allocated as senior captain (3 percent), captain (14 percent), first lieutenant (25 percent), and second and third lieutenants combined (58 percent). Two thirds of the billets were for line officers and one third for engineers. Thirteen positions were authorized for district superintendents for stations. These positions were equivalent to the following U.S. Coast Guard pay grades:

one captain, three first lieutenants, four second lieutenants, and five third lieutenants. Two constructor billets were also authorized at headquarters in the grade of first lieutenant.[25]

In anticipation of the possibility of war and service with the U.S. Navy, provisions were made in 1916 for establishing precedence among commissioned officers of the two services. Seniority for officers serving in the same grade was based upon date of rank. When war was declared in 1917, the strength of the navy was rapidly increased to meet mobilization demands and coast guard officers were assigned to navy billets. As the size of the navy was drastically increased, officer promotions were rapidly accelerated to meet the demands of the increased force structure. To meet needs, the navy made extensive use of temporary promotions. Much to the dismay of coast guard officers, there was no demand for accelerated promotions because the size of the U.S. Coast Guard's officer corps was not increased. Even if there had been an increase, the navy's authority for temporary promotions did not extend to the coast guard. As a result, coast guard officers frequently found themselves working for younger naval officers that had considerably less service and experience. This situation was not rectified until 1 July 1918, when the Naval Appropriations Act contained a provision to, "promote temporarily, with the advice and consent of the Senate, commissioned line officers and engineer officers of the United States Coast Guard." To provide coast guard officers an equal opportunity for promotion, even though the size of their officer corps was not increasing, they were assigned "running mates" in the U.S. Navy. When the assigned running mate, a naval officer of equivalent service and experience, was promoted, the coast guard officer was also promoted. Promotions for coast guard officers accelerated rapidly after July 1918.[26]

Pay and allowances for commissioned coast guard officers were fixed by Congress to be equal to army officers of comparable rank. The pay comparability with the army created another problem when naval officers were authorized 10 percent additional pay for sea duty. Coast guard officers of the same rank performing the same duties—often on the same ships—did not receive the same pay as their navy counterparts. This inequity was eventually corrected. When war was declared, the navy began assigning coast guard officers to navy billets ashore to make naval officers available for sea duty. Coast guard officers commanded naval training camps and section bases, served at navy bureaus, and were assigned to naval district staffs. One was chief of staff to the Twelfth Naval District commandant. Several officers, primarily engineers, were assigned to bureaus in the Navy Department and at shipyards. The U.S. Coast Guard had a mature and experienced seagoing officer corps; officers attained command rank at about forty years of age. As the ranks of the navy rapidly expanded, officers were drawn from coast guard units and assigned to navy ships, many as commanding officers. The vacancies created on cutters were filled with naval reserve officers undergoing training.[27]

The U.S. Coast Guard's enlisted ranks were made up of warrant officers, petty officers, and other men. In 1917, there were 358 warrant officers in six specialties: master's mates, gunners, machinists, boatswains, carpenters, and keepers (of stations). There were almost twice as many keepers as all other warrant specialties combined. Coast guard warrant officers were selected from among the petty officers and appointed by the secretary of the treasury as vacancies occurred. Petty officers were promoted from the enlisted ranks based on their performance. Master's mate was a warrant officer specialty unique to the U.S. Coast Guard; it was senior to all other warrant officers. The U.S. Navy did not have an equivalent rank and did not recognize the seniority of coast guard master's mates. The navy's proposal to reduce master's mates to chief boatswains mates caused considerable consternation in the U.S. Coast Guard's warrant officer corps.

Differences in the petty officer rate structures of the navy and coast guard also caused problems. The U.S. Coast Guard only had three petty officers grades—first class, second class, and third class; there were no chief petty officers. Senior first class petty officers on coast guard cutters had service experience equivalent to chief petty officers on navy ships and performed the duties of chief petty officers. Because there were only three petty officer grades, coast guard second and third class petty officers also had more experience and responsibility than navy petty officers of the same grade. The law specified that when serving with the navy, coast guardsmen should receive "the same rates of pay as are, or may hereafter, be prescribed for corresponding grades or ratings and length of service in the Navy." Consequently, when the U.S. Coast Guard was transferred to the U.S. Navy, its petty officers had less authority and received less pay than navy personnel with the same experience and training.[28]

Coast guard petty officer rating specialties were comparable to those of the navy, with one major exception—"surfman." This was the largest single rating and a specialty found only in the U.S. Coast Guard. Approximately one half of the service's enlisted force was assigned to stations; the other half was assigned aboard cutters. At stations, each enlisted man was called surfman, regardless of pay grade. The order of promotion to petty office aboard cutters for nonrated enlisted men on deck was: boy, first class boy, ordinary seaman, and seaman. In the engine room, nonrated men were first coal heavers and then firemen.[29]

Prior to the war, coast guard enlistments were generally for a period of one year. By July 1918, however, the service recognized that one-year enlistments were not sufficient to provide stability for wartime operations. Subsequently, terms of enlistment were established as "the period of the war, not to exceed three years." In addition to pay, enlisted men also received subsistence, an allowance for food, and an allowance for uniform clothing. Enlisted men were eligible to retire after thirty years of service and were required to retire at age sixty-four, the same as for officers. The U.S. Coast Guard's system of discipline was comparable to that of the U.S. Navy. Courts were organized and the procedures conducted substantially in accordance with naval courts. The coast guard mobilization plan directed that when the U.S. Coast Guard was transferred to the U.S. Navy "all regulations regarding Coast Guard courts are suspended and all matters which necessitate court proceedings shall be dealt with by naval courts."[30]

When the U.S. Coast Guard was created in 1915, a large number of the enlisted men serving aboard cutters were foreign born. Many had taken no action to become citizens of the United States. When the war in Europe spread, many foreign-born crewmen left the service, by discharge or desertion, to return home to fight for their countries. Their departures resulted in serious personnel shortages aboard cutters. Up until that time, the U.S. Coast Guard had no need for recruit training facilities. Previously cutter commanding officers had little difficulty in recruiting men to fill crew vacancies and the men recruited, many with prior nautical experience, were trained as necessary where they were enlisted. After mobilization, the demand for enlisted personnel increased rapidly. Beginning in 1917, the U.S. Coast Guard had to open recruiting offices for the first time to keep cutters manned. Once the United States entered the war, the demand for recruits became even greater. Wartime complements aboard cutters were increased and more men were needed at shore facilities to carry out expanded wartime duties, such as port security. By 1918, 1,446 coast guardsmen were required at the port of New York alone to supervise explosive loading and to enforce the port security provisions of the Espionage Act.[31]

The U.S. Coast Guard Academy, located at Fort Trumbull in New London, Connecticut, trained cadets to become commissioned officers. The facility was funded for a total of twenty-one cadets, of both line and engineer, and one civilian instructor. The academy taught a three-year course of instruction for line officers and a one-year course for engineers. One year of advanced education was required to enter the academy.[32] When the war began, the length of training was reduced to two years for line officers and nine months for engineer officers. Wartime demands for personnel for all the armed forces made it impossible to recruit experienced enlisted men. The U.S. Coast Guard established its first recruit training facility at the academy. Recruits received their outfit of uniform material and were given basic training in infantry drill and boat handling. The academy's cadets were used to assist with recruit training. By 1918, the academy had accommodations for five hundred recruits undergoing training. When Hamilton Cochran enlisted in the U.S. Coast Guard, he was sent to the academy for training. He said:

> By the middle of April, 1917, there were 200 recruits in training. We were instructed by Coast Guard cadets who were studying to become officers in the service and they were a fine lot of fellows. The first thing we were taught was the art of semaphore signaling which consists of sending messages by means of flags. A good part of each morning was spent in boat drill on the Thames River. Cadets had charge of the boats, teaching us the proper stroke, how to make a landing, and giving us commands pertaining to a boat under oars. Sometimes we had gun drill with a little three pounder that stood on a hill overlooking the parade ground. . . . Great stress was put on infantry drill and the manual of arms. We were kept at it day after day until

each company had become like a machine in executing the commands of the cadets. Finally by July, our training days had come to an end and we were ready to be assigned to the various cutters.[33]

After the United States entered the war, the U.S. Navy established an experimental station, just outside the grounds of the U.S. Coast Guard Academy. The station tested various devices for detecting submarines. Since there were no facilities for navy personnel at the station, they were quartered and fed at the academy. The navy later built two large barracks on academy grounds and converted casements at Fort Trumbull into offices for the station. A "listening in" school to train technicians to detect submarines was also begun at the academy. Two of the academy's six coast guard instructors were reassigned to meet the need for officers aboard cutters deploying to Gibraltar. Second Lt. (Eng.) Milton R. Daniels was ordered to *Seneca* and 3d Lt. Frank J. Gorman was assigned to *Manning*.[34]

The depot at Arundel Cove in Maryland was also used to recruit and process new enlistees. Once the other armed forces began drafting men, coast guard recruiting became easier. So many men volunteered for service in the U.S. Coast Guard, rather than be drafted into the U.S. Army, that recruiters were overwhelmed with more applicants than they could handle. When the Draft Law was passed, it contained provisions for men who had deserted from the services to return voluntarily to complete their enlistments. Secretary of the Navy Daniels allowed deserters to return and serve on probation. After completing the terms of their enlistment, former deserters received honorable discharges.[35]

COAST GUARD DUTIES

The U.S. Coast Guard's principal peacetime duties in 1917 were quite similar to those accomplished by the service at the end of the century. The *Annual Report of the United States Coast Guard for the Fiscal Year Ended June 30, 1917*, divided the duties into three mission areas: maritime safety, law enforcement, and military readiness. Maritime safety duties included: (1) rendering assistance to vessels in distress and saving life and property; (2) destruction or removal of wrecks, derelicts, and other floating dangers to navigation; (3) extending medical aid to American vessels engaged in deep-sea fisheries; and (4) international ice patrol of the Grand Banks. In 1917, the U.S. Coast Guard was the federal agency with primary responsibility for enforcing U.S. law in coastal waters and on the high seas. Law enforcement duties were: (1) protection of the customs revenue; (2) enforcement of law and regulations governing anchorage of vessels in navigable waters; (3) enforcement of law relating to quarantine and neutrality; (4) suppression of mutinies on merchant vessels; (5) enforcement of navigation and other laws governing merchant vessels and motorboats; (6) enforcement of law to provide for safety of life on navigable waters during regattas and marine parades; (7) protection of game and the seal and other fisheries in Alaska, etc.; and (8) enforcement of sponge-fishing law. Military readiness was the duty with the greatest importance in 1917. The law creating the U.S. Coast Guard in 1915 specifically assigned the duty of operating as part of the U.S. Navy in time of war or when the president shall direct.[36]

The missions listed in the *Annual Report* were the U.S. Coast Guard's principal duties. The service's cutters and trained crews, however, were seen by the government as ready resources, available to perform a variety of maritime functions. This had been a reality throughout the coast guard's history. In the 1917 *Annual Report* Captain Commandant Bertholf said, "It seems to be generally recognized that all the great departments of the Government should call upon the Coast Guard for any special work of a maritime nature for which no other vessels are especially maintained." On 6 April 1917, the U.S. Coast Guard's military capability to function as a part of the U.S. Navy became its primary duty. With the transfer to the navy, Bertholf said of the service's military role, "This attribute is now the paramount function of the Coast Guard, as all its facilities are now being employed in the prosecution of the existing war."[37]

When considering the coast guard role within the navy in World War I, it is important to appreciate the relative sizes of the two services. The U.S. Coast Guard had a small fleet of cutters and less than four thousand men on active duty when war was declared. During the war, the service experienced a modest increase in manpower. On 30 June 1918, there were 228 commissioned officers, 412 warrant officers, and 5,920 enlisted men. The U.S. Navy's strength, on the other hand, increased into the hundreds of thousands. The degree of coast guard integration within the navy was

greater in World War I than in any later conflict. The navy quickly recognized that the most important coast guard asset was the service's pool
of experienced mariners. The U.S. Coast Guard continued to man and
operate its cutters and stations, and individual coast guardsmen were reassigned to navy ships and units, wherever they were needed. They were
ordered to navy ships and staffs not as exchange or liaison personnel but
for duty. Coast guard officers commanded navy ships and naval air stations manned by navy crews. They were assigned as executive officers,
navigators, and chief engineers. On a smaller scale, navy officers and personnel were assigned to coast guard cutters and units, primarily for training. Coast guard cutters were assigned to navy commanders and carried
the same identification as navy ships (e.g., USS *Tampa*). This high degree
of wartime integration led to the proposal after the armistice that the U.S.
Coast Guard be transferred permanently to the U.S. Navy.

CHAPTER 2

CUTTERS TO THE WAR ZONE

The professional ability of the Coast Guard officers is evidenced by
the fact that twenty-four commanded combatant ships in European
waters, five vessels of the patrol force of the Caribbean Sea, and
twenty-three combatant craft attached to naval districts.

—SECRETARY OF THE NAVY JOSEPHUS DANIELS, *OUR NAVY AT WAR*

SS *WELLINGTON*

The British collier *Wellington* left Milford Haven, Wales, on Friday morning, 13 September 1918, as one of twenty-one merchant ships in Convoy O.M. (Outbound–Milford Haven) No. 99 bound for Gibraltar. A stiff breeze, blowing from the northwest, roiled the waters of Brides Bay. British destroyers and the coast guard cutter *Seneca* escorted the departing convoy. At times, rain squalls made it difficult for the escorts to see the merchant ships in their charge. On Sunday night, 15 September 1918, the convoy was well clear of coastal waters. The escort ships, assigned to the home waters danger zone, flashed a farewell and withdrew. The 204-foot *Seneca*, under the command of Capt. William J. Wheeler, USCG, was left as the convoy's lone ocean escort for the thousand mile voyage.[1]

The next day *Wellington*, a few hundred yards ahead of station, was leading the convoy's middle column of ships during the Bay of Biscay crossing. *Seneca*'s 16 September war diary reported that there was a sudden violent explosion at 11:30 AM.[2] The cutter's crew saw a column of water rise and collapse over *Wellington*'s bow. Crewmen on the collier reported seeing a submarine just before the explosion. The U-boat broke water and then submerged ahead of the ship. The torpedo struck *Wellington*, well forward on the starboard side. The detonation tore away the ship's forefoot and left a gaping hole in the bow, flooding no. 1 hold. Wheeler set general quarters and brought *Seneca* up to full speed. The cutter zigzagged while proceeding from its station ahead of the convoy to the torpedoed vessel. Wheeler maneuvered to avoid the oncoming ships, which had scattered after the explosion.[3]

When *Seneca* approached the collier, a lookout spotted the conning tower of a submarine on *Wellington*'s starboard quarter. The cutter's gun crews got off three quick rounds from their 4-inch guns before the U-boat submerged again. Other armed ships in the convoy also fired at the submarine, but no hits were scored. *Seneca* followed the submarine's wake and attacked, dropping eight depth charges. Wheeler said, "Numerous shells were fired from our 4-inch guns into clear spaces of water [among the scattered ships] to convince the submarine that he was being bombed from various parts of the convoy." The cutter fired thirty-five rounds and dropped another seven depth charges around the torpedoed ship to keep the submarine down.[4]

Most of *Wellington*'s crew of forty-two were new to the vessel. The ship was on its first voyage after having damage from an earlier torpedo attack repaired. When the torpedo struck, *Wellington*'s crew panicked and immediately began abandoning ship. Three boats pulled away from the collier at 11:55 AM. *Wellington*'s master, Captain Donovan, signaled *Seneca* by semaphore from one of the boats. He said he thought his ship would remain afloat, but that his crew refused to "remain by her" and asked if the cutter could help. Wheeler said, "The master and mate were violently opposed to leaving the vessel, but were practically carried off by the crew."[5]

Seneca's navigator, 1st Lt. Fletcher W. Brown, immediately requested permission to lead an expedition to salvage *Wellington*. Wheeler told Brown he would consider volunteers, but, "would order no one to such a desperate enterprise." When word of the salvage effort spread through the cutter, more men volunteered than could be spared to go. Acting Machinist William L. Boyce volunteered to take charge of the engine room. Wheeler authorized Brown and Boyce to select 18 volunteers, of appropriate ratings, from *Seneca*'s crew of 8 officers, 4 warrant officers, and 107 enlisted men. Brown's challenge would be to sail the crippled ship 350 miles to Brest, France, the nearest allied port. James J. Nevins, first class boy, asked to go with the volunteers, but was turned down. When the seventeen-year-old, called "Smiling Jimmy" by the crew, begged to go, Brown relented and let him come along. One of the volunteers was a navy gunner's mate named Paul Marvelle, who was temporarily assigned to *Seneca*'s crew.[6]

Wellington's boats came along both sides of *Seneca*. While the crew climbed the rope netting to the main deck, volunteers from the cutter scrambled down into one of the collier's boats. When Donovan, *Wellington*'s master, saw *Seneca*'s volunteers, he and two of his officers convinced nine of *Wellington*'s crew to return to the ship with them. Brown assigned duties to *Seneca*'s volunteers while they rowed back to the stricken ship. On *Wellington*, the coast guardsmen quickly took up their stations: a crew manned the gun aft and broke out ammunition in case the submarine returned; lookouts were posted; and 2d Class Electrician's Mate M. C. "Sparks" Mason, the wireless operator, headed for the radio room. Boyce and his six engineers went to work in the engine room. Donovan arrived in a second boat with *Wellington*'s men. With Donovan's concurrence, Brown took charge of the salvage effort. Donovan said he would navigate for Brown. *Seneca* left *Wellington* at 12:35 PM to rejoin the unprotected convoy. The collier, disabled and adrift, wallowed in the sea-way for half an hour until the engineers could raise enough steam to get it under way. Why the German submarine never returned to sink the crippled ship remains a mystery. When *Seneca* rejoined the convoy at 2:00 PM, Wheeler sent a message to the patrol force commander requesting that help be sent to assist *Wellington*.[7]

By 12:50 PM, Boyce's engineers had enough steam up to get under way. A fresh breeze of twenty knots was blowing out of the southwest when *Wellington* came ahead slowly, turned, and headed for France. Wheeler said *Seneca*'s volunteers took turns in the fire room, heaving coal to keep up

"*Seneca* Attempts to Save *Wellington.*" On 16 September 1918 a volunteer crew, including 2d Lt. Fletcher W. Brown, USCG, from the cruising cutter *Seneca* tried to salvage the torpedoed British collier. The next day the damaged ship, loaded with coal, sank in a raging storm in the Bay of Biscay. Of the twenty *Seneca* volunteers, eleven—ten coast guard and one navy—perished in the cold waters.
Painting by David Karl Stone

steam. Machinist Mate 1st Class Mike Ryan shoveled coal in the fire room for twelve straight hours. Men working in the fire room knew escape would probably be impossible if the ship was torpedoed again, or if the forward bulkhead suddenly failed. Eventually, the volunteers got the ship up to a speed of seven knots, despite its damaged bow. Before *Wellington*'s master had abandoned ship, he had thrown all the ship's codebooks overboard as he had been instructed. Without codes, Brown was reluctant to use the wireless. He sent only one message to *Seneca*. He radioed, in the clear, that the ship was under way, making seven knots on course north sixty east, and that he had no ciphers. Brown knew Wheeler would transmit the necessary information about his situation to the appropriate authorities. A short while later, Mason heard *Seneca* radioing Brest.[8]

First Mate Hellings and members of *Wellington*'s crew sounded the forward spaces every fifteen minutes. The water level in no. 2 hold, aft of the damage, rose to three and a half feet. To keep flooding under control,

Brown had to stop the ship periodically and run the pumps using a full head of stream. When the men were not heaving coal, taking sounding, or standing watches, they worked on building a large life raft on top of no. 3 hatch. Guy wires and tackle were cleared away so the raft would float free if the ship sank. Only one lifeboat had been hoisted in the davits. Unfortunately, the boat used by Captain Donovan and his crewmen to get back to *Wellington* had been cast adrift.[9]

In his official report, Brown commented on the particular performance of Russell Elam, a cook from *Seneca*. He said, "Immediately upon board-ing *Wellington*, he [Elam] disappeared into the galley, and in a short time had provided all hands with dinner, consisting of lamb, potatoes, carrots, bread, butter, and coffee." When he appeared on the bridge with Brown's dinner, he was clad in an immaculate white serving jacket, having omit-ted no detail of service.[10]

The U.S. Navy destroyer *Warrington*, out of Brest, France, was escort-ing a westbound convoy eighty miles south of *Wellington* when its captain received a message from the escort commander. The navy ship, capable of making thirty knots, was ordered to proceed to the collier's position and escort it to France. With the destroyer en route, flooding under con-trol, and *Wellington* making between five and seven knots toward France, Wheeler said, "They had virtually won from the enemy by sheer nerve." By sundown, however, the situation was changing rapidly. Clouds gath-ered and the barometer fell. A rising wind and seas from astern soon made it impossible to keep *Wellington* on course. The ship, down by the bow, persisted in coming head up into the seas. Brown considered rigging a sea anchor to keep the ship on course, but the materials he needed had been lost when the bow was damaged. With winds from the southwest mount-ing to gale force, Brown tried to maneuver the ship, stern first, toward France. He wanted to lighten the flooded bow by letting go the anchors, but waves were crashing over the bow and water was gushing up through the forward hatch, making the forecastle inaccessible.[11]

Wellington had what was known as a turret-type hull. Because its sides bellied out just above the waterline, the boat davits were low to the water and almost horizontal when the lifeboat was rigged out for lowering. Every time the ship, which was listing to port, rolled in the seaway, the davit heads came close to forcing the lifeboat under water. Brown ordered his men to launch the boat to save it. He told them to keep the boat alongside on a sea painter so the volunteers could board if they had to abandon ship. With the situation becoming more desperate, everyone was assembled on the port boat deck except Mason, the radio operator, who kept communications with *Warrington;* three engineers, who kept the pumps running; and Brown and Donovan, who were on the bridge. Eight men—seven from *Wellington*'s crew and *Seneca*'s Assistant Master-at-Arms Daniel E. Grimshaw—got into the boat for lowering. Grimshaw's duty was to unhook the crucial forward falls. *Seneca*'s men lowered the boat into the water and the falls were unhooked. While the lifeboat was riding the sea painter, one of *Wellington*'s crew suddenly took out a knife and slashed the line, casting the lifeboat adrift. The man was apparently afraid the boat would be crushed against the ship's bulging hull in the heavy seas. Hellings, *Wellington*'s first mate, was in charge of the boat. He tried to get the men to row back to the ship, but the stormy seas were too rough and the men in the boat were not able oarsmen. The boat was blown away in the darkness, leaving *Seneca*'s party and some of *Wellington*'s crew aboard the ship with only makeshift rafts to save them from the cold and turbulent seas if the collier went down.[12]

Captain Donovan managed to take star sights and fixed *Wellington*'s position at 11:30 PM. He corrected the ship's dead reckoning position and gave it to Mason, who radioed the updated information to the destroyer *Warrington* at 11:35 PM. *Wellington* began firing rockets at fifteen minute intervals to signal its position to the destroyer. At 2:30 AM, answering rockets from the 289-foot *Warrington* were sighted. The navy ship arrived on scene just as the moon slipped below the horizon and plunged the storm-tossed sea into total blackness. Brown radioed the destroyer that the collier's only lifeboat was adrift and requested that the men be rescued and the boat returned to *Wellington*. Lt. Cdr. Norman R. Van der Veer, USN, in command of *Warrington*, successfully located the lifeboat and took the eight men aboard. Unfortunately, while the boat was alongside the navy ship, it was crushed against the ship's steel hull in the rough seas and destroyed.

On board *Wellington*, the situation became grave. Bulkheads were beginning to give way to the pounding seas and flooding was increasing. The men gathered anything that would float and put it on deck. Brown found some long planks on the fantail and three rafts were hastily constructed. They were lowered over the port quarter and secured with lines. Despite the danger of collapsing bulkheads, Machinist Boyce and Oiler 2d Class George W. Christy went down into the engine room and opened valves to bleed off pressure so the boilers would not explode when the ship went down. With the lights of *Warrington* in sight, Brown signaled in Morse code with a flashlight that he had to abandon ship immediately. He asked the destroyer to work in close to pick up his men. *Wellington* began listing rapidly to port and Brown gave the order to abandon ship. Wearing life belts, the men jumped, one after another, into the fifty degree water. They surfaced briefly and disappeared into the night. Brown sent out one last message with his flashlight: "My men are in the water." While he was signaling, Jimmy Nevins saw that Brown was still wearing his heavy officer's rubber boots. Nevins pulled off the boots while Brown flashed the last of the message. With the ship settling down by the head and beginning a slow roll, Brown climbed over the port rail on the stern and leaped into the angry, black sea. At 4:00 AM on 17 September 1918, *Wellington* lurched into its final plunge and disappeared.[13]

Warrington made an unsuccessful attempt to lower one of its boats. After two men barely escaped serious injury, Van der Veer decided it was too dangerous to launch a boat. He said, "I searched for more lifeboats, coming as close to *Wellington* as I dare in the darkness. Going alongside in the wind and sea would have been suicide." The destroyer attempted to float down three life rafts with lines attached. Van der Veer reported, "From a few hundred yards to leeward, I watched the black hull turn turtle slowly settle in the water and then disappear from sight. It was very distressing not to be able to do anything at that moment for the men in the water." *Warrington*'s six officers and ninety-seven enlisted men waited until the first light of day to attempt to move among the floating debris and recover survivors. Van der Veer said, "When dawn broke finally, we began to see men in the water. . . . Maneuvering amidst the wreckage, liferafts, and [ring] buoys, we finally picked up eight men out of the water." Three of *Warrington*'s crewmen—Coxswain William J. Taylor, 1st Class Quartermaster Robert E. Noel, and 1st Class Fireman Walter I. Sherwood—went into the heavy seas with lines around their waists to rescue the men, who were now more dead than alive, from the frigid water.

Van der Veer said he recommended the navy men for life-saving medals for their efforts.[14]

First Lieutenant Brown was one of the first volunteers sighted in the water among the flotsam. A heaving line was flung to him and he grabbed it. He then lost consciousness and had no memory of being hauled aboard. He awoke in a bunk in the chief petty officer's quarters of *Warrington.* In his memoir, Brown wrote, "My men went off in rafts, but I remained signaling a destroyer until the collier started her final plunge. Three hours and half of cold, cramps, chills, and limbs made numb and aching from swimming—then unconsciousness." Coxswain James C. Osborn, another *Seneca* survivor, was picked up by the destroyer. Van der Veer reported the coxswain's particularly courageous actions:

> Osborn, supporting a shipmate—coxswain John A. Pedersen—swam to a small life raft and placed Pedersen, who was in a semi-conscious condition, on the raft, holding him, as well as he could, between his feet. Several times both Osborn and his shipmate were washed off the raft by the high seas, whereupon Osborn went to Pedersen's assistance and replaced him on the raft. Finally, while I was going to the assistance of another man, who seemed for the time being in a more desperate predicament than Osborn, the latter semaphored from his pitching raft, "I am all right, but he's gone unless you come right away." We got them both.

For his heroism in keeping his shipmate alive, Osborn was awarded the Gold Life-Saving Medal by Congress on 16 May 1919.[15]

Of the twenty *Seneca* crewmen who volunteered to attempt to save the *Wellington,* ten coast guardsman and one navy man perished in the stormy waters of the Bay of Biscay: William H. Best, water tender; William L. Boyce, acting machinist; Russell Elam, cook; Paul Marvelle, USN, gunner's mate; James J. Nevins, boy first class; Carl S. Newbury, acting coxswain; Martin M. Ovesen, acting water tender; William H. Prime, seaman; Merton Stellenwerf, acting coxswain; Raymond H. Tingard, water tender; and August Zuleger, master-at-arms. The nine members of *Seneca*'s crew that survived the ordeal were Fletcher W. Brown, first lieutenant; George W. Christy, oiler second class; R. J. Gorman, seaman; Daniel E. Grimshaw, acting assistant master-at-arms; M. C. Mason, acting electrician second class; A. Orhelein, seaman; James C. Osborn, coxswain; John A. Pedersen, coxswain; and Michael J. Ryan, acting machinist first class. Of the collier *Wellington*'s twelve volunteers, Captain Donovan and the four crewmen who went into the water drowned.

The British Admiralty expressed its admiration of the attempt to save the *Wellington:* "Seldom in the annals of the sea has there been exhibited such self-abnegation, such cool courage and such unfailing diligence in the face of almost insurmountable difficulties. America is to be congratulated."[16]

CUTTERS TRANSFERRED TO THE NAVY

When the United States declared war on 6 April 1917, coast guard cutters *Algonquin* and *Manning* were moored at the U.S. Coast Guard's depot (shipyard) at Arundel Cove, Maryland. *Algonquin* was completing extensive maintenance and repair work. *Manning* had arrived just a few days earlier from the Pacific coast, by way of the Panama Canal. When news of the declaration of war was received, Capt. Byron L. Reed, in command of *Algonquin*, and Capt. A. J. Henderson, in command of *Manning*, mustered their crews and read them the mobilization orders. In accordance with their instructions, they then reported their ships' positions to the commandants of the naval districts to which they were now assigned—*Algonquin* to the Fifth Naval District and *Manning* to the Sixth Naval District. Both cutters were commissioned in 1898. *Algonquin* was built at Cleveland, Ohio, to serve in the Great Lakes. During the Spanish-American War, however, the ship was cut into two sections and towed into the Atlantic Ocean for service with the U.S. Navy. *Algonquin* and *Manning* were essentially the same design. *Algonquin* was 206 feet in length and displaced 1,181 tons. *Manning* was 205 feet in length and displaced 1,155 tons. The cutters had beams of thirty-two feet and drew thirteen and a half feet of water. They had the lines of the Revenue-Cutter Service's earlier clipper cutters, but with plumb bows. They were the last cutters rigged for sail. Both had received extensive modernization. Their new oil-fired boilers and redesigned steam engines produced 2,400 horsepower, giving the cutters a maximum speed of sixteen knots and a longer range. During the

The cruising cutters *Algonquin* and *Onondaga* moored before the war. When the U.S. Coast Guard transferred to the U.S. Navy, cutter commanding officers reported to naval district commandants for duty. Cutter crews slept in hammocks. Note the bedding airing on *Algonquin*'s forestay. *Mariners' Museum, Newport News, Virginia*

Spanish-American War, *Manning* served with the U.S. Navy, carrying out blockade and escort duties off Cuba.[17]

Algonquin's first task after mobilization was to provide an armed detachment to help U.S. marshals seize three German merchant ships that were interned at the port of Baltimore at the outbreak of war. When overhaul at the depot was completed, *Algonquin* proceeded to the navy yard at Norfolk, Virginia, to be painted wartime gray. On 22 April *Algonquin* began patrolling the submarine nets at the entrance to the Chesapeake Bay. Four days later, the cutter was ordered back to the ship-yard to have four 3-inch guns and a fire control system installed. When the installation of the larger guns was completed, *Algonquin* took on ammunition and swung ship in Chesapeake Bay to calibrate its magnetic compass before returning to its patrol station off Cape Henry.[18]

In May 1917, *Algonquin* received orders to report to the Seventh Naval District commandant in Florida. Sailing against the Gulf Stream, the cutter arrived at the port of Key West on 13 May and was designated the flagship for Patrol Squadron Three. Operating out of the U.S. naval base at Guantánamo Bay, Cuba, *Algonquin* patrolled in the Caribbean with the squadron commodore embarked. Two and a half months later, *Algonquin* was designated for European duty and ordered to return to Norfolk. On 2 August the commander of Patrol Squadron Three shifted his flag to the U.S. Coast Guard cutter *Tallapoosa* and *Algonquin* departed Guantánamo Bay. After arriving at Norfolk, *Algonquin* was ordered to the shipyard at Newport News, to be fitted out for overseas duty.[19]

Twenty-year-old Hamilton Cochran put his college plans on hold when war was declared, and enlisted in the U.S. Coast Guard. After three months of recruit training at the U.S. Coast Guard Academy in New London, Connecticut, he and nineteen other recruits reported to the shipyard at Newport News for cutter duty. Cochran said, "Everything about the shipyard was in a furor of work. The steady rat-a-tat-tat of the riveting machines filled the air from early morning until far into the night. Every week, and sometimes more often, a new ship would slip off the ways to take its place in the ranks of the steadily growing American Merchant Marine. Finally, on the last day of August, after six busy weeks of preparation, our ship, provisioned for a long six months, steamed slowly down the Chesapeake [Bay] and around to New York." While the cutter was at the shipyard, Capt. H. G. Hamlet relieved Reed as commanding officer.[20]

Upon mobilization, *Manning* also received orders to proceed to Norfolk. Captain Henderson was ordered to report to the commanding officer of USS *Olympia*, flagship for the Patrol Force at Hampton Roads. After coaling at Baltimore, the cutter headed south in the Chesapeake Bay on 10 April 1917. While en route, *Manning* received orders to report to Patrol Squadron Six for duty. The cutter arrived at Hampton Roads and Henderson reported to Capt. C. B. Morgan, USN, aboard his flagship, USS *Albany*. *Manning* was painted gray on 12 April and commenced patrolling in the Chesapeake Bay two days later. The cutter was next assigned to Patrol Squadron Five, headquartered at Charleston, South Carolina. Arriving on 22 April, *Manning* commenced patrolling the waters off the Carolinas and Georgia. In early June the cutter was reassigned to Patrol Squadron Two at Newport, Rhode Island. *Manning* began patrolling along the coast of Rhode Island on 8 June, just when the Portuguese brig *Ilde de St. Hiago* foundered off Block Island. The cutter rescued all the brig's passengers and crew, took them into port, and was back patrolling on station the same day. *Manning* performed a variety of patrol and escort duties in the Second, Fifth, and Sixth Naval Districts until receiving orders in August to proceed to the naval shipyard in Charleston to be fitted out for European duty.[21]

On the day war was declared, *Ossipee* was en route to Boston from its "headquarters"—a term used for a cutter's homeport—at Portland, Maine. The 908-ton, 165-foot 10-inch cutter was manned by a peacetime crew of six officers, four warrant officers, and fifty-four enlisted men. Powered by a triple expansion steam engine and water-tube boilers, *Ossipee* had a modest speed of twelve and a half knots, but had an exceptionally long range. Its hull, with a beam of thirty-two feet and a draft of eleven and a half feet, was reinforced for breaking ice in the winter season. When Capt. William H. Munter moored *Ossipee* at Boston, he was ordered to return to Maine. Munter was given command of a defense area that included the mouth of the Kennebec River and the adjacent Maine coastline. After a brief stay in Portland, *Ossipee* commenced patrolling. One week later, the cutter was reassigned to the Nantucket detachment of the patrol forces. After coaling at Melville, Rhode Island, and painting the ship war colors, Munter got *Ossipee* under way and arrived on station 23 April 1917. On 5 May the cutter was ordered to proceed to Portsmouth, New Hampshire, to receive larger guns. After having its four 6-pound guns replaced with a battery of four 3-inch guns, *Ossipee* loaded ammunition and resumed patrol duties. The cutter served with the Nantucket detachment until ordered to the Boston Navy Yard to be outfitted for duty overseas.[22]

First Lt. Fletcher W. Brown, USCG, was at the U.S. naval base at Guantánamo Bay when war was declared. He was given orders to proceed to Portland, and report to the cruising cutter *Ossipee*. To get back to the United States, Brown had to make his way across Cuba, from the southern coast to the northern coast, and then find passage across the Florida Straits to the United States. He traveled on foot and by horseback because railroads destroyed during a recent revolution had not been rebuilt. Brown wrote of his journey, "The rainy season was on, with its attendant sea of mud, and I was equipped with only three white uniforms, but no leggings. No laundry was done en route. . . . My finances totaled thirty dollars, but from strangers en route, I obtained unasked [for] loans which enabled me to accomplish the journey."[23]

Seneca was moored at its headquarters at Tompkinsville, Staten Island, New York, on 6 April 1917. At 10:00 AM, an entry was made in the cutter's log, "Received radio [message] from Division Commander that tug and three barges were flying signals of distress off Mapeaque Beach, Long Island, and to proceed to their assistance." Capt. James H. Brown got *Seneca* under way at 11:24 AM and stood up the East River. While the cutter was searching along the coast of Long Island for the vessels in distress, a radio message was received. The 10:30 PM entry in the cutter's log reported, "Received Headquarters Radio instruction Plan One Acknowledge. Acknowledged and complied with as per previous instruction. One watch on deck, gun crews assigned, ammunition supplied, double lookouts stationed forward and aft, during watch. Double officer watch stood." *Seneca* searched through the night and all the next day, but found no indication of a vessel in need of assistance. The cutter anchored off of Montauk Point at 3:10 AM on 8 April. At 9:30 that morning Captain Brown called for volunteers to "paint the ship lead color from truck to waterline." All hands volunteered and the cutter was completely painted by 7:00 PM.[24]

At 1,445 tons displacement, *Seneca* was the largest of the cruising cutters. The peacetime crew was eight officers, four warrant officers, and seventy-five enlisted men. Built at Newport News in 1908, the cutter was uniquely designed for a special mission. The U.S. Coast Guard's 1917 *Annual Report* stated, "She is popularly known as the 'derelict destroyer,' from the fact that she is the only vessel in the world which is used exclusively for the purpose of destroying floating and sunken derelicts. The act of Congress approved May 12, 1906, provided that she should be 'specially fitted for and adapted to service at sea in bad weather, for the purpose of blowing up or otherwise destroying or towing into port wrecks, derelicts, and other floating dangers to navigation.'" *Seneca* was 204 feet long, had a beam of 34 feet, and a draft of 17 feet 3 inches. As a derelict destroyer, the cutter was designed to remain at sea for long periods of time, in all kinds of water. Although relatively slow with a maximum speed of twelve and a half knots, the cutter had a large fuel capacity.[25]

Upon returning to port, *Seneca* was ordered to proceed to the New

York Navy Yard at Brooklyn to receive larger armament; a battery of four 3-inch rapid-fire guns was installed. Leaving the shipyard, *Seneca* was directed to report to Squadron Four, Patrol Force, Atlantic Fleet, headquartered at Key West, Florida. On 22 May Brown reported to the squadron commodore and received orders to patrol the waters of Cuba and the Bahama Islands to search for German submarines. The United States suspected that U-boats were rendezvousing in the sheltered waters of the islands to receive supplies. On 18 July *Seneca* was reassigned to the Seventh Naval District, headquartered at Miami, and tasked with coastal patrol duties. When designated for service overseas, the cutter returned to New York. During *Seneca*'s month at the Morse Ship Yard being overhauled and refitted for escort duty, Brown was detached and Capt. William J. Wheeler reported to assume command.[26]

The cruising cutter *Tampa* was built at Newport News in 1912 and was originally commissioned as the revenue cutter *Miami*. Renamed *Tampa* in 1916, the cutter had coal-fired water-tube boilers and was powered by a triple-expansion steam engine. A large capacity for coal—approximately 260 tons—and large water tanks, gave *Tampa* the capability for extended cruising. Moored at the port of Tampa when the United States entered the war, the cutter's peacetime complement was eight officers, four warrant officers, and fifty-nine enlisted men. When Capt. Charles Satterlee received the Plan One message, he reported to the commandant of the Seventh Naval District and awaited orders.[27]

The coast guard cutter *Tallapoosa* arrived at the port of Tampa on 8 April 1917, and crewmen joined *Tampa* crewmen in forming an armed detachment to seize the Austrian steamer *Borneo*, from the port of Fiume. Austria was one of the Central Powers allied with Germany. Seized on the morning of 9 April, the steamer was turned over to customs authorities and the master and crew were handed over to local authorities for custody. After receiving a shipment of fifty gallons of slate-colored paint and ten gallons of heat-resistant slate paint for the stack, *Tampa* sailed on 15 April. The next morning, the cutter anchored, painted the ship war colors, and installed a fire control platform on the foremast. At night, the cutter "screened all lights" and ran darkened. Under the command of the Seventh Naval District, *Tampa* patrolled the coast of Florida in the Atlantic Ocean and the Gulf of Mexico. The cutter searched for German submarines, provided training for naval reservists, aided vessels in distress, and conducted maneuvers with other war ships in the district. On 30 July *Tampa* was selected as one of the six cruising cutters to be sent overseas, and sailed for Boston that day.[28]

The cutter *Yamacraw* was at the port of Norfolk when war was declared. Capt. Randolph Ridgely Jr. immediately reported the cutter's readiness for duty to the senior officer of the patrol forces of the Atlantic coast. The 1,080-ton cutter was built in 1909 at Camden, New Jersey. *Yamacraw* had a length of 191 feet 8 inches, a beam of 32 feet 6 inches, and drew 13 feet of water. A thorough overhaul had recently been completed at the U.S. Coast Guard's Arundel Cove depot. The cutter was assigned to Patrol Squadron Six, operating from the Virginia Capes to Nantucket Shoals Lightship. On 19 July the cutter was transferred to the Fifth Naval District, headquartered at Norfolk and operated out of Chesapeake Bay until ordered to prepare for service overseas. *Yamacraw* went to the Newport News Ship and Engine Building Company on 3 August for "outfitting for distant service." The cutter sailed for Europe on 30 August.[29]

Preparation for European Duty

The continuous flow of food, ammunition, and other supplies carried by ships sailing from Britain was vital to sustain military operations in Europe. Approximately six allied army corps were being supplied through Mediterranean Sea ports. The concept of escorted convoys to protect against attacks by German U-boats was being introduced with good success. To carry out convoy operations, easily maneuvered ships with good seakeeping capabilities and endurance for extended operations were needed. Seaworthy coast guard cutters, with their experienced crews, were well suited for ocean escort duty. The U.S. Coast Guard's six cruising cutters, designated for escort work in European waters, were initially ordered to report to Squadron Two of the Patrol Forces of the Atlantic Fleet based at Gibraltar. The cutters were later reassigned to Squadron One.[30]

At 4 PM on 30 July 1917, *Tampa* took in its last line and backed away from the wharf at Key West. The cutter sailed down the channel, crossed the reef to the open sea, and headed east along the keys, en route to the Boston Navy Yard. Captain Commandant Bertholf sent a letter to the commander of the eastern division about *Tampa*'s preparation for over-seas duty. The 3 August 1917 letter stated:

> The *Tampa* is now en route to Boston. Upon her arrival you will have her fit-ted for distant service. Make arrangements immediately to have her docked, bottom cleaned and painted, and the tail shaft examined at the same time. The decks shall be strengthened so as to mount four three inch guns which will be transferred from the [cutter] *Androscoggin*. Constructor [Frederick A.] Hunnewell will be directed to proceed to Boston in the near future and you will be guided by his advice as to the location of these guns and the construc-tion of the foundations. There is on board the *Tampa* an auxiliary dynamo which is to be installed in accordance with the enclosed sketch. Additional suc-tion pipes to the fire pump are also to be installed in accordance with the accompanying blue print, the material for which you can procure at the Navy Yard. It is particularly instructed that none of this work is to be done at the Navy Yard, but by private concerns and as the necessity for this work is urgent and immediate you will have the same done at the lowest cost obtainable.[31]

After an uneventful five-day voyage, *Tampa* entered Boston harbor and moored at 4:25 PM alongside coast guard cutter *Onondaga* at the Boston Navy Yard. The next day *Tampa* exchanged nine crewmen with *Onondaga*; *Tampa* received an electrician's mate, a cook, a coxswain, and six nonrated men in exchange for nine nonrated men. *Tampa* also exchanged power launches with the cutter—*Onondaga*'s launch was in better condition. On 8 August the gunners mates and deck force began unbolting the deck guns in preparation for receiving four 3-inch guns from the cruising cutter *Androscoggin* the next day. Charts and navigation publications for the Mediterranean Sea, British Isles, Scandinavia, and the Bay of Biscay were received along with codebooks, navy publications, and flags and pennants.[32]

All unnecessary gear, including gangway davits, awning stanchions, port screens, and old hawsers were offloaded from the cutter and stowed in building no. 38 at the navy yard. Once the gear was removed, *Tampa* got under way and proceeded to Atlantic Iron Works in East Boston. Additional personnel reported aboard while the cutter was at the ship-yard, bringing the complement up to eight officers, four warrant officers, and ninety-nine enlisted men. Ten depth charges were loaded aboard on

16 August. In the cutter's log, they were described as "depth discharges." Additional crockery was brought aboard to cover breakage for six months. While installing one of the 3-inch guns on the forecastle, Ordinary Seaman C. Schrughan had his foot crushed and was taken to the hospital. Colt machine guns were brought aboard and additional radio antennas were installed. The Boston Red Cross provided 110 comfort bags and 65 sweaters for the crew. L. G. Jelsik, after finishing bugler training at the U.S. Coast Guard Academy, reported aboard for duty.[33]

On 7 September 1917 *Tampa* was hauled out on the yard's marine railway and its hull was scraped and painted. Work continued on the installation of gun platforms, fire control system, magazines, searchlights, and a Marconi shortwave receiver. Additional medical supplies were received and stowed. When dry-docking was completed, the cutter shifted back to the navy yard where ongoing work was completed and ammunition was loaded aboard from a lighter. At the yard, a "smoke producer" was installed and the cutter received twenty-six sacks of mail. In an attempt to have all yard work finished, *Tampa* delayed getting under way from the navy yard until 8:30 PM on 15 September. Prior to getting under way, the cutter's log indicated that "yard force left ship with repairs uncompleted." The cutter proceeded to an anchorage at Presidents Roads, Massachusetts, for the night. During the next two days, *Tampa* conducted sea trials and gun drills. The next afternoon, with high winds blowing out of the north northeast, the cutter got under way. The cutter sailed in company with USS *Hubbard* to New York. Mooring at the navy yard in Brooklyn on 19 September, the crew was granted liberty. After taking on 175 tons of steaming coal, the cutter left the navy yard for anchorage in Gravesend Bay, New York.[34]

DEPLOYMENT

Ossipee, the first coast guard cutter to deploy to Europe, departed Boston on 15 August. After crossing the Atlantic Ocean and arriving at Gibraltar on 30 August, the cutter's commanding officer, Captain Munter, reported to the commander of the U.S. Patrol Forces for duty. He also made an official call on the senior British naval officer at Gibraltar. *Seneca* was the next cutter to sail for European waters. Departing 9 August, the cutter reached the Azores twenty days later. *Seneca* took on coal at Ponta

Delgada and departed the Azores after two days. Instructions, drills, and gunnery exercises during the transit readied the crew for combat operations. The cutter arrived at Gibraltar five days later. The cutter *Manning* sailed for the European war zone on 29 August. The crew had been increased for overseas duty to eight commissioned officers, four warrant officers, and ninety-six enlisted men. *Manning* arrived at Ponta Delgada, Azores, on 9 September. After *Yamacraw* completed outfitting at the Newport News shipyard on 30 August, it sailed for Europe the same day. *Yamacraw* joined *Manning* in the Azores and the two cutters departed for Gibraltar in company on 12 September. En route, *Yamacraw* sighted a U-boat, but the submarine submerged and was gone before any action could be taken. The cutters arrived at Gibraltar on 16 September and reported for duty.[35]

Captain Hamlet sailed *Algonquin* north to New York from the Newport News shipyard. He arrived on 3 September, and was relieved as commanding officer by Capt. George C. Carmine two weeks later. *Algonquin* sailed for Boston on 20 September. The cutter rendezvoused with the wooden-hulled navy minesweeper USS *Edwards*, to escort it to Europe. After a three-day port call at Halifax, Nova Scotia, the two ships headed east. Hamilton Cochran, a seaman aboard *Algonquin*, described the departure of the two ships:

> It was a fine clear day when we steamed out of the harbor and all hands were eager to encounter the excitement of being in the war zone. But the following day, the weather took a decided change and soon heavy black clouds massed themselves on the horizon. Several hours later we were in the midst of a terrific storm. . . . As night drew on, the storm increased in violence and it was necessary to put out oil bags, which helped to break the force of the huge waves which were breaking over the poor sweeper [USS *Edwards*]. She certainly was having a hard time of it. Meanwhile on our own ship we had plenty to think about. Oh what a lot of seasick, seagoing gobs we were! Lying about the decks, in the scuppers, anywhere was good enough.[36]

Edwards, formerly an oyster boat, did not carry enough coal to make the crossing to Europe and had to be towed. When the minesweeper, which was camouflaged like a black and white barber's pole, began taking

The 190-foot cruising cutter *Tampa*, formerly named *Miami*, was commissioned in 1912. The cutter's peacetime crew was increased by forty enlisted billets for a total of eight officers, four warrant officers, and ninety-nine enlisted men before deploying to the European war zone. *Mariners' Museum, Newport News, Virginia*

on water during the storm, *Algonquin* hove to next to it and waited for the weather to abate. On 3 October the cutter towed *Edwards* back to Halifax where it was determined the minesweeper was in no condition to make the crossing. On 5 October *Algonquin* once again departed Halifax, en route to the war zone. After ten days of steady steaming with good weather and moderate seas, the cutter reached the Strait of Gibraltar. Just after midnight, a lookout sighted a suspicious object off the starboard bow. General quarters rang throughout the cutter. *Algonquin*'s crew tumbled out of their hammocks and headed for their battle stations; everyone was certain it was a submarine. With all guns manned the cutter closed on the contact and discovered an old tramp steamer, hugging the Moroccan coast. *Algonquin* approached the Rock of Gibraltar on the morning of 16 October. Cochran was on deck when the ship drew near. In his journal, he wrote, "I shall always remember my first sight of Gibraltar as we proceeded up the Strait in the early morning with the bright sunshine bathing that huge mass of rock and making its every detail stand out against the flawless blue of the sky. Gibraltar is nothing more than a huge rock, looking as if it had been carved out of some gigantic mountain range by the wondrous hand of nature."[37]

Tampa was the last cutter to sail for Europe, departing on 22 September 1917. The officer of the deck recorded in the ship's log: "2:30 Piped down bags and hammocks and secured for sea. Up anchor and underway. Force forming in single column and standing through Ambrose Channel, various courses, 8 knots." The force consisted of the gunboat USS *Paducah* as the flagship, the converted trawler USS *Hubbard*, USS *Tampa*, and five French submarine chasers. Clearing the channel, the subchasers were taken in tow for the voyage to Halifax. The trip was delayed because the tow lines to the French vessels repeatedly parted. After three days in Halifax, the ships got under way on the afternoon of 6 October. The French subchasers were towed during the transit and cast off on 14 October to proceed under their own power. When the force approached the Azores, the ships were ordered to man their guns and commence zigzagging as a defense against submarines. The cutter *Tampa* moored to a buoy in Ponta Delgada harbor at 2:55 PM on 17 October, and granted liberty to one third of the crew. After coaling and taking on water, the cutter departed for Gibraltar four days later. *Tampa* entered Gibraltar harbor under passing rain showers on 27 October. Captain Satterlee moored at 7:45 AM and then reported to the commander of Squadron Two, Patrol Forces of the Atlantic Fleet for duty. *Tampa*'s arrival completed the deployment of coast guard cutters for service in the European war zone.[38]

CHAPTER 3

CONVOY ESCORT DUTY

The greatest disaster suffered by the Coast Guard, and the largest individual loss of life sustained by naval forces during the war, occurred on September 26, 1918, when the cutter *Tampa* was sunk with all hands on board in Bristol Channel.

—SECRETARY OF THE NAVY, 1918 *ANNUAL REPORT*

ARLINGTON NATIONAL CEMETERY

Treasury Secretary Andrew W. Mellon, Secretary of the Navy Curtis D. Wilbur, and U.S. Coast Guard Commandant Rear Adm. Frederick C. Billard dedicated a monument to coast guardsmen killed during the Great War on the afternoon of 23 May 1928. After the dedication, U.S. Coast Guard Academy cadets, standing on either side of the monument, came to attention and the navy band played. The cruising cutter *Seneca* and the new cutter *Tampa*, which transported the cadets to Arlington National Cemetery from the academy, were anchored in the Potomac River, along with the cutter *Apache*. When the music ended, *Apache* fired a twenty-one gun salute, while cutter crews manned the rails.[1]

The idea for a national shrine to honor coast guardsmen killed during World War I was first proposed by Capt. William J. Wheeler, USCG. Wheeler commanded the coast guard cutter *Seneca* and the navy gunboat *Paducah* in European waters during the war. Under his direction, funds were raised, a site at Arlington National Cemetery was obtained, and architect George Howe and sculptor Gaston Lachaise were commissioned for the project. The resulting monument was a white marble pyramid set on a rugged granite base. It stood twelve feet high and the sides of the triangular pyramid were fourteen and a half feet wide at the base. The monument, suggestive of a rocky coast and a marker warning of dangers to navigation, symbolized the U.S. Coast Guard's ideals of steadfastness and endurance. A sculptured sea gull in flight was in front of the monument and represented the service's watchful, untiring spirit. The U.S. Coast Guard seal and motto, "Semper Paratus," were carved into the face of the pyramid. Names of the 192 officers and men who lost their lives in the performance of their duties during the war were inscribed on the sides of the pyramid.[2]

On 11 November 1999, seventy-one years after the original dedication, another three men stood on the same hallowed ground. Transportation Secretary Rodney E. Slater, U.S. Coast Guard Commandant Adm. James M. Loy, and U.S. Coast Guard Master Chief Petty Officer Vincent Patton jointly laid a wreath at the base of the war memorial on Veterans Day. After placing the wreath, the three men stepped back under a gray sky and stood at attention while the doleful sound of taps echoed across the hills of Arlington National Cemetery. The wreath paid tribute to all of the U.S. Coast Guard's fallen heroes. When the last of the bugler's notes faded into the distance, the 320 people gathered on "Coast Guard Hill" for the ceremony on that cold and damp morning moved closer to the monument. Secretary Slater used the occasion of the annual Veterans Day wreath-laying ceremony to present Purple Heart Medals, awarded posthumously, to the 111 coast guardsmen of the original coast guard cutter *Tampa*. The officers and men of the cutter had never been awarded Purple Heart Medals. Family members of three of the crewmen—Ms. Mildred McGourty Blair, daughter of 2d Lt. John F. McGourty; Mr. John Henry Nix Sr., relative of Ship's Writer Jacob Darling Nix; and Mr. Ralph Poppell, relative of Seaman Felix George

"*Tampa* Sinking in World War I." On 26 September 1918, the cutter was relieved as ocean escort for Convoy H.G. No. 107 by the British home waters escort. While en route to Milford Haven, Wales, *Tampa* was torpedoed by the German submarine U-91 at 8:45 PM. The cutter sank, killing all hands. *Painting by John D. Wisinski*

Poppell—represented *Tampa*'s crew, in accepting the medals.[3]

The tragic loss of *Tampa* occurred just forty-six days before the end of World War I. The cutter completed the successful escort of merchant vessels in Convoy H.G. (home waters bound from Gibraltar) No. 107 from Gibraltar to England's Bristol Channel on 26 September 1918. Relieved by home waters danger zone escorts, *Tampa* departed the convoy at 6:45 PM and headed for Milford Haven, sixty miles away. The cutter sent a message, giving its estimated time of arrival. Two hours later, crews on ships in the convoy heard a loud explosion from the direction in which the cutter had departed. When *Tampa* did not arrive at Milford Haven, U.S. destroyers and British patrol vessels were sent to search for it. The coast guard cutter *Yamacraw* was at Pembroke Docks, Wales, when Capt. John G. Berry, commanding officer, learned that *Tampa* was overdue and possibly sunk. He immediately volunteered to get under way and search for survivors. The admiral in charge of Pembroke Docks thanked Berry for his offer to assist, but said five destroyers, including the USS *Wilkes, Davis,* and *Stockton,* and two divisions of trawlers were already searching the area. He said a large amount of flotsam had been found, but no survivors. Some of the debris picked up by patrol crafts no. 65 and no. 45 was marked *Tampa.* The admiral expressed condolences to Berry, "Myself and staff much regret the loss of this ship and her gallant commander Satterlee and her crew. On return of my vessels you shall have the latest information." In addition to floating debris, search vessels found two uniformed bodies that were unidentifiable. British listening-in stations on shore reported hearing German submarine activity in the area at the time *Tampa* was sunk.[4]

The U.S. Coast Guard's 1917 *Annual Report* described *Tampa* as having "an unusually large coal and water capacity, which enables her to make long-continued cruises in search of derelicts and in the assistance of distressed vessels." With a coal capacity of 260 tons, the cutter did not have to refuel at Gibraltar after escorting every southbound convoy. The coal used by the ships at Gibraltar had to be shipped in, so *Tampa* may have waited until arriving at ports in England, where coal was more readily available, to take on fuel. If that was the case, *Tampa* was likely steaming with some empty bunkers, en route to Milford Haven to recoal. This could explain why there were no survivors from the torpedo attack.

The disastrous loss of all hands when German submarine U-91 torpedoed *Tampa* may have resulted because the cutter was ripped open by a massive internal explosion. The Navy Department report on the loss of *Tampa* stated, "It is reported by other vessels of the convoy that the *Tampa* . . . had gone well ahead of the convoy, and that about 8:45 PM the shock of an explosion was felt." For the shock to be felt twenty miles away, the explosion had to have been enormous. If the torpedo struck the cutter in the vicinity of empty bunkers, the impact of the detonation would have stirred up clouds of suspended coal dust in the bowels of the ship. Any flash or flame could have triggering a coal dust explosion. A chain reaction explosion deep in the ship would have torn the hull open, sending *Tampa* to the bottom in minutes.[5]

A total of 131 persons lost their lives when *Tampa* sank; 111 of these were coast guardsmen: 7 officers, 4 warrant officers, and 100 enlisted men. Four U.S. Navy personnel assigned to *Tampa* also died. Two were medical personnel: Lt. (j.g.) H. H. Teter (Medical Corps), USN, and Pharmacist's Mate 2d Class C. L. Dalton, USN. Two were watch officers aboard for training: Ens. Edward Reavely, USN, and Ens. David Hoffman, USNR. Sixteen British passengers—one naval officer, ten enlisted men, and five civilians—aboard the cutter for the trip from Gibraltar to England, were killed when *Tampa* sank.[6]

Upon learning of the loss of the *Tampa*, the British Admiralty addressed a letter to Vice Adm. W. S. Sims, commander of U.S. naval forces operating in European waters: "Their Lordships desire to express their deep regret at the loss of the USS *Tampa*. Her record since she has been employed in European waters as an ocean escort to convoys has been remarkable. . . . Appreciation of the good work done by the USS *Tampa* may be some consolation to those bereft and Their Lordships would be glad if this could be conveyed to those concerned." During European service, *Tampa* escorted eighteen convoys from Gibraltar. Of the 350 ships escorted, only 2 were lost through enemy action. Just three weeks before *Tampa* was lost, Capt. Charles Satterlee and his crew received special recognition from Rear Adm. A. P. Niblack, commander of patrol squadrons based on Gibraltar. From his flagship, the tender USS *Buffalo*, Niblack addressed a special letter of commendation to *Tampa* on 5 September praising the cutter for exemplary performance in carrying out escort duties. He noted that the cutter was never disabled and was always ready whenever called upon. Niblack wrote, "This excellent record is an evidence of a high state of efficiency and excellent ship's spirit and an organization capable of keeping the vessel in service with a minimum of shore assistance. The squadron commander takes great pleasure in congratulating the commanding officer, officers, and crew on the record which they have made." The U.S. Coast Guard Commandant Ellsworth P. Bertholf sent letters to the next of kin of the crew of the *Tampa*. The 8 October 1918 letter to Mrs. Bertha L. Earp, said, "This office is deeply grieved to announce the loss of the Coast Guard Cutter *Tampa* with all hands in Bristol Channel, England, at 8:45 p.m., September 26, 1918. The dispatches show that your husband, First

Lieutenant J. M. Earp, was on board the *Tampa* at the time and that hope has been abandoned of finding any survivors of the catastrophe. . . . in the sinking of the *Tampa*, the naval force has suffered its greatest individual loss during the war."[7]

INITIAL DUTIES IN EUROPEAN WATERS

When coast guard cutters first arrived in the war zone, they were employed as danger zone escorts, protecting merchant convoys approaching or departing from Gibraltar. Danger zone escorts accompanied outbound convoys for thirty hours after sailing from Gibraltar, leaving them under cover of darkness on the second night. Escorts met inbound convoys when they were a day out and brought them into Gibraltar. To the north, in British waters, home waters danger zone escorts from English and Welsh ports carried out the same operation, except they stayed with outbound convoys longer. Convoys arriving from Britain were re-formed at Gibraltar and escorted to ports in the Mediterranean Sea. USS *Ossipee*, the first coast guard cutter to reach Gibraltar, sailed from Boston and reached Base 9 at Gibraltar on 30 August 1917. After mooring in the harbor, *Ossipee*'s commanding officer, Capt. William H. Munter, reported to Rear Adm. H. B. Wilson, USN, aboard his flagship, the cruiser USS *Birmingham*. Wilson commanded the patrol squadron based at Gibraltar and was the senior American naval officer present. *Ossipee* was assigned to Patrol Squadron Two for duty. Munter then paid a call on the senior British officer present. The cutter sailed four days later with its first convoy, as one of the ships of the danger zone escort. *Seneca* arrived at Gibraltar at 5:30 PM on 4 September, and moored to buoy no. 14 inside the harbor. Captain Wheeler reported to the flagship and was also assigned to Patrol Squadron Two. After recoaling and taking on provisions, *Seneca* sailed on its first escort duty nine days later, accompanying a merchant convoy to the nearby port of Tangier, Morocco, and returning the next day. In addition to danger zone escort duties, cutters were also used in the Mediterranean Sea during the first month after their arrival. They escorted convoys to Oran, Algeria, Tangier, Morocco, and Bizerte, Tunisia.[8]

The cutters *Manning* and *Yamacraw* entered the harbor at Gibraltar, just after noon on 16 September. The commanding officers of the newly arrived cutters reported to Admiral Wilson for duty and were assigned to the western division of Patrol Squadron Two. After coaling and out-fitting, on the third day *Manning* sailed from Gibraltar to escort its first convoy through the danger zone, staying with the ships until they were 215 miles west of Gibraltar. *Yamacraw* sailed on its fourth danger zone escort on 5 October with USS *Machias* and the cutter *Ossipee*. That night, *Yamacraw*'s crew heard two explosions just after 11:00 PM; a German U-boat had torpedoed one of the merchant ships of the con-voy. *Yamacraw* was detached from the escort and ordered to return to rescue survivors from the stricken ship. The German torpedoes broke the back of the merchantman and it rapidly sank in the darkness. Only four survivors were recovered. The next morning the submarine made a second attack on the convoy, but its attempt to torpedo a ship was unsuccessful.[9]

The last two coast guard cutters assigned to European duty arrived at Gibraltar in October 1917. *Algonquin* moored in the harbor on 16 October. After mine chutes (depth charge racks) were installed on its stern and other repairs were completed, *Algonquin* sailed with its first convoy on 27 October. That same day *Tampa* arrived and moored in the harbor.[10]

BASE 9, GIBRALTAR

Gibraltar is a rocky peninsula on the north side of the Strait of Gibraltar, the vital waterway separating Spain and North Africa. The British first established a naval base on Gibraltar in 1704. The penin-sula was connected to the southern coast of Spain by a one half mile long sandy spit, called "neutral ground." A British gate stood at the Gibraltar end of the spit and Spanish soldiers guarded the northern end. The base was strategically located at the eastern end of the strait, enabling Britain and its allies to control ship movements between the Atlantic Ocean and the Mediterranean Sea. The Rock of Gibraltar—called "Gib" or "The Rock" by the sailors—was a limestone formation 2 3/4 miles long, 3/4 of a mile wide, and 1,408 feet high. The town and harbor were located on the northwest side of the peninsula. Hamilton Cochran, a coast guard seaman aboard *Algonquin*, kept a journal of his experiences during his European duty. He described Gibraltar: "The north and east sides are very steep and precipitous, rising almost straight up from the water. However on the other two sides of the rock, it rises a great deal more gradually and on the western slope will be found the harbor and town. The town itself is not much more than a jumble of white and yellow and blue houses with queer narrow winding streets, while the buildings rise one above the other with fascinating irregularity."[11]

When cutter crews first went ashore at Gibraltar, the sights and sounds in the strange land were fascinating. The brightly colored, Spanish-style houses had courtyards decorated with flower gardens and small balconies overlooking the streets. Ships from all over the world arrived at Gibraltar to be assembled into freight convoys. Coast guardsmen on liberty mingled with sailors from several nations on Main Street. The novelty of the new port soon wore thin, however, and the monotony of convoy duty became a reality. Before long, Cochran said, "There was absolutely no decent place to go for recreation, except a couple musty, dusty, so-called homes for British soldiers and sailors. The most exciting thing to do there was to play checkers or read a month old English newspaper. The average two fisted American sailor, going ashore after weary days at sea, demands more amusement than that. Of course there was the Theatre Royal, but unless you understood Spanish, you could not make out what they were jabbering about."[12]

During in-port periods, coast guardsmen managed to find ways to entertain themselves. Cutter crews organized baseball and basketball teams and competed among themselves and with ships of other services. Pulling boat races were held in the harbor. Captain Wheeler said, "Amateur theatrical performances held in Gibraltar early in the war revealed an astonishing amount and variety of talent from the Coast Guard. A performer from the *Seneca*, whose services were often requisitioned, both in Gibraltar and in the British Isles, was an ex-cowboy, a lariat artist with considerable experience on the stage."[13]

Seaman Frederick R. Foulkes was assigned to the cutter USS *Manning*. In a letter to his father, he joked and wrote about life aboard ship. He said,

We have a dog aboard for which I am supposed to be the cause. Yesterday, the Captain ordered me ashore to get him a muzzle. I mean a muzzle for the

A coast guardsman on watch stands next to a forward deck gun aboard the 205-foot cruising cutter USS *Manning*, anchored at Milford Haven, Wales. *Manning* was one of the U.S. Coast Guard's six cruising cutters assigned to ocean escort duty in the European war zone. *U.S. Coast Guard Historian*

dog. I did not mind as I was not on liberty yesterday and therefore went ashore on time belonging to Uncle Sam. "Rags," as we call the dog, does not like his new face guard. Especially after the cat found out he could not bite her, for she has chased him a merry chase. . . . I have a fine coat of tan now as I spend my afternoons, which give me one o'clock liberty, in swimming. The water is a little cool, but the sun is hot and the air is fine. . . . You can tell your friends that your sea-going son is still alive and does not seem to deteriorate with sea service. As they say, " It is a great life if you don't weaken."

In another letter home, Foulkes wrote to his mother about the scarcity of personal supplies. He said, "I would like to have some Pepsodent Tooth Paste. . . . A couple of boxes of Week End chocolates would go down fine once in a while. We can get no candy over here at all. A good nut cake or fruit cake would not make me mad either."[14]

Ocean Escorts

With the arrival of *Algonquin* and *Tampa*, the six coast guard cutters attached to Patrol Squadron Two took on a new mission: ocean escort of freight convoys sailing between Gibraltar and ports in Great Britain. *Seneca* sailed for Britain on its first ocean escort duty on 19 October 1917 as the lone escort for the eleven merchant ships of Convoy H.G. No. 23. During the voyage, two of the ships in the convoy collided; the steamer *Usher* sank as a result of damages. *Seneca*'s commanding officer said the freight convoy system was just beginning when the cutters arrived at Gibraltar and that there were a number of problems and difficulties. At night, ships in the convoys ran darkened and could only use light or radio signals in an emergency. The masters and crews of the merchant ships, coming from many different countries, were unfamiliar with the new system and were very reluctant to sail in such close proximity to other ships without lights. The slow speed and poor maneuverability of the bulky merchant vessels made it difficult for them to maintain station, especially at night with no lights and no communications. When bad weather, low visibility, and the constant threat of submarine attack were added to the equation, convoy escort work became a harrowing business.[15]

Prior to a convoy's departure, a conference was held with the masters of all the merchant ships, escort commanding officers, and the convoy commodore. Written instructions were distributed to all participants. The instructions included a diagram of the convoy, names and positions of all the ships in the convoy, and mast heights for each ship. Mast heights were necessary for station keeping; conning officers used stadimeters to maintain proper distances between ships. At one conference, the master of a Russian ship said through an interpreter that he was not sure he could comply with the order to sail with a darkened ship. He explained that every order he gave on his ship had to be approved by the soviet commission and he was not sure they would approve the order regarding lights. Wheeler said, "He was assured that if his vessel showed any lights [at night], she would be sunk by gunfire." This apparently impressed the soviet commission; no lights were shown on the Russian ship after dark.[16]

Due to the shortage of appropriate ships for ocean escort duty, only one vessel was usually assigned to each freight convoy; each convoy had six to thirty ships. A British naval officer was assigned as convoy commodore for each convoy and sailed on a merchant vessel in the front line. The single escort ship generally maintained a station six to eight hundred yards ahead of the columns of ships. The columns were spaced four to eight hundred yards apart, with ships in line separated by intervals of four hundred yards. The escort zigzagged back and forth ahead of the convoy and kept the lead ships in alignment, abeam of each other. Wheeler said, "It necessitated the utmost vigilance on the part of the officer conning the escort ship and utmost confidence in the steering gear, necessarily overworked by constant zigzagging." The most dangerous part of each voyage was when the newly formed convoys first departed and were still in the danger zone. In addition to the submarine threat, which was highest in this area, there was the constant danger of collision between ships operating in close proximity without communications. Danger zone escorts were stationed on the flanks and astern of the newly formed convoys, not just to protect them from submarine attacks, but to keep them together as well. Escorts continually had to round up stragglers, particularly at night, and get them back into position in the convoy; this was done without the benefit of lights or radio communications.[17]

The threat of a collision was greatly increased for escort ships, because timid merchant ship masters worked their way out of the body of the convoy after nightfall to take a position off the flank column to reduce the possibility of their ship being involved in a collision. Most prevalent during the early months of the convoy system, this maneuver created a serious danger for conscientious escort skippers. Escorts stayed close to the outboard column of ships to avoid losing contact with the convoy in the darkness. Wheeler reported that "the escort would suddenly be confronted by the specter in the form of a truant vessel, looming up ahead with no running lights to indicate which was the safest way to shift the helm. Close shaves were too numerous to mention and the nervous tension experienced by a zealous skipper of a patrol boat, during hours of darkness and thick weather, was extreme. Why more patrol boats were not sunk in collisions is a mystery." The capability of merchant masters to adapt to operating in close proximity improved greatly from the beginning of a convoy to the end. Coast guard crews had the highest respect for the predominantly British merchant mariners who manned the freight ships and demonstrated their proficiency under extreme conditions.[18]

Seaman Cochran described sailing with a convoy. He said, "An outbound convoy leaving Gibraltar was always an impressive sight. Along about noon, the ships would start out of the harbor and steam slowly toward the Straits, flying their code flags which indicated their number and position in the convoy. Small speedy submarine chasers darted about here and there, giving instructions to the heavily laden vessels and keeping a watchful eye on any suspicious streak of foam." In late afternoon, when the shadows from the mountains of Morocco grew longer, the convoy would be in formation at half speed, heading for the open sea. Once clear of land, the flagship would raise a three-flag-hoist, signaling an increase to convoy speed. Cochran said:

> We know that we are started once more on our dangerous mission. As evening draws on, the ships take a close formation which is a risky business for there is always danger of a collision. On several occasions, vessels in our convoy were forced to put back to Gibraltar in seriously damaged condition due to colliding in the dark. No lights of any kind were permitted and it was a serious offense for a man to light even a match on deck. Presently, through the darkness on our starboard hand, there flashes a bright light. It is Tariffa, the last beacon we pass on the Spanish coast. Soon the lookout reports another flash which is our old friend, Spartel Light on the rugged Moorish coast. Now we know we are practically through the Straits and really at sea.[19]

On a foggy night in December 1917, two ships in a convoy collided. The Italian steamship *Torona* rammed the British freighter *Sahara* from astern. *Sahara* sent a message to ocean escort *Seneca*: "That Italian astern has run into me and cut my stern bulwark down to the deck. . . . We find one Italian aboard. We don't know what has become of the rest." The message to *Seneca* was immediately followed by one from *Torona* that said, "Senuka come quick!" The cutter worked its way around the flanks of the convoy in the thick weather and came abeam of the Italian ship. *Torona* was still under way and holding its approximate station. *Seneca* steamed alongside the Italian ship until daybreak. In the first light of morning, Wheeler saw that the ship was flying the Italian flag at half mast. The flag was in the lowered position in mourning for its mate who was lost overboard in the collision at night. The Italian mariner, who ended up on *Sahara*'s stern, turned out to be *Torona*'s missing second mate.[20]

Convoys

Northbound and southbound convoy routes were varied widely to deceive German U-boats and avoid the possibility of collisions between darkened convoys that were traveling in opposite directions. Longer routes and the necessity for convoys to travel at the speed of the slowest ship resulted in seven- to twelve-day transits between Gibraltar and ports in Wales and England. Cutters generally remained in port from three days to two weeks between convoys to take on fuel, resupply, and make repairs, as well as provide rest for their crews. During sixteen and one half months in the war zone, the cutter *Algonquin* escorted nineteen convoys and was under way with convoys 45 percent of the time. Thirty- to forty-five-day in-port maintenance periods were scheduled for the cutters for overhaul, repair, and refitting as necessary. Maintenance and repair work was normally accomplished at facilities at Gibraltar or at ports in Great Britain. When there was no room in British dockyards in the summer of 1918, *Algonquin* was sent to Lisbon, Portugal, for repairs.[21]

As the months passed, convoy speeds steadily decreased. The overworked merchant ships sailed continuously for three years and needed overhaul and repair, but time could not be spared. While escorting one convoy, *Seneca* hailed a British ship by megaphone and requested it get up more speed to get into position. The Scottish master replied, "I dinna ken. I dinna ken. This ship is nae liner. She is an auld box." The slowest

Forty-three-year-old Capt. Charles Satterlee, commanding officer of USS *Tampa*, had his picture taken during a visit to London in 1918. After Satterlee's death aboard *Tampa*, the U.S. Navy named a destroyer in his honor. USS *Satterlee* (DD-190) was transferred to the British navy at the beginning of World War II. Renamed *Belmont*, it was torpedoed by a German U-boat and was lost with all hands. *U.S. Coast Guard Museum*

convoy Wheeler sailed with traveled at a speed of five and one quarter knots and the fastest at a speed of just over nine knots.[22]

When *Tampa* departed Gibraltar with its first convoy on 4 November 1917, light winds were blowing from the southeast and the seas were smooth. Two days into the voyage, an entry in the ship's log read, "Zigzagging. Bright moonlight, starlight night. At midnight reduced speed to 60 rpms. Dropped back of convoy until it was out of sight." Presumably, this maneuver was to check for German submarines that might be trailing the ships and waiting for a chance to attack after the danger zone escorts had departed. *Tampa* crossed St. Brides Bay into Milford Haven with the convoy on 14 November and moored at Pembroke, Wales, completing its first ocean escort without incident. After mooring, Captain Satterlee traveled to London to make a call on Vice Admiral Sims at his headquarters. Three days later, *Tampa* departed with a southbound convoy. Just after midnight on 21 November 21, lookouts on *Tampa* saw lights shining astern. Satterlee set general quarters, increased to full speed, and turned to investigate. He discovered that two merchant ships in the convoy, SS *Bilbster* and SS *Mauban*, had collided in the darkness. *Bilbster*'s port bow was stove in and *Mauban* could not get under way. *Tampa* took *Bilbster*'s crew of thirty-six aboard and SS *Corbin* evacuated the crew of *Mauban*. Twelve of *Bilbster*'s crew volunteered to return to their ship and were able to get the ship under way. After ordering *Bilbster* to make for the nearest port and requesting a tug to take *Mauban* in tow, *Tampa* rejoined the convoy.[23]

Between convoys, cutters at Gibraltar got under way for antisubmarine gunnery practice. An incident in July 1918 indicated the effectiveness of the target practice. Convoy H.G. No. 90, consisting of twenty-five ships, was northbound from Gibraltar on 13 July when one of the ships sounded the submarine warning signal and hoisted flags indicating "submarine to star-board." *Seneca* dropped two depth charges on the flank of the convoy and then headed for what appeared to be the wake of a periscope and upper part of a conning tower at a range of five thousand yards. The cutter closed on the object and opened fire, expending twenty-eight rounds. Wheeler reported in his war diary: "The object was hit, but on closer approach it was found to be a dead whale floating on its side showing a white line and a darker upper portion, bearing a striking resemblance to the conning tower and wake of a submarine." The cease fire order was given at 4:30 PM. When *Seneca* approached the object, Wheeler could see that his gun crew had scored four good hits on the carcass at the surface of the water.[24]

One of the cutters came up with a novel approach for providing prac-tice for machine gun crews. A boathook staff was fitted with a bridle and attached to the wire of the cutter's deep-sea sounding machine. One end of the staff was weighted so that when it was towed with two hundred fathoms (twelve hundred feet) of wire paid out, the other end rode about a foot out of the water. A tin can was attached to make it look like a periscope. While the cutter zigzagged on the flank of the convoy, gun crews rotated at the after machine guns, firing at the simulated periscope. In the summer of 1918, cutter armament was improved; 3-inch guns were replaced with a battery of four 4-inch 50-caliber 1918 model guns. The guns were installed at shipyards in England. Yard crews worked around the clock to make the installations, without disrupting convoy schedules. Y-guns for projecting depth charges were also installed on the cutters.[25]

PORT CALLS

Cutters escorted convoys to and from ports in Great Britain: Milford Haven and Pembroke Docks in Wales; and Falmouth, Davenport, and Plymouth in England. After ships had been in the war zone for six months, allied sailors were allowed one free trip on the British railway system. Seaman Foulkes, aboard the cutter *Manning*, wrote in a letter to his father:

> Well father I have really sad news this time. I am going to touch you for some money. I have a good reason though you see on account of my allotment I have never been able to save much money. I have always been able to hold my own (with little fluctuations). . . . Of course I want to see London in her war dress and need some spondulix [money] to do it with. $25 would fix me up fine as fellows have gone there with about that much and even paid their fare. A postal money order is no good over here. The best way to send it that I know of is by registered mail. You can take the twenty-five out of the money I am sending home, so I will feel as though I am doing Europe myself. Only, I guess, I had better be careful Europe does not *do* me.[26]

While cutters escorted convoys to both ports in Wales and ports in England, crews preferred to go ashore at the English ports. Cochran said,

> On many of our convoys from Gibraltar, we went right up the English Channel. . . . When this was the case, our destination was Plymouth and all hands were greatly pleased whenever we visited this place, for Plymouth is quite a lively town and affords many amusements and pleasures not found in the small, out-of-the-way Welsh village of Pembroke Dock. Moreover, we usually got a short leave in Plymouth and a number of us went up to London and enjoyed viewing the sights of that historic old city.[27]

One coast guardsman, commenting about his shipmates meeting English girls, said, "The American sailors are greatly more interested in the capturing of European girls, than in the getting of the terrible 'Hun.' A convincing proof is that our English mail is nearly as large as the American. At least, it works out that way lately." In a letter to his mother, Foulkes probably caused some concern at home: "My spirits are not the best, as I just received a fifteen days' quarantine [restriction to ship] today. I sure did want to get ashore today, too. . . . Do you think I am too young to marry? I guess I am, so don't worry. But I am afraid some of the boys will fall. I don't blame them for there are some nice girls over here."[28]

When *Algonquin* sailed to Lisbon for dockyard maintenance in 1918, the cutter arrived on the Fourth of July. The officers and men were invited to an Independence Day reception at the American embassy. During the six weeks in Lisbon, *Algonquin*'s crew, along with the crews of two U.S. Navy ships also at the port, participated in an athletic event in the city. Cochran said the ships "gave a big field meet for the benefit of the citizens, who thronged the stadium and were very much interested in everything that took place. Our ship succeeded in winning the tug o war, for which the *Seculo*, Lisbon's foremost newspaper, presented us with a handsome loving cup, suitably engraved in Portuguese."[29]

HMS *COWSLIP* RESCUE

Convoy escort duty was primarily a continuous chain of monotonous back-to-back port and starboard watches, punctuated by brief periods of action and great excitement. One of these times occurred on 16 April 1918, after *Seneca* sailed from Milford Haven, Wales, with a convoy of twenty-four ships. It was the cutter's tenth trip as an ocean escort. After leaving the home waters danger zone, *Seneca* was once again the sole protector of a convoy sailing across the Bay of Biscay and down the west coast of the Iberian Peninsula. Nearing the end of the voyage, contact was made with the Gibraltar danger zone escort on the afternoon of the eighth day and additional escorts soon joined the convoy. The danger zone escort consisted of American destroyers, British Q ships, and small craft. Two British 262-foot-long "flower"-class ships, *Cowslip* and *Chrysanthemum*, were among the escorts; the two ships took stations on either quarter of the convoy.

A cool breeze, blowing off the ocean from the east at fifteen knots, lowered the air temperature to fifty-nine degrees. Just as the ships passed offshore from the lighthouse at Cape Trafalgar on Spain's southern coast, a steady downpour began and the winds freshened from the south, stirring up choppy seas. The escorts closed in to maintain contact with the convoy in the lowered visibility; *Seneca* zigzagged astern. *Cowslip* was five hundred yards away, guarding the starboard quarter. The convoy favored the African shore as it headed into the Strait of Gibraltar. At 2:45 AM on 25 April, a lookout on *Cowslip* sighted a large, fully surfaced German cruiser submarine. Unfortunately, the German U-boat had seen *Cowslip* first and launched a well-directed torpedo that struck the British escort just abaft the midship section. The detonation almost tore the 1,200-ton British ship apart. All *Cowslip*'s officers—except the captain and officer of the deck who were on the bridge—were killed instantly when the torpedo exploded under the wardroom. *Cowslip*'s forward 4.7-inch gun got off one shot before the torpedo struck. Because the night was thick, *Seneca*'s commanding officer was already on the bridge. Wheeler immediately closed on the location where the torpedo had come from and dropped depth charges, but the enemy submarine succeeded in escaping in the poor visibility.[30]

The concussion from *Seneca*'s depth charges awakened 2d Lt. Fletcher W. Brown. He wrote, "I jumped from my bunk, seized my binoculars and automatic [pistol], and clad only in pajamas, rushed on deck to the after battery which I commanded. As the *Seneca* circled close to the sinking ship, the hissing steam, mingling with the many cries, all cloaked in darkness, wrought in one's imagination a picture not soon forgotten." U-boats were known to lurk near torpedoed ships, ready to attack vessels that came to rescue the stricken vessel's crew, so escorts were prohibited from stopping to pick up survivors. Brown said, "But the Law of the Sea is strong and, in Coast Guard officers, is deeply ingrained, for the saving of life has been our chief work. The night-borne cries fell on sympathetic ears." *Cowslip*'s gun crew fired again when the submarine reappeared briefly on the surface. When *Seneca* approached, *Cowslip* signaled a warning with flashing light: "Stay away! Submarine in sight, port quarter." *Seneca*, however, remained behind to attempt to rescue the survivors from the British ship, while the convoy and other escorts continued toward Gibraltar. *Cowslip*'s crew calmly set the ship's depth charges on safe to prevent them from detonating when the ship sank, lowered their remaining boat, put life rafts in the water, and waited for rescue.[31]

The explosion had nearly broken *Cowslip* in two; the stern section settled while the bow hung high in the air. The British survivors gathered on the bow. Brown—still wearing his pajamas and automatic—was put in charge of *Seneca*'s whaleboat with a picked crew of oarsmen. Brown said, "The order to lower away was eagerly awaited. The *Seneca* momentarily checked her speed, then vanished from our sight in the darkness and resumed her bombing [with depth charges]." Brown reached *Cowslip* and, using the oars to hold the whaleboat bow-on, moved close under the ship's port bow while British sailors slid down a line into the boat. Beset by strong cross-currents, Brown said, "The constant use of the oars and the steering oar were necessary as the *Cowslip*'s forefoot formed, with the turbulent sea, a gigantic pair of scissors which every moment threatened to accomplish our destruction." *Cowslip*'s own lifeboat, with nineteen survivors aboard, came alongside *Seneca*. When the survivors were taken aboard, P. W. Patterson, the cutter's veteran boatswain, and a crew of coast guard oarsmen remanned the boat and rowed back to the ship. Patterson picked up eighteen survivors from two life rafts and took a small dinghy with seven more in tow.[32]

Brown signaled *Seneca* and the cutter stopped at 4:00 AM, pausing only long enough to transfer the survivors. Brown said, "Although there was no other means of leaving the doomed ship, only the number [of men] I designated attempted to gain our boat. That, with one exception, was as splendid an exhibition of discipline as I have ever witnessed. As we shoved off from the *Cowslip* came the words of the popular British song, 'Goodbye.'" When Brown headed back to *Cowslip* in the darkness, he did not know if he would find the ship still afloat. When he reached the British ship, its bow was flung even higher in the air as it readied to make its final plunge. Brown reported:

> Our little boat was quickly filled, yet, though others remained aboard they did not attempt to gain this last chance to be saved. "Can you take more?" came from the darkness above. "How many are left?" I called. "Three!" "Come on." Wedged between my pajamered legs, so that I was fairly riding his back was one man. For once in handling a steering oar, my feet were firmly anchored. Under the thwarts and crouched in the bottom, in every possible space were jammed these uncomplaining British sailors. . . . The *Cowslip* gave us but scant time to get clear before she slid beneath the seas.

Cowslip's captain, Lt. Cdr. S. R. Lane, RNR, was the last to leave the ship just before it sunk at 4:28 AM. On his final trip back to *Seneca*, Brown had twenty-two survivors in his boat in addition to his own oarsmen. *Seneca* hoisted the boat at 4:45 AM and proceeded at full speed to rejoin the convoy. Five officers and a steward were killed when the torpedo struck *Cowslip*. The cutter successfully rescued all the remaining eighty-one crewmen, at night in the open sea under the constant threat of a submarine attack. The convoy reached Gibraltar without further incident. *Seneca*'s 7:30 AM log entry read, "Entered harbor and made fast at Ordnance Wharf. Cassano, Seaman 2nd USN restricted 30 days for failing to obey order of a petty officer." Despite the drama and excitement of that morning's rescue, life and discipline aboard the cutter continued.[33]

Submarine Incidents

Sightings of periscope wakes, submarine wakes, or surfaced submarines were frequent and most often occurred when convoys reached the danger zones where German U-boats lay in wait. World War I submarines operated on the surface a great deal of the time and frequently took slow-moving merchant ships under fire with their deck guns. When sightings occurred, cutters set general quarters, increased to full speed, and headed for the submarine's location. Sometimes gun crews were able to get off a few quick shots before the U-boats disappeared beneath the surface. Working in 1922 on a history of the U.S. Coast Guard during World War I, Cdr. Richard O. Crisp said, "Escort ships of all convoys kept their guns' crews ready at quarters at all times night and day. On the occasion of an alarm, general quarters was sounded which brought the entire crew on duty." Cochran described the setting of general quarters on board *Algonquin*: "It is rather disagreeable to be startled out of a deep sleep by the furious ringing of the alarm bell and the rush of hurrying feet through the dark. No lights were allowed on any part of the ship. Some of us were only half dressed as we stood at our stations in the biting wind." Gun mounts were routinely exercised each watch. Depending on the visibility and sea conditions, the low profile of a surfaced submarine was usually not seen until it was only three miles away; periscopes were seldom seen at more than a mile away. Crisp said, "All vessels sighting submarines, or wakes of same, were directed to fully report all such matters, and to give in addition warnings of same." When a sighting was made, an "ALLO" message was sent out, warning other ships of the presence of a submarine. The message was followed by a written report.[34]

At 7:20 AM on 19 November 1917, *Tampa* was heading south with its second convoy when a German submarine took the steamer *Suzanne Marie* under fire with its deck guns. *Tampa* went to the ship's assistance and fired six shots at the U-boat before it submerged. Five days later, another submarine was sighted by the convoy and *Tampa* fired twenty-one rounds at the reported position. During surface actions, a spotter stationed in the cutter's main top called down information on the "fall of shots" to the gunnery officer. The gunnery officer called out sight corrections to the batteries by means of speaking tubes running from the bridge to the guns. The speaking tubes were attached to the ears of the sight setters so they could hear the corrections over the sounds of the guns. Protection of the ships transporting vital supplies and materials to support the war effort was so important that escorts were directed not to stop to pick up survivors of torpedoed merchant vessels if there was a possibility a submarine could still be in the vicinity. When a ship was torpedoed, it was customary for the entire convoy to proceed, leaving the unfortunate ship and crew to save themselves.[35]

On 15 December 1917, *Ossipee* was escorting a thirty-ship convoy to Britain. At 4:30 in the afternoon, a U-boat launched a torpedo at the cutter. A watch officer aboard *Ossipee* reported: "Viewed from the deck, its [torpedo] wake seared a white path that disappeared beneath our starboard quarter. As fast as her limited speed would permit, the *Ossipee* reached the indicated locality of the enemy and dropped a bomb. You know the kind we had in those first days—the type in which the detonator was inserted before the bomb was thrown overboard by hand. The hun did not renew the attack." The convoy's ships scattered during the attack and did not have time to reform before dark. That night a gale ravaged the Bay of Biscay and several vessels foundered. Second Lieutenant Brown said, "The *Ossipee*, though but one hundred and sixty feet in length, rode out the storm with but the loss of one life boat." Brown was later transferred to *Seneca* on Christmas Day 1917.[36]

Seneca joined a convoy sailing directly from the Mediterranean to Great Britain, without stopping at Gibraltar, in April 1918. Traveling at a speed of nine knots, it was the fastest convoy the cutter escorted. On the night of 29 April, the convoy was off Cape St. Vincent, on the southwest corner of Portugal. The cutter was zigzagging ahead of the convoy, when Brown, officer of the deck, said, "A yell from those on the port side of *Seneca*'s bridge left no doubt as to its meaning." He immediately gave the command "Hard astarboard." Brown said, "Like a chalk line on a blackboard appeared the wake of a submerged torpedo. Apparently it would strike us abreast our bridge. The only order that could possibly help had been given. 'By a hair' is but an expression, yet that was our margin of safety in this instance." The cutter swung just enough so that the torpedo passed no more than fifty feet ahead of the stem. "Hard aport" was next given to avoid the oncoming ships of the convoy. The cutter's captain said, "A second torpedo fired at a closer range passed immediately under *Seneca*'s stern. Apparently proximity saved the vessel." When the general alarm sounded, Captain Cornwell, RNR, a passenger aboard the cutter, reached the deck in time to see the second torpedo approach and pass under the ship. He said, "I felt my hat go six inches straight into the air!" Submarine attacks on convoys were more frequent in the Mediterranean Sea than in the Atlantic Ocean. When *Seneca* escorted two convoys on short trips in the Mediterranean, it experienced two submarine attacks that resulted in one ship being sunk.[37]

Attacks often occurred at night when submarines could see the silhouettes of ships in the moonlight. Cochran described such an attack on *Algonquin*, which occurred while he was on watch as a lookout:

It all happened ten or fifteen minutes after I had come on watch. The sea was rather calm and it was easy to detect any disturbance in the water. We had been zig zagging continuously throughout the night and just as we were turning on the starboard tack, I saw the thing coming. A wide streak of swiftly moving foam, which looked like a path of fire because of the phosphorus in the water, was headed directly for the ship. I knew in an instant it was a torpedo. . . . My tongue stuck to the roof of my mouth and I seemed to lose control of my knees. But, I managed to shout down to the bridge, "Torpedo headed for our starboard bow, sir!" An order from the officer of the watch and our bow slowly turned away from the fast approaching missile. All this happened in a few seconds, but it seemed hours before the ship turned, just in time to see the torpedo rush past, clearing our stem by not more than a few yards.[38]

LIFE ABOARD THE CUTTERS

Convoy duty was most difficult in the winter months when the nights were long, the weather stormy, and the seas turbulent. Severe conditions taxed the endurance of the crews on the small U.S. Coast Guard vessels; the largest cutters were just over two hundred feet in length. On 8 November 1918, Cochran wrote in his journal:

> Three and a half days out from Gib and bound, they say, for Plymouth. The first day of our voyage was ideal, but the next two were horrible with a nor'easter raging. At one time yesterday afternoon, we plowed into a huge wave just as it was breaking. With a crash that shook the whole ship, it surged over the fo'c'sle head, completely submerging the guns and the forward companionway. Luckily the gun crews had taken their stations on the bridge or they surely would have been washed overboard during the heavy weather. At dusk last night, the ships bound for the Americas shoved off, leaving but fifteen ships in the convoy. Today the sea is quite calm, the nor'easter subsiding as quickly as it came.

The mixture of monotony, punctuated by periods of high excitement, distorted the passage of time. Second Lt. James Marsden Earp, called Marsden by his family, was a deck watch officer aboard *Tampa*. In an 8 September 1918 letter to his brother Arthur, he wrote, "You may recall it was the fifteenth of last September that I left Boston to start for this side so that I am just finishing out the first year. As I say a year it seems to have passed rapidly, but when I think how the time has dragged from month to month it means another thing." Eighteen days later Earp was killed when *Tampa* was torpedoed.[39]

Cutter crews were increased by a third over peacetime complements, and all billets were filled. Crews were made up of a nucleus of veterans, augmented with enthusiastic recruits, many of whom had left college to enlist. Crews were divided into two watch sections that stood four-hour port and starboard watches; the sections relieved each other. The afternoon watch was divided into two 2-hour dog watches. Standing one 2-hour watch each day meant that duty sections did not have to continually stand the same watches. Cochran said, "During our four hours off watch, we had to do our eating and sleeping, as well as wash ourselves and our clothes. It was always a scramble to get through with the two latter in order that we might turn in our hammocks after the arduous hours on watch." When the weather was mild, many of the men swung their hammocks, known as "dream bags," out on deck in the fresh air. The guns were always manned and the gun crews paced the deck at night to stay awake. Both day and night, ten lookouts were stationed at various parts of the ship, including the crow's nest and the searchlight platforms. Escort crews knew that the ships of the convoy depended on them to be vigilant and that U-boats struck when least expected. The heightened readiness of the lookouts resulted in many false alarms, caused by sighting debris, wreckage, and trash in the water at great distances. Sometimes, the wake of a whale or blackfish was mistaken for the enemy. This was particularly true at night in the southern latitudes where the phosphorescent trail made by a swift moving porpoise differed little from the streak of foam left by a German torpedo. Cochran said, "Any object, no matter what it was, was always reported to the officer of the watch on the bridge, whether it was a school of fish or a flock of curious seagulls hovering over some unseen thing in the water."[40]

With larger crews, living conditions aboard the cutters were even more crowded. Cochran commented, "The man coming from a large battle ship to a small converted yacht or a revenue cutter would find life on shipboard very different. The comfortable quarters and conveniences found on a larger ship are conspicuous by their absence and he should consider himself lucky to be able to find a place to swing his hammock." While conditions on the cutters were not good, crews knew their lives were much better than those of the men in the trenches of Europe. "Fortunately, we had no cooties, but cockroaches were a common pet and a popular pastime was racing between these sociable little insects," Cochran said. "Sometimes, they would be found in the soup or the coffee and the man who was unable to fish them out without a murmur was not considered much of a seagoing sailor."[41]

LANDING PARTY

Algonquin was moored at Gibraltar in June 1918. As the sun came up, the cutter's crew was unexpectedly ordered to make preparations to get under way. Speculation about the unscheduled mission quickly spread through the ship. Just as the crew finished its morning mess, a launch set out from the wharf at Gibraltar. By the time the boat came alongside and a British army officer climbed aboard, the cutter had slipped its mooring and was under way. *Algonquin* crossed the Strait of Gibraltar, steamed west, and anchored at noon off the port of Tangier, Morocco. An old Spanish gun-boat was lying at anchor in the harbor. Cochran was assigned as one of the oarsmen for the surfboat that was put over the side. He said, "After our boat had gone half way to the pier, a small boat met us. It contained the French consul's attaché and he accompanied our officer to the dock. They both went up town together while we roamed about the queer place as we pleased. Returning after a little while, our officer ordered us back to the ship. With him came a French naval lieutenant and this increased the mystery more than ever."

The cutter quickly weighed anchor and got under way. The next morning before dawn, *Algonquin* approached the lighthouse at Cape St. Vincent on Portugal's southwestern tip. With the lighthouse on its port side, the cutter made its way past submarine nets into the cove at Sagres and anchored. Small fishermen's huts were scattered on the rocky hill overlooking the small cove. The fishermen earned their living catching sardines for the small canning factory that stood near the cove. The cutter's boats were lowered and preparations were made to put a landing party ashore. Cochran was again assigned to one of the boats. He said, "Instantly, all was hustle and bustle. Belts and leggings were buckled on, revolvers passed out, and a landing party chosen . . . manning the surf boat[s] we pulled ashore." The landing party formed up and hiked inland. The going was tough over rocky terrain and under a blazing sun. After several miles, the party came to rugged hills, cut sharply by ravines and gorges. "We had to carry several heavy instruments," Cochran said, "which the various officers had brought along." When the landing party approached their objective, the men were told to have their weapons ready. Cochran said:

> By this time we had entered a narrow ravine which turned sharply to the right several hundred yards ahead. With as much quiet as is possible, we approached the turn and waited while one of our officers scouted ahead. Soon he returned. In obedience to his whispered command, we crept along and around the bend. . . . Hidden in a thick clump of cedars was a small shack and, strung across the narrow sides of the ravine, the aerial of a powerful wireless plant. Quickly surrounding the house, we found it empty and the wireless instruments gone . . . there were signs of a hasty departure. After setting fire to the shack and dismantling the aerial, we made our way back to the ship.

The approximate location of this clandestine German radio station, which had been intercepting and jamming allied radio traffic and transmitting shipping information to German U-boats, was determined by the use of a newly developed radio direction finder. Cochran said, "Spain and Portugal were thick with spies and the operators of the secret station had most likely gotten wind of our expedition and had fled shortly before our arrival."[42]

SS *Queen* Sinking

Seneca departed Pembroke Docks, Wales, on 25 June 1918 and joined the twenty-four merchant ships of Convoy O.M. No. 79, southbound for Gibraltar; again the cutter was the lone ocean escort. When dawn broke on the morning of 28 June, the seas were relatively calm under cloudy blue skies, with a moderate breeze blowing out of the east. At 6:52 AM, the cutter's crew heard an explosion and saw a spout of water rise from the starboard side of the convoy's flagship, SS *Queen*. General quarters was sounded and *Seneca* came up to full speed. Maneuvering between the columns of ships, the cutter headed for the stricken *Queen*. The large and stately steamship, with the commodore still aboard, settled rapidly down by the stern. In less than ten minutes, the ship disappeared below the surface of the sea, taking the convoy commodore, Capt. V. deM. Cooper, RN; all of the ship's officers but two; and nearly half the crew with it. When *Seneca* arrived on scene, survivors from *Queen* were clinging to an

A view of the cruising cutter *Seneca*'s main deck on the port side looking forward. The pulling boats, secured in their davits, were used to rescue survivors from torpedoed ships. The large air scoops provided ventilation below decks. They were mechanically rotated, from below, to control the air intake. *U.S. Coast Guard Historian*

overturned lifeboat and pieces of debris in the cold waters of the Bay of Biscay. Wheeler had no idea where the attack had come from; no one had seen any sign of a submarine or the wake of a torpedo.

The cutter lowered the no. 1 boat with Second Lieutenant Brown in charge. Brown said, "I frequently wonder if George Washington, in crossing the Delaware, was as carefully attired as he is depicted to have been. There is nothing comfortable, nor poetic, in performing rescue work clad in pajamas, yet . . . I again, similarly robed in June 1918, found myself in command of the same whale boat, being lowered on the run in the middle of Biscay Bay, to pick up those struggling survivors." After the boat was away, all four of *Seneca*'s guns were fired into the water between ships to make the submarine think it was being depth charged. Brown picked up eight men from the water and another thirteen from the shattered lifeboat. He said, "I noticed one man in particular who was having difficulty in keeping afloat. Passing several corpses, buoyed by life belts, I reached the swimmer and found him to be lad of about sixteen or seventeen years old. He was completely exhausted and could not have remained afloat much longer." *Seneca* took six survivors aboard from the raft dropped into the water when it first arrived on scene. Twenty-seven of the *Queen*'s crew of fifty-two were rescued. *Seneca* hoisted its boat aboard at 7:38 AM and overtook the convoy that had sailed on under the command of the vice commodore. Of the attack, Wheeler said, "The conservatism of the German submarine doctrine was apparent from this sinking. With twenty-three large freight ships still in the convoy, protected by one cutter, the submarine failed to follow up the attack."[43]

During European duty, *Seneca* escorted 30 convoys, with a total of 580 ships. Wheeler said this was probably typical for ocean escorts, but *Seneca* had more than its share of submarine attacks possibly because it was known to be the slowest cutter. On three or four occasions the cutter believed itself to be under attack when torpedoes passed close by. *Seneca* fired on what were thought to be submarines in six instances and dropped depth charges on what were believed to be submerged submarines on eight other occasions. *Seneca* dropped over one hundred 300-pound depth charges in attacks on submerged submarines. The concussions frequently knocked out the lights on the cutter. Wheeler reported:

> During the period in which the *Seneca* was employed in convoy [escort duty], a total of some twenty-one alarms concerning submarines, or their imminent proximity, were made to the convoy, either by the *Seneca* herself or some other vessel, only one of which was then proven to be false—the case of a dead whale. . . . Concerning the other twenty alarms, evidence is given in the official reports of the sighting of submarines, their periscopes or wakes, or the wakes of torpedoes in thirteen cases; thus leaving but seven cases in which the convoys were alarmed and where the actual presence of the enemy was markedly in doubt in the minds of those present.

The war records of the other five cutters serving with the U.S. Navy in European waters indicated that their experiences were similar. In fourteen months, the cutters escorted thousands of ships between Gibraltar and the British Isles with a minimum of losses. The loss of so many coast guard shipmates during the war, however, made it difficult for cuttermen to rejoice in their accomplishments. The U.S. Coast Guard's losses, in proportion to its size, were greater than the losses suffered by any other branch of the U.S. armed forces in World War I.[44]

CHAPTER 4

HOME WATERS

A fringe of vessels is being flung up and down the coast, composed of
destroyers, submarine chasers, converted yachts, trawlers, motorboats
and vessels, both naval and mercantile, that are being pressed into
active service in connection with the full mobilization of the Navy, the
Naval Militia, the Naval Reserve, and the Coast Guard.

—*New York Times*, 10 April 1917

HALIFAX EXPLOSION

The 147-foot coast guard cutter USS *Morrill* departed its homeport of
Detroit, Michigan, at 4:00 PM on 10 November 1917. Under the command of 1st Lt. George E. Wilcox, the 420-ton cruising cutter, with an
iron hull and wooden superstructure, was bound for the Atlantic Ocean
and the naval shipyard at Philadelphia. The cutter's crew consisted of six
officers, four warrant officers, and fifty enlisted men, from both the U.S.
Coast Guard and the U.S. Navy. Half the officers—a surgeon and two
watch officers—were from the U.S. Naval Reserve. Prior to the war, cutter crews were made up entirely of coast guard officers, warrant officers,
and enlisted men. The only exception had been surgeons assigned from

the U.S. Public Health Service. After war was declared, this arrangement quickly changed and navy officers, petty officers, and enlisted men— mainly reservists—augmented cutter crews.[1]

Irv P. Beall, USCG, was a first class petty officer assigned to *Morrill*. He was one of three men aboard the cutter who were designated as "electricians-radio." He described Wilcox as "a fine captain he was, too, loved and respected by the ship's entire crew and others who knew him. His crew would have gone through 'hellfire and brimstone' if he had given the order, and some of us did just that!" After an uneventful trip through the St. Lawrence Seaway, *Morrill* arrived at Quebec City. Wilcox intended to remain overnight and get under way in the morning. Canadian naval authorities at the port, however, asked that *Morrill*'s departure be delayed so that the cutter could escort six small Canadian minesweepers to Halifax, Nova Scotia. The six vessels were steam-driven drifters outfitted for coastal minesweeping duty in Canadian and British waters. After a six-day delay, *Morrill* and the six Canadian vessels departed Quebec, en route to Halifax. The group remained overnight at Gaspe, Quebec, at the mouth of the St. Lawrence River, before crossing the Gulf of St. Lawrence. Reaching the eastern side of the gulf, the Canadians continued on to Halifax, while *Morrill* put into Charlottetown, Prince Edward Island, to celebrate Thanksgiving.[2]

Morrill entered Halifax harbor on the afternoon of 5 December, and approached the Canadian cruiser HMCS *Niobe*. *Niobe* was the flagship and naval headquarters for the port admiral. Wilcox used a megaphone to request permission to moor alongside the pier, aft of *Niobe*. His request was denied because another ship was expected to moor there shortly. Wilcox was told to anchor out and bring *Morrill* alongside *Niobe* the next morning. The cutter backed away, turned, and crossed the harbor to the north, anchoring near Dartmouth Cove. Arrangements were made to take on coal and water in the morning. Early the next day, a water tender came and moored along the cutter's starboard side. When some of the cutter's crew noticed smoke rising across the harbor, they asked the water boatman what it was. With a shrug of his shoulders, the man replied, "Oh, it's probably a fire over in the dockyard." At 9:00 AM Halifax time *Morrill*'s quartermaster struck eight bells; the cutter did not change its clocks to local time because Wilcox intended to be in port only two days. A few

At 145 feet, *Morrill* was the U.S. Coast Guard's smallest cruising cutter. When the French ship *Mont Blanc*, loaded with explosives, blew up in the harbor at Halifax, Nova Scotia, at 9:10 AM on 6 December 1917, *Morrill's* landing party was the first to reach the devastated city and provide relief to its people.
U.S. Coast Guard Historian

minutes later, Beall said, "There came across the placid water of the harbor, a huge rumbling roar, a blast—followed a few seconds later by a second explosion."[3]

Earlier that morning, Pilot William Hayes had gotten the 5,043-ton Norwegian steam ship *Imo* under way from Bedford Basin, bound for the open sea four miles away. The freighter, which had arrived from Rotterdam in ballast two days earlier, was en route to New York to pick up a cargo of Belgian war relief supplies. As the ship approached the area of Halifax harbor known as the Narrows, the French steamer *Mont Blanc* was approaching from the opposite direction. Pilot Frank MacKay was taking the old French Line freighter to anchorage at Bedford Basin. *Mont Blanc* had arrived at the entrance to Halifax harbor from New York the night before, but it was too late for it to pass through the protective submarine boom. Capt. Aime Le Medec anchored the 3,121-ton ship outside the harbor for the night. *Mont Blanc*'s manifest showed a load of bulk explosives. Cargo included twenty-three hundred tons of picric acid; wet picric acid in barrels filled the forward holds and dry picric acid in barrels and bags, along with cases of gun cotton, were crammed into the forward 'tween decks. Four hundred tons of TNT filled the after hold and 424 barrels of benzol were stowed on deck.[4]

The morning air was clear and both ships were in plain view. The vessels approached each other at a turn in the channel and MacKay on *Mont Blanc* sounded one short blast on the ship's whistle, signaling for a port to port passage. He then slowed the ship's engines. Contrary to the Rules of the Road, procedures for avoiding collisions, the Norwegian ship responded with two short blasts of its whistle, signaling a starboard to starboard passage. Despite the crossed signals and uncertain intentions, the ships continued to approach each other. When the ships were 150 feet apart, *Mont Blanc* stopped its engine and sounded two short blasts in response to *Imo*'s two blast signal for a starboard to starboard passage. When the ships were only fifty feet apart and nearly parallel, starboard to starboard, *Imo* reversed its engines and sounded a three blast backing signal; *Mont Blanc* did the same. With a collision eminent, both masters swung their bows to starboard to take the impact of the collision as far forward as possible. *Imo* was almost stopped when its bow lightly struck *Mont Blanc* on the starboard side, abeam of hatch no. 1. A passing Canadian naval dispatch boat stopped to inspect the damage. The boat crew reported that the impact caused a wedge-shaped cut in *Mont Blanc*'s hull plating from waterline to main deck. The boat crew said they could see the barrels of picric acid through the hole and they were still neatly stacked. As *Imo* backed away, its crew saw a small flame at the bottom of the gash in *Mont Blanc*'s hull. Then thick black smoke began rising from the French ship's deck.[5]

Captain Le Medec immediately ordered all hands to abandon the burning ship, which was loaded with explosives. Two boats were lowered and the French crew quickly filled them. *Mont Blanc*'s momentum took the ship slowly toward the piers at Halifax. Le Medec's crew rowed frantically for Dartmouth on the other side of the harbor. *Mont Blanc*'s bow grounded gently next to pier no. 6 at Halifax, just as its crew reached shore on the Dartmouth side of the harbor. The French crew left their boats and hastily formed up for a muster to be taken; Pilot MacKay was with them. The crew then took shelter in nearby trees. Capt. Horation Brannen, aboard the tug *Stella Maris*, was in the Narrows and saw the collision and fire. He anchored the scows he was towing and headed down channel to assist the ships. The tug's crew rigged fire hoses and Brannen worked his way between *Mont Blanc* and the pier to get at the fire. The heat was too intense, however, and he had to back away. The current forced the burning ship hard against the pier and the fire spread to storage sheds ashore. Two boats arrived on scene from the small, three-funneled British cruiser *Highflyer*, which was anchored in midstream, abeam of *Niobe*. *Highflyer*'s captain and crewmembers climbed aboard *Mont Blanc* and began to rig fire hoses. The British captain asked Brannen to put a line on *Mont Blanc* and tow it away from the piers.[6]

At 9:10 AM, explosives aboard *Mont Blanc* detonated. The explosion sounded like a rumbling roar to people in downtown Halifax. The greatest impact of the blast was felt in Richmond, the northern part of Halifax. The concussion crumbled buildings, burying inhabitants under piles of rubble. On the other side of the harbor, the north end of Dartmouth was similarly destroyed. Remarkably, survivors nearest the blast later said they could not recall hearing anything. The explosion sent up a giant mushroom cloud that rose miles into the sky. It was reported as the largest man-made explosion in history. The French ship *Mont Blanc* literally disappeared. The only parts of the ship ever found were a ninety-five millimeter stern gun that landed in Albro Lake behind Dartmouth; a piece of anchor that landed at Spryfield, two miles from Halifax; and pieces of steel plate that penetrated *Imo*'s hull. There were no traces of the British cruiser's captain, crew, or boats. The tug *Stella Maris*, driven ashore, was in shambles.

After the initial collision, Pilot Hayes intended to turn *Imo* back to Bedford Basin. When the explosives detonated, he was headed down channel to where there was enough sea room to turn. On *Imo*'s bridge, Capt. Haakon From, Hayes, and four ship officers were blown overboard by the blast and killed. Boats from *Highflyer* picked up badly injured survivors from the Norwegian ship. Even the crewmen from *Mont Blanc*, sheltered in the woods on the Dartmouth side of the harbor, were not safe. The blast killed one man and injured several others. The old cruiser *Niobe* took the full force of the explosion. Its upper decks were a mass of twisted steel. One of four stacks was gone and the second was flattened against the third, which was crushed and leaning against the fourth. The new British steamship *Caracus* had been moored upstream at pier no. 8. Torn loose from its moorings, the ship sank in the channel. Forty-nine of the fifty-five crewmembers were killed. The merchant ship *Middleham Castle* was in the shipyard at Halifax when the burning *Mont Blanc* grounded at the pier. *Middleham Castle*'s third mate, John Mayers, was walking toward the fire and was about one hundred yards away when he heard the explosion. He turned and ran toward his ship. Mayers said that while running he had the sensation of being lifted into the air and passing, and being passed by, things that were flying before he blacked out. When he regained consciousness, he was lying on the ground a half mile away on Fort Needham Hill and was only wearing his boots.[7]

Beall and several shipmates were on *Morrill*'s forecastle watching the heavy black smoke rise from *Mont Blanc*. Beall recalled, "About 9:05 Halifax time the vessel blew up, knocking us all to the deck. I crawled under the legs of the gun mount to escape the falling pieces of metal, while high in the air there were thousands of small explosions." A piece of metal fell out of the sky and went through the deck of the water boat alongside *Morrill*. A large object resembling a ship's boiler passed over the cutter and landed in the water a few hundred yards away. Beall said, "It threw up a column of water resembling that of an exploding mine." All the windows in *Morrill*'s deckhouse and pilothouse were shattered by the blast. The thick glass in the hull's portholes did not break. Several *Morrill* crewmen were cut by flying glass. These were the only injuries. "So great was the effect of the explosion that our little ship was virtually lifted out of the water," Beall said, "then settled back with a half-rolling, half-pitching motion, her body shivering, with broken glass tinkling all over her decks."[8]

After checking the cutter and finding no serious damage, Wilcox ordered 2d Lt. Henry G. Hemingway to immediately assemble a landing party to help people ashore. Wilcox told Hemingway to report to the senior British naval officer present and offer the services of *Morrill* and the landing party. The landing party consisted of twenty-five men—about half of *Morrill*'s crew. It included two navy officers, Assistant Surgeon J. J. Hardy and Ens. C. M. Kreitenstein, as well as coast guard warrant officers, Gunner John deCosta, and Boatswain Charles Lundgren. Beall was one of the enlisted men selected for the landing party. He said, "The whole crew wanted to go, but some one had to watch the store." After Hardy finished dressing the wounds of the men cut by flying glass, the party departed. As soon as the boats cleared the cutter, Wilcox called for steam to be ready aboard *Morrill* and brought the anchor to short stay, in case the cutter was needed to tow vessels clear of the danger zone. *Morrill*'s two lifeboats were towed ashore by the cutter's motor launch; there were too many men in the boats to use the oars. When Hemingway attempted to land the boats near *Niobe*, he was warned off by people on shore and sent downstream. Fire threatened the magazines ashore near the cruiser and there was danger of another explosion. *Morrill*'s boats put ashore some distance from *Niobe* and Hardy set up a dressing station to treat the injured. Hemingway sent the motor launch back to *Morrill* for more linen for bandages; it was apparent the landing party would need all that could be spared. Wilcox practically stripped the cutter of linens, sending sheets, pillowcases, tablecloths, napkins, and toweling. Men from the landing party also found a supply of bandages and medicines at a deserted hospital.[9]

When a British navy captain came to the dressing station with a head injury, Hemingway said, "I explained to this officer that we were from a ship of the United States and that I had orders to report to the senior British naval officer present. . . . He depreciated the necessity of making such a report, asserting . . . that we could do considerable good by starting right in where we were." After caring for the injured in the area, Hemingway and Hardy prepared to move closer to *Niobe*, where the damage was worse. Before they left, a one hundred man landing party from the navy ship USS *Old Colony* arrived. They had also been warned away from landing near *Niobe* because of the threat of another explosion. Hemingway conferred with Lieutenant Clark, USNRF, from *Old Colony* and, because there was only one surgeon, they decided to combine the two landing parties. Together, they moved into the damaged area and set up a dressing station. Stretcher bearers went out and brought the injured to be treated by the surgeon. "Then," Hemingway said, "word being received that the danger from the explosion of the magazines was over, we proceeded to a position near the *Niobe* where we remained for about an hour taking care of the cases, as they were brought in."[10]

The party now consisted of two doctors—a doctor from *Niobe* having joined the group—men from *Morrill* and *Old Colony,* and several British seamen who had no other unit to report to. The party made enough stretchers so that there was one for every four men. A box containing medical supplies was fitted with handles and carried like a stretcher. Each man in the party also carried a supply of bandages. Hemingway scouted ahead. He said, "I walked out into the devastated area to get an idea of the proper direction for our search, looking over the situation and making inquires." They moved out as a unit into the most heavily damaged sections of the city, searching through demolished houses for the injured. When *Old Colony* was brought into the pier to serve as a hospital ship, word was sent to the relief party for Doctor Hardy to report to the ship so he could treat the injured that were being brought there. Hemingway said, "After his [Dr. Hardy's] departure, the stretcher bearers proceeded with their work, rendering first aid and when possible carrying the badly injured to the main streets where they were turned over to ambulances or other conveyances and sent to the various hospitals." While looking for injured people, the shore party became separated, but by this time, the men knew what they had to do and Hemingway let them act on their own initiative. With the use of a donated truck, Hemingway took a group of men from *Old Colony* and went into the sparsely populated northern districts of the city. The explosions had been particularly devastating there and no assistance had arrived yet. Hemingway said that the group "carefully and systematically examined the buildings in the section where it appeared that no others had been before us, rendered first aid in several cases, and gathering a load of badly injured, ordered the truck to return to the city with instructions to go to the Camp Hill Hospital."[11]

With night approaching, Hemingway passed word for the recall of *Morrill*'s landing party, instructing them to return to *Niobe*'s dock. He said, "As the men assembled, they returned to *Morrill,* in our boats. Before my return, I visited the USS *Old Colony* where . . . I found Dr. Hardy earnestly employed in the operating room, assisted by some of the men from *Morrill.*" When Hemingway learned that the bandages were running out and that Hardy needed a hypodermic syringe, he remembered the abandoned cadet hospital and returned there to gather the needed supplies. He also found other medicines and solutions among the debris. After delivering the materials to Hardy, he returned to the *Morrill*. With the return of the first landing party, a second was immediately organized and went ashore, under the command of First Lieutenant Wilcox, to continue the work.[12]

The blast killed 1,635 and injured another 9,000. One hundred and ninety-nine people lost their sight as a result of the explosion. Sixteen hundred buildings were totally destroyed and another twelve thousand buildings, within an area of sixteen miles, were severely damaged. The property damage was estimated at $35 million dollars. To make matters worse, that night a raging blizzard dropped heavy snow onto Halifax, creating a grave situation for the citizens who were still in shock. During the storm, the steamer *North Wind* lost both anchors and was cast adrift in the harbor. The freighter blew down on *Morrill* in the snow and darkness, ramming the cutter on the port side. *North Wind*'s bow cut a wedge-shaped gash into the cutter's hull, extending from the main deck down to a foot above the waterline. The impact also broke the pilothouse and chart room loose from the deck, moving them six inches to starboard. On 10 December Wilcox moored *Morrill* at a pier in Halifax to make repairs. The hole in the cutter's side was patched with several layers of sail canvas. The canvas was held in place by mooring lines passed under the cutter's hull. Several turns of the *Morrill*'s four-inch towing hawser were passed over the pilothouse and chart room to secure them in place. Canvas was nailed over the broken windows. Beall said, "Our good old ship was bundled and tied up like a young lad going to school in a snow storm in Minnesota." With emergency repairs completed, the damaged cutter departed Halifax on 18 December, with orders to proceed to the U.S. Coast Guard's depot at Arundel Cove (Curtis Bay), Maryland, for repairs. After a harrowing winter voyage through ice and snow, *Morrill* limped into the depot on 4 February 1918.[13]

COASTAL PATROL

When war was declared, coast guard cutters and crews were used to assist federal agents with the seizure of German ships interned in American ports. After this task was completed, the security of coastal waters became a primary concern. Coast guard cruising cutters were assigned to coastal patrol duties and smaller cutters were used to patrol harbors and inlets. The cruising cutters *Algonquin, Manning, Ossipee, Seneca, Tampa,* and *Yamacraw* were engaged in patrolling Atlantic Ocean and Gulf of México coastal waters before being deployed to Europe for convoy escort duty. Cruising cutters patrolled for submarines off the entrances to ports and waterways. At the port of New York, the 206-foot cruising cutter *Mohawk,* with a crew of eight officers and sixty-three enlisted men, was assigned to patrol the approaches to New York's Ambrose Channel. The cutter performed this duty continuously, only coming into port for coal and supplies. *Mohawk*'s commanding officer, Capt. James G. Ballinger, USCG, a graduate from the Naval Academy in Annapolis, Maryland, was put in command of the squadron of patrol ships guarding the entrance to the port of New York. When he was reassigned to duty as captain of the port of Norfolk, Virginia, he was relieved by his executive officer, 1st Lt. Howard E. Rideout. *Mohawk* was on patrol three miles southeast of Ambrose Lightship on the morning of 1 October 1917 when a heavy fog set in. At 8:20 AM, lookouts aboard the cutter saw the British tank ship *Vennachar* suddenly emerge from the thick fog, close aboard. The tanker, part of a convoy of ships arriving at New York, struck *Mohawk,* its bow cutting into the cutter's hull. Severely damaged and flooding rapidly, the cutter's crew was called to abandon ship stations and a distress message was sent on the ship's two kilowatt transmitter. A muster was quickly taken and six boats were lowered. All hands embarked in the boats and rowed clear of the cutter, taking the ship's records with them. The crew was picked up by the steamship SS *Sabalo* and the 144-foot converted yacht USS *Mohican.* USS *Bridge,* a 423-foot ship of the Naval Overseas Transportation Service, arrived on scene and attempted to tow the foundering cutter into shallower water. The damage was too great, however, and *Mohawk* sank, stern first, at 9:35 AM; *Bridge* cut away the tow hawser as the cutter went down. *Mohawk* settled on the bottom with just its topmasts showing above the water.[14]

The wooden-hulled 1,605-ton cruising cutter *Androscoggin* was at its headquarters at Portland, Maine, when war was declared. The cutter's commanding officer, Capt. Henry G. Fisher, reported to the commandant of the First Naval District for duty and was ordered to sail for Boston. After having a battery of 3-inch guns and a fire control system installed at the navy yard, the cutter went to the shipyard at Provincetown, Massachusetts. Extensive repairs were made to the wooden hull under the ship's engines and boilers. With hull repairs complete, the 210-foot cutter returned to Maine as part of the First Naval District's patrol forces. *Androscoggin* continued coastal patrolling until reassigned to rescue, towing, and convoy duties in October 1917. In the spring of 1918, there were increasing reports of German U-boat activity in the waters along the east coast of North America and more ships were outfitted for operations against submarines. A Y-gun, for projecting depth charges, was installed on *Androscoggin* and the cutter began patrolling in New England waters. From June 1918 until the end of the war *Androscoggin* cruised the waters from Boston to St. John, Newfoundland, searching for German U-boats.

The 205-foot cruising cutter *Gresham* was at the Boston Navy Yard undergoing repairs when the U.S. Coast Guard was transferred to the U.S. Navy. After having a battery of four 3-inch guns installed, the cutter sailed for Norfolk on 11 June 1917. *Gresham* was assigned to Squadron Five of the Fifth Naval District's naval forces. The twenty-year-old cutter, capable of making seventeen knots, performed a variety of duties, including submarine net patrol, search and rescue, and merchant vessel convoying. With a wartime complement of 103 men, the cutter also served as a training platform for naval reserve officers. On 7 June 1918, a Y-gun was installed on *Gresham* and it began patrolling for submarines in addition to its other duties.[15]

Dockside repairs were completed on the 170-foot, 670-ton cruising cutter *Comanche* on 13 April 1917. Under orders from the commandant of the Eighth Naval District, headquartered at New Orleans, Louisiana, Capt. Henry Ulke got *Comanche*, painted wartime gray, under way and proceeded to Galveston, Texas, where the cutter took on ammunition. Ulke was assigned to patrol for submarines along the coast of the Eighth Naval District, giving special attention to the approaches to the ports of Galveston and Port Arthur, Texas. The wooden-hulled *Comanche*, formerly named *Windom*, with a complement of five officers and forty-four enlisted men, performed patrol and guard duty along the southern coast of the United States from the west coast of Florida to the Mexican border. The cutter was well adapted for patrolling. Recently rebuilt and fit-

A landing party from the cruising cutter *Comanche* mustered at New Orleans. Armed coast guard landing parties accompanied U.S. marshals when they seized interned German ships at the beginning of the war. *Bettelou Biting Hand photo*

ted with new water-tube boilers, the cutter was designed to burn fuel oil. John J. Bitting, Jack to his shipmates, was born in Sherman, Texas. With dark brown hair and brown eyes, he had just turned eighteen when he traveled to Sabine, Texas, to enlist in the U.S. Coast Guard. Only 5 feet 7 inches tall and weighing 135 pounds, Bitting was assigned to the cruising cutter *Comanche*. Before going into the engine room, he spent six months on deck as an ordinary seaman. According to his daughter, "He was very proud of having been a short while in the war and in the 'black gang' [engineers]."[16]

At the end of September 1917, the 178-foot cruising cutter *Tuscarora* was transferred from its headquarters at Chicago to Newport, Rhode Island. The cutter arrived at its new homeport on 27 October and reported to the commandant of the Second Naval District for duty. When not assigned to other missions, *Tuscarora* patrolled Station A, in the vicinity of Block Island, Rhode Island.

The small cruising cutter *Acushnet*, under the command of 1st Lt. Eugene Blake, was transferred from its headquarters at New Bedford, Massachusetts, to the navy submarine base at New London, Connecticut.

The 152-foot seagoing tug patrolled the waters at the entrance to the
Thames River until 14 June 1917 when it was reassigned to patrol the
defensive area off Watch Hill, Rhode Island. *Wissahickon*, a ninety-six-foot
harbor cutter, was transferred to New London from New York on 24
August 1917 and ordered to patrol the waters of Long Island Sound near
Cornfield Lightship. Repairs to the cruising cutter *Seminole* were being
completed when war was declared. The cutter's commanding officer, Capt.
Frederick J. Haake, reported to the commandant of the Sixth Naval District
at Charleston, South Carolina, for duty and was directed to proceed to the
Charleston Navy Yard. After having a battery of 3-inch deck guns installed,
the 188-foot, 860-ton *Seminole* began patrolling along the coasts of North
Carolina, South Carolina, and Georgia, with emphasis on the ports of
Charleston and Wilmington, North Carolina. The cutter was also tasked
by the district commandant with convoying seized German merchant vessels and responding to ships in distress. In November 1917, *Seminole* was
transferred to the Fifth Naval District. The cutter arrived at Norfolk on 24
November 1917 and began patrolling off the Virginia Capes.[17]

After seizing the Austrian steamship *Borneo* in Hillsboro Bay, Florida,
on 9 April 1917, the cruising cutter *Tallapoosa* was ordered to patrol the
approaches to Tampa Bay, with particular emphasis on the entrance at
Egmont Key. Built in 1915, the 166-foot cutter was one of the U.S. Coast
Guard's newest ships. *Tallapoosa*'s commanding officer, 1st Lt. James F.
Hottel, was given an additional duty by the commander of the Seventh
Naval District's sixth section. He was assigned to inspect motor boats to
be used by the U.S. Navy in patrolling Tampa Bay. Hottel also enrolled
men in the U.S. Naval Reserve. After patrolling Florida coastal waters
until the end of July 1917, *Tallapoosa* was transferred to Patrol Squadron
One headquartered at Guantánamo Bay, Cuba. In September 1918,
Tallapoosa sailed north to Boston, where a battery of 3-inch guns was
installed, along with depth charges and releasing gear. On 7 November
1918, the cutter was transferred to Halifax, Nova Scotia, for operations
against German submarines.[18]

The cruising cutter *Itasca* was built in 1893 and christened USS *Bancroft*;
the 190-foot ship served as the Naval Academy's training ship. When the
ship was determined to be too small for the academy's training needs, it was
designated a gunboat. *Bancroft* was transferred to the Treasury Department

in 1906. Completely overhauled and renamed *Itasca*, the vessel was used for training cruises for Revenue-Cutter Service and then U.S. Coast Guard cadets. When war was declared, the cutter's cadet training duties were curtailed and the ship was assigned to wartime patrolling. From its headquarters at San Juan, Puerto Rico, *Itasca* patrolled the waters of the West Indies, searching for submarines. On 23 December 1917, the steel-hulled cutter was reassigned to the Sixth Naval District and for the next three months patrolled off the coast of South Carolina. At the end of March 1918, *Itasca* was again transferred, this time to the Fourth Naval District, headquartered at Philadelphia. A battery of three-inch rapid-fire guns was installed and a Y-gun for projecting depth charges was mounted. After leaving the Philadelphia Navy Yard, *Itasca* patrolled the southern coast of New Jersey and the entrance to Delaware Bay from its base at Cold Springs on New Jersey's southern tip.

Two weeks before his twenty-second birthday, Francis P. Smith joined the U.S. Coast Guard. Smith was sworn in at the coast guard recruiting office in Chicago, by Boatswain L. H. Luksich on 6 April 1918. Because of his age and prior experience as a fireman for the city of Chicago, he was enlisted as a fireman (nonrated engineer). Two days after enlisting, Smith said goodbye to his mother, Brigette, at their home on the south side of Chicago. The slender young man—just under five feet eleven inches tall, with black hair and brown eyes—boarded the train for New York at 2:30 PM on Saturday 6 April. After seeing the sights of New York, he reported to the New York recruiting office at 8:15 Monday morning. Smith was processed at the receiving ship at New York, and assigned to the cruising cutter *Itasca*. As a fireman, his monthly pay was $46.50. Smith reported aboard the cutter at the Philadelphia Navy Yard on Tuesday morning, 14 May. Two months later, he wrote a letter to the captain commandant, requesting that his name be put on the list for the next draft of men to be sent for foreign service. Smith was never selected to go overseas, remaining aboard *Itasca* until he was discharged as a water tender third class on 7 April 1919.[19]

Submarine Net Duty and Harbor Patrol

The large number of coast guard cutters at repair facilities when war was declared indicated a planned effort to get necessary work done before the beginning of hostilities. *Apache* was undergoing repairs in its homeport of Baltimore on 6 April 1917. The 185-foot cruising cutter's repairs were completed on 21 April and it sailed for Norfolk. The iron-hulled *Apache* was painted gray at the Norfolk Navy Yard and commenced patrolling the submarine nets between the Virginia Capes. The ten-mile-long nets, which stretched across the entrance to the bay from Cape Charles to Cape Henry, were anchored at the bottom and supported at the surface by an assortment of floating casks, beer kegs, and buoys. Gateways in the net permitted the passage of ships and boats. A guard boat was stationed near each gate day and night to instruct vessels on how to pass through. All transiting merchant ships had to obtain permission to pass through the net. Naval ships transited through the gates after exchanging recognition signals with the guard vessels. As many as twenty vessels at a time were required to patrol the net and guard its entrances. Patrol vessels were kept busy preventing merchant ships from running over the nets, tearing them, and fouling their propellers in the cables. Squadrons of minesweepers worked in the channels leading to the gates; they swept several miles to seaward and for a shorter distance inside the net. Naval forces at the net were formed into squadrons, with the senior squadron commander in overall charge. Capt. Richard O. Crisp, USCG, captain of the *Apache*, commanded Squadron Five of the Fifth Naval District. He was the senior squadron commander at the Cape Henry net. On 11 December 1917 *Apache* was relieved of net duty and ordered to sail to Charleston and report to the commandant of the Sixth Naval District. The cruising cutter *Gresham* arrived at Norfolk from Boston on 13 June 1917, and began submarine net patrol duty at the entrance to Chesapeake Bay.[20]

Shortly after war was declared, commissioned officers who commanded smaller harbor cutters were relieved and reassigned to more important duties. They were replaced on the cutters by warrant officers. Master's Mate Nels Johnson relieved 1st Lt. (Eng.) John I. Bryan of command of the iron-hulled harbor cutter *Gutherie* the day after war was declared. Five days later, *Gutherie* was ordered from Philadelphia to Fort Delaware, Delaware, for submarine net duty. Operating from various ports, the 88-foot, 149-ton *Gutherie* guarded the entrance to Delaware Bay and Philadelphia. *Winnisimmet*, a ninety-six-foot harbor cutter, was undergoing extensive repairs at Charlestown Navy Yard in Massachusetts when the order to mobilize was received. Departing the yard on 9 July 1917, *Winnisimmet* proceeded to Presidents Roads, where it was assigned as a Boston harbor entrance patrol vessel. The cutter, under the command of U.S. Coast Guard warrant officers, performed various patrol duties within Boston harbor until the end of the war. The twenty-two-year-old steam launch *Tybee* reported to the navy section commander at Savannah, Georgia, on 6 April 1917. After helping seize a German merchant ship, the cutter patrolled local waters and served as a boarding vessel until the end of hostilities.[21]

Second Lt. (Eng.) Martin A. Doyle commanded the small 41-ton harbor cutter *Penrose*, headquartered at Pensacola, Florida. When war was declared, the cutter commenced guard and patrol duty at the entrance to the harbor, checking all shipping entering the port. Doyle, with a naval engineering background, was also assigned by the commandant of the Eighth Naval District to inspect work being done at the navy yard on the two seized German merchant ships—the 3,916-ton *Vogesen* and the 1,769-ton *Rudolph Blumberg*. He was further tasked to inspect aircraft engines at the naval air station. *Penrose* carried out patrol duties at the port of Pensacola until the end of the war. The ninety-two-foot harbor cutter *Davey*, with a complement of one officer and thirteen enlisted men, was headquartered at the port of New Orleans. After assisting with the seizure of a German steamship, the cutter's commanding officer, 1st Lt. Benjamin L. Brockway, was reassigned to "other important duty" and Boatswain William Kendrick took command. Operating out of Pilot Town, Louisiana, the cutter patrolled the passes at the mouth of the Mississippi River. On 16 April 1917, a boarding party from *Davey* arrested six German sailors who were plotting to take over the American schooner *Salem*. The cutter, with a maximum speed of ten and a half knots, continued guarding the Mississippi River passes until the end of the war. At the port of Mobile, Alabama, the sixty-one-foot harbor cutter *Alert*, under the command of 2d Lt. (Eng.) George W. Cairnes, patrolled the entrance to Mobile Bay. But the wooden-hulled *Alert*, built in 1907, was in need of repair and ill-suited for the rough waters at the entrance to the bay. The cutter was subsequently reassigned to boarding duty within the bay.[22]

The harbor cutter *Golden Gate*, with 1st Lt. California C. McMillan in command, was assigned to the commandant of the Twelfth Naval District

at San Francisco. The cutter assisted with the internment of German cit-
izens found on various vessels in San Francisco Bay. On 13 September
1917, a Naval Reserve Force (NRF) officer took command of *Golden
Gate*. The cutter patrolled San Francisco Bay between Fort Point and
Lima Point. From March 1918 until the end of September 1918, *Golden
Gate* transported armed guards to merchant vessels in the bay. On 1
August the cutter returned to harbor entrance patrol duties. With a crew
of twenty-two, *Golden Gate* was commanded by NRF officers until the
U.S. Coast Guard was returned to the Treasury Department. The small
harbor cutter *Hartley*, under the command of Boatswain August
Anderson, was also assigned to the Twelfth Naval District. It carried out
patrol and boarding duties in San Francisco Bay until the end of the war.[23]

The harbor cutters *Arcata*, *Scout*, and *Guard* were headquartered at
ports in Washington's Puget Sound. The wooden-hulled, sixty-one-foot
Scout was commanded by Boatswain Ben Lichtenberg, a warrant officer.
Scout was ordered to proceed from Port Townsend to Port Angeles and
report to the section commander, Capt. G. R. Slocum, USN. After repairs were made to the cutter at the Bremerton Navy Yard, it was painted
gray and commenced guard and patrol duty on 26 April. In addition to
wartime duties, the patrolling cutter arrested smugglers, intercepted
Chinese aliens who were attempting to enter the United States from
Canada, and seized a shipment of opium. Under the direction of the section commander, *Scout* operated from different headquarters in Puget
Sound until the end of the war. *Arcata*, headquartered at Port Townsend,
and *Guard*, headquartered at Friday Harbor, Washington, were also
assigned to guard and patrol duty. They patrolled the waters around their
homeports and in the Straits of Juan de Fuca. When war was declared,
the lieutenants commanding the two cutters were replaced by warrant
officers. First Lt. Frank L. Austin, from *Arcata*, reported to navy cruiser
Columbia for duty as navigator, and 2d Lt. Paul H. Harrison, from *Guard*,
was assigned to command the coast guard barracks at Cape May, New
Jersey. The 110-foot, 241-ton cutter *Mackinac* was assigned to the Great
Lakes, with headquarters at Sault Ste. Marie, Michigan. When the
United States declared war, the cutter was out of service, decommissioned
for the duration of the ice season. *Mackinac's* commanding officer, 1st Lt.
Edward S. Addison, acknowledged the order to mobilize and reported his

cutter's position to the commandant of the Great Lakes naval districts—
the Ninth, Tenth, and Eleventh. The cutter was placed back in commission on 24 April 1917, and commenced patrolling St. Mary's River as ice
conditions permitted. On 10 November the cutter was transferred to
New York for duty in the Third Naval District.[24]

MINESWEEPING AND MINE PLANTING

The iron-hulled harbor cutter *Hudson* was famous for its heroic rescue of
the disabled navy torpedo boat *Winslow* while under fire from Spanish
shore batteries at the Bay of Cardenas, Cuba, during the Spanish-
American War. One of the first cutters built with full compartmentation,
the twenty-four-year-old cutter was capable of making fifteen knots.
Hudson and the steel-hulled harbor cutter *Wissahickon* were on duty at the
port of New York when the United States declared war on Germany. The
cutters—both ninety-six feet in length—were immediately sent to the
Brooklyn Navy Yard to be fitted out as minesweepers. On 16 April 1917,
the cutters commenced minesweeping operations in Ambrose Channel at
the entrance to New York harbor. *Wissahickon* was reassigned to patrol
duty in August. After the installation of a rapid-fire one pound gun,
Hudson was reassigned to patrol the submarine net at Port Jefferson on
Long Island's northern coast. In December 1917, *Hudson* returned to
New York harbor for duty with the U.S. Coast Guard's New York division. In December 1918, the cruising cutter *Apache* was fitted out as a
minesweeper and reassigned to Charleston from submarine net duty at
the Virginia Capes.

When *Morrill*'s damages, caused by the 6 December 1917 explosion of
Mont Blanc and the collision with *North Wind* at Halifax, were repaired,
the cruising cutter was assigned as flagship for the Fourth Naval District's
minesweeping squadron. *Morrill*'s commanding officer, Capt. (Temp.)
George E. Wilcox, was assigned to command the squadron on 1 May
1918. The squadron's fourteen minesweepers operated from Barnegat,
New Jersey, to the Delaware Capes. The minesweepers were heavily
engaged in removing mines planted along the coast by German submarines. This duty continued for several months after hostilities ended.
Because of his diligent work, Wilcox was commended by the Fourth

Naval District commandant, Rear Adm. J. M. Helm, USN. In a 26 May 1919 letter to the chief of the U.S. Navy's Bureau of Navigation, Helm said, "The German submarines seemed to favor this part of the coast. His [Wilcox] duties were both strenuous and hazardous. In addition to keeping the channels swept, he located and removed three different groups of mines; one group in the mouth of the Delaware in June 1918; one group off Barnegat Bay, from June to October; and another group north of Winter Quarter Shoal, in August 1918. . . . It seems to me that this officer performed real war service, attended with personal risk of life and great responsibility, and is entitled to something higher than the ordinary decoration given to officers where lives were not in danger." In May 1917 *Seminole* was converted for minesweeping at the Charleston Navy Yard. On 13 June 1918, the cutter became the flagship for Minesweeping Squadron Five at the entrance to Chesapeake Bay, continuing these duties until the end of the war. In February 1918, the 1090-ton cruising cutter *Gresham* was fitted out for mine planting operations, but was never used for that mission.[25]

TOWING, ESCORT, AND SUPPORT

On 19 September 1917, the cruising cutter *Acushnet* was reassigned from guard and patrol duty at the entrance to Long Island Sound to the port of New York. Operating out of New York, the 152-foot cutter towed vessels carrying war supplies to various ports in New England. It also transported aviation supplies from Newport, Rhode Island, to naval air stations as far south as Hampton Roads, Virginia. On 12 December *Acushnet*, under the command of 1st Lt. Eugene Blake, sailed to St. Lawrence Bay in Canada to help cargo ships get through the ice. After escorting the Shipping Board's vessel *War Victory* to New York, *Acushnet* returned to St. Lawrence Bay, continuing to tow and escort Shipping Board vessels though the ice-covered waters of the Gulf of St. Lawrence until 3 February 1918. Towing duties continued until 5 March when the ship was ordered to load ordnance stores at the Washington Navy Yard. *Acushnet* delivered the ordnance supplies to the Charleston Navy Yard, departing for the return trip to Washington, D.C., the same day. A week later, *Acushnet* again loaded ordnance supplies and delivered them to the U.S.

Navy at New York, where the cutter went into the shipyard for repairs. When the shipyard availability was completed, *Acushnet* resumed towing duties. The cutter convoyed transiting submarines, engaged in salvage operations, and performed coastal guard duty until the end of the war. It was in the shipyard at Boston when the armistice was signed.

Cruising cutter *Androscoggin* interrupted coastal patrol and rescue work on 12 October 1917 to convoy HMS *Shearwater* and small British submarines from Sandwich, Massachusetts, to Halifax. Six months later, the cutter was again assigned to escort duty, sailing from New London, Connecticut, to Bermuda, with a convoy of submarine chasers. *Androscoggin* left Bermuda on 8 April 1918 and sailed to Guantánamo, Cuba. The cutter took a barge in tow and loaded personnel for transport to Norfolk. Like *Acushnet*, *Androscoggin* was used to transport guns and ordnance supplies from the Washington Navy Yard to New London. *Androscoggin* was at Quebec, waiting to escort three Canadian minesweepers, when the armistice was signed.[26]

The 206-foot cruising cutter *Onondaga* was unique because it was not assigned to a naval district commandant. It continued to operate directly under the commandant of the U.S. Coast Guard throughout the war. When the U.S. Coast Guard was mobilized, the cutter was out of commission at the depot at Arundel Cove. Officers and a crew were assigned and the cutter was recommissioned on 18 May 1917. *Onondaga* returned to its headquarters at New London, where Capt. Frederick C. Billard, who was also superintendent of the U.S. Coast Guard Academy, took command of the cutter. The cutter was used to convoy vessels turned over to the U.S. Coast Guard for use during the war, and to transport personnel between coast guard units. *Onondaga* delivered newly trained recruits from the U.S. Coast Guard Academy to the six cruising cutters being outfitted for duty in the European war zone, making special trips to the various ports where the cutters were located. The cutter towed the army harbor vessels *Richard Caswell* and *Coquet* from Wilmington, North Carolina, to New York, where they were turned over to the U.S. Coast Guard for use during the war. When the cutter *Mackinac* was transferred from the Great Lakes to the east coast, *Onondaga* escorted and towed it, as necessary, from Quebec to Long Island Sound.[27]

On 30 April 1917, *Seminole* escorted the seized 318-foot, 2,974-ton

German steamship *Hohenfeldt* from Savannah, Georgia, to Charleston. The next month, the cutter convoyed two more seized German vessels— 388-foot, 4,901-ton *Kiel* and 339-foot, 3,974-ton *Nicaria*—from the Cape Fear River in North Carolina to Charleston. On 2 December *Seminole* convoyed eleven outbound British merchant ships from Norfolk to a distance of fifty miles offshore. When the ships were clear of the waters where submarine attack was most likely, the cutter returned to the Virginia Capes. Two months later, *Seminole* sailed from Norfolk to Cristobal, Panama, via Guantánamo, Cuba, to pick up a barge and tow it back to Norfolk. On 4 April 1918, *Seminole* left Newport News with the army transport *Meade* in tow, en route to Boston; the tug *Tasco* assisted with the tow. The vessels ran into heavy weather off Nantucket Shoals and could not make any headway against the strong winds and current. When the seas threatened to drive the ships aground on the shoals, *Seminole* anchored *Meade* and evacuated its crew. By the time the weather cleared on 13 April, *Seminole* was running short of coal and the steamship *Germantown* had to be used to tow *Meade* the rest of the way to Boston.[28]

Repairs to the cruising cutter *Snohomish* were completed at the Bremerton Navy Yard in February 1918. The 152-foot cutter, which was constructed in 1908 as a first-class seagoing tug, was equipped with steam-towing apparatus. On 18 February 1918, *Snohomish* departed for San Francisco, towing navy barge no. 305 and escorting USS *Mohave*, which had two barges in tow. The vessels reached San Francisco, on 23 February. *Snohomish*, with barge no. 305 again in tow, sailed for Norfolk via the Panama Canal five days later, successfully arriving on 15 April. *Snohomish* next towed U.S. submarine chaser no. 140 from New London, Connecticut, to Bermuda. The voyage was made in company with USS *Arapaho*, which towed submarine chaser no. 33. The ships reached Bermuda four days later and remained there until 15 May 1918. They departed, in company with USS *Prarie*, escorting several French submarine chasers to the Azores. *Snohomish* took on coal and provisions at Ponta Delgada, and departed for the return trip to Bermuda on 31 May. The cutter traveled in a convoy with USS *Prarie*, USS *O'Connor*, and navy tugs *Iroquois*, *Dreadnought*, and *Arapaho*, which towed the disabled steamer *Luckenback*. *Snohomish*, *Dauntless*, and *Iroquois* left Bermuda on 24 June, towing *Luckenback* to New

York. *Snohomish* continued towing ships and barges between ports on the east coast and Bermuda until the end of the war.[29]

While at Guantánamo in August 1918, Capt. (Temp.) James F. Hottel received orders to sail the cruising cutter *Tallapoosa* to Cienfuegos, Cuba, and take the seized German steamship *Constantia* in tow. The cutter delivered the ship to the naval station at New Orleans on 8 September. *Tallapoosa* was then assigned to Key West, where the U.S. Navy used the cutter for search and rescue work and for towing. *Tallapoosa* towed barges from Key West to Norfolk, from New Orleans to Bermuda, and from Panama to Norfolk. After having repair work done at the coast guard depot at Arundel Cove, *Tallapoosa* towed naval ordnance barge *Sargent* from the Washington Navy Yard to naval facilities at New London, Connecticut, and Portsmouth, New Hampshire. *Tuscarora* was assigned to the Second Naval District, headquartered at Newport, Rhode Island. When not on patrol and guard duty, the 178-foot cruising cutter was used for towing and escort work. *Tuscarora* served as an escort on three trips to Bermuda from the east coast, convoying forty-three ships to the islands and seven back to the United States. *Unalga* was ordered to duty in the Twelfth Naval District after completing its usual summer cruise in Alaskan waters. The 190-foot cruising cutter, with Capt. Frederick G. Dodge in command, arrived at its new headquarters at San Pedro, California, on 17 October 1917. *Unalga* was assigned to duty as a submarine tender until the spring of 1918 when it was designated to make a Bering Sea cruise. Four NRF ensigns sailed with the cutter as watch officers during the cruise in Alaskan waters. On 17 October 1918, *Unalga* returned to San Pedro and resumed duties as a submarine escort and tender.[30]

TRAINING

Capt. Preston H. Uberroth commanded the 198-foot, 1,700-ton cruising cutter *Bear* in April 1917. He reported for duty to the commandant of the Twelfth Naval District at San Francisco when war was declared. The wooden-hulled cutter was ordered to continue making annual cruises to Alaskan waters from April to November to enforce U.S. laws and protect national interests. When not deployed to Alaska, *Bear* was used to train navy enlisted men at the San Pedro naval base in southern California.

McCulloch was also headquartered at San Francisco. With a 219-foot length, the cruising cutter was the U.S. Coast Guard's largest ship. The commandant of the Twelfth Naval District assigned the cutter to patrol and training duty along the coast of southern California. *McCulloch*, with a wartime complement of 130 officers and enlisted men, departed San Pedro on a training cruise on 12 June; three naval reserve ensigns were aboard for training as officers of the deck. The cutter was under way in a dense fog in the Santa Barbara Channel in the early morning hours of 13 June. *McCulloch*'s commanding officer, Sr. Capt. John C. Cantwell, was in his cabin when passenger ship SS *Governor*, making fourteen knots, came out of the fog. The steamship struck *McCulloch*'s port bow, cutting a deep gash into the hull at the waterline. With the cutter rapidly taking on water, all hands were called to their abandon ship stations. After a muster was taken, the crew took to the boats. *Governor* successfully recovered the cutter's entire crew. Acting Water Tender John A. Johannson was the only man seriously injured in the collision. He was sleeping in his bunk, which was near the point of impact. When *Governor* reached port, Johannson was rushed to the hospital at San Pedro. He died from his injuries three days later.[31]

The cruising cutter *Tuscarora* was reassigned from Milwaukee to Chicago when war was declared. The cutter, under the command of 1st Lt. William T. Stromberg, patrolled in the Great Lakes and provided training for naval reserve officers and enlisted men. The cutter also boarded and inspected vessels on the lakes and examined merchant seamen for qualification as life boatmen on passenger and freight ships. *Tuscarora* continued duty in the lakes until ordered to proceed to the Atlantic coast on 30 September 1917. *Apache* was reassigned from submarine net duty at Chesapeake Bay to Charleston. Before departing from the Fifth Naval District, the cutter was fitted out for minesweeping. *Apache* arrived at Charleston on 13 December, and the new commanding officer, 1st Lt. George C. Alexander, reported to the commandant of the Sixth Naval District. Alexander was told that, in addition to minesweeping, the cutter would be used as a school ship for training navy ensigns. Additionally, *Apache* was frequently called to respond to vessels in distress. The rescue work provided operational experience for the navy trainees being prepared for overseas duty. In the winter of 1917–1918, the cruising cutters *Gresham* and *Seminole* were also used to train naval reserve officers for shipboard duty.[32]

In addition to training cadets at the U.S. Coast Guard Academy, the cruising cutter *Onondaga* trained new coast guard enlistees. The cutter made several cruises along the Atlantic coast training cadets as watch officers and enlisted men for duty aboard cutters. Many of the early enlisted trainees were assigned to the six cruising cutters being outfitted for duty in European waters. With a draft of only five and a half feet, the cruising cutter *Pamlico* was used to patrol the shallow waters of North Carolina's Pamlico Sound, from its headquarters at New Bern. When war was declared, the cutter's commanding officer, 1st Lt. James A. Alger, reported to the commandant of the Fifth Naval District. He was ordered to cruise the waters of the district to enroll officers and enlisted men for service in the naval reserve. Because the U.S. Navy was looking for suitable boats to purchase, Alger and his chief engineer were also assigned to inspect motorboats at the ports where the cutter called. At the end of October 1917, the 158-foot *Pamlico* was transferred to Chesapeake Bay. Operating from Pinner's Point, Virginia, the cutter made short cruises in the bay, providing instruction for naval reserve officer trainees being prepared for duty overseas. The cutter continued its training role until the end of the war.[33]

SEARCH AND RESCUE

Navy commanders recognized and used the skills and experience of coast guard crews to respond to vessels in distress. Although assigned to other missions, they were used extensively for rescue work. In addition to patrolling from its headquarters at Portland, Maine, *Androscoggin* was used for wreck and rescue work, cruising as far north as St. John, Newfoundland. In March 1918, the cutter went to the assistance of British steamship *Turret Crown*, disabled in the North Atlantic. *Androscoggin* safely towed the merchant ship into Boston on 9 March 1918.[34]

The cruising cutter *Gresham* carried out search and rescue missions for the Fifth Naval District in addition to patrolling the submarine net. On one occasion, when *Gresham*'s commanding officer, Capt. Benjamin M. Chiswell, was ashore disabled by influenza, 1st Lt. (Eng.) John N. Heiner, the cutter's next senior officer, took command of the ship. Heiner—an engineer with only three years commissioned service—was ordered to take *Gresham* to sea to rescue a ship in distress. Despite his limited experience, Heiner successfully rescued the ship and returned safely to Norfolk. The cruising cutter *Seminole*, assigned to coastal patrol duty in the Sixth Naval District, frequently engaged in rescue missions. In one case, the cutter was called to refloat a steamship aground on the bar at Brunswick, Georgia. On 8 January 1918, *Seminole* departed Norfolk to search for navy barges lost in stormy seas in the Atlantic Ocean. The cutter reached Bermuda eight days later. Operating from Bermuda, it continued searching for the next thirteen days, without success. While *Seminole* never found the barges, it did locate the disabled steamer *Wilmington*, under tow by another ship, and escorted it to Bermuda. The commandant of the Second Naval District at Newport, Rhode Island, frequently used the cutter *Tuscarora* to respond to requests for assistance from distressed vessels.[35]

In February 1918, the 206-foot cruising cutter *Onondaga* was under way, transporting coast guard personnel between units and convoying vessels between ports on the Atlantic coast. Coast guard cadets and new enlistees were aboard for training. On 20 February the cutter was offshore from Cape Hatteras when a distress message was received from the British steamship *Venturia*. *Venturia* reported running aground at Cape Hatteras in dense fog. *Onondaga* worked its way toward shore in the low visibility until it located Diamond Shoal Lightship. Having fixed the cutter's position, Capt. Frederick C. Billard cautiously maneuvered along the coast in the fog and darkness until he located the stricken ship. *Venturia*'s master signaled to the cutter that he wanted to abandon ship. In a 1922 account of the rescue, Crisp wrote, "Although there was considerable sea on, and the position of the stranded ship a dangerous one, the surf boat was lowered with Boatswain Charles Martinson in charge, with an able crew sent to the side of the *Venturia*. Here, in spite of a heavy sea running along the ship's side, the boat was loaded with a part of the crew which were safely brought to the cutter. Six more trips were made by Boatswain Charles Martinson in like manner before the entire crew was taken off the stranded ship." *Onondaga* successfully rescued *Venturia*'s entire crew of forty-six. At the time of the rescue, *Venturia* was on transport duty for the British Admiralty. The Lords Commissioners of the Admiralty expressed appreciation for the rescue in a letter to the U.S. naval forces commander. The letter requested that the admiral "convey to the officers and men concerned an expression of their great appreciation on the very valuable service rendered by the United States Coast Guard vessel *Onondaga* in rescuing the crew." Gow, Harrison and Company, *Venturia*'s owner, also sent a letter to the secretary of the navy expressing appreciation for the rescue.[36]

NAVY VESSELS

To meet wartime needs, the U.S. Navy acquired ships from other government agencies and private owners. The U.S. Navy asked the U.S. Coast Guard to assign experienced personnel, especially officers, to command and operate these newly obtained ships and yachts. Coast guard enlisted personnel were generally not available to man the ships because they were needed to fill increased wartime complements aboard cutters. In fall 1917, the U.S. Navy's Bureau of Navigation requested that Coast Guard Headquarters assign officers to man U.S. Navy ships as well as seven large yachts, which were acquired by the navy and being outfitted for overseas duty. First Lt. James A. Alger, USCG, was assigned to command the 140-foot *Halcyon* with 2d Lt. Gordon T. Finlay, USCG, as his executive officer. The ship's condition, however, was found to be unsuitable for service overseas. *Halcyon* was not put into commission and its coast guard officers were reassigned. Two of the scheduled yachts were found to be unserviceable and were stricken from the rolls before any coast guard officers were assigned. The U.S. Navy acquired the 192-foot, wooden-hulled sailing yacht *Xarifa* on 9 August 1917. First Lt. Eugene Blake, USCG, was ordered to report as commanding officer. Five more coast guard lieutenants were assigned to complete the officer complement. They reported aboard the yacht in a shipyard at Port Jefferson, New York. *Xarifa* was later found to be unsuitable for overseas duty and the six officers were reassigned. Three were ordered to navy ships—two cruisers and a transport. Two were assigned to coast guard cruising cutters, and the third was sent to the U.S. Coast Guard Academy for duty. *Zara*, a 152-foot steam yacht was built in 1891. When commissioned as a

U.S. Navy ship, it was sent to the Brooklyn Navy Yard to be outfitted for overseas duty. The U.S. Coast Guard provided five officers and the U.S. Navy supplied fifty-seven enlisted men to man the ship. First Lt. Leon C. Covell, USCG, was assigned as commanding officer. When the ship was taken to sea for trials, it was determined to be unseaworthy and the plan to send the ship overseas was abandoned. The coast guard officers were reassigned to other duties and *Zara* was used for local duties in Long Island Sound.[37] Only two of the seven yachts—*Galatea* and *Rambler*—actually deployed overseas. The activities of these ships, manned with coast guard officers, are described in Chapter 5.

On 15 October 1917, Capt. John G. Berry, USCG, was ordered to take command of the twenty-year-old USS *Dorothea*. At the time, the ship was assigned to patrol the Mexican coast and the southern coast of the United States. One month after taking command of *Dorothea*, Berry and his crew of navy officers and men were transferred to USS *Eagle*, which was stationed at Base 16 at Key West. The 156-foot *Eagle* was a converted yacht, manned with a crew of sixty-seven officers and men. Part of the American Patrol Detachment, *Eagle* was assigned to patrol the Florida Straits and coastal waters of Cuba and Hispanola. On 21 April 1918, 1st Lt. Eben Barker, USCG, relieved Berry as commanding officer of *Eagle*; four months later he was replaced by Capt. (Temp.) Edward D. Jones, USCG. Jones was in command of *Eagle* when the war ended and continued to command the ship for another seven months. Another coast guard officer, 1st Lt. Cecil M. Gabbett, was ordered to command *Dorothea* on 18 May 1918. By that time, the ship was at Havana, Cuba, where it was being used to train Cuban naval officers. *Dorothea* periodically returned to Key West for supplies and repairs. After the war ended, the ship was assigned to transport duty in Cuban, Puerto Rican, and Dominican Republic waters. For a brief period, the ship was under the command of the military governor at Santo Domingo, Dominican Republic. Gabbett remained in command of *Dorothea* for several months after the armistice. When 1st Lt. John L. Maher, USCG, was relieved of command of the cruising cutter *Pamlico* on 27 October 1917, he took command of the Fifth Naval District's third section, headquartered at Cherrystone Island, Virginia. As a part of his assignment, Maher also commanded the 164-foot barracks ship USS *Maggie*. He was relieved of these duties on 1 March 1919.[38]

The 234-foot *Albatross* was transferred from the Department of Commerce's Fish Commission to the Navy Department and commissioned as a patrol gunboat (PG) on 19 November 1917. *Albatross* was attached to the American Patrol Detachment and assigned to patrol the southern coast of the United States. On 1 March 1918 Capt. Claude S. Cochran, USCG, took command of *Albatross* and its navy crew of 110 officers and men. The ship continued patrol duties in southern waters, protecting shipments of oil and supplies in the Gulf of Mexico and the Caribbean. Cochran commanded *Albatross* until the armistice was signed on 11 November 1918. The inspector of naval districts on the Atlantic coast, Rear Adm. C. McR. Winslow, USN, used the converted yacht *Aloha* as his flagship. Sailing from his headquarters at the port of New York, he inspected naval districts from Maine to Texas. First Lt. Harold D. Hinckley, USCG, took command of the 218-foot *Aloha* on 1 July 1918. The ship, which had previously been commanded by naval officers, mounted two 4-inch guns and two 3-inch guns and was manned by an 86-man navy crew. Shortly after taking command, Hinckley was promoted to captain and remained in command until the ship was decommissioned and returned to its original owners on 29 January 1919.[39]

On the west coast, the U.S. Coast and Geodetic Survey (USC&GS) ships *Explorer* and *Patterson* were transferred to the U.S. Navy on 22 May 1918. When acquired, the vessels were sent to the Puget Sound Naval Shipyard at Bremerton for repairs. First Lt. Thomas A. Shanley, USCG, selected to command *Patterson*, was detailed to supervise repairs being made to both ships. He also arranged for the outfitting of the 163-foot, 719-ton *Patterson*. The 135-foot *Explorer* was commissioned on 3 June 1918, with Lt. W. H. Stanford, USNRF, in command. Shanley took command of *Patterson* and its crew of forty-nine when it was commissioned on 20 June 1918. At the request of the Department of Justice, the Thirteenth Naval District commandant ordered the two lightly armed ships to deploy to Alaska in the summer of 1918 to assist officials and round up "slackers," men who avoided the draft. Col. Theodore Roosevelt called slackers "miserable creatures who should be hunted out of the society of self-respecting men and women." *Patterson*, with a complement of forty-nine, departed Puget Sound on 3 July. Because of his prior experience in Alaskan waters, 2d Lt. Joseph R. Besse, USCG, was ordered to relieve Stanford as commanding officer of *Explorer* before the ship deployed to Alaska. *Patterson*, with a maximum speed of nine knots, arrived at Unalaska, Alaska, on 17 July 1918, and was renamed *Forward* one month later. *Forward* continued to cruise coastal waters and called at Alaskan ports, performing duties for the Department of Justice, until returning to the Puget Sound Navy Yard in September 1918. When work at the yard was completed, Shanley sailed *Forward* south to San Diego. *Forward* was designated flagship for Rear Adm. W. F. Fullum, commander of the second division of the Second Fleet, at San Diego in October 1918. *Explorer* continued to patrol in Alaskan waters as a navy ship until it was returned to USC&GS six months after the end of the war.[40]

Coast guard officers were also assigned to duty aboard navy cruisers and gunboats. On 30 May 1918, Capt. William V. E. Jacobs, USCG, assumed command of escort ship USS *Niagra*, with a crew of 195 men. Jacobs had previously commanded the U.S. Coast Guard's cruising cutter *Itasca*. The 282-foot, 2,690-ton *Niagra* was attached to the cruiser and transport forces under the command of Adm. Albert Gleaves. During the months of June and July 1918, the twelve-knot ship escorted two squadrons of troop and cargo ships from New York to Halifax. On 15 July *Niagra* sailed from New York, escorting a squadron of four ships to Ponta Delgada in the Azores Islands. On the return trip to Bermuda, it convoyed the crippled navy ship USS *Barry*. When Jacobs reached Bermuda, he was ordered to escort the French cable ship *Pouyer Quertier* to Fort de France, Martinique, in the West Indies. At Fort de France, Jacobs reported to Admiral Grout, the French commander of the Atlantic, for duty. Beginning in September 1918, *Niagra* patrolled West Indian waters in search of German submarines and escorted ships between ports in the islands. *Niagra* continued these duties until the armistice was signed. The 188-foot gunboat *Petrel* (PG-2) was built in 1888 and had a complement of 138 men. The ship, armed with four 4-inch guns, was being used as a station ship at the naval station at Guantánamo Bay when war was declared. *Petrel* was ordered back to the United States to serve with the American Patrol Detachment at Boston. Second Lt. (Eng.) Sidney B. Orne, USCG, reported aboard *Petrel* on 12 January 1918, and was assigned as the ship's chief engineer. Second Lt. Roy P. Munro, USCG, reported aboard two weeks later. When Orne became sick, he was detached from the ship on 28 August and transferred to the receiving ship at New

York for temporary duty. Orne died one month later of bronchial pneumonia at St. Vincent's Hospital in Brooklyn. Munro remained aboard *Petrel* until after the war ended. He was transferred from the ship on 11 September 1919, and resigned from the U.S. Coast Guard two months later.[41]

The 3,769-ton, 354-foot protected cruiser *Albany* (CL-23) was the flagship of Squadron Six, Patrol Force, Atlantic Fleet in April 1917. When the United States declared war on Germany, *Albany*, with a 365-man complement, was assigned to the Cruiser Force, Atlantic Fleet, with the mission of escorting convoys between the United States and Europe. Second Lt. Michael J. Ryan, USCG, was a deck watch officer when he joined the ship. Ryan was promoted to first lieutenant on 18 September 1917 and was assigned as gunnery officer of the *New Orleans*–class cruiser. The heavily armed ship mounted three 18-inch guns, six 6-inch guns, and four 4.7-inch guns. Second Lt. S. S. Yeandle, USCG, who graduated from the U.S. Coast Guard Academy two years after Ryan, reported aboard *Albany* on 8 December 1917, and was designated the ship's navigator. He served as navigator until he was detached on New Year's eve 1918. Yeandle wrote about his service on the cruiser in a letter: "The *Albany* was employed on convoy duty exclusively during this period, making eleven round trips with cargo and troop convoys from New York to France." Second Lt. Frederick A. Zscheuschler reported aboard the cruiser *Chattanooga* on 20 December 1917. He served as a deck watch officer aboard the 3,200-ton, 309-foot ship until after the end of the war. The cruiser was manned by a crew of 339 and armed with ten 5-inch guns and eight 6-pound guns. *Chattanooga* escorted convoys across the Atlantic Ocean to rendezvous with war zone escorts. Zscheuschler, whose name was changed to Zeusler, was a temporary captain when he was detached on 5 March 1919.[42]

Second Lt. David P. Marvin, USCG, joined the 339-man complement of protected cruiser *Denver* (C-14) on 7 December 1917. The 309-foot, 3,200-ton cruiser, armed with ten 5-inch guns, escorted eastbound convoys from New York and Norfolk. Destroyers from Europe met the convoys of troop and cargo ships at mid-ocean rendezvous points and escorted them to ports in England and France. Marvin, who was promoted to temporary captain on 21 September 1918 was initially assigned to *Denver* as a deck watch officer. By the time he was detached a year later, however, he was the

The 13,680-ton armored cruiser USS *San Diego*, zigzagging en route to New York, struck a German mine off the coast of Fire Island, New York, on 19 July 1918. The ship sank in twenty-six minutes, with the loss of 6 of its 1,114-man wartime complement. Second Lt. Henry G. Hemingway, USCG, had reported aboard *San Diego* from *Morrill* in May 1918. *U.S. Naval Historical Center*

ship's executive officer. Third Lt. George W. McKean, USCG, reported aboard *Cleveland* (C-19), a *Denver*-class cruiser, on 12 January 1918. He served as a deck watch officer until he was detached on 6 March 1919, four months after the armistice was signed. Three coast guard officers were assigned aboard the 413-foot cruiser *Minneapolis* (C-13). Recommissioned when war began, the ship had been out of service for more than ten years. First Lt. Leon C. Covell, USCG, joined the 477-man crew on 14 January 1918, and was assigned to duty as navigator. *Minneapolis* mounted four 18-inch guns, one 8-inch gun, two 6-inch guns, and eight 4-inch guns. The cruiser initially escorted ships in the western Atlantic and patrolled the coast of the United States. On 24 February *Minneapolis* was assigned to transatlantic convoy duty. When Covell was detached on 19 July, Capt. Lloyd T. Chalker, USCG, replaced him as navigator. First Lt. Jesse F. Sexton, USCG, reported aboard for duty on 12 July. Both Chalker and Sexton were transferred from *Minneapolis* two weeks after the war ended.[43]

The cruiser *San Diego* escorted convoys bound for Europe. Second Lt. Henry G. Hemingway, who had been decorated for his work during the 6 December 1918 Halifax explosion, reported aboard *San Diego* on 29 May 1918. Seven weeks later, the ship was en route from Portsmouth, New Hampshire, to New York in clear weather with smooth seas. Zigzagging ten miles southeast of New York's Fire Island Light, *San Diego* struck a German mine. At 11:30 AM on 19 July the mine detonated on the armored cruiser's port side, just forward of the port engine room's forward bulkhead. The 504-foot, 13,680-ton warship, armed with two 18-inch guns, four 8-inch guns, fourteen 6-inch guns, and eighteen 3-inch guns, capsized and sank in 28 minutes. Four steamships stopped to pick up survivors. Fortunately, only 6 of the 1,114 officers and men aboard the ship were lost. *San Diego* was the largest U.S. warship lost during the war. Hemingway, who was not injured, was reassigned to temporary duty on the receiving ship at the port of New York. The next day minesweepers located six German mines in the vicinity where *San Diego* went down.[44]

CHAPTER 5

ON NAVY SHIPS IN
THE WAR ZONE

The professional ability of the Coast Guard officers is evidenced by the fact that twenty-four commanded combatant ships operating in European Waters, five vessels of the patrol force in the Caribbean, and twenty-three combatant craft attached to naval districts. . . . The Navy Department, naturally enough, assigned to the command of combatant ships only officers whose experience and ability warranted such detail and only those officers in whom the Department had implicit confidence.

—JOSEPHUS DANIELS, SECRETARY OF THE NAVY

MARIETTA

At 6:00 AM on the morning of 27 April 1919, twelve small U.S. Navy ships departed the port of Brest, France, bound for Hampton Roads, Virginia. Movement Order No. 111, issued by the commander of U.S. forces in France, designated Capt. Harry G. Hamlet, USCG, as the convoy commander. Hamlet commanded the 1,000-ton, 189-foot gunboat *Marietta*.

The other ships of the convoy were *Rambler, MacDonough, Teresa,* and eight minesweepers. *Rambler* was a converted yacht and *Teresa* was a Naval Overseas Transportation Service cargo vessel. The minesweepers, converted Menhaden fishing trawlers, were *Anderton, Courtney, Douglas, Hinton, Hubbard, James, Lewes,* and *McNeal.* When the ships of the convoy passed Les Pierres Noires Lighthouse at 8:30 AM, they left the French coast behind. The seas were calm and the sky was overcast, with a light wind blowing from the northwest. Hamlet set an initial course of 257 degrees true and a speed of eight knots.[1]

While the ships proceeded on their westerly track, the winds gradually increased "as was to be expected at this time of the year," Hamlet said. He anticipated that the winds would continue to increase until noon and then diminish, becoming calm as the sun set. Noon passed. The winds continued to increase and the seas to build. When the smaller ships started taking heavy seas on their starboard bows, Hamlet reduced the convoy's speed to seven knots "in order not to strain any of the vessels," he said. At 1:00 PM, *Marietta* received a signal from Lt. Cdr. F. L. Johnson, USN, on 177-foot *Rambler,* reporting that his ship was having engine problems. Fifteen minutes later, a lookout aboard *Marietta* called out that *Rambler* had broken the "man overboard flag," at its yardarm. Hamlet immediately turned *Marietta* to port and signaled for ships in the right column to commence searching for the lost man. Crews took their man overboard stations and additional lookouts were posted. The white life ring and gray life raft, thrown into the water when the man was swept over the side, were quickly located. The life ring was retrieved, but the raft was left in the water to mark datum for the search. The ships concentrated their efforts around the life raft.

Heavy seas pounded the small vessels as the storm increased in intensity. *Marietta* was searching for the missing man when the minesweeper *Courtney* signaled, "I am leaking badly in the floor plates." Hamlet ordered the minesweeper's commanding officer, Lt. (j.g.) Harry N. Sadler, USN, to return to port, saying, "Make best of your way to Brest." Hamlet then signaled Lt. James B. Dryden, USN, on the minesweeper *McNeal* to "escort the *Courtney* to Brest. If necessary, take her in tow so that she can use all her steam on the pumps." *McNeal* was the minesweeper with the most powerful engines. With the weather continuing to worsen, *Marietta* ordered all the minesweepers to reverse course at 2:22 PM and return to Brest. Hamlet assigned *Rambler* and *MacDonough* to escort the minesweepers back to port. *Marietta* and the 276-foot *Teresa* continued to search for *Rambler*'s missing seaman, Carl J. Mohr. Dryden on *McNeal* next signaled *Marietta*, saying that his ship was in trouble. Hamlet told him, "If you need towing assistance, get another sweeper ahead of you to give you a line." The minesweeper *Hinton* took *McNeal* in tow and the sweeper *Anderton* took over the tow of *Courtney*. By 4:50, all the minesweepers were headed back to Brest. Patrol craft *Rambler* and *MacDonough* escorted them and tugs were on their way out from Brest to assist. When *Courtney*'s commanding officer sent an urgent call saying he was sinking, Hamlet diverted *Marietta* and *Teresa* from their search to go to his rescue.[2]

The two ships arrived on scene and found *Courtney* riding low in the water, with *Anderton* standing by. Hamlet told Lt. Cdr. R. H. Allen, USNRF, in command of *Teresa*, to proceed to windward of the foundering vessel, put out an oil slick, and then drift down on *Courtney* to remove her crew. Hamlet reported, "This maneuver was very skillfully performed by USS *Teresa*." After taking *Courtney*'s crew aboard, *Teresa* took *Courtney* in tow, as a derelict. *Anderton* was sent on toward Brest with the other minesweepers. With the convoy now divided into two separate groups, *Marietta* took a station halfway between them, in position to respond to a call for help from either group. When the minesweeper *Douglas* fell behind, its commanding officer, Lt. (j.g.) A. J. McKenzie, signaled that his ship was in trouble and needed a tow. *Teresa* released its tow of the unmanned *Courtney* and went to assist *Douglas*. *Marietta* circled back to check on *Courtney* and arrived just in time to see the abandoned minesweeper slip below the surface of the rough seas, stern first, at 7:12 PM. Hamlet ordered *Teresa* to take *Douglas* in tow, while he circled the position where *Courtney* went down to make sure no one had been left aboard the ship. When *Marietta* rejoined *Teresa*, Hamlet saw that *Teresa* was preparing to remove *Douglas*'s crew, but was having a difficult time in the raging storm. By the time *Teresa* successfully removed all the men from *Douglas*, there was another call for help. Lt. (j.g.) John R. Roil, captain of the minesweeper *James*, was signaling that he urgently needed help. Hamlet told *Teresa* "to make all possible speed" in proceeding to assist *James*.

With a full gale now blowing, *Marietta* stood by *Douglas*. Hamlet intended to take the abandoned minesweeper in tow in the morning, if conditions improved and if the ship was still afloat. At 10:20 PM, a heavy squall with driving rain swept through the area and *Douglas* disappeared in the darkness. When the squall cleared, the minesweeper was gone. At 11:30 PM, Hamlet concluded that *Douglas* had gone down and proceeded to rejoin the other minesweepers. He found the disabled *James*, with *MacDonough* and three minesweepers that had come out from Brest to assist—*Penobscot*, *Yarnell*, and *Murray*—standing by. *Teresa*, with survivors from *Courtney* and *Douglas* aboard, had departed for port. When dawn arrived on the morning of 28 April, the sweeper *Penobscot* passed a line to *James* and commenced towing it toward Brest. Hamlet said, "The tow line soon parted and the USS *Penobscot* continued on her course and was out of sight in a heavy swell." *James* was shipping water and its crew was exhausted from continually bailing. Rising water in the bilges had put out the boiler fires the night before; *James* was a dead ship. With no steam for the pumps and no heat, the minesweeper's crew was suffering from fatigue and exposure.

Hamlet realized *James* could not remain afloat much longer and decided, despite the hazards, to attempt to remove the crew. He knew it was impossible to take *Marietta*, with its protruding hull gun mounts, alongside the stricken vessel in the heavy seas. Hamlet took control of his gunboat and made an approach on *James*, which was wallowing low in the water, rolling and pitching. The gunboat's crew managed to get a messenger line across to the foundering ship; a heavier line was bent onto it and passed across to *James*. The minesweeper's crew secured the line to a small Carley life raft and tied a tending line to the other end of the raft. Hamlet held the underpowered 1,000-ton gunboat in a precarious position close aboard the disabled minesweeper while the raft was hauled back and forth through the churning seas. *Marietta*'s crew used oil freely to dampen the turbulent waters for the small raft, which could hold no more than six men at a time. Each time the raft reached *Marietta*'s side, lines knotted with bowlines were passed over the survivors and they were hauled aboard. It took nearly three hours before the minesweeper's crew of two officers and forty-five enlisted men were all safely transferred to *Marietta*. During the rescue, *MacDonough* and the minesweeper *Murray* stood by. The minesweeper *Yarnell* ran low on fuel and had to return to Brest. On their return trip to Brest, the ships were diverted to search for the 135-foot navy tug *Gypsum Queen*, which had sent out a distress signal.

The tug, out of Brest, was caught in the same storm—one of the worst to hit the French coast in recent memory. After towing the minesweeper *McNeal* to safety, *Gypsum Queen* had put back to sea to render further assistance. The storm drove the tug aground on rocks two miles from Ar-Men Lighthouse at 1:00 PM on 28 April. Thirteen men managed to abandon ship in one lifeboat, but they were unable to get back to the tug to pick up the captain and remaining crew. *Gypsum Queen*'s commanding officer ordered the boat to make for shore to get help. Just as the boat turned toward shore, the men saw *Gypsum Queen* blow up. The boiler explosion killed two officers and fourteen men. The men in the lifeboat survived. When released from the search for survivors from *Gypsum Queen*, *Marietta*, *MacDonough*, and *Murray* returned to Brest. *Marietta* moored at 12:55 AM on 29 April 1919.

The forty-five enlisted men rescued from the USS *James* sent a letter to Hamlet, expressing their gratitude to him, his officers, and crew. The letter, signed by each man, stated, "When it seemed that all chance of being saved was gone and that a number of us would be lost, your valor and coolness during this period of extreme stress showed itself and, owing to the heroic measures and daring chances taken by you and the stick-to-it employed in the work of rescue, not a man of the *James* was lost." The letter closed: "We take this opportunity of expressing to you our profound admiration for your wonderful work, which we will never forget and, to the last man, we feel that we owe an everlasting debt of gratitude to you." *Marietta*, with a crew of 10 officers and 130 enlisted men, remained in France until June 1919; the gunboat then departed for the United States by way of the West Indies. The ship arrived at New Orleans on 1 July, and was decommissioned twelve days later. Hamlet was reassigned to the receiving ship at New York and then to Coast Guard Headquarters. For the heroic rescue of the entire crew of the *James*, Hamlet was awarded the Gold Life-Saving Medal by Congress on 5 January 1920.

Navy Ships

To meet the demand for experienced officers—particularly commanding officers—for ships being mobilized for war, the U.S. Navy called on the U.S. Coast Guard. Coast guard warrant officers and officers of the naval reserve were used to replace officers reassigned from cutters. Seventy-three Naval Reserve Force (NRF) officers were assigned to cruising cutters for duty. As the war continued, more coast guard officers were assigned overseas to command navy ships in the war zone. They were frequently used to replace naval officers who were promoted to higher positions. Coast guard officers served on four gunboats and six patrol craft at Base 9, Gibraltar. Nine of the ten commanded the ships they were assigned to. Another four officers at Gibraltar served on cruisers. Several coast guard officers were assigned to ships, primarily converted yachts, operating out of ports on the coast of France, nine as commanding officers and one as chief engineer. Several of the former yachts were larger than coast guard cruising cutters, but they did not have the endurance or seakeeping qualities of the rugged cutters. A coast guard officer put into commission and commanded a navy supply ship that was used to support naval air stations in France. Five officers were assigned to large mine planter ships based at Scotland, filling billets as executive officer, chief engineer, navigator, and watch officers.[3]

BASE 9, GIBRALTAR

Gibraltar was used primarily as a base for British and U.S. ships escorting convoys in the Atlantic Ocean and Mediterranean Sea and for vessels patrolling the strait for submarines. Coast guard cruising cutters, capable of distant cruising, were used to escort convoys on the longer ocean voyages. The converted yachts were tasked with escorting convoys on shorter runs in the Mediterranean Sea. Capt. Randolph Ridgely Jr., USCG, was in command of the cruising cutter *Yamacraw* when he was ordered to take command of the gunboat USS *Castine*. He relieved Cdr. William C. Asserson, USN, as commanding officer of the 1,177-ton, 204-foot gunboat on 8 August 1918. Asserson was reassigned to be the chief of staff for Base 9. The twenty-four-year-old *Castine* was armed with eight 4-inch guns mounted in enclosures protruding from the sides of the hull. Four 6-pound guns were mounted on the main deck. The ship had a raised forecastle and fantail and two tall masts. The pilothouse was aft of the forward mast. A single tall smokestack rose from the low deckhouse. Manned by a crew of 11 officers and 143 enlisted men, *Castine* was assigned to Squadron Two, Patrol Force. The day after Ridgely took command, *Castine* sailed from Gibraltar, escorting a convoy of ships to Genoa, Italy. The gunboat continued to escort convoys in the Mediterranean Sea until the armistice was signed. First Lt. Roger C. Weightman, USCG, was Ridgely's executive officer aboard *Castine*. After the war ended, *Castine* was ordered back to the United States. The gunboat departed Gibraltar on 21 December 1918, as an escort for a flotilla of eighteen submarine chasers. An additional fourteen submarine chasers joined the convoy at Ponta Delgada in the Azores. The 274-foot, 4,000-ton USS *Hannibal*, a tender for submarine chasers from Portsmouth, England, was the convoy's flagship. The convoy's five escorts were all commanded by coast guard officers. A fuel ship, a mother ship, and three tugs also sailed with the convoy. The ships arrived at St. Thomas in the Virgin Islands on 17 January 1919 without incident. The convoy was disbursed at St. Thomas and the vessels proceeded to various ports in the United States. *Castine* sailed to New Orleans, where Ridgely was relieved of command on 26 April 1919.[4]

The 200-foot *Paducah*, another gunboat based at Gibraltar, was attached to Squadron One, Patrol Force. The 1,084-ton *Paducah* had twin screws and was capable of making thirteen knots. Its primary mission was escorting convoys to and from ports in the Mediterranean Sea. Capt. Muller S. Hay, USCG, took command of *Paducah* at the end of the summer in 1918. He remained in command of the ship until after the armistice, when he and Capt. William J. Wheeler, USCG, exchanged commands. Hay took command of the cruising cutter *Seneca* and Wheeler assumed command of *Paducah*, which was scheduled to return to the United States. Wheeler had been in the war zone since 4 September 1917, while Hay had only been overseas for a few months. *Paducah*'s crew of 10 officers and 174 enlisted men mustered on 3 December 1918 for the change of command. *Paducah* departed Gibraltar on 11 December, escorting the 420-ton destroyer USS *Decatur*. The ships refueled at the Azores and *Paducah* took *Decatur* in tow for the remainder of the voyage to Bermuda. The gunboat arrived at Bermuda on New Year's Day 1919, and departed before nightfall. *Paducah* proceeded to Portsmouth, New Hampshire, where it was decommissioned on 2 March. Wheeler was reassigned to Coast Guard Headquarters.[5]

On 30 March 1918, 1st Lt. Charles F. Howell, USCG, was ordered to command the patrol craft *Arcturus*. Howell had gained his experience in the war zone while serving as a deck watch officer on convoy duty aboard cruising cutters *Algonquin* and *Seneca*. *Arcturus*, a 177-foot converted yacht, was armed with two 3-inch deck guns and depth charges. Manned by a crew of five officers and sixty-two enlisted men, the 456-ton ship was attached to Squadron 2, Patrol Force. Howell commanded the ship until he was reassigned to command *Venetia* on 2 August 1918, relieving Cdr. Lewis B. Porterfield, USN, as commanding officer. The 226-foot converted yacht was a single screw ship capable of making thirteen knots; it was armed with four 3-inch guns and depth charges. *Venetia* put into the shipyard at Gibraltar for refitting on 16 August 1918 and sailed on 14 September, escorting an eleven-ship convoy to Genoa. *Venetia* returned with a convoy of nineteen ships. During the next six weeks, the ship continued to sail from Gibraltar, escorting four more convoys to and from the ports of Genoa and Bizerte, Tunisia. The converted yacht was anchored at Funchal, Madeira Islands, west of Africa, when the armistice was signed. *Venetia* returned to Gibraltar before it sailed for the United States with a squadron of submarine chasers. Getting under way from "The Rock" on 21 December 1918, *Venetia* towed submarine chasers SC-223 and SC-330. The ship left the squadron at St. Thomas, Virgin Islands, and proceeded independently to Guatánamo Bay, Cuba. After departing Cuba, *Venetia* passed through the Panama Canal on 3 February 1919, and arrived at San Francisco three weeks later, where Howell was detached. *Venetia* was moved to the Mare Island Navy Yard on 27 February 1919 and decommissioned.[6]

Cythera was another large converted yacht that was based at Gibraltar and assigned to escort duty. Capt. Raymond L. Jack, USCG, reported aboard the 1,000-ton, 215-foot ship on 16 August 1918; he relieved Lt. Cdr. George E. Lake, USN, as commanding officer the next day. Four days later, *Cythera* sailed from Gibraltar, escorting a convoy of merchant ships, on the four-day passage to Bizerte. *Cythera* was armed with three 3-inch guns and depth charges, and was manned by a crew of 10 officers and 103 enlisted men. First Lt. (Eng.) Milton R. Daniels, USCG, first served aboard *Cythera* as executive officer and then as chief engineer. Daniels had deployed to Gibraltar with the cruising cutter *Seneca* in fall 1917 as a sec-

The 215-foot steam yacht *Cythera* was one of several large civilian vessels obtained by the U.S. Navy and armed for escort duty overseas. *Cythera* was attached to Squadron Two, Patrol Force at Gibraltar and escorted convoys to and from ports in the Mediterranean Sea. The ship's commanding officer and executive officer were coast guardsmen. *Milton R. Daniels Jr.*

ond lieutenant. He told his son Milton that he enjoyed serving aboard *Seneca* very much, saying, "She was a good ship." Daniels was initially reassigned from *Seneca* to the navy's twenty-seven-year-old gunboat *Machias*. It was the same class as *Castine* and carried the same armament. The ships were originally built as schooner-rigged gunboats at Bath Iron Works in Maine in the early 1890s. For a brief period Daniels served as an engineer aboard the 204-foot *Machias* before the ship was ordered back to the United States for refitting on 29 August 1918. Daniels told his son the ship had sunk at one time and was in very bad condition. He said, "She had terrible boilers. They were so badly deteriorated that it was impossible to maintain a full head of steam. It was no fun being on that ship."[7]

Cythera convoyed ships between Gibraltar and Genoa until 19 September 1918 when it was sent through the strait into the Atlantic Ocean to meet and escort a U.S. transport en route to the Mediterranean Sea. *Cythera* then resumed convoy work between Gibraltar and Bizerte. Sailing from Bizerte with a convoy on 1 October, the first two days of the voyage were uneventful. On the third night, however, the convoy was attacked twice by a German submarine. The first attack occurred at 8:08 PM when the merchant ship *St. Luc* was torpedoed. *Cythera* was the closest escort to the ship when the torpedo struck and exploded. Within thirty seconds *Cythera*'s rudder was over and the ship was headed for the point where the torpedo had been fired. The ship passed over the spot and dropped a depth charge that was set to go off at a depth of ninety feet. *Cythera*'s commanding officer turned and made two more attacks on the position in quick succession. The order to drop a fourth depth charge was not heard on the fantail, however, because of the high winds. All the depth charges exploded, but the results of the detonations were unknown. During the attacks, Jack had to maneuver *Cythera* to avoid the other escorts that came to rescue the crew of the rapidly sinking ship. The ships were able to recover only a few survivors from *St. Luc;* the others perished in the dark waters. Less than an hour later, at 9:00 PM, the U-boat struck again. *Cythera* was two hundred yards astern of the SS *Ariel*, standing toward its starboard quarter, when the torpedo hit *Ariel*'s starboard bow and exploded. *Cythera*, already on high alert, immediately went to the attack. In less than two minutes, two depth charges were dropped. Unfortunately, neither of the charges detonated. *Cythera* circled the submarine's suspected position and dropped four more depth charges; these functioned properly. The ship continued to drop depth charges at intervals to keep the submarine submerged while ship's boats picked up survivors. *Cythera*'s boats successfully rescued *Ariel*'s entire crew of thirty-five, including the convoy commodore, Capt. John Dewberry, Royal Navy Reserve. Daniels told his son about the incident: "Old John Dewberry was still wearing his binoculars when they fished him out of the water. When he came up the side of the ship, Old John said to me, 'Ah! You see Number One, I've come over to pay you a visit.'" The convoy reached Gibraltar on 5 October without further incident.[8]

Cythera departed Gibraltar with its last convoy, en route to Genoa on 5 November 1918. The ship arrived at Genoa on 10 November, and was there when hostilities ended the next day. Daniels had good memories of his Mediterranean duty. He recalled going to the opera in Genoa while *Cythera* was in port. He said the Italian audience was very vocal in their dislike of the performances of certain actors. The ship returned to Gibraltar on 15 November, and made one more round trip to Algiers, Algeria, before having the camouflage on its hull painted over and its mine releasing gear and depth charge racks removed. *Cythera* sailed for the United States with a squadron of submarine chasers on 21 December, and arrived at the Brooklyn Navy Yard on 5 February 1919. Two weeks later, Jack was detached from the ship with orders to report to coast guard cutter *Tuscarora*.[9]

Capt. John G. Berry, USCG, was in command of the converted yacht *Eagle*, patrolling along the southern coast of the United States, when he received orders overseas. Dated 17 April 1918, the orders directed him to proceed to Gibraltar and take command of the USS *Surveyor*. When Berry arrived at Base 9, his orders had been changed and he was told to take command of *Cythera*. Before he could carry out those orders, they were again changed. He was subsequently directed to take command of the 181-foot converted yacht *Lydonia*. He reported aboard the ship at Gibraltar on 13 June, and relieved Lt. Cdr. R. P. McCullough, USN, as commanding officer the same day. Under Berry's command, the 497-ton ship, armed with four 3-inch guns and depth charges, escorted convoys between Bizerte and Gibraltar. *Lydonia* was the senior escort ship for three of Berry's eight convoys. Berry was reassigned to command the coast guard cutter *Yamacraw*, based at Gibraltar, on 11 August. He was relieved as commanding officer of *Lydonia* by Capt. Philip F. Roach, USCG. After a ten-day overhaul period, *Lydonia* resumed convoy escort duties. The ship escorted four convoys between Gibraltar and Genoa, and five between Gibraltar and Bizerte before the war ended. The ship was en route to Bizerte when the armistice was signed. *Lydonia* returned to Gibraltar and sailed for the United States with a squadron of submarine chasers on 21 December. Roach was detached from the ship at Norfolk on 6 February 1919, and ordered to Coast Guard Headquarters.[10]

At seventeen knots, USS *Druid* was one of the faster converted yachts used for escorting convoys. When Capt. LeRoy Reinburg received orders to the 217-foot *Druid*, he was serving aboard coast guard cutter *Ossipee*, escorting ships between Britain and Gibraltar. He took command of *Druid* and its crew of 7 officers and 106 enlisted men on 28 July 1918. Under Reinburg's command, the ship, which was armed with depth charges and two 3-inch guns, continued to escort convoys between Gibraltar and the Mediterranean ports of Genoa, Marseilles, and Bizerte. On 30 October *Druid* was assigned as flagship for what was known as the

Gibraltar barrage. The barrage was a squadron of vessels assigned to the Strait of Gibraltar for the purpose of intercepting and destroying German submarines attempting to escape from the Mediterranean Sea after the surrender of Austria and Turkey. *Druid* was under way with the barrage from 31 October to 10 November, and had frequent contacts with the enemy—always at night. On the night of 8 November, three enemy submarines were sighted on the surface, attempting to transit the strait to the Atlantic Ocean. In rough seas and heavy rain, *Druid* and other ships of the barrage attacked the submarines. The HMBS *Privet* reported firing a 4-inch round through the conning tower of one of the submarines. During the engagement, a heavy bump was felt under the stern of *Druid*. Reinburg suspected that it was one of the U-boats and dropped several depth charges over the position. He never knew if the depth charges damaged any of the submarines. On the morning of 9 November, the British battleship *Britannia* was standing through the strait into the Mediterranean Sea when it was torpedoed by a German submarine. *Druid* stood by the sinking ship while destroyers from Base 9 removed the crew and the bodies of the dead before the battleship sunk. *Druid* returned to Gibraltar when the armistice was signed.[11]

After the war ended, *Druid* made several trips from Gibraltar to Tangier, Morocco. On one occasion, Reinburg furnished an armed guard to protect U.S. diplomatic representatives at the port. On 16 December 1918 *Druid* departed Gibraltar in company with *Wheeling, Arcturus, Surveyor, Wenonah*, and the cruising cutter *Yamacraw*. The ships recoaled at Ponta Delgada in the Azores and departed for Bermuda. The squadron ran into a hurricane on Christmas Eve and the ships had to heave to for two days, riding out the storm. During the worst of the weather, the executive officer of the 163-foot motor patrol boat USS *Wenonah* was swept overboard by the raging seas and lost. The ships finally reached Bermuda on 28 December. *Druid* departed for the United States with *Arcturus* and *Wenonah* on New Year's Eve; Reinburg was the senior of the three commanding officers. After an uneventful voyage in good weather, the three ships reached New London, Connecticut. At the end of January 1919, Reinburg was detached from *Druid* and given command of the reserve squadron at New London. The squadron consisted of twenty-two converted yachts and six submarine chasers.[12]

First Lt. Ralph W. Dempwolf received orders to Europe in August 1918. When he reported to the Third Naval District at New York for transport to the war zone, he was directed to take passage on the Portuguese transport *Tras Os Montes*. The ship was loaded with army personnel—3,000 troops and 150 officers—under the command of Brig. Gen. S. M. Foote, USA. After reporting aboard, Dempwolf quickly realized the ship was poorly manned by an inexperienced Portuguese crew. He told Foote of his apprehensions and offered to assist in any way he could. After discussing the situation with the general, Dempwolf said, "We personally informed the authorities of the Army and Navy at New York of the chaotic conditions on board the transport." Because of the need to get the troops to Europe as soon as possible, Dempwolf said, "Admiral Usher (USN) advised us to use every endeavor to straighten matters out and get the vessel to the other side with the troops." He told Dempwolf to assume command of the ship at any time that Foote deemed it necessary. *Tras Os Montes* sailed from Brooklyn with a convoy on 25 August, bound for London. From the very beginning of the voyage, the Portuguese ship was unable to keep up with the convoy. *Tras Os Montes* continually lagged five to ten miles astern of the other ships, presenting an easy target for a German submarine.[13]

Realizing that the U-boat threat would become worse when the convoy approached European waters, Dempwolf took action. He said, "I managed, with the assistance of General Foote, to find some twenty-four locomotive firemen among the troops. These men were detailed, at my suggestion, to the fireroom for duty. Coal heavers from among the troops were also detailed." Dempwolf also learned that of the eleven U.S. naval officers aboard the ship, three naval reserve officers were engineers. "I took it upon myself to detail these officers to the engineroom to assist the Portuguese officers," Dempwolf said. "And, through this means, I obtained first hand information of the conditions in the engine department of the vessel." Conditions began to improve and the ship was able to keep pace with the convoy. Dempwolf assigned the naval officers junior to him to regular bridge watches. When the convoy was eighty miles south of Queenstown, Ireland, the White Star liner *Persic*, which was steaming three hundred yards abeam of *Tras Os Montes*, was torpedoed without warning. *Persic*'s master successfully coaxed the crippled ship to Lands End, England, where he beached it without loss of life. Dempwolf reported, "While we were steaming away from the scene of the attack at full speed, I saw the submarine come to the surface for a few seconds and it appeared that she had been disabled by depth charges from the British destroyers."[14]

The convoy separated at the English Channel and *Tras Os Montes* proceeded to London, where the troops disembarked on 10 September. Foote informed Vice Adm. W. S. Sims, commander of U.S. naval forces operating in European waters, of Dempwolf's performance aboard the troopship. He said that the Portuguese crew was inexperienced in handling a ship the size of *Tras Os Montes* and that Dempwolf's "services were of great value in aiding in the navigation of the ship and handling of the crew." Sims wrote a letter to Dempwolf: "The Force Commander is pleased to note the commendatory manner in which on a recent voyage of the steamship *Tras Os Montes* you lent your services and were of considerable value to Brigadier General S. M. Foote, USA, in acting in the capacity of liaison officer between the commander of the troops and the master of the vessel."[15]

The 423-foot, 3,750-ton cruiser *Birmingham* reported to Gibraltar for duty in August 1917 as the flagship of Rear Adm. A. P. Niblack, commander of U.S. forces at Gibraltar. Niblack later shifted his flag to the station and repair ship USS *Buffalo* when it arrived at Gibraltar in summer 1918. Capt. (Eng.) California C. McMillan, USCG, was assigned to *Birmingham* on 28 August 1918 and designated the ship's chief engineer. The cruiser was assigned to convoy duty, escorting ships between Gibraltar, the British Isles, and France. Dempwolf reported aboard the heavily armed *Birmingham* in September 1918 and was assigned as the cruiser's senior deck watch officer. He served in that capacity until he was transferred to the 990-ton gunboat USS *Wheeling* as an observer. McMillan remained aboard *Birmingham* and returned to the United States with the ship in January 1919. He continued as head of the engineering department until he was transferred on 27 February. Temporary Capt. (Eng.) Charles H. Johnson, USCG, reported aboard *Birmingham* after the armistice was signed and served in the engineering department until 5 June when he was detached and reassigned to Coast Guard Headquarters.[16]

Dempwolf's duty aboard *Wheeling* was in preparation for taking command of USS *Surveyor*, a former U.S. Coast and Geodetic Survey vessel.

By the time he took command of the 186-foot, 1,143-ton ship on 7 November 1918, Dempwolf had been promoted to temporary captain. The ship, manned by a complement of 10 officers and 75 enlisted men, was armed with two 3-inch deck guns and depth charges. On 10 November Dempwolf received orders to sail with a convoy to Genoa. When the armistice was signed the next day, the orders were canceled. On 16 December *Surveyor* sailed with a squadron of six ships returning to the United States. After leaving the Azores, the squadron ran into heavy weather en route to Bermuda. *Surveyor,* convoying the USS *Arcturus,* arrived at Bermuda on 28 December. *Surveyor* left *Arcturus* and sailed for the United States the same day, arriving at Norfolk on New Year's Eve.[17]

FRENCH WATERS

After war was declared in 1917, the U.S. Navy asked the U.S. Coast Guard to provide officers to man seven large yachts that had been acquired for duty in the European war zone. After underway evaluations, only two of the yachts were found to be suitable for deploying overseas. The larger of the two yachts, the 192-foot *Galatea,* was brought from the Great Lakes to Boston to be repaired and outfitted for deployment. The U.S. Coast Guard assigned five officers to the ship, with 1st Lt. Harold D. Hinckley, USCG, in command. *Galatea,* armed with three 3-inch guns and depth charges, was manned by a crew of five officers and fifty-two navy enlisted men. The ship, capable of making fourteen knots, was placed in commission at Boston on 16 November 1917. The converted yacht sailed from Boston to Philadelphia, where additional repairs were made at the navy yard. When outfitting for overseas duty was completed, the yacht departed for Bermuda on 15 December en route to Brest, France. *Galatea* sailed with Patrol Detachment Three, a squadron of ships consisting of converted yachts, tugs, and submarine chasers.[18]

Hinckley was placed in charge of the "Galatea" division of the detachment. His division consisted of *Galatea,* tugs *Concord* and *Gypsum Queen,* and French submarine chasers 170, 314, and 318. The detachment arrived at Bermuda on 20 December, where more ships joined the squadron. Patrol Detachment Three sailed for the Azores on 5 January

1918, and, after seventeen days of bad winter weather, arrived at Ponta Delgada. The squadron commodore, Capt. David F. Boyd, USN, sent a letter to the coast guard commandant praising Hinckley's performance during the voyage. He said, "Captain Hinckley in the *Galatea* commanded one division with ability, entire steadfastness and good judgment; and in all operations I could place implicit confidence in him. The latter does not relate solely to the routine or ordinary sea events to which any capable officer can measure up; but rather to those anticipated and experienced with incompetent and frightened tug officers, green French crews who were unable to keep the machinery of the chasers going, other boats and divisions in hard luck—and this in a North Atlantic winter gale, lasting throughout the trip."[19]

As a result of the pounding *Galatea* took during the voyage to the Azores, the ship was determined to be unseaworthy and not permitted to proceed any further. Hinckley was detached and ordered to the troop transport *Hancock*. Upon his departure, 2d Lt. Gordon T. Finlay, USCG, assumed command. *Galatea* was assigned to Base 13 at the Azores and performed duties in the waters around the islands. Frustrated in their attempt to reach the war zone, the remaining coast guard officers on *Galatea* made their feelings known to Coast Guard Headquarters. On 28 June 1918, Capt. Charles E. Johnston, USCG, wrote from headquarters to the U.S. Navy's Bureau of Navigation, saying, "There are still four good Coast Guard officers on the *Galatea*. . . . They feel they have been lost in the shuffle." On 1 August all the coast guard officers were detached and the ship was put out of commission.[20]

Of the yachts the navy asked the coast guard to provide officers for, *Rambler* was the only one to successfully reach European waters. First Lt. Thomas M. Molloy, USCG, reported aboard *Rambler* at the port of New York, where the ship was being outfitted for overseas duty. He took command of the 177-foot, 288-ton ship ten days later, on 22 September 1917. The ship's other four coast guard officers reported aboard during the last week of September 1917. With repairs completed, *Rambler* was commissioned on 18 October, and sailed for Newport, Rhode Island, twelve days later, convoying two French submarine chasers. *Rambler* was assigned to Squadron Five of the Patrol Forces and sailed for Bermuda on 4 November. The squadron departed Bermuda two weeks later and, after enduring winter weather and heavy seas, arrived at the Azores on 8 December. *Rambler*, powered by oil-fired boilers, had to remain in the Azores when the squadron sailed two days later because there was no fuel oil available. A supply of oil reached the islands in January 1918, and *Rambler* finally sailed from the Azores with Squadron Three of the Patrol Forces on 9 February 1918. After a port call at Leixoss, Portugal, *Rambler* arrived at Brest on 21 February. The ship was assigned to duty with the Brittany patrol, under the command of the French admiral headquartered at Brest. In the following months, *Rambler* escorted convoys along the French coast between the ports of Brest, Quiberon, and Pallice. The ship also made monthly antisubmarine patrols between Ushant and Raz de Sein.[21]

While *Rambler* was escorting a convoy, a navy dirigible signaled the ship. It indicated that a German submarine had just submerged and pointed out an oil slick where the U-boat had disappeared. Molloy immediately attacked, dropping depth charges around the spot where the submarine had gone under. The results of the attack were unknown. On another occasion, one of the escorts with *Rambler* sighted and attacked a submarine. The U-boat was so severely damaged by depth charges that its captain had to go into a Spanish port; the German submarine was interned there until the end of the war. In August 1918, Molloy was assigned to command a small squadron of navy vessels, with *Rambler* as his flagship. *Rambler* was twice commended while under Molloy's command. The first commendation was for making all repairs and keeping the ship running without the assistance of the repair ship. Molloy attributed this to the resourcefulness of his chief engineer, 2d Lt. (Eng.) Harvey F. Johnson, USCG. Johnson was later transferred to USS *Aphrodite*. The second commendation was for rescue work the ship's crew performed at Quiberon, France, on 24 April 1918, when the 3,819-ton ammunition ship SS *Florence H*, loaded with four thousand tons of smokeless powder, caught fire. The fire raged until the ship split open and sank in the harbor. Flaming masses came shooting out of the hull and projectiles whistled through the air as *Rambler* and other ships in the harbor went to the rescue of the ammunition ship's crew. Forty-five of *Florence H*'s crew were killed in the explosion. Molloy was detached from *Rambler* on 25 August, with orders to command USS *Nokomis*. His executive officer,

1st Lt. Earl G. Rose, USCG, took command of *Rambler*. On 16 September Rose and his crew rescued survivors from the British steamship *Philomel*, torpedoed by a German U-boat. *Rambler* continued to escort convoys until the war ended. After the armistice, Rose was detached from the ship on 15 November, and ordered to return to the United States for duty with the U.S. Navy's Bureau of Navigation.[22]

The 1,500-ton, 302-foot converted yacht USS *Aphrodite* was attached to a squadron of the patrol forces operating from Base 20 at Rochefort, France. Capt. Frederick C. Billard, USCG, was acting superintendent of the U.S. Coast Guard Academy and commanding officer of the training cutter *Onondaga* when he received orders for overseas duty. Upon Billard's arrival in London, he was directed to take command of *Aphrodite* and its crew of 11 officers and 121 enlisted men. First Lt. (Eng.) Harvey F. Johnson was the ship's executive officer when Billard took command on 13 September 1918. *Aphrodite* continued to escort merchant convoys along the coast of France and was later assigned as the flagship for an escort squadron operating out of the port of Bordeaux. *Aphrodite* was performing this duty when the armistice was signed on 11 November. After the war ended, the ship was ordered to sail north to visit German ports and show the flag. While passing through the North Sea, *Aphrodite* struck a German mine. The detonation damaged the ship, but Billard was still able to continue his voyage and carry out his mission. *Aphrodite* was the first American ship to pass under the guns of the great German fortifications at Heligoland and the first ship to navigate the Kiel Canal. After completing his assignment in German waters, Billard returned to the French coast where he performed various naval duties. During the winter, Billard became ill and was unable to continue in command of *Aphrodite*. On 3 March 1919 he was detached and ordered to report to the naval hospital at London. Regaining his health, Billard was ordered back to the United States on 5 May.[23]

USS *Emeline* was another converted yacht. A well constructed, seaworthy vessel of 407 tons and 196 feet in length, *Emeline* mounted two 3-inch 50-caliber deck guns and one Y-gun, with twenty-four 300-pound depth charges. On 29 July 1918 Vice Adm. Henry B. Wilson, USN, commander of the U.S. forces in France, issued orders directing 1st Lt. Leo C. Mueller, USCG, to relieve Lt. W. D. Chandler Jr., USN, as commanding officer of *Emeline*. Mueller took command of the ship—manned by a crew of ten officers and seventy-five enlisted men—at Brest on 4 August. *Emeline* was attached to a group of patrol force escorts that consisted of one destroyer and three converted yachts. The group escorted convoys of freight ships between Brest and La Pallice. While Mueller was in command, *Emeline* escorted approximately one thousand ships in twenty-six convoys. In addition to convoy work, *Emeline* also patrolled for submarines in the water of Iroise, a bay between the headlands at the entrance to Brest. Ships patrolling the Iroise frequently engaged German submarines. *Emeline* also served as a station ship off the entrance to Brest harbor, meeting inbound troop ships and assisting them in making landfall. *Emeline* guided troop ships into the harbor so they did not have to slow down or stop to fix their position in the hazy weather along the French coast. The transports that *Emeline* assisted carried more than one hundred thousand troops. On the morning of 8 November 1918 fourteen troop transports arrived. *Emeline* assisted them in entering port and informed them of their anchorage assignments. Cdr. Richard O. Crisp, working on a 1922 manuscript about the U.S. Coast Guard during World War I, said, "The picture made by these troop ships with the upper decks, masts, and even the smokestacks covered with cheering troops, was an inspiring scene."[24]

On several occasions, the convoy *Emeline* was escorting had to delay its departure until the ship channel could be swept of mines planted by German submarines during the night. Initially, the British and French favored sailing cargo ships at night, using the darkness to conceal and protect the ships from submarine attack. The Americans, however, believed the ships were better protected during daylight when patrolling aircraft from the chain of air stations along the French coast could fly cover and detect and attack U-boats as they lay in wait. When nighttime losses greatly exceeded the ships lost during daylight hours, the allies were convinced and the ships sailed during the day, putting into port at night when possible. *Emeline*'s experience while escorting a convoy in October 1918 was typical of escort duty. Not long after *Emeline* got under way with the convoy, an American dirigible passed overhead and radioed that it had just been fired on by a German submarine that had made no attempt to submerge while the aircraft was in range of its guns. Later that day, a steamship was torpedoed and sunk five miles ahead of *Emeline*. Additional lookouts were posted and the convoy's speed was increased. *Emeline*'s crew looked forward to an opportunity to engage a U-boat, but no contact was made. That evening, *Emeline* discovered an American seaplane with two aviators aboard, drifting twenty miles off the French coast. The ship towed the aircraft back to the air station at Croisic. Several mines were later sighted during the voyage and their locations were passed to French minesweepers. It was unsafe for convoy escorts to stop to destroy mines themselves because the mines indicated the presence of German submarines.[25]

After the war ended, *Emeline* sailed for the United States in December 1918 with a squadron of ships consisting of *Nokomis, Sultana, Vedette,* and *Corona.* Due to a machinery failure, *Emeline* had to leave the squadron and return to Brest for repairs. Repairs were quickly made and the ship got under way again. *Emeline* overtook the ships and rejoined the squadron when it was one hundred miles from the Azores. The ships took on fuel, water, and provisions at Ponta Delgada and sailed for Bermuda, arriving there on Christmas Eve. *Emeline*, in company with *Corona*, arrived at New London, Connecticut, on New Years Day. Mueller was detached from the ship on 1 February 1919 and assigned to the cruising cutter *Yamacraw*.[26]

The 239-foot, 1,100-ton converted steam yacht USS *May* was armed with one 4-inch gun, two 3-inch guns, and depth charges. The twenty-seven-year-old ship had a speed of thirteen knots and was manned by a crew of ten officers and sixty-seven enlisted men. Capt. James Pine, USCG, was ordered overseas on 6 August 1918 and took command of *May* five weeks later at the port of Bordeaux. Under Pine's command, the ship was assigned to escort inbound and outbound convoys of merchant ships through submarine-infested French coastal waters. Admiral Wilson's convoy doctrine established the priority for protecting ships as: (1) troop ships, full; (2) store ships, full; (3) troop ships, empty; and (4) store ships, empty. No troopship en route to France was ever successfully attacked by a submarine if it was escorted by American ships. Only five empty westbound ships were successfully attacked; three were sunk and two made it back to port. *May* continued escort work until the war ended. The ship remained in France until December 1918. *May* departed for the United States as an escort for a detachment of smaller vessels, and arrived

Under the command of Capt. James Pine, USCG, the 1,100-ton converted yacht *May* operated out of Brest, France, escorting ships through U-boat infested French coastal waters. The ship was manned by a 77-man crew and armed with one 4-inch gun, two 3-inch guns, and depth charges. *U.S. Naval Historical Center*

at New York City on New Years Day 1919. Pine was ordered to sail *May* to New London, where the ship joined the reserve squadron. When *May* was selected for duty in Santo Domingo, Dominican Republic, Pine was detached on 3 March 1919, and ordered to take command of *Corona*, another reserve squadron ship.[27]

First Lt. Joseph H. Crozier, USCG, was in command of the navy supply ship *Bella* when he received orders to command the escort *Nokomis* on 1 August 1918. He commanded the 243-foot, 1,265-ton *Nokomis* for two weeks before being reassigned to transport duty. Capt. Thomas M. Molloy was ordered from *Rambler* to take command of *Nokomis* on 25 August. Two tall masts and a single smokestack rose from the ship's deckhouse, which covered two thirds of the former yacht's flush weather deck. The stately vessel had flared bows, an overhanging counter stern, and was capable of making sixteen knots. It was armed with depth charges and four 3-inch guns—two forward and two aft. *Nokomis* was based at the port of Bordeaux, and was used to escort convoys to and from the open waters of the Atlantic Ocean through coastal waters where German U-boats lay in wait. Escorts designated convoys en route to France as "homeward bound" and convoys for the United States as "outward bound." *Nokomis* cruised as far as 450 miles from France to rendezvous with incoming convoys. Under Molloy's command, the ship continued to carry out escort work until the war ended. After the armistice, *Nokomis* sailed to Brest, where it joined a squadron preparing to depart for the United States. The ship served as flagship for Cdr. R. P. Craft, USN, who commanded the squadron. The ships sailed for the Azores on 5 December, where they took on fuel. The squadron arrived at Bermuda on Christmas Eve and sailed again on Christmas Day. *Nokomis* entered Chesapeake Bay on 29 December, and was made flagship for a squadron of ships under the command of Rear Adm. Thomas Washington, USN. Malloy continued in command of *Nokomis* until 16 April 1919, when he was reassigned to command the troop transport *H. R. Mallory*, engaged in bringing army forces back from Europe.[28]

USS *Noma* was another large converted yacht engaged in escorting inbound and outbound convoys though the coastal waters. Armed with depth charges and four 3-inch guns, *Noma* convoyed transport and cargo ships to and from France's Gironde River. Capt. Gordon T. Finlay, USCG, reported aboard the 262-foot, 1,250-ton *Noma* from the gunboat *Marietta* on 26 September 1918. He was the second most senior of the twelve officers assigned to the ship, and served as executive officer and navigator, before taking command on 27 October. *Noma* continued escort work until the end of the war. After the armistice, the ship was ordered to Brest to prepare for the return trip to the United States. *Noma* arrived there the day before Thanksgiving. While at Brest, Finlay received new orders, directing him to sail to Plymouth, England, and report to Rear Adm. W. L. Bristol, USN. At Plymouth, *Noma* was designated as the admiral's flagship, and dispatched on a special mission to Constantinople, Turkey, on 18 January 1919. After stops at Brest, Gibraltar, Malta, and Taranto in Italy, the ship arrived at the Turkish capital on 12 February. Next assigned to the U.S. naval forces in Turkey, *Noma* was used to transport members of the American Relief Commission in the Near East, including Mr. Howard Heinz of the U.S. Grain Corporation, to countries in Eastern Europe. *Noma* called at the ports of Constanta, Rumania, 9–14 March; Varna, Bulgaria, 3–6 April; and Batumi, Russia, 21 April–1 May. When *Noma* departed Varna, it carried $3.25 million in gold that was received as security for flour shipments to the Bulgarian government. *Noma* returned to Constantinople and Finlay kept the gold aboard until 21 May, when he transferred it to another navy ship, before sailing for the United States. *Noma* arrived at New York on 3 July 1919, and was placed out of commission twelve days later. Finlay was reassigned to the Third Naval District.[29]

The twenty-one-year-old *Wanderer* was another converted steam yacht. The 197-foot ship, capable of making twelve knots, was manned by seven officers and forty-nine enlisted men. Like other escorts, it carried depth charges and mounted two 3-inch guns. Second Lt. John J. Hutson, USCG, was transferred from the escort *Rambler* and reported aboard *Wanderer* on 30 June 1918. He relieved Lt. Cdr. P. L. Wilson, USN, as commanding officer a week later. The ship, based at Brest, escorted convoys, consisting of five to thirty merchant ships, between the ports of Brest and La Pallice. The voyage usually took two days, and included a stop at Quiberon. While under Hutson's command *Wanderer* escorted more than four hundred ships of all nationalities. It also patrolled the waters at the entrance to Brest, between Raz de Sein and Ar-Men and around the Pierres Noires Lighthouses, in search of submarines. The ship carried out escort and patrol duties until the war ended. After the armistice, *Wanderer* sailed with a squadron of vessels, returning to the United States. The squadron departed the first week of December 1918 and arrived at New London, Connecticut, on New Years Eve. Hutson, now a captain, remained in command of *Wanderer* until 13 February 1919, when he was detached and ordered to the cruising cutter *Seminole*. Second Lt. W. C. Maglathlin, USCG, was chief engineer of *Utowana*, another escort based at Brest. The 169-foot *Utowana*, originally built as a yacht in 1891, was converted to a fishing trawler just before the United States entered the war. *Utowana* began war service in France in February 1918, performing escort and patrol duties. Maglathlin was later reassigned to *Nokomis*, where he served as chief engineer until after the war ended.[30]

MINE PLANTERS AND SUPPORT SHIPS

In the spring of 1918, the United States assisted the allies in creating the Northern Mine Barrage, a gigantic minefield stretching across the North

Sea from Scotland to Norway. The minefield was laid to discourage and prevent German submarines from reaching the Atlantic Ocean. Secretary of the Navy Josephus Daniels credited the hidden menace of the mines with demoralizing German U-boat crews. It was a silent killer, hidden and dangerous, faced by every German submarine putting out to sea or returning to port. The U-boats had no means for detecting or avoiding the mines. Seventeen U-boats were damaged by mines and had to return to their base. Possibly six more were sunk. Daniels said, "This was a terror the undersea boatmen were unwilling to face. The revolt of the U-boat crews spread to other branches of the naval service and the entire German navy began to disintegrate." A total of 70,263 mines were planted, from the surface down to a depth of 240 feet, at a cost of $80 million. The minefield was 250 miles long and between 15 and 35 miles wide. Just before the United States entered the war, President Wilson had discussed how to deal with the U-boat menace with Daniels. He asked Daniels, "Why don't the British shut up the hornets in their nests?" The mine barrage did just that.[31]

Eight merchant ships, including four Morgan Steamship Company liners, were obtained by the U.S. Navy and converted into mine planters. The ships were assigned to Squadron One, Mine Forces, Atlantic Fleet. Mine Squadron One consisted of nine mine planters and two tugs. The ships were outfitted as mine planters in the United States and deployed to bases in Scotland. Coast guard officers were assigned aboard five of the large mine planter ships. The steam liners *El Cid* and *El Siglo*, built at the turn of the century for Southern Pacific–Morgan Steamship Company, were acquired by the U.S. Navy from the Shipping Board on 23 November 1917. They were sent to the Morse Dry Dock and Repair Company at Brooklyn to be fitted out as minelayers. *El Cid*, renamed *Canonicus*, was 405 feet in length and displaced 6,300 tons. *El Siglo*, renamed *Canandaigua*, was smaller at 380 feet and 6,080 tons. After three months at the shipyard, the ships were commissioned on 2 March 1918. Third Lt. John Trebes Jr. reported aboard *Canonicus*, a week later, joining the crew of 19 officers and 349 enlisted men. With outfitting and training completed, *Canonicus* sailed from Newport, Rhode Island, on 12 May 1918 with Mine Squadron One. The ship arrived at the Firth of Inverness two weeks later. Capt. Philip W. Lauriat was assigned to *Canandaigua* on

The minelayer USS *Canandaigua* and a U.S. Navy destroyer are under way in the rough waters of the North Sea. Coast guard officers served on five mine force ships engaged in planting the Northern Mine Barrage, an antisubmarine minefield. The barrage contained more than seventy thousand mines and stretched from Scotland to Norway. *Mariners' Museum, Newport News, Virginia*

28 September and served as executive officer. The ships operated out of Inverness and Invergordon, Scotland, planting mines for the Northern Mine Barrage. After the armistice, *Canonicus* was ordered back to the United States. Before the ship departed, Trebes was transferred to *Roanoke*, another mine planter. *Roanoke*, formerly named *El Dia*, was a sister ship of *Canandaigua*. All the former Morgan liners were armed with one 5-inch and two 3-inch guns. *Roanoke* returned to the United States in early 1919 and went to the navy yard at Portsmouth, New Hampshire, to be refitted as a troop transport. When work was completed, *Roanoke* reported to the cruiser and transport forces on 10 March. Trebes made four voyages between the east coast of the United States and France, returning 5,500 U.S. troops. He was transferred to another transport on 30 August 1919, fifteen days before *Roanoke* was decommissioned.[32]

The 5,690-ton, 420-foot repair ship *Black Hawk* departed Boston in June 1918. Arriving at Base 18 at Inverness, Scotland, the ship was designated flagship for Rear Adm. Joseph Strauss, USN, commander of the Atlantic Fleet's mine forces. Not including the admiral's staff, the ship had a complement of 27 officers and 444 enlisted men, and was armed with four 5-inch guns and one 3-inch gun. Capt. (Eng.) John B. Turner, USCG, was the ship's chief engineer. When the war ended, *Black Hawk* shifted its base to Kirkwall in the Orkney Islands and supported the North Sea sweep, an operation to remove the mines. The ship returned to New York in November 1919. *San Francisco* was originally built as a protected cruiser in 1889. In June 1908, the 4,391-ton, 325-foot ship was refitted as a mine vessel. The bridge was enlarged, masts were heightened, and original batteries and torpedo tubes were removed. Minelaying tracks were installed on the second deck with mine ports in the stern. The ship was overhauled extensively in March 1918. It was designated a minelayer and assigned as flagship for Mine Squadron One. *San Francisco* was manned by 21 officers and 363 enlisted men. The ship departed Newport, Rhode Island, on 12 May 1918, and reached Scotland two weeks later. *San Francisco* joined in planting the Northern Mine Barrage. Capt. Edward D. Jones, USCG, served as navigator aboard *San Francisco* until 29 August 1919.[33]

Coast guard officers were also assigned to navy ships supporting operations in the war zone. The English-built cargo ship *Bella* was purchased by the U.S. Navy on 22 February 1918. The 2,500-ton, 235-foot ship was commissioned at the U.S. naval air station at Paulliac, France, on 15 March 1918, with 2d Lt. Joseph H. Crozier, USCG, in command. Crozier was transferred from the cruising cutter *Yamacraw* to take command of the ship. Before entering the Revenue-Cutter Service, Crozier had served with the U.S. Navy as a volunteer officer on the USS *Lebanon* during the Spanish-American War. *Bella*, with a complement of seven officers and forty-four enlisted men, was used to transport aviation supplies and equipment. In recognition of his service aboard *Bella*, Crozier was given command of the large escort ship *Nokomis* on 1 August 1918.[34]

The 6,530-ton, 406-foot auxiliary cruiser *Buffalo* was refitted as a destroyer tender at the Philadelphia Navy Yard. Third Lt. Loyd V. Kielhorn, USCG, from the cruising cutter *Tallapoosa*, was ordered to *Buffalo* on 11 April 1918, where he was assigned as navigator. The ship's conversion was completed in June 1918 and *Buffalo* was outfitted for duty in European waters. The ship, manned by a crew of 24 officers and 326 enlisted men, arrived at Gibraltar and was assigned as station and repair ship for escorts and submarine chasers. On 18 December 1918, Kielhorn

The U.S. Navy purchased the fifteen-year-old British cargo ship *Swan Hunter* in February 1918. The ship was commissioned USS *Bella* in France on 15 March 1918 with 2d Lt. Joseph H. Crozier, USCG, in command. The 2,500-ton ship delivered supplies and equipment to naval air stations in Europe.
Mariners' Museum, Newport News, Virginia

was detached from *Buffalo* and reassigned to the U.S. Coast Guard Academy. Capt. Gordon T. Finlay was transferred from the *Galatea*, at Base 13 in the Azores, in August 1918. He was assigned to the 6,114-ton, 392-foot destroyer tender USS *Dixie* at Queenstown, Ireland. He joined the ship's complement of 45 officers and 1,217 enlisted men and served as a deck watch officer until he was transferred to the gunboat *Marietta*. From *Marietta*, he was assigned to the escort *Noma*, where he was executive officer and then commanding officer.[35]

CHAPTER 6

AVIATION

Aviation came to the Coast Guard through the passage of the Naval
Appropriation Act, approved August 29, 1916, authorizing the Coast
Guard to establish, equip and maintain air stations, not to exceed ten
in number, on the Atlantic and Pacific coasts, the Gulf of Mexico and
the Great Lakes. Before action could be taken to acquire land for the
first air station, however, the United States entered the War.

—REAR ADM. RUSSELL R. WAESCHE, COMMANDANT, U.S. COAST GUARD

U-BOAT ATTACK

A fog bank settled over calm waters four miles east of Cape Cod's south-
eastern elbow on 21 July 1918. Just inshore from the fog, the 452-ton
tug *Perth Amboy* worked its way south with four barges. The tug's crew
could see seaside cottages beyond the beach at Orleans, Massachusetts,
off to starboard. *Perth Amboy* was en route to New York City from
Gloucester, Massachusetts, with Lehigh Valley Railroad coal barges—
including *Langsford* No. 703, No. 740, and No. 766—in tow. Only one
of the barges was loaded; it carried a cargo of stone. Some of the barge
crews had their families aboard with them. A total of forty-one people

were on the tug and tows—including three women and five children. At 10:30 AM vacationers who had flocked to the seashore that Sunday morning, were shocked to see the ominous shape of a large German cruiser submarine emerge from the fog.[1]

Without warning, Korvettenkapitän Richard Feldt opened fire with two 5.9-inch deck guns. *Perth Amboy*'s captain, J. H. Tapley, was in his cabin when the shooting began. He rushed out on deck and saw U-156 coming out of the fog a few hundred yards away. John Botovich manned the tug's steering wheel. He said, "I was standing in the pilot house of the tug when the submarine opened fire. So far as I know, no one on the tug saw her until she hurled the first shell. A shell came right into the pilot house and passed through it. It made a big crash; the next thing I know I was being picked up on the deck." Botovich's right arm was nearly severed by a piece of shrapnel. John Vitz, who was also in the pilothouse, had his right hand blown off. Maj. Clifford L. Harris, commander of the Cape Cod battalion of the state guard, witnessed the attack from onshore. He said, "Four or five shots were fired into the pilot house. The tug began to burn after the first or second shot. I could see the flames coming up out of the forward hatch. In all, about twenty shots were fired at the tug, but it did not sink."[2]

The lookout in the tower of Coast Guard Station No. 40 at East Orleans saw the attack and immediately notified the station keeper, Warrant Officer Robert F. Pierce. Pierce alerted his boat crew to prepare to launch the surf boat and telephoned the naval air station at Chatham, Massachusetts, ten miles to the south. His terse message said, "Submarine sighted. Tug and three barges being fired on and one is sinking three miles off Coast Guard Station 40." The submarine, with its crew of eighty, was still firing on the vessels when Pierce and his men launched their boat and rowed out to help the people on the tug and barges.[3]

When the barge crews saw the 361-foot U-boat shelling the tug, they quickly put their boats in the water. Once the wooden tug was in flames, the submarine turned its deck guns, one forward and one aft of the conning tower, on the barges. A shell exploded on *Langsford*, the second barge in the tow, wounding Capt. Charles Ainslie in both arms. The German submarine closed on the barges while continuing to fire. Crews from the tug and barges struggled to row clear of the vessels; shrapnel and debris fell in the water around them. In his official report, Keeper Pierce said:

> When about two thirds of the way off to the sinking tug and four barges, we met the boat from the *Perth Amboy* with all her crew which had escaped. The crews of the barges had left and were pulling for Nauset Harbor in their life boats. They landed three miles from our station to the north. When the Coast Guard boat approached, Captain Tapley of the tug *Perth Amboy* told him, "Do not go any further. We have all our crew here and all have left the barges."

Pierce put his no. 1 surfman, W. D. Moore, into the lifeboat to treat the injured seamen. One man was lying in the stern of the boat with a shattered arm, unconscious from the loss of blood. Moore put a tourniquet on his arm and stopped the blood flowing from an arterial hemorrhage. Moore then treated the wound of a second man lying next to the first.[4]

Only two newly arrived HS-1L seaplanes were available at the naval air station when the coast guard called. The air station's commanding officer, Capt. (Eng.) Philip B. Eaton, USCG, had launched all other aircraft to search for one of the station's two Class B blimps, which was missing. When the air station received the telephone call, the two remaining planes were quickly readied for launching. The first HS-1L water taxied out, but could not take off because of spark plug problems. The second plane, manned by Ens. Eric Lingard, pilot; Ens. Shields, observer; and Petty Officer Howard, "mechanician," took off successfully. The aircraft carried a Mark IV 120-pound TNT bomb. Shields said, "When we set out, we did not really believe it was a submarine; we had so many false reports. Then we saw smoke across the horizon—soon the flame of guns. Then we saw the outlines of the burning boats, one on end, another sinking and a big thing not 500 yards off, blazing away complacently as if there was no air station within a thousand miles."[5]

When the HS-1L, a biwing seaplane powered by a Liberty "pusher" engine, got closer, the crew got a good look at the U-boat. The submarine did not see them coming. Shields said, "The submarine was an immense one; it looked like a destroyer or a small cruiser, three hundred feet long at least and it carried two six inch guns and one or two high angle guns, as we later discovered. They did not appear to see us until we were almost upon them. As we nosed down toward them, there was a great deal of commotion and hustling around on deck. The gun nearest the conning tower disappeared in the deck and the submarine was in motion, slowly forward. It appeared they did not have time to put all the guns away before they started to submerge."

With adrenaline pumping through their bodies, the air crew lined up the "flying boat" for the attack. Shields said,

> We passed over the U-boat amidships, some 800 feet above it. I had the sights dead on the deck and pulled the release; it failed to work. I waved a signal to fly back at a lower altitude and as the plane came down on the submarine again, proceeding so as to pass over it from stern to bow. [Petty Officer] Howard tested the release; it was stuck. A moment more and we would be yards out of range. Suddenly and without thinking . . . Howard sprung out of the cockpit and into the blast of the wind which sweeps the deck of a liberty in flight, leaped onto the side, six feet, and caught one arm about the interplane strut. Then, leaning head downward, he released the bomb under the wing with his fingers. It was all done so quickly, we did not know what he was about. The bomb, with its charge of TNT, dropped straight and splashed within a few feet of the U-boat. It did not explode.[6]

Shields helped Howard back into the cockpit while Lingard circled and climbed. The submarine submerged briefly and then, brazened by the failure of the bomb to explode, resurfaced and put an antiaircraft gun into action. Shields handed Lingard a note that read, "They are firing shrapnel." The plane continued to circle while keeping the submarine in sight. "Then," Lingard said, "We now saw the prettiest sight I ever hope to see. Right through the smoke of the wreck, over the life boats and all, there came the captain's plane, flying straight for the submarine, and flying low. We saw their [U-boat's] high-angle gun flashing too; but he [Eaton] came right ahead."[7]

The TNT bombs carried by the seaplanes were powerful enough to open seams if dropped within one hundred yards of a submarine. Naval doctrine called for the bombs to be dropped at an altitude of no less than one thousand feet, for the safety of the aircraft. Eaton, flying R-9 float plane no. 991, closed on the submarine at an altitude of four hundred feet. He said, "As I bore down upon the submarine, it fired. I zigzagged and dove as it fired again. They were getting underway and scrambling down the hatch when I flew over them and dropped the bomb. The bomb fell within thirty yards of the U-boat's port quarter. Had the bomb functioned the submarine would have been literally smashed. I circled about and tried to stay over the spot where the U-boat was, but it was too hazy and smoky. At this point of the coast, the water is 95 fathoms deep by chart. The submarine submerged far down, turned and escaped." Had more planes been available at the air station to attack the U-boat, some of the bombs may have detonated. When the other aircraft returned from their search for the dirigible, they were quickly refueled and took off to look for the submarine. The search continued until nightfall, but was unsuccessful. There was little hope in relocating the 3,200-ton U-boat, which could travel submerged at 19 knots for 120 miles. U-156's forays along the Atlantic coast of the United States lasted until August 1918, at which time the U-boat departed to return to Germany. The attacks would also be the raider's last. While attempting to penetrate the Northern Mine Barrage to reach home waters, U-156 struck a mine and sank with all hands.[8]

The next day, Secretary of the Navy Josephus Daniels requested a report from the commandant of the First Naval District, Rear Adm. Spencer S. Wood, as to why the bombs failed to explode when dropped. The air station had previously reported bombs failing to detonate when dropped during bombing practice. The Navy Department immediately initiated an inspection of its entire stock of naval airplane bombs to determine the reliability of detonation and the Ordnance Bureau began considering alterations to the bombs used in aerial operations to ensure the certainty of their detonation.[9]

THE BEGINNING

The U.S. Coast Guard's first interest in the use of aircraft to accomplish its missions began in summer 1915. Second Lt. (Eng.) Norman B. Hall and 3d Lt. Elmer F. Stone were assigned to coast guard cutter *Onondaga*. The cutter, under the command of Capt. Benjamin M. Chiswell, was headquartered at Hampton Roads, Virginia. One of the cutter's primary duties was searching for overdue fishing schooners. Winter storms wreaked havoc with the old and poorly maintained schooners operating along the Atlantic seaboard. After a storm, *Onondaga* would get under way to look for vessels dismasted by the high winds and then tow them into port. After observing flight operations at a nearby flying school, Hall and Stone recognized the potential benefits of searching for disabled vessels from the air. They convinced their commanding officer that rescues could be greatly expedited by using an aircraft to locate vessels needing assistance.[10]

The flying school, operated by the Curtis Aeroplane and Motor Company, was located at Boat Harbor Point in Newport News, Virginia, not far from the cutter's moorings. Thomas A. Baldwin, a pioneer balloonist and pilot, managed the school. It was used primarily for training Canadian military pilots for war service in Europe. When Hall and Stone went to Baldwin to discuss their idea of using an aircraft for overwater searches, he arranged for them to be flown on a number of experimental flights in a Curtis flying boat. Even though the seaplane lacked the capability for offshore navigation and had to remain in sight of land, its advantages for overwater searches were obvious. Chiswell and his two young officers saw the important potential aviation held for assisting the U.S. Coast Guard in accomplishing its missions; they were determined to convince Washington of the need for aircraft.[11]

Coast Guard Headquarters was receptive to Chiswell's enthusiastic appraisal of the value of aircraft. Capt. Charles A. McAllister, chief engineer of the U.S. Coast Guard, drafted a legislative proposal for the creation of a coast guard aviation section at headquarters. On 21 March 1916, Captain Commandant Ellsworth P. Bertholf approved orders for Stone to receive "instructions in relation to aviation" in the Norfolk area. Stone's orders read,

> Referring to orders of this date, assigning you to special duty at Norfolk, Va., you will be governed by the following: (1) You will investigate aviation matters having a bearing upon the Coast Guard, giving special attention to those phases of aviation that have a direct bearing upon assistance of vessels in distress and search for derelicts. (2) You will keep in touch with the commanding officer of the *Onondaga* and will confer and cooperate with him in such matters as involve the use of aircraft in conjunction with the usual

activities of the Coast Guard. (3) This office will have no objection to your taking a course of aviation, provided that it will not interfere with your duties as outlined above and that the Government shall be put to no expense thereby. (4) You will submit reports of your progress and results at the end of each quarter.

The same day that Stone's orders were issued, Bertholf sent a letter to Chiswell, suggesting that "whenever experiments are to be made by that officer [Stone] involving the cooperation of aircraft with Coast Guard cutters, you confer with him and arrange to have him act in conjunction with the *Onondaga*."[12]

Lt. (j.g.) R. G. Thomas, USN, of the hydrographic office in Norfolk became aware of Stone's and the U.S. Coast Guard's growing interest in aviation. He communicated this interest to the office of Secretary of the Navy Josephus Daniels. Daniels sent a reply to Thomas: "If the Captain Commandant of the Coast Guard Service will make a request on the Navy Department for an opportunity for the training of his officers, the Department will be very glad to add two Coast Guard officers to the class at Pensacola. A new class will be formed April 1st, and it would be advantageous if these requirements should be received in time for the officers to take up the course on that date." As a result of this correspondence, Coast Guard Headquarters canceled Stone's initial orders and requested navy flight training for him and for 2d Lt. (Eng.) Charles E. Sugden. The two officers were ordered to report to the navy aeronautical station at Pensacola, Florida, for the April 1916 class.

When *Onondaga* made a port call at Washington, D.C., in April 1916, Chiswell saw an opportunity to further U.S. Coast Guard interest in aviation. He invited Glenn H. Curtis, aviation pioneer and aircraft manufacturer, and Assistant Secretary of the Treasury Byron R. Newton, a known aviation enthusiast, aboard the cutter for lunch on Sunday, 16 April. During their meal, the three men discussed the possibility of the U.S. Coast Guard using "flying lifeboats." The concept involved flying a boat to the scene of a distress to rescue survivors. On scene, the boat's wings would be jettisoned and the craft would function as a motorized surfboat or lifeboat. Two days after the meeting, Chiswell wrote a letter to Constructor Frederick A. Hunnewell at Coast Guard Headquarters:

If practicable, please mail me as soon as convenient plans, specifications and blue prints of a type of motor surfboat which you regard as best adapted to . . . convert a surfboat into a flying boat with wings and a motor so arranged that they could be quickly eliminated when the boat lighted on the water and within a few minutes it would be, instead of a flying boat, an ordinary motor surfboat. If the lifeboat is better adapted, send lifeboat. He [Glen H. Curtis] promised to think about it and I am going to encourage him. If it is possible to perfect something of that kind I believe it would be the biggest find for the Coast Guard of the century and might be the means of saving hundreds of lives.[13]

As interest in aviation increased, Captain McAllister expanded the U.S. Coast Guard's legislative proposal. The new proposal called for the construction of ten coast guard air stations on the Atlantic and Pacific coasts, the Great Lakes, and the Gulf of Mexico. The proposal was made a part of the 1916 Naval Appropriations Act and was approved by Congress and signed by the president on 29 August 1916. In addition to the air stations, the act provided for a coast guard aviation school and an aviation corps of ten line officers, five engineer officers, and forty enlisted mechanics. To prepare for the coast guard use of aircraft, Second Lieutenant Hall was ordered from *Onondaga* to the Curtis Aeroplane and Motor Company's factory at Hammondsport, New York, on 28 October. Hall, who was trained as a naval architect, went to the factory to study aircraft design and construction. While air stations and an air corps were authorized by Congress, the funding necessary to implement the plan was not appropriated. When war was declared and the U.S. Coast Guard was transferred to the U.S. Navy, all plans for coast guard aviation were unfortunately put on hold.[14]

FLIGHT TRAINING

The U.S. Navy's aeronautical station at Pensacola opened in January 1914 as the navy's only aviation facility. By 1916, it was still a primitive training station, with an assortment of training aircraft—flying boats and seaplanes. When Stone and Sugden began their course of instruction, less than forty naval officers had completed flight training and the course of

The U.S. Coast Guard's original aviators were photographed at Naval Air Station Pensacola, two weeks before the United States declared war. Left to right: Master-at-Arms Charles T. Thrun, Oiler 1st Class J. F. Powers, Ship's Writer George Ott, Master-at-Arms C. Griffin, Surfman John Wicks, 3d Lt. Robert Donohue, 2d Lt. (Eng.) Charles E. Sugden, 2d Lt. Eugene Coffin, 1st Lt. Stanley V. Parker, 2d Lt. (Eng.) Philip B. Eaton, 3d Lt. Elmer F. Stone, No. 1 Surfman Ora Young, Coxswain W. R. Malew, Surfman J. Myers, Asst. Master-at-Arms J. Medusky, Signal Quartermaster R. F. Gillis, Surfman W. S. Anderson, and Signal Quartermaster L. M. Melka. *U.S. Coast Guard Historian*

instruction was still being developed. The training program at Pensacola was forced to stand down in June 1916 because of the high level of accidents experienced. The U.S. Navy was concerned about the quality—design and construction—of their training aircraft. After delivery of new N-9 pontoon planes late in 1916, training safety at the facility improved significantly. Students also began training in classes instead of individually or in small groups, and the curriculum was expanded. Up until that time, the ground school only taught the technical aspects of aviation. Courses in navigation and seamanship were not considered necessary because all the trainees were Naval Academy graduates already trained in those subjects. The training program for enlisted aircraft mechanics was also improved, and the course of instruction was formalized.[15]

An additional sixteen coast guardsmen were ordered to the navy aeronautical station at Pensacola in 1916—four officers and twelve enlisted men. These men comprised the U.S. Coast Guard's aviation group during World War I. The six coast guard officers assigned to Pensacola completed flight training and were designated naval aviators: 3d Lt. Elmer F. Stone, No. 38; 2d Lt. (Eng.) Charles E. Sugden, No. 43; 3d Lt. Robert Donohue, No. 54; 1st Lt. Stanley V. Parker, No. 57; 2d Lt. Eugene A. Coffin, No. 59; and 2d Lt. (Eng.) Philip B. Eaton, No. 60. The U.S. Coast Guard did not assign aviator designator numbers until after the war. The enlisted men assigned to Pensacola for training were Surfman W. F. Anderson, Signal Quartermaster R. F. Gillis, Master-at-Arms C. Griffin, Coxswain W. R. Malew, Asst. Master-at-Arms J. Medusky, Signal Quartermaster L. M. Melka, Surfman J. Myers, Ship's Writer George Ott, 1st Class Oiler J. F. Powers, Master-at-Arms Charles T. Thrun, Surfman John Wicks, and No. 1 Surfman Ora Young. Of the enlisted personnel, Thrun, Anderson, and Melka went on to become coast guard aviators after the war.[16]

Second Lieutenant Coffin, who requested assignment to Pensacola for flight training in April 1916, recalled his training experience in a letter, written some years later. He wrote, "I was one of the lucky few who went down there. I was ordered to report to the senior Coast Guard officer at Pensacola who was C. E. Sugden. I arrived there in November of 1916." Coffin took his first flight in an airplane with Lt. Cdr. Earl Spencer, USN, who was in charge of the flying school at Pensacola. Coffin said, "He [Spencer] was then the husband of Wallis Warfield, later to become Mrs. Simpson and then the Duchess of Windsor. She was there [Pensacola] with her husband and was a little slip of a thing, very pleasant. They had been married only a month or so." After the flight, Spencer gave Coffin's morale a boost by praising him in front of the other trainees, saying that he thought he was a natural born aviator. Coffin recalled,

During my first six months at Pensacola, we were not at war and things were done leisurely with no pressure at all on anyone. Spencer would come down in the morning and look at the sky and if there happened to be a cloudy sky, he would decide it was not a good day for flying and go back uptown. However, in 1917 when we entered the war, all this was changed. Spencer was replaced by an officer named R. W. Cabaniss who was a driver. Student aviators came in droves and were killed off at the rate of about one a week—they were too eager.[17]

Coffin crashed an airplane in April 1917 while he was practicing landings. He said, "While I was still under instruction, Lieutenant Stone and I spun into the bay from six hundred feet—the first tailspin they had ever seen. The plane was completely washed out and I had a broken nose and split upper lip." Of the navy aircraft used for training, he said, "Those Curtis training planes were really something! When there was no breeze to head into, it took anywhere from ten to twenty minutes to get them off the water. Full speed in the air was 70 MPH and it took all of a half hour to climb to 6,000 feet."

Stone was the first coast guard officer to complete flight training. He received his wings on 22 March 1917 and was designated a seaplane aviator on the U.S. Navy's roster. When Coffin completed his training in June 1917, he was ordered to remain at the Navy Aeronautical Station Pensacola; the name of the facility was not officially changed to Naval Air Station Pensacola until 18 December 1917. Coffin was in charge of a recruit battalion. He said recruits arrived at the station for training at the rate of one hundred a week.[18]

WARTIME AVIATION DUTY

The 504-foot armored cruiser *Huntington* (ARC-5) was mounted with two 18-inch guns, four 8-inch guns, and fourteen 6-inch guns. The day before war was declared, *Huntington* was detached from the reserve force and put into full commission at Mare Island, California. After launching catapults were installed on the ship's quarterdeck and the boat deck was equipped to accommodate four seaplanes, the cruiser departed for Pensacola. Seventeen days later it arrived at the air station. *Huntington* spent the next two months training for, and evaluating the feasibility of, operating airplanes and balloons from a ship under wartime conditions. Coast guard aviators Stone and Donahue were assigned to the testing and, before the cruiser set sail for Hampton Roads, they were transferred to *Huntington* as members of the aviation detachment. *Huntington* proceeded from Hampton Roads to New York, where it joined a convoy of six troop ships bound for France; the convoy departed on 8 September 1917.[19]

Several successful balloon observation flights were flown from the ship, but on 17 September a squall forced the tethered balloon into the water. When the balloonist became entangled in the rigging, Patrick McGunigal, a navy ship fitter, jumped into the sea to free the pilot from the overturned basket. The cruiser returned to Norfolk on 30 September and took on supplies before sailing to New York. *Huntington*'s commanding officer was not impressed with the potential for using aircraft from a warship and had the catapults and seaplanes removed from the ship. Before *Huntington* departed for Halifax, Nova Scotia, Donahue was detached on 11 October and assigned to Naval Air Station Montauk Point, on New York's Long Island. Stone, nicknamed "Archie," was transferred on 12 October to Naval Air Station Rockaway in New York. Stone was then assigned to the U.S. Navy's Bureau of Construction and Repair as a test pilot.[20]

After the war, Stone was selected as a pilot for the historic transatlantic flight of Navy Curtis (NC) Seaplane Division 1. Reportedly, he was recommended for the assignment by Glenn Curtis. Stone was the senior pilot of aircraft NC-4, which was commanded by Cdr. Albert C. Read, USN. The remainder of the six-man crew consisted of Lt. (j.g.) Walter K. Hinton, USN, pilot; Lt. James L. Breese, USN, reserve pilot and engineer; Ens. Herbert C. Rodd, USN, radio operator; Chief Machinist Mate Eugene "Smokey" Rhoads, mechanic. Rhoads was the only enlisted man in the crew. The three aircraft—NC-1, NC-3, and NC-4—departed Naval Air Station Rockaway at 10:00 AM on 8 May 1919. At 1:50 PM oil pressure in NC-4's center after engine dropped and ignition was cut. The aircraft continued on three engines, at a slightly reduced speed. An hour later, a connecting rod in the center forward engine let go and NC-4 had to land in the water, eighty miles east of Cape Cod. The seas were calm and NC-4, using its two wing engines, was able to taxi on the surface. Making ten knots, the plane reached Naval Air Station Chatham just as the sun was rising. Stone, who was qualified for engineering duty, Breese, and Rhoads worked around the clock replacing the center forward engine, repairing the center after engine and getting the plane ready to continue the flight. Bad weather and more mechanical problems delayed

Navy flying boat NC-4 landed at Lisbon, Portugal, on 27 May 1919 after its historic transatlantic flight. The aircraft, with 1st Lt. Elmer F. Stone as senior pilot, was the only one of the three planes of Curtis (NC) Seaplane Division 1 to successfully complete the flight across the ocean. *U.S. Coast Guard Historian*

NC-4's departure until 14 May, when it took off for Halifax, Nova Scotia, to join the other two planes. The following day the three aircraft flew to Trespassey Bay, Newfoundland. The three aircraft took off from Newfoundland just before 8:00 PM on 16 May. With the sun setting, they headed for Horta in the Azores—a distance of 1,200 nautical miles. During the flight, NC-1 and NC-3 got lost in dense fog; NC-4 was the only aircraft to successfully reach Horta. The other two planes were forced to land at sea and could not continue the journey. On 20 May NC-4 flew 150 miles east across the Azores, from Horta to Ponta Delgada. The plane flew the final eight hundred miles of the historic journey on 27 May. NC-4 landed at Lisbon, Portugal, at 7:02 PM. Three months later, Stone received a letter from the secretary of the navy: "I wish to heartily commend you for your work as Pilot of the Seaplane

NC-4 during the recent trans-Atlantic flight expedition. The energy, efficiency, and courage shown by you contributed to the accomplishment of the first trans-Atlantic flight, which feat has brought honor to the American Navy and the entire American nation." The letter was signed by Franklin D. Roosevelt, acting secretary of the navy.[21]

The coast guard officers who completed aviation training were older and more experienced than the navy trainees at Pensacola. U.S. Coast Guard Academy graduates, they had prior years of shipboard duty. Parker, the oldest of the coast guard aviators, had ten years of service before reporting for flight training. Eaton had eight years of service and Sugden had seven. Stone and Donahue, the youngest officers assigned to flight training, graduated from the academy in 1913 and each had three years of sea duty. The age and experience of the coast guard aviators was certainly a consideration in their assignments to positions of responsibility during the war.[22]

NAVAL AIR STATION ILE TUDY, FRANCE

In response to a request from the French government, the United States agreed to build a naval air station at Ile Tudy, France, to augment the French air station at Cape Penmarch, south of Brest. Concentrated German submarine activity in the area was taking a heavy toll on allied shipping; vessels were being sunk at the rate of one a day. Building materials needed to construct the station had to be shipped directly from the United States. Delays in the arrival of needed materials extended the time to complete the work. American servicemen did much of the construction work themselves because French contractors were overwhelmed by other war-related construction projects. Fortunately, there was a large pool of construction talent and experience available among the station's officers and men, who came from all walks of life. They built four large hangars in a row. A taxiway, in front of the hangars, ran perpendicular to the shore and led to a launching ramp. Buildings for administration, barracks, and officers quarters were built behind the hangars, along the shore. Naval Air Station Ile Tudy was completed on 14 March 1918, and placed in commission under the command of 1st Lt. (Eng.) Charles E. Sugden, USCG. Twenty-one aircraft were assigned to the station, which had a complement of 22 officers and 363 enlisted men. French-made Donnet-Denhaut seaplanes were initially used for flight operations.[23]

The air station's mission was the escort and protection of coastal convoys and convoys going to and from the United States. Air stations were situated along the French coast so that overlapping protection could be provided for convoys. After coastal air patrols commenced, only three ships were lost in the French waters between Cape Penmarch and Ile d'Yeu during the remaining ten months of the war. The first aircraft attack on an enemy submarine, flown from a U.S. naval air station, was made by a plane from Ile Tudy. Because of its location, aircraft from Ile Tudy saw more action against submarines than any other overseas air station. Each day, a northbound and a southbound convoy passed through the air station's sector. The waters just offshore from Cape Penmarch were deep and free of reefs and sandbars, providing a haven for German submarines. The U-boats, which came close to shore and lay in wait for coastal shipping, were nicknamed "Penmarch Pete" by ship crews. The majority of submarine sightings received by the air station came from the Cape Penmarch area. Naval Air Station Ile Tudy's historian described the air station's routine:

> A section of two planes escorted each convoy. As the sector was too long to be covered by two planes, it was necessary to send out another section to relieve the first, when the convoy was approximately halfway through the area. This necessitated using at least eight planes per day for convoy work alone. In addition, there was always a section known as "Alert" ready to take the air from daybreak until dark in response to any "Allis" [submarine sightings] received. When the convoy was picked up, the planes would first circle over it. Then while one plane would remain around the convoy the other would fly as far as ten or fifteen miles ahead, zigzagging broadly on both sides.

The planes alternated, circling the convoy and searching ahead. They repeating the same maneuver over and over. The planes made a final search around the convoy before they were relieved by the next section of two aircraft.[24]

On 23 April 1918, two aircraft from Ile Tudy air station joined a southbound convoy of twenty ships six miles north of Cape Penmarch. The two Donnet-Denhaut seaplanes were flown by navy pilots: Ens. K. R. Smith and Quartermaster 1st Class R. H. Harlem. Because visibility was reduced by fog, the two planes first flew to the rear of the convoy to check for stragglers and then made a wide circle around the main body of the convoy. When Smith spotted what appeared to be the wake of a submarine under way at a high rate of speed, he closed and attacked. He dropped two bombs just ahead of the beginning of the wake. The bombs created a large explosion in the water and then air bubbles began to surface. Harlem, in the second plane, was so convinced of the success of the attack that he did not drop his bombs. He marked the spot with a smoke float and began to circle while Smith flew to the USS *Stewart*, a destroyer escorting the convoy. Smith dropped a message block reporting the attack onto the ship. *Stewart* set general quarters and proceeded to the location of the attack. The French gunboat *Ardente* also arrived on scene and quickly dropped three depth charges. Crews in the two planes circling overhead saw pieces of wreckage and large quantities of oil float to the surface. Aircraft from Ile Tudy continued to see oil coming to the surface at the location for the next two weeks. French authorities officially credited Ensign Smith and his observer, Chief O. E. Williams, with sinking a German submarine. They were cited in the Order of the Day and each awarded a Croix de Guerre with Palm. Five months earlier, Smith had had a close call when he was forced down at sea. In the first armed patrol by a U.S. naval aviator in European waters, he had flown a French Tellier seaplane out of LeCroisic to investigate a report of a German submarine in the Bay of Biscay. He experienced mechanical problems and had to make an emergency landing on the open sea. He, along with his crewmen—Electrician's Mate Wilkinson and Machinist Mate Brady—drifted for two days aboard the damaged plane before they were found by a French destroyer. Within minutes after their rescue, the seaplane sank.[25]

On 27 September 1918, two planes from Ile Tudy air station were on patrol near Cape Penmarch when they sighted what appeared to be a submarine. When they attacked, their bombs set off a violent underwater disturbance. The incident was assessed as a submarine "probably damaged." For his distinguished service in command of the air station at Ile Tudy, Sugden was recommended for the rank of Chevalier of the Legion of Honor by Lt. Cdr. V. Vaschalde, commander of the French navy's aerial patrol of the Loire. The award was presented by the French government.[26]

Naval Air Station Key West, Florida

First Lt. Stanley V. Parker, USCG, reported to Navy Aeronautical Station Pensacola and was appointed a student aviator on 10 March 1917. After completing seaplane training at Pensacola, he was designated a naval aviator and sent for additional training in lighter than air (LTA) aircraft. Parker was ordered to Key West, Florida, on 11 December 1917 and took command of Naval Air Station Key West when it was commissioned on 18 December. Some patrol operations were flown from Naval Air Station Key West, but it was primarily an elementary flight training facility.[27]

Naval Air Station Rockaway, New York

Naval Air Station Rockaway was established to provide antisubmarine protection for the critical approaches to New York harbor. Commissioned on 15 October 1917, the air station was originally built for seaplane patrols and kite balloon training. A hangar for dirigibles was later added. Parker, promoted to captain on 1 July 1918, received orders on 6 August to report to Naval Air Station Rockaway for duty. Shortly after his arrival, he took command of the station, with Coffin as his executive officer. Parker remained in command of the station until 31 May 1919. While commanding officer, preparations for the first transatlantic flight were made at the station. On 4 October 1918, the first of the NC flying boats to be used for the flight to Europe made its initial flight from Rockaway.[28]

Naval Air Station North Sydney, Nova Scotia, Canada

Convoys sailing from the United States and Canada en route to Europe were assembled at Sydney, Nova Scotia, in the large natural harbor on the northern tip of Cape Breton Island. Naval Air Station North Sydney was established to protect the ships as they were forming into convoys and to escort the convoys when they departed. The seaplane station was commissioned on 31 August 1918 with 1st Lt. Robert Donahue, USCG, in command. Twelve days earlier, Naval Air Station Halifax, Nova Scotia, to the south, was placed in commission by Lt. Richard E. Byrd, USN, who later gained fame as a polar explorer. After the armistice, Donahue was detached from Naval Air Station North Sydney on 23 December 1918. He was reassigned as commanding officer of the Naval Air Station Montauk Point, Long Island, New York. He held this command until 16 June 1919.[29]

NAVAL AIR STATION CHATHAM, MASSACHUSETTS

Naval Air Station Chatham was located on the southeast corner of Cape Cod. It was built on fifteen acres of land and its shore was protected by a long sandbar. The station's large barracks building and hangars were visible from the town of Chatham five miles away. The station had two dirigibles and seven seaplanes. The complement was 245 men. Second Lt. (Eng.) Philip B. Eaton, USCG, took command of the station on 19 June 1918, and was promoted two grades to the temporary rank of captain of engineers—equivalent to the U.S. Navy's rank of lieutenant commander—on 1 July. Eaton was detached from the station on 6 June 1919, seven months after the war ended.[30]

When the U.S. Coast Guard was transferred back to the Treasury Department by executive order in August 1919, coast guard personnel "engaged in the operation and construction of aircraft for the Navy" were reassigned to coast guard billets. Interest in flight operations continued after 1919 and attempts were made to develop a coast guard aviation capability using aircraft borrowed from the U.S. Navy. While these early flight operations were promising, the U.S. Coast Guard was unsuccessful in obtaining funding from Congress to support continuation. In 1925 Congress, concerned about enforcing prohibition laws, appropriated funds for the U.S. Coast Guard to purchase its own aircraft for search operations.[31]

CHAPTER 7

COASTAL STATIONS

It may be readily appreciated that it was of the utmost importance that
the Navy Department should have, particularly on the Atlantic and
Gulf coasts, numerous observation posts manned by competent and
trustworthy men who would immediately report the presence off the
coast of enemy craft and of vessels of a suspicious character that might
be sighted. This requirement was admirably met by the personnel of
the Coast Guard stations. There were on the Atlantic and Gulf coasts
199 of these stations whose crews maintained a constant, alert watch
from their observation towers at all times and patrolled the beach
through hours of darkness and fog.

—Report to Secretary of the Navy Josephus Daniels

Tankship *Mirlo*

The British tanker *Mirlo* rounded Cape Hatteras and headed north just
east of North Carolina's Outer Banks on the afternoon of 16 August 1918.
The 6,679-ton ship, carrying a cargo of gasoline and refined oil, was
bound for Norfolk, Virginia, from New Orleans, Louisiana. The lookout
in the wooden tower on top of Coast Guard Station No. 179 at

Chicamicomico, North Carolina, watched as the ship made its way along the coast, seven miles offshore. Suddenly, at 4:40 PM, when the ship was one mile from Wimble Shoal Buoy, a geyser of water erupted at its starboard quarter. The lookout sounded the alarm and then heard the rumble of the explosion from across the water. The tanker continued on course with black smoke billowing from its stern. Then flames shot into the air and more explosions were heard. The crippled ship's bow swung toward shore and then to seaward, before it came dead in the water.[1]

The station's keeper, John A. Midgett, immediately called out all hands and ordered the horse hitched to the boat wagon. Midgett's daughter watched from the sand dunes while the station's crew hauled power surfboat no. 1046 down the beach. A northeast wind blew from seaward, driving a heavy surf onto the shore. She said they "trundled their boat to the sea, lifted it from its wagon, carried it to the thundering surf, and rowed it against 30-knot winds into the wall of breakers off the shore." The boat crew was swept away from their oars by the waves when they tried to launch. Midgett's daughter said, "I stood on the beach and watched my father and a crew of five, . . . on the third attempt, they made it through the breakers." Their twenty-six foot Beebe-McLellan self-bailing motor surfboat cleared the beach just after 5:00 PM. Once the boat was through the surf, the crew started the twelve-horsepower gasoline engine and boated their oars. Midgett stood in the stern sheets and steered for the flaming ship.[2]

Two miles from the burning tanker, Midgett saw one of *Mirlo*'s boats emerge from the smoke. Seventeen men were aboard the boat, including the ship's master, Capt. W. R. Williams. Williams told Midgett that his ship had been torpedoed. He said two more of the ship's boats were back in the midst of the burning oil—one of them had capsized. Williams said he thought all the men in the capsized boat were dead. Midgett directed him to take his boat toward shore, "and await my arrival." He told Williams not to attempt a landing through the surf, because the sea was strong and there was danger of his capsizing his boat without assistance. Midgett then headed for the burning wreckage and flaming oil. There were two great masses of flame, about one hundred yards apart, with the sea covered with burning gas and oil for hundreds of yards. When the wind briefly cleared the smoke, Midgett saw a lifeboat between the flames; it was bottom up, with six men clinging to it. Midgett said, "The heavy swell was washing over the boat. With some difficulty, I ran our boat through the smoke, floating wreckage, and burning gas and oil and rescued the six men from the burning sea; who informed me that at many times they had to dive under the water to save themselves from being burned to death. All had been burned, but none seriously."[3]

The survivors said they saw the other men from their boat perish in the burning seas. Despite assurances that all the others were dead, Midgett continued to search in the vicinity of the wreck until he was confident no one else was still alive. Then he set out to find the remaining boat. In his report, he wrote, "I headed our boat before the sea and wind in hopes of finding the missing boat and in a short time the third boat with nineteen men was sighted. It was overloaded and so much crowded that the men in it could not row and were just drifting with the wind and sea. This boat was about nine miles S.E. of the station. I ran alongside and took her in tow and proceeded to where I directed the first boat to be. This boat was soon reached and taken in tow; with thirty-six men in the two boats being towed, and six men in the station boat, in addition to my own crew."[4]

Midgett towed the two boats—one with Captain Williams and sixteen men and the other with Boatswain Donalds and eighteen men—until they were just offshore, about two miles south of the station. With the wind freshening from the northeast and the sea rising on the beach, Midgett said, "It was dark and for safety I decided to make a landing. I had the two boats anchored about six hundred yards off shore and began transferring the shipwrecked crew to land in the station boat." Midgett made four trips through the breakers in the station's surfboat. Members of his crew who had been left ashore and the keeper and crew from nearby Coast Guard Station No. 180 at Gull assisted in landing the survivors. The British sailors were taken to the Chicamicomico station by horses from the two stations.[5]

Hot meals were waiting for the shipwrecked sailors and the rescuers when they reached the station. The British sailors were given dry clothing that had been either donated to the station or provided by the surfmen. Midgett's daughter said she "helped peel the potatoes and his [Midgett's] mother assisted his future brother-in-law, John E. Herbert, . . . prepare the food, the warm blankets, the hot rum, and other aid for the shipwrecked sailors, many of whom were badly burned." After eating, the British crew was given places to sleep. Midgett's log entry at the end of the day simply stated, "I landed last trip at 9:00 PM, and arrived at station at 11:00 PM. Myself and crew very tired."[6]

The next morning, the winds had abated and the seas were calm. Navy seaplane A-765 landed just offshore from the station at 10:00 AM and the station's boat took *Mirlo*'s master out to the plane. Williams was flown to Norfolk to make a report on the sinking of his ship. When USS *Legonia* arrived offshore from the station, the remaining survivors from the tanker were taken out to the ship for passage to Norfolk. Williams reported that *Mirlo* was sunk by a torpedo, and the station's tower lookout said he saw the explosion toward the stern of the tanker, indicating a probable torpedo strike. There were still questions as to whether the ship went down after hitting a German mine planted by a submarine. U-117, under the command of Kapitänleutnant Droscher, was known to have been operating in U.S. waters off the mid-Atlantic coast on a minelaying mission at the time the ship was sunk.[7]

Secretary of the Navy Josephus Daniels commended Midgett and the crew of motor surfboat no. 1046 and, after the war, Congress recognized their heroism by voting to award them Gold Life-Saving Medals for "courageous and heroic action." The commandant awarded the medals to the crew at a public ceremony at Elizabeth City, North Carolina. The recipients were John A. Midgett keeper; Zion S. Midgett, no. 1 surfman; Arthur V. Midgett, surfman; Clarence E. Midgett, surfman; Leroy S. Midgett, surfman; and Prochorus L. O'Neal, surfman. The British government also recognized the courage of the crew, sending them congratulatory letters and presenting them with gold medals. On 2 November 1921 the U.S. Coast Guard forwarded the gold medal to Keeper Midgett. The enclosed letter said, "The Commandant takes pleasure in forwarding herewith the gold medal for gallantry and humanity in saving life at sea which has been awarded to you by the British Government." In addition to the gold medal, the British Board of Trade also presented Midgett with a silver cup, inscribed, "Presented by the British Government to John A. Midgett, Keeper of Coast Guard Station No. 179, Rodanthe, North Carolina. In acknowledgment of the able leadership in effecting the rescue of the shipwrecked crew of the SS MIRLO on the 16th August, 1918."[8]

WARTIME

War was already raging in Europe when the U.S. Coast Guard was created in January 1915. At that time, the United States still proclaimed its neutrality, but government leaders were conscious of the increasing potential for the eventual involvement in the conflict. The act creating the U.S. Coast Guard directed that the service would operate as a part of the U.S. Navy in time of war. In anticipation of this happening, Secretary of the Treasury William G. McAdoo and Secretary of the Navy Josephus Daniels jointly ordered that plans be prepared for the U.S. Coast Guard's operation within the U.S. Navy. Capt. William H. G. Bullard, USN, and Captain Commandant Ellsworth P. Bertholf, USCG, submitted a report to the two secretaries on 20 March 1915. In the report, they described how coast guard resources could best be used by the navy during wartime. With respect to coastal stations, manned by former Life-Saving Service personnel, the report called for them to continue operations with additional coastal watch and communications duties. The report also recommended that some of the surfmen, if properly trained and equipped, could be used to guard navy coastal radio stations and others could serve on small gunboats or boats for landing troops through the surf.[9]

The military potential of Life-Saving Service stations had been addressed earlier by Franklin MacVeagh, former secretary of the treasury. In a 5 May 1910 report, he said,

> In time of war the life-saving stations are admirably adapted for military outposts and pickets. This fact was so apparent at the outbreak of the Spanish-American War. . . . They performed a principal part of the Naval coast guard service throughout the campaign, and according to the report of Captain John R. Bartlett, United States Navy, superintendent of the Coast Signal Service, rendered aid of great importance by advising the Navy Department of the movements of Government vessels by means of the service telephone lines, which are connected with the general telegraph lines of the Country.[10]

In 1917 there were 272 coast guard stations distributed along the shores of the United States: 190 stations on the Atlantic and Gulf of Mexico coasts, 19 stations on the Pacific coast, and 63 stations in the Great Lakes. The stations were divided geographically into districts with a superintendent in charge of each district. Station keepers were warrant officers and each station's no. 1 surfman was a petty officer. The remaining surfmen at the stations were nonrated enlisted men. When war was declared on 6 April 1917, telegrams sent to the stations directed them to execute Plan One. Station keepers reported for duty to the commanders of the naval districts to which they were assigned and then notified Coast Guard Headquarters of their actions. The U.S. Navy took command of all the former Life-Saving Service facilities, including stations, boathouses, communication systems, and storehouses. The network of coastal stations, with their communications capability, provided a coordinated warning system for the maritime borders of the United States.[11]

After the U.S. Navy took command of the stations, crews were increased and day and night beach patrols were extended. More men were required to accomplish the additional wartime duties that had to be carried out even when a boat and crew were under way for a rescue. After the transfer, a dual system for the operation and administration of the stations evolved. The U.S. Navy was primarily concerned with the defense and communications capabilities of the stations and less interested in their rescue functions. Military inspections were carried out by representatives of the commandant of the naval district in which the station was located. These inspections addressed uniform equipment, fire arms and ammunition, communications systems, flags for signaling by hand and by hoist, military drills, and target practice. U.S. Coast Guard district superintendents retained the responsibility for inspecting stations for their readiness to perform rescues. They checked the condition of boats and equipment; beach apparatus; station buildings and grounds; horses, wagons, and carts. They also conducted boat and rescue apparatus drills. Reports from both navy inspectors and coast guard district superintendents were sent to naval commanders, with copies to the coast guard commandant.[12]

FACILITIES AND EQUIPMENT

The U.S. Coast Guard had three types of stations—life-saving stations, lifeboat stations, and houses of refuge. Life-saving stations were primarily located along the shores of the Atlantic coast from Maine to South Carolina. They were usually "open beach" stations where crews launched their boats directly through the surf to rescue distressed mariners. Lifeboat stations were built on the sheltered shores of bays and inlets, with access to open waters. They were near cities or towns with breakwaters, piers, and channels with water deep enough to operate larger boats. Lifeboat stations were mainly located in the Great Lakes and on the Pacific coast. The third type of facility was a house of refuge. In 1917, only eight houses of refuge remained; they were all located on the Atlantic coast of Florida. Houses of refuge were originally located in remote coastal areas to provide shelter and supplies for shipwrecked sailors. These small facilities were maintained by caretaker crews. After the war began, the houses of refuge were fully manned and operated as stations. All coast guard stations had some sort of lookout tower to observe coastal waters and the shore. The most common arrangement was a tower built on the top of the main station building. In some cases, a station had a separate tower erected near the main building to provide better visibility.[13]

All stations had boats assigned; these included lifeboats, surfboats, and other types. The boats were painted white above the waterline on the outside and a "straw color" on the inside. Gunwales, guards, bitts, masts, spars, and thwarts were finished with spar varnish. Hardwood water breakers, flag staffs, trim, gratings, portable stretchers, molding, and hand grabs were also varnished. In addition to boats, stations were equipped with beach apparatus and rescue gear, consisting of line-throwing guns, hawsers, breeches buoys, life cars, heaving sticks and lines, and life preservers. The stations used flags and pyrotechnics for signaling. The standard outfit of equipment for each station depended on station size and needs. As coastal charts became more accurate and better methods of navigation were developed in the early 1900s, fewer large ships ran aground along the U.S. coast. The changing nature of maritime emergencies and the deployment of more capable power craft resulted in a greater reliance on boats for rescues; the need for beach apparatus for rescues became less important. The types of boats assigned to stations varied depending on their suitability for local surf and sea conditions. Larger lifeboats were too heavy to be launched from the beach into the surf; they required launching ways located in sheltered waters. Surfboats were smaller and light enough to be transported along the beach for launching directly into the surf. The boats used by stations were divided into two classes: those with gasoline motors and those powered by oars or sails. Of the U.S. Coast Guard's 709 rescue boats in 1917, one third were powered by gasoline engines. Boats were further subdivided, based on their hull construction: open, self-bailing, and self-righting. In addition to rescue boats, another 262 miscellaneous small craft and supply boats were used by the stations.[14]

Self-righting and self-bailing motor lifeboats built after 1908 were thirty-six feet in length and powered by forty-horsepower gasoline engines. Motor lifeboats built before 1908 were thirty-four feet in length. Thirty-nine of the U.S. Coast Guard's seventy-four motor lifeboats were used on the Great Lakes. The smaller motor surfboat was either self-bailing or open. Beebe-McLellan surfboats, both powered and unpowered, were self-bailing. Self-bailing boats had flotation compartments in the hull that caused the boats to ride high enough to allow shipped water to flow out of freeing ports. Twenty-six-foot motor surfboats were powered by twelve-horsepower gasoline engines. Unpowered surfboat types included: Beebe-McLellan; Beebe, open; Monomoy; Excelsior; Race Point; and Jersey. The largest class of rescue boat used by the U.S. Coast Guard was the unpowered Beebe-McLellan type. It accounted for 40 percent of the service's inventory. While it was the most numerous, it was not the most popular boat due to its size and weight. Surfmen complained that the boats were too heavy to launch through the surf and, once through the surf, they were more difficult to row because the double bottom reduced the height of the thwarts.[15]

DUTIES

Before the war, station crews were small, with little more than enough men to man one rescue boat. The larger lifeboat stations generally had eight men, while life-saving stations had only six men to man their surfboats. Directives provided detailed guidance on how stations were to be organized. Each surfman at a station was provided a copy of *Instructions for Coast Guard Stations*. The 180-page, 4-inch by 6-inch booklet set forth how a station was to operate, how buildings and boats were to be maintained, when and how exercises and drills were to be held, and what equipment was to be on hand. A carryover from the Life-Saving Service, the *Instructions* were the station's regulations. Station crews were divided into watches of two men each. Watches were stood after working hours, when crews were not up and immediately ready to respond to distress situations. Tower watches were stood from sunset to 8:00 PM, 8:00 PM to midnight, midnight to 4:00 AM, and 4:00 AM to sunrise. During daylight hours, the keeper assigned men to man the tower. To ensure alertness, crewmen manning the lookout towers were required to stand while scanning the horizon for the duration of their watches. They kept a rough log of passing ships and recorded all telephone communications. To check on the attentiveness of lookouts, station keepers often required watch standers to strike bells each half hour, as was done aboard ship. Article 81 of the *Instructions* contained rules for tower watches:

> He shall not sit down, lie down, sleep, read, entertain visitors, or do anything else that will tend to interfere with the proper discharge of his duties. He shall immediately report to the officer or other person in charge of the station all occurrences which involve or seem likely to involve, danger to or loss of property. He shall not leave the lookout unless properly relieved. He shall not take into the lookout any book, paper, or pamphlet, or other reading material, or any chair, stool, bench, or other seat nor shall he permit any such article or articles or any person not connected with the service in the lookout while he is on watch.[16]

All surfmen had to be able to swim and had to pass a swimming test. Each man had to accomplish the following as a single exercise: swim 100 yards, dive properly from the surface and swim 50 yards on his back; dive from the surface of the water and bring up a 10-pound object from a depth of at least 7 feet; carry a supposedly drowning person of at least his own weight 20 yards with a two-hand carry and 20 yards with a one-hand carry; swim 50 yards dressed, with shoes, trousers, and coat, and then remove the clothing in the water, without touching bottom.[17]

Patrolling the shore to look for vessels in distress was a basic part of a surfman's duties. Patrols had been a common routine for stations when they were part of the former Life-Saving Service and were continued by the U.S. Coast Guard. Set patrol routes were laid out in each direction along the shore from a station. Distances varied, depending on the topography of the coastline, but did not usually exceed four miles. At sunset, the first man from each station in a district started out on patrol, traveling in the same direction. While one man was on patrol, his watch mate took the station watch, standing in the tower or on the beach near the station, depending on conditions. If the station was connected with a telephone line, the station watch stayed within hearing distance of the bell. In addition to keeping a watch to seaward, he also kept a lookout for signals from the patrolman. When the first patrol returned, he took the station watch and his watch mate began a patrol in the opposite direction. Near the end of the watch, the next two men were called, so they could be dressed and ready for duty, before the first two men turned in.[18]

A check system was sometimes used to provide evidence of the integrity of patrols. Where stations were close enough for adjacent patrols to cover the entire distance between them, a halfway point was established. At the halfway point, each patrolman deposited a brass disk called a check. The check, bearing the station name and the patrolman's number in the crew, was picked up by the adjacent station's patrolman when he arrived at the halfway point. He, in turn, left his check. The first patrolman of the next night returned the checks that had been picked up the previous night. Where patrols did not connect, patrolmen carried a watchman's clock that was punched with a key kept in a safe at the end of the route. Telephones were also used by patrolmen. They were located at halfway houses or at the end of the routes where patrolmen could call and report to the stations. Patrolmen carried Coston signal flares to warn vessels standing too close to shore, or to signal a ship in distress that help was coming. Night patrols were an important and difficult part of a surfman's duties. Patrols were most needed when the weather was the worst. During winter gales, surfmen trudged along windswept shores, wearing foul weather gear and carrying lanterns. At stations located in populated areas, such as harbors and ports, where a vessel in distress would be observed and reported, fixed lookouts were used rather than beach patrols.[19]

Training was an important part of a station's daily routine. To maintain the proficiency of the crew, drills were scheduled weekly. These included boat drills, signal drills, resuscitation drills, fire drills, and practices rigging beach apparatus. Drills were usually held in the morning between 8:00 AM and noon. Afternoons were devoted to the upkeep of the station. Boat drills and signal drills were mandated to last at least one hour and other drills and instructions at least a half hour. Beach apparatus was equipment used to bring people ashore from vessels that grounded offshore, usually during a storm. Rigging the gear involved firing a line to the ship; the line was attached to the mast. A breeches buoy or a rescue car was then run along the line to bring people ashore. In 1917, stations still practiced rigging beach apparatus. The drill required firing a line to a drill post that simulated the mast of a distressed ship and transporting a man in a breeches buoy. Article 191 of the *Instructions* required the following drills weekly: two boat drills, five signal drills, one beach apparatus drill, one fire drill, and one resuscitation drill. Station crews were also required to be proficient in motorboat laws, pilot rules, coast guard regulations, and compass. At least once a week, the officer in charge was required to determine the proficiency of each crew member in these subjects by testing them, using the questions contained in the appendix of the *Instructions*. No drills or instructions were held on Saturday, a day devoted to cleaning the station. The *Instructions* provided that "when circumstances permit, Saturday afternoon shall be regarded as a half holiday."[20]

Stations in the vicinity of naval air stations were frequently called on to assist with disabled aircraft. In September 1918, coast guard stations assisted in rescuing three planes from Naval Air Station Chatham at Cape Cod, Massachusetts. At 9:00 AM on 8 September 1918, HS-1L No. 1693 developed engine trouble and had to land in Winthrop's Broad Sound. The crew from Coast Guard Station No. 24 at Nahant rowed out to the plane and towed it to shore, where they hauled it above the high-water mark. The plane's pilot, Ens. Thomas T. Hoopes, used the station phone to call the air station and report the situation. The coast guard station posted two guards to prevent onlookers from coming too close or taking pictures of the plane. The aircraft's crew spent the night at the station and the next morning the air station sent a party to repair the plane. Two days later it took off and returned to the air station. Less than a week later, HS-2L No. 1849 was forced to land at sea. The seaplane landed two and a half miles north of Coast Guard Station No. 37 at Pamet River at 10:00 on 12 September. The men from the station got a line out to the plane and hauled it to shore. Using the station's horse, they dragged the plane above the high-water mark. Due to weather, surf, and beach conditions, it took fifteen hours before the crew had the plane safely secured. Mechanics from the air station removed the plane's wings so they would not be damaged by the high winds. Unrepairable, the aircraft was towed back to the air station a week later for a major overhaul. The lookout on watch at Coast Guard Station No. 39 at Nauset sighted a distress signal

A surfboat from the Fire Island coast guard station rows out to the stranded troop transport USS *Northern Pacific*. The 9,708-ton ship ran aground at 2:30 AM on New Year's Day 1919 while returning with troops from Europe. Coast guard surfboats brought 450 soldiers and nurses ashore through the surf before the seas calmed enough for rescue vessels to come alongside the listing ship.
Mariners' Museum, Newport News, Virginia

on 11 September 1918. The signal came from an R-9 float plane out of Naval Air Station Chatham; it was forced to land in rough seas two miles away. The station's crew started down the beach with a surfboat and rescue gear on a horse-drawn wagon. The horse gave out en route and the men from the station had to pull the wagon the rest of the way. By the time the men reached the plane, it was already in the surf. They brought the aviators ashore and, using rollers and planks, hauled the R-9 up on the beach. Bad weather prevented the plane from being towed back to the air station until 18 September.[21]

SS *NORTHERN PACIFIC* RESCUE

Just before 2:30 AM on New Years Day 1919, the lookout in the tower of the coast guard station at Fire Island saw the glow of a ship's lights through the fog. The lights were close to shore and not moving. From the separation between the lights and the height above the ocean, the lookout knew it had to be a large ship. He immediately called the station keeper. The 12,835-ton, 525-foot transport *Northern Pacific* was en route to New York with three thousand troops returning from Europe. The ship was traveling at a moderate speed when it ran hard aground on a sandbar two hundred yards off the beach. The transport settled heavily on the bar and took on a fifteen degree list to port. Keeper John D. Tuttle and his no. 1 surfman hurried down to the beach to evaluate the situation while the rest of the crew broke out the rescue gear. Heavy breakers rolled onto shore. With the ship apparently in no immediate danger, the crew brought their gear down to the beach and waited for dawn. The transport's commanding officer, Capt. Louis J. Conelly, USN, sent a message to naval authorities: "Northern Pacific is in no danger. Relatives of soldiers and crew need have no fear for their safety. Soldiers will in all probability be landed tomorrow or whenever winds shift to the northwest or west."[22]

When dawn came, the men could see the full extent of the camouflaged ship; it was lying parallel to the beach, starboard side to. Additional gear was brought to the scene from adjacent coast guard stations. During the day, three lines were fired to the ship with a Lyle gun. Two of the lines parted when the transport shifted on the sandbar. With the condition of the ship stable, it was deemed too risky to bring people ashore by breeches buoy. Surfboats from the stations made it out to the ship and surfmen boarded the transport to arrange the evacuation of troops. The boats returned with mail from the ship. Throughout the day, boats put out through the surf and returned with soldiers. *Northern Pacific* served as a breakwater for the surfboats, shielding them from the easterly winds and seas. The seas were so rough that they carried away the transport's no. 14 lifeboat. By noon there were four destroyers standing by offshore, but waves breaking on the seaward side of the transport and shallow water on the starboard side prevented rescue vessels from coming alongside to pick up troops. Vice Adm. Albert Gleaves, commander of cruiser and transport forces, directed the rescue effort from aboard his flagship, the cruiser *Columbia*. By sundown, surfboats from the stations, powered by oars, had only managed to land 254 troops through the surf. On one trip a surfboat capsized and two soldiers were in danger of drowning. They were rescued by people waiting on the beach. Before the day was over, a rescue force of two cruisers, the transport *Mallory*, the cruising cutter *Seneca*, twelve destroyers, and a fleet of tugs and harbor cutters was on scene. The next day it was still too rough to get vessels alongside *Northern Pacific*, so surfboats and a breeches buoy were used to bring ashore another two hundred people, including nurses. Rowing the boats through surf, trip after trip, was exhausting the surfmen. Waves continued to break along the length of the port side of the huge ship. One of the coast guardsmen who went aboard *Northern Pacific* said, "The transport shudders every time a wave hits her and sends nerve-racking sounds reverberating through her interior. Between the noise and the motion, some of the sick men have reached such a state they scream when anyone approaches them."[23]

On 3 January 1919—the third day—the winds veered to the northwest and died down; the seas became calmer. Coast guard harbor cutters and 110-foot navy submarine chasers from New York were able to come alongside the transport to remove the soldiers. They shuttled the troops to waiting destroyers. As many as three subchasers and cutters would come alongside the transport at one time, for soldiers to climb down rope ladders to their rolling decks. Those who had difficulty climbing down the ladders had lines secured about their waists to prevent them from falling. At 2:45 PM, *Columbia*'s motor launch capsized and washed onto the beach. Many soldiers being removed from *Northern Pacific* had been wounded in combat. Those missing limbs had to be lowered to the rescue vessels in baskets. The more seriously wounded troops were taken to the transport *Mallory*. When the hospital ship *Solace* arrived, the stretcher cases were transferred to it. Twenty-one hundred soldiers were removed from the transport on the third day. Among the thirty-one ships in the vicinity of the grounded transport were three large Merritt Chapman wrecking tugs, waiting for the weather to improve to attempt to refloat the transport. By 4 January the winds and seas calmed and the last 240 soldiers, all seriously wounded, were removed and transferred to the hospital ship *Solace*. Seventy-five of *Northern Pacific*'s crew remained aboard the transport. Several days latter, the ship was successfully refloated and taken into New York.[24]

STATION NO. 162, VIRGINIA BEACH, VIRGINIA

A typical rescue station, Coast Guard Station No. 162 was built on the sandy shore of the Atlantic Ocean, five and a half miles south of Cape

Henry Lighthouse. The adjacent stations were no. 161 at Cape Henry, four and three quarter miles to the north, and no. 163 at Dam Neck Mills, four and a half miles to the south. When war was declared, each station was manned with just enough men to make up a single boat crew. The Virginia Beach station had a crew of six—a keeper and five surfmen. The station's main building was relatively new. It was constructed in 1903 to replace the old station that had been built in 1878 when the Life-Saving Service was established. The station had five buildings, including the old station building. The main building, which sheltered the boats, was set back on the sand dunes 160 feet from the ocean. A storage and toilet building was located just behind and to the north of the main building. Because of the threat of fire in the wooden main building, all cooking was done in a separate cookhouse, sixty yards behind the main building. When the new station was built, the old building was moved back from the water on log rollers to a site next to the cookhouse; a water tank was located between the two buildings. The last building, a stable and cart house, was behind the cookhouse.[25]

Building no. 1, the main building, was a large two-story bungalow with a third floor attic and an 8-by-12-foot lookout tower on top of the roof. The building measured 24 by 56 feet and was constructed of wood and had white cedar shingles. Red cedar posts on concrete footings supported the building above the sandy soil. Construction of the building was completed on 2 April 1903 at a cost of $7,500. The boat room took up half the ground floor. It had a concrete floor and three large doors: a 10.5-by-11.5-foot door on the east side that faced the ocean and 14-by-11.5-foot and 12.5-by-8-foot doors on the west side. The remainder of the first floor was used for a crew's mess room, a washroom, and the keeper's office and sleeping room. The second floor was divided into two sleeping rooms for the surfmen, and a large storeroom. Two windows on the north side, two on the south side, and dormer windows facing the ocean and inland, provided light for the second floor. The lookout tower was accessed through the attic. The tower had two windows on each of its four sides. Kerosene oil lamps were used to light the building and woodstoves provided heat. Building no. 1 and the old station building were two stories; the others were one story. Building no. 2 was a 12-by-18-foot wooden building divided into four rooms, all about the same size. Three rooms were used for storing coal, oil, and firewood. The fourth room was a privy

Keeper Thomas J. Barnes and the crew of the Virginia Beach coast guard station standing in front of the station's main building. The tower on top of the building was manned by a lookout twenty-four hours a day to watch over coastal waters for vessels in distress. *Mariners' Museum, Newport News, Virginia*

with two toilets. Water for the toilets came from the town's water supply. The cookhouse, building no. 3, was also made of wood with pine planking. In a 1916 report, it was indicated to be in poor condition. Water for cooking came from the water tank and food was prepared on a wood-burning cookstove. A hired cook prepared the food or one of the surfmen was assigned to cook. Building no. 4—the stable, feed house, and cart house—was a two-hundred-square-foot wooden structure divided into three spaces. Half the building was used for cart storage. The other two rooms were of equal size and were used as a stable for the station's large draft horse and for its feed. The Virginia Beach station's horse was always named John or Old John. The two-story original station building, designated building no. 5, was primarily used for storage.[26]

The station's two rescue boats, a Beebe-McLellan self-bailing power surfboat and a Beebe-McLellan self-bailing surfboat, were kept on wagons in the boat room, ready for launching. The wagons had wide wheels for traveling over sand. The beds of the wagons had rollers to get the boats on and off. It took the station crew five minutes to get a boat to the water for launching. A dinghy and other life-saving equipment were also kept in the boat room. The life-saving equipment included an apparatus cart with a Lyle gun and breeches buoy. The station had a twenty-one-foot drill post with a platform and crossarm to practice firing a line to a grounded ship and rigging for a breeches buoy rescue. The American flag flew from a tall flag tower on the south side of the station. The tower had a fifty-foot main pole with a twenty-five-foot galvanized topmast. A flag flying from the seventy-five-foot pole was visible to a ship more than ten miles offshore.[27]

When war was declared, the station was under the command of forty-one-year-old Keeper Thomas J. Barnes. He had been keeper since July 1914. Although Barnes was a warrant officer in the U.S. Coast Guard, keepers were usually referred to as "captain" by their crews and the local population. John W. Sparrow, a petty officer, was no. 1 surfman and second in command to Barnes. The remaining four surfmen were nonrated enlisted men. They were Joseph W. Barco, Leonard T. Garrison, Little J. Henley, and Thomas W. Simmons.[28]

LIGHTHOUSE SERVICE

On 6 April 1917, the Lighthouse Service was also mobilized and transferred to the U.S. Navy by executive order of the president. The service, which would later become a part of the U.S. Coast Guard, had 46 steamers that were used as lighthouse tenders, 4 light vessels, and 21 lighthouses manned and administered by its 1,132 personnel. Secretary of the Navy Daniels said that the Lighthouse Service "vessels did a large part of the work on the defensive entrance areas, laid mines, and were employed as patrols. . . . The larger lighthouse tenders were almost continuously in the danger-zone and were employed to buoy the wrecks of torpedoed ships." The lighthouses and lightships were also important as coastal lookouts.[29]

In August 1918, Germany's newest and largest cruiser submarine, the

U-140, was deployed to American waters. Fregattenkapitän Waldemar Kophamel commanded the U-boat. It carried thirty-five torpedoes and four thousand rounds of ammunition for its two deck guns—a six-inch forward and a four-inch aft. U-140 surfaced on the afternoon of 6 August 1918 within sight of Light House Service Lightship No. 71, on station at Diamond Shoals off Cape Hatteras. The submarine's target was the 3,024-ton steamship *Merak*, which was carrying a load of coal from Newport News to Chile. Sailing under a U.S. flag, *Merak* was a Dutch vessel that had been taken over by the Shipping Board. The submarine opened fire on the freighter with its deck guns, firing thirty rounds at *Merak*. An officer on *Merak* said, "We took up a zigzag course toward shore, hoping to escape. We hit on the shoals, however, and as shells from the submarine were falling all about us, some striking the bridge, we abandoned the ship, taking to the boats. With the freighter hard aground and her crew fleeing in two life boats, Kophamel turned his attention to the 124-foot lightship."[30]

It was 2:50 PM when the crew of the lightship first heard gunfire to the north northeast and saw U-140 on the surface one and a half miles away. First Mate Walter L. Barnett was mate-in-charge while the lightship's master, Capt. Charles Swanburg, was ashore on liberty. Forty-seven-year-old Barnett ordered the two navy radiomen assigned to the lightship to begin transmitting a warning to all shipping in the area, giving them the position of the submarine. U-140 opened fire on the lightship at 3:25 PM. Six shots were fired from a distance of two miles. Barnett said, "Her first shot took away our wireless, but the next five were aimed wide and missed us." At 3:30 PM, Barnett gave orders to abandon the lightship. He said,

We had been painting our yawl-boat that morning and she was hauled up on the davits with nothing inside but a small canvas sail. I called for her oars and had the yawl lowered to the water. . . . Within ten minutes we had the whaleboat overboard and the twelve of us shoved off from No. 71. We had seven oars, six fourteen-footers for rowing and a sixteen-foot sweep oar. I put the large oar over the stern and six of the crew grabbed the others and we headed west'ard as fast as we could row. Roberts, the chief engineer, had left his false teeth behind and none of us had saved anything but the clothes we had on our backs, but nobody seemed bothered too much about that.[31]

U-140 broke off its attack on the lightship when it saw another merchant ship to the north. The submarine fired fourteen rounds from its six-inch gun at the ship, but the fire was ineffective and the ship escaped. The U-boat returned to the lightship and fired seven rounds into its hull, sending it to the bottom. The lightship's crew—mate-in-charge, engineer, cook, three firemen, four seamen, and two navy radio operators—was five miles away when they saw the lightship go down. The submarine next returned to *Merak* and planted bombs to destroy it. After dealing with the freighter, the U-boat approached *Merak*'s boats and ordered them to stop. An officer in one of the boats said, "The submarine came to within a boat's length and an officer speaking perfect English asked our name, nationality, cargo, and where we were from. He did not seem to place us and told one of his men to go below and get Lloyd's register. Examining the book, he said, 'Oh! Your ship was a Hollander, was it?' He then asked if we had a sail and on being told we did, he advised us to hoist it, with the remark that the coast was only ten miles to the westward." Later reports indicated that the lightship's warnings had enabled twenty-five vessels to take shelter in Lookout Bight, thus escaping possible attack by the U-boat. Barnett and his crew sighted land just before dark and landed their boat through the surf at 9:30 PM near the Cape Hatteras wireless station. From the wireless station, Barnett reported the details of U-140's attack to naval headquarters.[32]

CHAPTER 8

PORT SECURITY

The Coast Guard has continued to enforce the rules and regulations in the matter of anchorages and movements of vessels in New York Harbor, in the St. Mary's River, and certain other navigable waters. Under the Espionage Act, jurisdiction over these matters passed from the War Department to the Treasury Department, and the Secretary of Treasury has designated certain Coast Guard officers as captains of the ports of New York, Philadelphia, Norfolk, and Sault Ste. Marie [in Michigan].

—*ANNUAL REPORT OF THE SECRETARY OF THE NAVY,* 1918

EXPLOSION AT THE AMMUNITION PLANT

T. A. Gillespie and Company, in Morgan City, New Jersey, was the largest shell-loading plant in the United States and probably the largest in the world. Railroad tracks ran through the twenty-three-hundred-acre plant site, and piers on Cheesequake Creek were used for loading barges that transported the ammunition to ships waiting in New York harbor. Every day hundreds of railroad cars arrived at the plant. The cars were loaded with empty artillery shell casings shipped from plants in Pennsylvania and with TNT to fill the shells shipped from chemical works in New Jersey.

Capt. Godfrey L. Carden, USCG, was the controversial commander of the U.S. Coast Guard's New York division. As captain of the port of New York, Carden reported directly to the secretary of the treasury even though the service operated as part of the U.S. Navy. After the explosion at Halifax, Nova Scotia, on 6 December 1917, Carden imposed stringent and unpopular regulations on the loading and movement of ammunition ships in New York harbor.
U.S. Coast Guard Museum

Construction of the plant's 200-by-75-foot wooden frame and corrugated iron buildings began in March 1918; production started four months later. By October 1918, thousands of workers at the plant were producing thirty-two thousand artillery shells a day. The shells ranged from three inches to sixteen inches.[1]

On the evening of 4 October 1918, Master's Mate K. S. McCann, USCG, was on watch at the Perth Amboy, New Jersey, office of the first company of the New York division. Temporarily in command of the company, McCann was standing at the office window when he saw the sky light up in the direction of South Amboy. In his official report, he wrote, "I called the Coast Guard cutter *Patrol* on the telephone, Keeper Lester D. Seymour answering immediately. Asking him about the fire, he said that it was in the vicinity of Cheesequake Creek." Fearing the fire was near the Gillespie shell loading plant, McCann immediately sounded assembly and mustered the company's seventy-five men. "I was just taking off the receiver to call the Coast Guard watchmen on the [plant's ammunition] barges at Cheesequake Creek," he said, "when the first explosion came rocking every house for miles around and throwing people off their feet, and breaking every window in the city." McCann quickly commandeered four civilian cars and began shuttling his men to the scene of the explosion. He then called Capt. Godfrey L. Carden, commander of the New York division, at 7:45 PM and told him about the explosion. He reported that men from his company were en route to the plant and to Cheesequake Creek, where barges loaded with artillery shells were moored.[2]

When Carden heard that more explosions were probable, he ordered 1st Lt. Joseph E. Stika to proceed immediately to Perth Amboy and take charge of the U.S. Coast Guard's response. Stika and thirty coast guardsmen from the New York barge office boarded the ninety-four-foot harbor cutter *Calumet* and got under way for Perth Amboy. Carden also ordered 3d Lt. Frederick J. Birkett to go from Staten Island to Perth Amboy to help with the situation. The commanding officer of the New York division's sixth company at Sandy Hook, New Jersey, sent Cadet R. T. McElligott and thirty-five men aboard the harbor cutter *Richard Caswell* to the scene of the explosion and fire. Carden said, "In all, about two hundred men were made available to Stika, comprising details from the First, Third, and Sixth Companies." Men of the first company arrived at the plant first—even before the police or ambulances. Plant managers told the warrant officers in charge of the coast guard party that most of their guards ran from the plant after the first explosion. With no one of authority at the scene, the coast guardsmen took charge and proceeded to establish a guard around the compound to keep civilians, who were gathering at the gates, back. Then they went to work, bringing out the wounded and dead. They stopped vehicles on the street and used them to take the injured to the hospital for treatment. With fire raging out of control in the buildings and the expectation of more explosions, the coast guardsmen began clearing families out of the nearby houses. When Ordinary Seaman C. F. Bennett returned from the Gillespie plant, he reported to McCann that the warrant officers needed more men.

McCann called Carden and asked for reinforcements. The local hospital also called McCann, requesting coast guard assistance to control the hundreds of people crowding the hospital looking for relatives who worked at the plant. He sent his last four men to the hospital. McCann said, "Ordinary Seaman C. F. Bennett, driving the first auto which I commandeered, made trip after trip through barrages of steel, having a door blown off the car, a headlight and the roof of the car riddled, and narrowly escaped death time and again in carrying out the wounded and dead and bringing in the guards. After driving the car steadily until 1:00 AM, October 5th, he relieved a driver of an ambulance, running it steadily until 9:00 AM, October 6." When Bennett was relieved, he was ordered to go to bed.[3]

Two warrant officers from coastal rescue stations were on temporary duty with the first company when the disaster occurred. Keeper Jesse G. Hearon took a detachment of men and established security at the Cheesequake gate of the plant. He also assigned men to guard the ammunition magazines there. His men carried wounded workers out of the rubble and Hearon sent them to the hospital. His men kept onlookers back from the plant because blasts were continuing to occur. Coast guardsmen were repeatedly barraged with flying steel. When explosions erupted, the men took shelter behind trees, on the ground, and behind anything that would provide protection from the shrapnel. While Hearon was talking to a worker from the plant, the man was struck down by a piece of flying steel and killed. Boatswain (Life-saving) William S. Bennett took another detachment of men and secured the west gate. His men performed the same duties as the men at the Cheesequake gate. Bennett and his party found themselves in the most dangerous location. They were at the part of the plant where the fire caused artillery shells to burst, sending shards of steel flying through the air. A shell fragment hit a Gillespie employee, who was with the coast guardsmen, in the head over the temple, knocking him to the ground. Bennett was standing nearby when the man was struck and seriously injured.[4]

McCann ordered two warrant officers—Gunner Charles L. Wright and Signal Quartermaster A. V. Horton—to take the harbor cutter *Bluffer* and proceed up Cheesequake Creek to where ammunition barges were moored at the plant. He told them to remove the watchmen and attempt to tow the barges, loaded with explosives, away from the fire. He then called the cutter *Patrol* and gave Keeper Seymour the same order. The two small cutters made their way to the plant through the darkness. After the cutters advanced through the drawbridges, a projectile—driven by the force of another blast—lodged itself between the bridgehead and the electrical cables. The unexploded projectile cut off electrical power to the bridges, trapping *Patrol* and *Bluffer* in the creek. The cutters continued to the barges and picked up the watchmen. Then the crews stood by, ready to render whatever assistance they could. Fortunately, the wind was blowing in the other direction and did not spread the flames to the ammunition barges or the storage buildings at the pier. Six barges were loaded with 16,288 cases of 75-mm shells and 6,944 coastal artillery shells. Another two barges were empty. Although the barges were not immediately threatened by the fire, shell fragments from the explosions continued to rain down on them.[5]

Because the closed drawbridge prevented the harbor cutters from leaving the creek, Warrant Officers Wright and Horton set out on foot toward the fire to render assistance. They first came to a freight train loaded with TNT that was in the path of the approaching flames. The warrant officers ran over to a group of plant workers gathered at the fence. Among the men, they found an engineer who could operate the locomotive and persuaded him to return with them. While they were backing the train away from the fire, the engineer was cut down by a piece of flying steel. He was seriously injured, but not killed. Once the train was moved a safe distance from the blaze, Wright and Norton continued on to the ruins of building no. 6-1-1, where the fire apparently had started. The building was used to melt and blend TNT and other explosives. The result, anitol, was then ladled into the shells. While they were at the building, overheated projectiles continued exploding in the area. McCann said, "They [Wright and Horton] proceeded to the scene of the last explosion and dug out fourteen bodies, all beyond recognition, the legs and feet pulling off the bodies when they would lift them to the stretchers. The above men are recommended for special commendation." McCann sent Ship's Writer R. E. Messner to the plant to form a detachment of guards to keep people back from the scene of the fire and clear of the area where glass continued to fall and downed trolley wires were a hazard. The guards were armed and instructed to prevent looting in the disaster area.[6]

At 10:00 PM Lieutenant Birkett received orders to proceed immediately from Staten Island to the scene of the fire. He took a train to Tottenville, Staten Island, and then got a ride in a car to the Gillespie plant. When he arrived, men of the first company were guarding the entrances. When Birkett took charge from the warrant officers, he was informed that a detachment of soldiers, under the command of Capt. Watson, USA, was attempting to relieve coast guardsmen at the gates. Birkett declined Watson's offer of relief, saying that every man would be needed in the emergency, but he welcomed the army's assistance. Coast guardsmen were positioned in the most dangerous locations at the plant, guarding the magazine and the entrances. Fragments from exploding shells and other pieces of debris continued to fall all about them. Birkett said, "So perilous were their positions, that I gave Gunner Wright instructions to withdraw his men, when the case seemed hopeless."[7]

Lieutenant Stika reached the plant at 1:30 AM on 5 October and relieved Birkett as the senior officer on scene. Birkett left to return to his duty station at Staten Island. When he got outside the plant, he joined the flood of thousands of people who were ordered to leave their homes in South Amboy and the surrounding area because of the danger of more explosions. Birkett said, "All my way down to Perth Amboy, I observed miles and miles of refugees; in fact, they extended in one continuous line from the outer limits of South Amboy to Perth Amboy. The great majority were walking. Countless children, invalids, and aged people were being carried by the stronger ones and with the interspersed farm wagons loaded with families' earthly possessions, it made one think of what takes place in the advance of a victorious army."

Cadet McElligott arrived at the Gillespie plant with forty-five coast guardsmen from the sixth company at 1:45 AM. They were assigned to duty in and around the danger zone. In his official report, Stika wrote, "Unit 6-2-1 could not be saved as had been hoped, so the firemen were forced to withdraw and our guards in the vicinity were given orders to drop back out of the danger zone. A detail of 6th Company men, under Keeper William I. Purnell and of the 5th Company, under Acting Gunner Katzbauer, were left at a safe distance in reserve. This detail supplied guards for automobiles commandeered on the Keyport Road for the purpose of carrying the sick and wounded and the women and children to Keyport." McElligott and Bugler [William F.] Cavaston went with Stika to set up a headquarters in a small bungalow just inside the gate of the plant.[8]

At 2:10 AM building no. 6-2-1 exploded, followed by building no. 6-3-1 exploding. The explosions were so violent that they rattled windows in Manhattan twenty miles away. Stika said, "The force of these explosions wrecked my headquarters, to the extent that only a minor explosion was needed to bring the walls to the ground. We retired to the main gate, using telephone poles for shelter during the heavy blasts." Building no. 6-4-1 blew up at 3:15 AM. During the conflagration and explosions, the cutters *Patrol* and *Bluffer* stayed with the ammunition barges in Cheesequake Creek. The fumes from the explosions and burning chemicals were overpowering. Stika commented that "whole shells, which sometimes exploded, were falling dangerously close and for that reason, the rain of shrapnel fragments and sparks was increasing. . . . the crews stood by their vessels in spite of the fact that the seven barges loaded with explosives as well as twenty odd freight cars on the wharf, not ten feet away from them, also loaded with explosives, were almost certain to ignite and blow up any moment. Keepers Harry F. Smith and Seymour were on the *Patrol* and Coxswain Neehan and Oiler Blundon on the *Bluffer*."[9]

The sixty-nine-foot harbor cutter *Takana*, moored at lower Manhattan, received orders to proceed to Perth Amboy. The cutter, capable of making ten knots, got under way and arrived at Perth Amboy at midnight. The cutter's 5 October 1917 log said, "At 12:15 AM observed a large fire at the powder works, but heard no explosions. At 12:30 AM left Perth Amboy and stood down to the Great Beds Light and was standing by there when at 2:00 AM heard a great explosion about two miles distant followed by a second explosion in about thirty minutes—then a continuous roar of explosions with heavy explosions at frequent intervals. Debris and shells falling around the vessel." *Takana* remained in the area and rendered assistance to vessels damaged by the blasts. It pushed a sinking barge onto the mud flats.[10]

Capt. Harry G. Hamlet, USCG, commanded the Third Naval District's Section Base No. 6, a large training and operating base at Bensonhurst, New York. He received orders from the commandant of the district at 10:00 PM on 4 October 1918 to send a relief party to Morgan City. Hamlet assembled a detachment of twenty-five navy enlisted men, together with warrant officers and a surgeon, under the command of Ens. G. M. McKay, USN. Hamlet stopped boiler repair work on the navy ship USS *Joyance* and had it prepare to get under way. The navy relief party departed aboard *Joyance* at 12:15 AM. They arrived on the scene two hours later and went to work.[11]

Seventy-five coast guardsmen from the second company, under the command of Cadet Louis W. Perkins, arrived at the plant at 9:00 AM. They immediately relieved the exhausted men of the first, fifth, and sixth companies, who had worked throughout the night. At 10:00 AM, there was a thunderous explosion when the main storage warehouse blew up. This raised fears that the main magazine, containing eighty thousand pounds of TNT, would explode. The earlier explosions, involving only a fraction of that amount, were felt as far as forty miles away, breaking windows in lower Manhattan. The order was given to complete the evacuation of South Amboy and the surrounding towns. Stika said, "Up to this time, there appeared to be no danger in South and Perth Amboy, outside of flying splintered glass and wood from windows, bricks from chimneys, and plaster from ceilings. Most of the inhabitants had gone, but the stragglers were gathered up and sent away. The crews of *Bluffer* and *Patrol* were notified, but they decided to remain." Authorities in New York City halted traffic through the tunnels to Manhattan, fearing the explosion of forty tons of TNT would cause the tunnels to collapse. People were ordered out of tall buildings and off the streets where falling glass would be a danger. After the danger to the main magazine passed, Stika received orders from Carden at 1:00 PM on 5 October that the U.S. Coast Guard was to be relieved by the U.S. Army. By the time the coast guardsmen left their positions, the explosions and fire that had leveled the plant were dying down. Only four buildings survived the flames spread by a southwest wind. They were new buildings erected on the other side of the creek and not yet in use. Coast guardsmen of the second, fifth, and sixth companies turned over their positions to the army and withdrew, returning to their headquarters. The *New York Times* said, "Several thousand soldiers were on guard, holding the danger zone for miles on every side of the explosion in a state of siege, guarding all roads and aiding in the work of salvage and rescue at the plant." At 2:00 PM on 5 October the crew of the harbor cutter *Bluffer* managed to get the vessel under the locked drawbridges and returned to their headquarters.[12]

Stika and some men from the first company remained in the area. They guarded the barges in Cheesequake Creek and, at the request of the Red Cross, operated ambulances, set up first aid stations, and prepared housing for refugees. On 7 October a fire reflashed in a pile of debris and unexploded shells. T. A. Gillespie and Company asked for volunteers to go into the plant and move nine rail cars loaded with TNT. The cars were on a siding near the fire. Stika took Asst. Master-at-Arms Francis M. Noble as brakeman, Ordinary Seaman John Grimes as engineer, and Bugler William F. Cavaston as fireman, and went into the plant to get steam up on an engine. Acting Coxswain Harry J. Ryan, Seaman William V. Walsh, and two army soldiers successfully repaired, strengthened, and replaced missing pieces of track so the locomotive could move the cars away from the danger. McCann said, "Lieutenant Stika and bugler W. F. Cavaston have been continuously [three and a half days] on the go with only about twelve hours sleep, since reporting at about 1:30 AM Saturday morning and are pretty well worn out. [Sick] Bayman N. L. Harmon of the 2nd Company has also been continuously on the go rendering first aid in Red Cross ambulances, getting his first sleep today." On the afternoon of 7 October the U.S. Army's Ordnance Department issued a statement, saying that all danger at the plant had passed.[13]

At the recommendation of the commander of the New York division and the commodore commandant of the U.S. Coast Guard, the U.S. Navy's Board of Awards approved the award of the Navy Cross to twelve coast guardsmen for their "conspicuous act of heroism and devotion to duty on the occasion of the disaster at the T. A. Gillespie Shell Loading Plant." They were 1st Lt. Joseph E. Stika, 3d Lt. Frederick J. Birkett, Boatswain (Life-saving) William S. Bennett, Keeper Jesse G. Hearon, Gunner Charles L. Wright, Master-at-Arms Francis M. Noble, Signal Quartermaster A. V. Horton, Acting Coxswain Harry J. Ryan, Seaman William V. Walsh, Ordinary Seaman C. F. Bennett, Ordinary Seaman John Grimes, and Bugler William F. Cavaston.[14]

ESPIONAGE ACT

Another ammunition explosion had occurred in the New York area before the United States entered the war. A munitions terminal was located at Black Tom Island, New Jersey, a small island on the New Jersey side of the Hudson River, just across from Manhattan. It was a primary staging point for ammunition being shipped to the war in Europe. At 2:00 AM on 31 July 1916 the explosion erupted, shattering windows in offices and apartments in New York City. Property damage was estimated at $22 million. While sabotage was suspected, nothing was ever proven. Investigators believed the initial explosion occurred on one of the loaded barges. The incident was important because it drew attention to the vulnerability of America's ports and caused congressional leaders to propose legislation to protect facilities from sabotage.

Less than a year later, the Espionage Act of 1917 was signed by the president on 15 June 1917. The act shifted responsibility for the adoption and enforcement of regulations governing the anchorage and movement of vessels in specific navigable waters from the Army Corps of Engineers to the Treasury Department. While the U.S. Coast Guard had already been transferred to the U.S. Navy, Secretary of the Treasury William G. McAdoo was still responsible for assigning specific coast guard officers the responsibility for security at four critical ports: New York, Sault Ste. Marie (Great Lakes), Hampton Roads (Norfolk), and Philadelphia. The officers were also designated as supervisors of anchorages at the ports where they were assigned. While the coast guard officers continued to serve with the navy, they were directly responsible to the Secretary McAdoo for port duties. The term "Captain of the Port" was first used for this position at the port of New York.[15]

Overseas, Capt. Detlef F. A. de Otte, USCG, was ordered by the commander of the U.S. forces in France to duty as supervisor of the harbor of Brest, France. His duties included providing for the coaling, oiling, and watering of vessels; transporting troops to and from ships; supervising tugs, boats, and barges; assigning anchorages; and coordinating port matters with French authorities. From April 1918 to February 1919, this duty involved providing services for 370 warships, transports, and supply vessels with a total tonnage of 6,814,725, at the port of Brest. The transports carried over 700,000 troops and the supply ships delivered more than 257,000 tons of cargo.[16]

GREAT LAKES

The security of the vital waterway connecting the internal commerce of the Great Lakes to the Atlantic Ocean was a major concern during World War I. Secretary of the Navy Josephus Daniels, in his annual report, said, "The tremendous amount of shipping that passes from upper to the lower lakes, through the canals, locks and waterways of the St. Mary's River system, make it most important to carefully regulate this traffic." The channels and locks were vulnerable to accidents and a potential target for sabotage. Blocking the channels, particularly the dredged channels of the Detroit, St. Clair, and St. Mary's Rivers, would have had a major impact on the transport of essential war materials. To protect the waterways, Capt. Edward S. Addison, in command of the harbor cutter *Mackinac*, was ordered to increase and extend his patrol of the St. Mary's River. Captain de Otte was in command of the cruising cutter *Morrill* at Detroit when the United States entered the war. He was ordered to commence patrolling the Detroit River. Responsibilities for these patrols were later taken over by the commandants of the Great Lakes naval districts. De Otte and Addison were designated navy section commanders and provided with navy patrol boats, personnel, and equipment for use in securing the waterways. Addison was also designated captain of the port of Sault Ste. Marie. The American locks at Sault Ste. Marie were the responsibility of the army engineers and were guarded by soldiers throughout the war. During the entire war period, there were no serious incidents involving shipping on the Great Lakes waterways.[17]

New York Harbor

When war was declared, the responsibility for the operation of cruising cutters and harbor cutters was transferred from the coast guard division commanders to navy district commandants, leaving division commanders with little to oversee. The New York division was an exception, however. While army engineers had jurisdiction over the movement of vessels in the harbor, Sr. Capt. Horace B. West, commander of the New York division, was the supervisor of anchorages and had ongoing responsibilities in the increasingly busy port. When responsibility for the port of New York was transferred to the secretary of the treasury, by passage of the Espionage Act of 1917, Secretary McAdoo designated West as captain of the port of New York. On 12 December 1917, Capt. Godfrey L.

Carden relieved West as New York division commander and captain of the port. Carden, who had commanded the cruising cutter *Mohawk*—headquartered at New York—was familiar with conditions at the harbor and with the shipping community. As division commander, Carden reported to the commandant of the Third Naval District, but as captain of the port he was directly responsible to Secretary McAdoo. Even before the United States declared war on Germany, New York had been the primary port for the exportation of explosives to Europe.

After the devastating explosion at Halifax in December 1917, there were grave concerns for the safety of the densely populated areas surrounding New York harbor. Because of the serious potential for a catastrophic explosion, extraordinary precautions were implemented by Carden. This need for caution was fully supported by local authorities. To protect and secure the port, Carden requested, and received, an increasing number of resources. The additional personnel and vessels—cutters, tugs from the army engineers, and vessels from the navy—quickly made the New York division the largest command in the U.S. Coast Guard. An anchorage board—made up of army, navy, and coast guard officers—was established in New York. The board recommended locations for anchorages at the port of New York and surrounding waters to Secretary of the Treasury McAdoo. When approved, the recommendations were incorporated into the harbor regulations. Carden, as captain of the port, was responsible for enforcing the harbor regulations, as well as special regulations regarding the handling of explosives. New York's Gravesend Bay became a major explosive loading anchorage. Carden's enforcement of the stringent regulations was frequently controversial. His strict adherence to the regulations antagonized and alienated civilian and military personnel alike. Ship masters complained that his interpretation of ship movement regulations were arbitrary. In September 1918, the U.S. Navy unsuccessfully recommended to the Treasury Department that Carden be relieved as captain of the port. While Carden's methods were controversial, the success of his operation was unquestionable. There were no serious explosions in New York harbor at any time during the war. Secretary of the Navy Daniels commented about the huge volumes of ammunition and high explosives that were shipped through the port of New York. He said, "The safe handling and loading of such vast quantities of the explosives in this congested harbor have demanded and received the most careful and untiring efforts. This work has been largely entrusted to officers and men of the Coast Guard and it is gratifying to note that there has not been a single accident or mishap connected with this vast undertaking, either in the harbor of New York or on other navigable waters, during the period of the war."[18]

Personnel

Additional commissioned officers, warrant officers, and enlisted men were assigned to the New York division until it was increased to 7 companies of 154 men each. This was in addition to the crews of the harbor vessels. In his annual report, Secretary Daniels said, "Owing to the great increase in the shipment of ammunition and other explosives, it has been necessary to increase the number of personnel attached to the New York Division, Coast Guard, to a total of 1,446 officers and enlisted men, in order to provide a force sufficient to enable the captain of the port to properly supervise and safeguard the transfer and loading of explosives in that harbor." Men of the division not assigned to cutters were billeted and fed at the various locations where companies were headquartered. These locations were the barge office; ferry buildings; the Manhattan up-town armory; Perth Amboy, New Jersey; Sandy Hook, New Jersey; and Gravesend Bay, New York. Detachments of coast guardsmen were transported by harbor cutters to ships coming into New York harbor to load or offload explosives. Onboard, they controlled access to the ships, allowing only authorized persons to board. They also monitored the handling of the explosives to ensure that regulations were strictly followed.[19]

Vessels

Seven cutters—two cruising cutters and five harbor cutters—were assigned to the New York division before the U.S. Coast Guard was transferred to the U.S. Navy on 6 April 1917. The cruising cutter *Seneca* was deployed to Europe and the cruising cutter *Mohawk* was assigned to patrol the approaches to New York. Prior to the war, the harbor cutters *Manhattan*, *Guide*, and *Patrol* were assigned to anchorage patrol in New

The U.S. Coast Guard's New York division mustered with weapons and field gear. With 7 harbor cutters and 1,446 men, the division was the service's largest operational command during World War I. *U.S. Coast Guard Museum*

York harbor. The harbor cutters *Hudson* and *Calumet* were used for customs boardings. After passage of the Espionage Act of 1917, the cutters were assigned port security duties and worked directly for the captain of the port. Built in 1873, *Manhattan* was the U.S. Coast Guard's oldest cutter still in service. The 102-foot, 145-ton cutter continued anchorage patrol duties until 1 December 1917, when it left New York for the last time. *Manhattan* sailed to the coast guard depot at Arundel Cove, Maryland, and was taken out of commission. *Patrol* was a newly constructed, wooden-hulled harbor cutter. Sixty-nine feet in length and displacing twenty-three tons, the cutter was commanded by a warrant officer and manned by a crew of eight. *Patrol* was assigned to patrol harbor anchorages where freighters were loaded with munitions for shipment overseas. The seventy-foot, forty-one-ton harbor cutter *Guide*, with a crew of seven, also patrolled explosive loading anchorages. In addition to patrol duties, the cutters transported guards to the ships and barges that were loading ammunition at the port of New York.[20]

When war was first declared, the 179-ton, 96-foot *Hudson* and 194-

ton, 96-foot *Wissahickon* were outfitted for minesweeping. They were used to sweep for mines in Ambrose Channel at the entrance to the port of New York. In July 1917, *Hudson* was assigned to a new headquarters at New Haven, Connecticut. Operating out of New Haven, *Hudson* patrolled the submarine net at Port Jefferson, New York. *Wissahickon* was transferred to New London, Connecticut, in August 1917, and given the mission of patrolling Long Island Sound in the vicinity of Cornfield Lightship. When the U.S. Coast Guard was given greater responsibility for port security, the two cutters were ordered back to New York for duty with the expanding New York division. *Hudson* arrived at New York on 1 December and *Wissahickon* on 11 December 1917. The cutters were used at the port to patrol explosive loading anchorages and ferry personnel to and from ammunition ships and barges.[21]

The iron-hulled *Calumet* was out of commission, undergoing repairs at the coast guard depot on 6 April. The 170-ton, 94-foot cutter was placed back into commission on 28 August. Master's Mate F. T. Ford relieved 1st Lt. Ralph W. Dempwolf as commanding officer before the cutter sailed for New York on 4 September. Upon arrival at the port, Ford reported to the coast guard division commander and the twenty-three-year-old cutter was assigned guard duty in the anchorage areas. In the early part of 1918, the 104-foot, 350-ton New York harbor tug *Emma Kate Ross* was taken over by the U.S. Coast Guard for the use by the captain of the port. Boatswain S. B. Natwig, a warrant officer was placed in command. The tug performed various duties in protecting the safety of the harbor, including patrolling anchorages and supervising the loading of explosives.[22]

On 1 March 1918, the cruising cutter *Onondaga* sailed from Wilmington, North Carolina, with two former army engineer vessels, *Richard Caswell* and *Coquet*, in tow. The two small vessels were turned over to the U.S. Coast Guard for use by the New York division. *Onondaga* arrived at New York on 10 March and the vessels were turned over to the division commander. After repairs were made on the harbor vessels, they were commissioned as coast guard cutters. They were commanded by coast guard warrant officers and performed essentially the same duties as the division's other harbor cutters, working in the ammunition loading anchorages until after the end of the war. *Coquet* was also used as a guard boat at the Raritan arsenal. Even after the signing of the armistice, the harbor cutters were required to continue working in the ammunition anchorages for several months, because munitions were still being shipped under the provisions of existing contracts. *Richard Caswell* and *Coquet* were later returned to the War Department.[23]

The harbor cutter *Mackinac* was ordered on 10 November 1917 to sail from its headquarters at Sault Ste. Marie for duty at the port of New York. First Lt. Eben Barker relieved 1st Lt. E. S. Addison as *Mackinac*'s commanding officer before the cutter sailed on 29 November. After getting under way, ice conditions in the river forced the cutter and its crew of eleven to winter over at Quebec City, Canada. On 11 May 1918, the 110-foot, 241-ton cutter, now under the command of 1st Lt. Lloyd T. Chalker, departed Quebec and arrived at New York harbor on 25 May. *Mackinac* was assigned guard duty at the explosive loading anchorages. The U.S. Navy also made the 69-foot USS *Takana* available to the U.S. Coast Guard for duty at New York. The 68-ton, 10-knot harbor vessel was manned with a coast guard crew, with Keeper F. W. Downs, a warrant officer, in command. *Takana* worked for the captain of the port of New York, patrolling ammunition loading anchorages until several months after the end of the war when it was returned to naval authorities.[24]

HAMPTON ROADS, VIRGINIA

Extensive naval facilities were concentrated at Hampton Roads and the port of Norfolk was a major naval operating base. Activities in the waters of the Chesapeake Bay were closely controlled by the U.S. Navy. Capt. James G. Ballinger, USCG, reported to the commandant of the Fifth Naval District for duty and as Secretary of the Treasury McAdoo's representative at Hampton Roads on 17 August. A Naval Academy graduate, Ballinger worked closely with the U.S. Navy in carrying out his duties. He used coast guard harbor cutters to guard the ammunition loading anchorages and to patrol the port's other anchorages. Because of the navy's heavy involvement in the area, Ballinger had much less autonomy in carrying out his duties than did Carden in the port of New York.[25]

PHILADELPHIA, PENNSYLVANIA

Philadelphia was the fourth port area where a coast guard captain of the port was assigned by Secretary of the Treasury McAdoo. Capt. Francis S. Van Boskerck, USCG, was assigned to the commandant of the Fourth Naval District at Philadelphia, on 6 April 1917. When he reported, he was assigned duty as the aide for information and censor. He was later assigned the additional duty of captain of the port of Philadelphia. The 149-ton, 88-foot harbor cutter *Gutherie* was the only coast guard vessel available at Philadelphia for Van Boskerck's use. *Gutherie* carried out captain of the port duties at Philadelphia from 2 December 1917 until 10 March 1918 when the cutter was reassigned to submarine net patrol duty at the entrance to Delaware Bay. Van Boskerck later gained notoriety when he wrote the words and music to the U.S. Coast Guard's song, "Semper Paratus," after the war.[26]

From its initial responsibilities in World War I, port security became a major coast guard mission, with personnel and resources used to secure and protect ports and waterways in the United States and overseas.

CHAPTER 9

SEIZED GERMAN SHIPS
AND TROOP TRANSPORTS

At the end of our first year of service as the Cruiser and Transportation Force, I desire to congratulate the Flag Officers, Captains, officers and enlisted men on the excellent work they have accomplished. . . . The preparation in three months of the fleet of ex-German ships, which for three years were idle, and worse, at their piers, was in itself a great accomplishment. The organization supply and sanitation of types of ships entirely new to the Navy, for a service overseas of the most vital importance, not only to this country but to our allies, presented serious and complex problems, which have all been happily solved by your intelligence, zeal and ability.

—REAR ADM. ALBERT GLEAVES, USN, CRUISER AND TRANSPORT FORCE, ATLANTIC FLEET, 5 JUNE 1918

KD-III

Three interned German ships were in the harbor at San Juan, Puerto Rico, on 6 April 1917. Two of the vessels, the Hamburg-American Line's 356-foot, 3,537-ton steamship *Odenwald* and its 900-ton tender *Präsident* were German merchant ships. The third ship, however, was different. The British collier *Farn* had been captured by the German navy raider *Karlsruhe*. The 400-foot *Farn*, renamed *KD-III* by the Germans, was loaded with Welsh coal. When the ship was captured, *Karlsruhe*'s captain remanned the ship with German navy officers and enlisted men from his crew. He used the British ship as a tender to support the raider's operations. When *KD-III* developed engine problems in January 1915, it was forced to enter San Juan harbor in distress, where it was interned by the U.S. government. Captain Lubinus, his officers, and men were permitted to remain living aboard *KD-III*; soldiers from the Puerto Rican infantry regiment at San Juan were assigned as guards on board the ship.[1]

At noon on 6 April 1917, the day war was declared, a sergeant from the Puerto Rican guard aboard *KD-III* came to the U.S. Coast Guard's 190-foot cruising cutter *Itasca*. He told the cutter's commanding officer, Capt. William V. E. Jacobs, that he had heard suspicious noises coming from *KD-III*'s lower engine room. He said that when he went to check, he found the steel doors to the engine room locked. When he requested the key from the German captain, he was given an evasive answer about the key being unavailable. Jacobs immediately suspected the Germans were attempting to scuttle the ship in the harbor. He sent his senior engineer officer, 1st Lt. (Eng.) Carl M. Green, with an armed party to *KD-III*. His instructions to Green were: "Prevent the sinking by all means in your power."[2]

Green selected a boarding party and loaded tools into the cutter's boat. En route to *KD-III*, Green stopped at the interned German ship *Präsident* and picked up 2d Lt. John P. Gray, USCG. Gray was in charge of the custody crew aboard *Präsident*; its German crew had been removed. When Green reached *KD-III*, he recalled, "I found the engineroom locked and the fireroom entrance secured by wire. I sent a man to the German officers to get the key to the engineroom door." When Green heard the sound of rushing water coming from beyond the door, he ordered his men to break it down. Just then, Lubinus and Chief Engineer Auer arrived with the keys and opened the door. Green reported, "Stepping inside on the upper gallery of the engineroom, I was about to go below when the German captain put his arm in front of me and said, 'You cannot go below. The ladders are all taken down.'" Green said to Lubinus, "You have opened the valves, have you?" The German shrugged his shoulders and replied, "We have done what we could."[3]

When Green and his engineers climbed down on the main engine to the lower engine room, they found a stream of water, sixteen inches in diameter, spouting fifteen feet in the air. "Water could also be heard rushing in at the after end of the long shaft alley," Green said, "and also into the fireroom." The Germans had removed the covers to the sea valves. The water was already two feet over the fire room deck plates and the ship was beginning to list to port. Green sent his men into the shaft alley and the fire room to attempt to slow the flow from the open sea valves. "Meanwhile," he said, "my men in the engineroom attempted to stop up the main sea valve, the cover of which had also been removed, by using canvas and mats. But, all these attempts met with failure and the water was gaining rapidly." While Green was below, Gray rounded up the German crew and held them on the forecastle under armed guard.[4]

The Germans were very thorough in their attempt to sabotage the ship. They removed the covers, discs, and stems from all the sea valves. They opened the manifolds that allowed the seawater to run into all the compartments and double bottoms of the ship. Parts to the valves were thrown into the water in the bilges so they could not be seen or retrieved. All the ladders in the engine room and fire room had been unbolted and removed. The Germans used sledgehammers to smash the steam pumps so they could not be used to dewater the ship. Green said, "My men finally succeeded in stopping the flow of water through the valves in the shaft alley and the fireroom." He had them close off the spaces by securing the watertight doors. But efforts to stop the flooding from the main sea valve were still unsuccessful and the water level was rising steadily. The ship was now beginning to list dangerously to port. Green said, "A boat was hurriedly sent to *Itasca* for materials and tools and a blank flange of wood was made to fit between the studs remaining on the large sea valve. After some difficulty, the nuts to these studs were found and some square washers." The engineers finally succeeded in forcing the wooded disc between the studs on the sea valve, holding it in place with a wooden beam secured across it. Green said, "This work was carried on under water, the men laboring in the roaring stream, which pouring into the ship, threatened her destruction. Many trials were made before the disc was forced into place. Finally, nuts and washers were gotten onto the studs, after many failures, and the inrush of water was stopped, save for a few slight leaks."[5]

By the time the flooding was under control, the ship had fourteen feet of water in its after hold and eighteen feet forward. Commercial divers were used to plug the outboard strainer openings in the hull and the steam pumps and sea valves were repaired. Green supervised all the work on the ship. After *KD-III* was pumped out, it was put back into operating condition and sailed from San Juan under its own power. The ship and its cargo of coal were used to support the war effort. Green and his men risked their lives to save the ship, which was in danger of capsizing at any minute. The men worked continuously in waist- to neck-deep water and had to dive below the surface to force the flange into place. Secretary of the Navy Josephus Daniels recognized the heroic efforts of *Itasca's* salvage team and sent a special letter of commendation to Green, entitling him to wear a silver star on his Victory Medal. Captain Lubinus, Lieutenant Hentschel, and Engineer Auer were arrested on charges of conspiracy to sink *KD-III* in the navigable waters of San Juan harbor.[6]

SHIPS SEIZED

When America declared war on Germany, there were fifty-seven German merchant ships interned at twenty-one ports in the United States. Another thirty-four were at island ports under U.S. control; twenty-three German ships were at three ports in the Philippines. The largest concentration of interned ships was at the port of New York. Twenty-seven ships were at moorings in Manhattan, Brooklyn, and Staten Island and at the New Jersey ports of Hoboken and Newark. When the 206-foot cruising cutter *Mohawk* reported to the commandant of the Third Naval District for duty on 6 April 1917 it was assigned to keep watch on five of the interned ships. Capt. James G. Ballinger, the cutter's commanding officer, was ordered to prevent the ships from escaping to sea. Second Lt. John S. Baylis, USCG, was assigned to the U.S. Coast Guard's New York division and was directly involved in the seizure of German ships at the port. In his report to the division commander, he said,

> At 3:45 AM, today received information from the Collector of Customs to report to him at Pier No. 2 Hamburg-American Line, Hoboken. The troops [from the U.S. Army's Twenty-Second Division] came aboard immediately, 165 in all, and about 4:00 AM, left Governors Island. The [harbor cutter]

Guide with 30 soldiers was directed to report to Mr. Lamb at 135th Street and, after landing the troops, to return to the battery. The *Manhattan*, *Hudson*, and *Wissahickon* proceeded to Pier No. 2, Hamburg-American Line, Hoboken, where I conferred with Mr. Dudley Field Malone, Collector of Customs, about 5:00 AM, for further instructions.[7]

Just after 5:00 AM Malone received a telephone call from Washington, D.C., directing him to carry out his orders to seize the German ships in the harbor. In a matter of minutes, under a gray sky with drizzling rain, authorities executed prearranged plans. Malone boarded the 54,282-ton German cruise liner *Vaterland* and told Capt. Hans Ruser, commodore of the Hamburg-American Line fleet, "We have come to take possession of the ships and we are going to do it with the least possible inconvenience." Ruser replied, "We are ready." Baylis reported that he and Captain Roselle, USA, in command of the troops, boarded eighteen of the German ships with Collector Malone while he seized them in the name of the U.S. government. Baylis said, "The crews of these vessels were directed to pack their personal effects and assemble on the docks as soon as possible. . . . At 10:00 AM, all the Germans, about 1080 in all, were aboard the Immigration steamers and the troops were put aboard the cutters." The cutters escorted the steamers to Ellis Island where the Germans were landed at 10:30 AM. The cutters then took the soldiers back to Governors Island. The harbor cutters *Manhattan* and *Wissahickon* were used to take German seamen found on the ships of other countries into custody. A total of 303 officers and 1,100 crewmen from the ships were placed under guard and taken to quarters on Ellis Island in New York harbor. After the ship captains were given receipts for their ships at the customs house, the cutter *Hudson* took them from Battery Park to Ellis Island. At the Immigration Bureau's facility, the German officers were housed in one of the hospitals and ate in the small dining hall that was used for second class passengers. The twenty-eight German ship captains had their meals at the restaurant on the island. Ruser was lodged in special quarters. The crews of the German ships slept in one of the main detention buildings and were fed at the large dining hall.[8]

Armed parties from coast guard cutters at the various American ports accompanied U.S. marshals when they boarded the German ships. Most

ships had been interned at the ports since 1914 when the hostilities in
Europe began. Seizing the ships was American's first overt action against
Germany. Coast guardsmen from the cruising cutters *Algonquin* and *Apache*
helped seize three German steamships—11,440-ton *Bulgaria*, 10,058-ton
Rhein, and 9,835-ton *Necker*—interned at Baltimore. Armed parties, each
with an officer in charge, boarded the ships with U.S. marshals. The
German crews offered no resistance and the vessels were taken without
incident. After the crews were removed, customs officials found kegs of
gunpowder and a quantity of rifles and pistols locked in a room behind the
pilothouse on *Necker*. Gunpowder was also found on *Bulgaria*. The chief
engineer of *Rhein* told officials that the crew had disabled the ship's engines
six months earlier. At Philadelphia the 88-foot harbor cutter *Gutherie*
assisted customs officials with the seizure of the 6,026-ton *Prinz Oskar* and
the 6,600-ton *Rahetia*. Marines from the Philadelphia Navy Yard boarded
the ships and rounded up the German crews. *Gutherie* transported the
Germans to the immigration station at Gloucester, New Jersey.[9]

The 188-foot cruising cutter *Seminole* was headquartered at Wilmington,
North Carolina, when the United States entered the war. The cutter's
first duty was to assist marshals in seizing two interned Hamburg-
American Line ships at the port. Two armed parties were selected from
the cutter's complement of eight officers and fifty-nine enlisted men. The
first party, under the command of 2d Lt. Michael J. Ryan, boarded and
seized the 339-foot steamship *Nicaria*, while a second armed party, with
3d Lt. Edward H. Smith in command, boarded and took control of the
4,494-ton steamship *Kiel*. As with the other interned vessels, the German
crews had sabotaged the machinery. To disable the engines, German
crews cut the heads off the bolts holding the equipment together so it
would fly apart the first time it was used. Boilers were ruined by dry firing. Armed guards from the cutter were left aboard each ship. At
Savannah, Georgia, the 63-foot harbor cutter *Tybee* was commanded by
2d Lt. Sidney B. Orne. He and his crew of five assisted customs officials
and marshals with the seizure of the 2,974-ton German steamship
Hohenfelde. The cruising cutter *Tallapoosa* was ordered from its headquarters at Mobile, Alabama, to Tampa, Florida, the day after war was
declared. When the 166-foot, 912-ton cutter arrived at Tampa, its commanding officer, 1st Lt. James F. Hottel reported to Capt. Charles

Satterlee aboard the cruising cutter *Tampa* for orders. On 9 April 1917, armed parties from the two cutters boarded and seized the Austrian merchant ship *Borneo*, anchored in Hillsboro Bay. At Pensacola, Florida, crewmen from the 67-foot harbor cutter *Penrose* helped U.S. marshals remove the crew of the Austrian merchant ship *Lucia* on 9 April. To the west, at the port of New Orleans, the 171-foot cruising cutter *Comanche* and the 92-foot harbor cutter *Davey* sent a combined armed party, consisting of four commissioned officers and twenty-five enlisted men, to assist U.S. marshals and customs agents in seizing two German ships, the 420-foot *Breslau* and the 329-foot *Andromeda*.[10]

The 110-foot, 240-ton harbor cutter *Golden Gate*, with a wartime complement of twenty-two, was headquartered at San Francisco. The cutter was used to board ships of different nationalities in San Francisco Bay. Germans serving as crewmen aboard the ships were taken into custody. In Washington State's Puget Sound, the wooden-hulled, gasoline-powered harbor cutter *Scout* was ordered from its homeport at Port Townsend, on the western side of the sound, to Eagle harbor where the 4,424-ton *Saxonia* and 2,164-ton *Steinbek* were interned. At 1:00 PM on 6 April 1917, the German merchant ships were boarded and their masters and portions of their crews were removed and taken to Seattle. The 61-foot *Scout*, a former customs service vessel, was sent back that afternoon to reboard *Saxonia* to determine if the German crew had sabotaged its machinery and boilers. When no damage was found, the cutter returned to Seattle. Crewmen aboard the seized German steamships were civilian merchant mariners and offered little resistance to the armed boarding parties. The crews, acting under orders from their government, however, had seriously damaged machinery and equipment on almost all the ships. When repaired, the seized German ships proved to be extremely valuable resources for the United States.[11]

TROOP LIFT

When the United States declared war on Germany, the country faced the daunting challenge of transporting American fighting men overseas. Early estimates indicated that as many as four hundred thousand American troops would be needed in Europe. These estimates quickly escalated. At a meeting of the Army Transportation Service at London in October 1917, assumptions were made on the number of American troops to be transported to France: one hundred thousand by October 1917; three hundred thousand by 1 March 1918; five hundred thousand by 15 May 1918; eight hundred thousand by 1 September 1918; one million by 1 December 1918; and two million by 1 December 1919. The actual number would prove to be even higher. The secretary of the navy said, "The idea of a United States overseas expeditionary force numbered by millions would have been generally regarded as a remote if not impossible contingency. Consequently, no extensive peace-time preparations had been made for such an undertaking." The United States had no ships capable of transporting such an enormous military expeditionary force. Although the United States had a flourishing coastal and inland shipping industry with trained officers and crews, the country's high-seas merchant marine was very small. Within the U.S. Navy, there was only a minimum troop lift capability: two troop transports for marines—*Henderson* and *Hancock*. The newly constructed 7,750-ton, 484-foot *Henderson* had just come off the ways at the Philadelphia Navy Yard and was still being fitted out. It was not commissioned until 24 May 1917. With a crew of 233 officers and men, the new transport was initially outfitted to carry twenty-five hundred troops. The second transport, *Hancock*, was about the same size as *Henderson*, but nearly thirty-nine years old and barely seaworthy. It could carry one thousand troops. The few transports the U.S. Army had were not suitable for transatlantic service.[12]

Rear Adm. Albert Gleaves, USN, was in command of Destroyer Force, Atlantic Fleet, with headquarters at Newport, Rhode Island. He was summoned to Washington on 23 May 1917 and informed by Secretary of the Navy Daniels that he would command the first expedition of four convoys that would transport troops and supplies to France. On 29 May Gleaves was officially designated commander of convoy operations in the Atlantic. Lacking suitable transports for the expedition, Gleaves had to find ships. He said, "It was necessary to commandeer such ocean-going vessels as could be found and alter them as quickly as possible for carrying troops." The U.S. Navy commandeered merchant ships and quickly armed and outfitted them. The ships had lookout stations, communications systems, and berthing for troops installed. Each of the four convoys was made up of troop or cargo ships, and was escorted by cruisers, destroyers, and auxiliaries.[13]

Gleaves delayed the expedition's departure from 8 June until 14 June so the convoys would arrive off the French coast when there was no moon. The oiler *Maumee* deployed from Boston a few days before the expedition departed to be in position to refuel the escorting destroyers in mid-ocean. The concept of underway refueling had been developed just before the war began. Gleaves returned to Washington for his final instructions on 4 June. When he was leaving, Daniels, said, "Admiral, you are going on the most important, the most difficult, and the most hazardous duty assigned to the Navy." The first three convoys of the expedition, designated Group I, II, and III, sailed from New York at two-hour intervals beginning at daybreak on 14 June 1917. The fourth convoy's departure was delayed for twenty-four hours, waiting for belated dispatches and stores. Convoy Group I consisted of four troopships and six escorts. The escorts included one armored cruiser, one auxiliary cruiser, three destroyers, and a converted yacht. The second and third convoys were each made up of three transports and five escorts. Convoy Group IV consisted of four cargo ships and seven escorts. An armored collier, loaded with coal, sailed as one of the escorts with Convoy Group III.[14]

Before the expedition departed, Gleaves issued instructions to all ships: "Every man has to be as familiar with them as with the Lord's Prayer." The reference to prayer, in relation to the convoys, was not an accident. The German Admiralty had boasted that its submarines would see that "not one American soldier will set foot in France." Gleaves's instructions to the convoys called for the use of maximum speed through the danger zone. Ships' guns were to be manned continuously, with constant communication between officers of the deck, lookouts, fire control watch, and gun crews. In addition to continuous zigzagging, the ships were completely darkened at night and radio use was minimal. Smoke from the ships' stacks was carefully controlled and nothing was thrown overboard lest it indicate the direction of the convoy's movement. A trained officer on the bridge of every ship was always ready to maneuver the ship to avoid torpedoes. Day and night signals were prearranged for maneuvering ships if a submarine was sighted, and rules were established for using guns and depth charges. The ships held abandon ship drills daily and watertight boundaries were kept set. The troops were assembled at abandoned ship stations, fully equipped and ready to leave the ship, at dusk and dawn—times most favored by submarines for attack. Troop transports were stationed in the center of the convoy groups and screened by the escorts.[15]

Reports from the British and French navies indicated the expedition would face the greatest danger of enemy submarine activity when the convoys reached longitude 20 degrees West and were within a five hundred mile radius of the Azores Islands. The first U-boat attack occurred on the night of 22 June when Convoy Group I passed north of the Azores. A lookout aboard *Seattle* spotted the phosphorescent wake of a submarine as it fired two torpedoes. Gun crews on the auxiliary cruiser *De Kalb*, formerly the German ship *Prinz Eitel Friedrich*, opened fire when they saw the wakes of the torpedoes. One torpedo passed ahead and one astern of *De Kalb*. After passing *De Kalb*, the torpedoes just missed the transport *Havana*. On signal, the convoy dispersed in the darkness, with ships of the right and left columns turning to starboard and port, respectively. The convoy reformed at daybreak and continued to France. Convoy Group II encountered two submarines at 11:50 AM on 26 June, one hundred miles from the French coast. An additional escort of six American destroyers had already joined the convoy. When the submarines were sighted, the destroyers turned toward them. The U-boats submerged and were not seen again. Convoy Group IV was attacked on 29 June. The freighter *Luckenback*, loaded with a cargo of ammunition and gasoline, managed to turn just in time to avoid being hit by a torpedo. Gun crews on the armed collier *Kanawha* gave a cheer when the torpedo passed clear of the freighter. The last of the ships of the first expedition arrived at the French port of Nazaire on 2 July 1917 without the loss of a single man. The Germans had been successfully misled as to the destination of the expedition. The U.S. naval attaché in Paris, Cdr. W. R. Sayles, had made plans as though the convoys were arriving at Brest, France, a port more suitable for handling large ships. Just before the expedition would have reached Brest, German submarines mined the harbor entrance. Instead of Brest, however, the ships of the expedition sailed to the smaller port of Nazaire, where the transports had to wait for high tide before they could enter the harbor. Facilities for offloading the ships was limited. The marine regiment embarked in the transports *Hancock*, *Henderson*, and the auxiliary cruiser *De Kalb* turned to and offloaded their own ships. After the expedition was completed, Gleaves observed, "In my mind a most important lesson taught by the voyage was that the transportation should be done entirely by the Navy, and I believe further that this was the unanimous opinion of all of the Army officers with whom I discussed the subject."[16]

To meet the need for sealift capability to support the war, the Emergency Fleet Corporation and the Shipping Board were created in the United States. The organizations were charged with building, equipping, and manning the merchant fleet that would be needed to transport troops and supplies. Gleaves said they "did their best, and indeed accomplished wonders in quickly building and equipping a vast merchant fleet; but in obtaining civilian crews to operate the ships, they were heavily handicapped by labor conditions and the lack of trained seamen." Faced with the inability to man the fleet of troop transports and supply ships it was assembling, the Shipping Board turned to the U.S. Navy for assistance. Unlike Britain, which drew upon its merchant fleet to provide seamen for its navy in time of war, the United States had to look to its navy to provide men to man its merchant ships. The ability of the U.S. Navy to successfully operate an enormous merchant fleet was a significant factor in the success of the United States during the war.[17]

Even before war was actually declared, an organization was evolving within the Navy Department to address issues of ships operating in the war zone. Faced with the threat of German submarines, the department in March 1917 established a policy of defensively arming merchant ships and provided navy gun crews. Navy personnel were assigned to 384 merchant ships. They manned guns and served as signalmen and radio operators aboard the ships. The U.S. Navy also had to face the issue of civilian crewmen manning navy auxiliaries, vessels that would be expected to operate with the fleet in the war zone. On 7 May 1917, the U.S. Navy began replacing civilian officers and crews on naval auxiliaries with navy personnel. In many cases, the change was accomplished by enrolling existing crews of qualified merchant officers and seamen into the U.S. Naval Reserve. The secretary of war and the secretary of the navy addressed the conversion of merchant ships to troop transports on 12 July 1917 in a joint letter to President Wilson: "The War and Navy Departments jointly recommend further that should it be found necessary to take over additional vessels for permanent employment as transports during the present war, vessels so taken over shall be commissioned in the Navy." The president approved the recommendation.[18]

The dividing line for authority in the operation of troop transports was at the dock. The U.S. Army supervised the docks in the embarkation and debarkation ports, transporting and loading the troops and cargo. The U.S. Navy was in charge afloat, manning, operating, and repairing the transports. The navy provided coal and provisions and routed convoys and their escorts. Operating a fleet of troop transports was a new undertaking for the navy; ships had to be obtained and officers and crews had to be assigned and trained. An infrastructure of docks, storehouses, lighters and tugs, coaling equipment, and repair facilities also had to be created, as well as an organization to administer it. The Naval Overseas Transportation Service (NOTS) was officially established on 9 January 1918. Seventy-two troop and cargo ships were assigned to the service. Branch offices for managing the fleet were established at major Atlantic coast ports. During the war, NOTS operated forty-two troop transports. After the armistice, the transport fleet was expanded to 149 ships, manned with 4,238 officers and 59,030 enlisted men.[19]

CONVOYS

Once the Naval Overseas Transportation Service had enough ships, transports were grouped into convoys of four to eight ships, all capable of making approximately the same speed. The convoys sailed at intervals of approximately eight days and were accompanied by an escort of cruisers and destroyers. Destroyers from Europe came out to meet the convoys and escort them through the waters where the submarine threat was the greatest. Convoys carrying troops were assigned more escorts than cargo convoys. In particularly dangerous waters, the number of escorts for transports could be ten times as high. Special routing was also used to protect transports. Troopships followed different routes than cargo convoys and their movement was planned to pass through the most dangerous submarine areas during darkness. An official explanation of the policy stated,

> As only fifteen percent of the vessels in Atlantic convoys carried troops, it
> became desirable, so far as practicable, to route troop transports in special

lanes through which cargo convoys did not pass. This greatly increased the safety of troop transports, as it practically forced submarines to concentrate their efforts in the areas through which cargo vessels [comprising 85 percent of the shipping] passed. If a German submarine took station in a troop transport lane, he might have remained for weeks without sighting a troop convoy. . . . If the submarines had known the positions of these troop lanes and had concentrated on them, they would have found a relatively small number of ships, all of high speed, hence difficult to attack. Furthermore, they would have been encountered a destroyer escort three times as strong as the escort protecting cargo ships.

Voyages from the United States to France averaged twelve days, except for the transports *Leviathan, Northern Pacific,* and *Great Northern,* which could steam at better than twenty knots. These three ships usually sailed together without escorts.[20]

After several conferences and frank discussions with transport captains, the commander of Cruiser and Transport Force, Atlantic Fleet published "Regulations and Doctrine Governing the Movement of Troop Convoys" on 1 January 1918. The extensive regulations contained 102 articles and covered all aspects of convoy operations. When steaming in waters where there was a high threat of submarine attack, convoys were directed to form a line abreast, not to exceed four ships. This formation was more difficult to attack; column formations were avoided in submarine waters. Where there was a danger from mines, ships traveled in a column. Transports in convoy maintained stations eight hundred yards apart. Lookouts were crucial as a defense against submarines. A surfaced submarine could be seen as far as the horizon. Submarines awash were visible for a distance of five miles. The periscope of a submerged submarine could be seen at no more than two miles. The wake of a torpedo was visible at two thousand yards in smooth water. In addition to posting lookouts aloft and on each side of the ships, twelve—and some times twenty-four—lookouts were assigned in the area of the bridge. Each man was given a specific sector of the compass, from 15 to 30 degrees, to continually watch. A lookout's watch was usually one hour and never more than two. Sunset and daybreak were the most critical time for lookouts. On one transport, a ship's officer tested one of the troops assigned to lookout duty by saying, "My good fellow, what are you looking for?" The Irish-American soldier, from the 69th Regiment of New York's National Guard, replied, "I'm looking for what I don't want to find, sir!"[21]

Guns on troop transports were manned at all times. Gun crews slept and ate their meals at their guns. They had to be able to reach their gun in fifteen seconds. Shelters for gun crews were built in the vicinity of the guns. The shelters were heated and had bunks or benches for their crews to lie on while fully clothed. Radiomen were always on watch to receive messages. No messages were transmitted, however, except in the case of extreme emergency involving the safety of the ship. No lights were allowed to show from the ship between sunset and sunrise. Flashlights were collected from the troops and locked up before the ship sailed. No one was allowed to smoke on deck after dark. No matches were permitted aboard ship. Cigarettes had to be lit from "smoking lamps" that were only lit at appropriate times. News of the war and information about events at home were copied from the radio. Transport commanding officers were advised that "press may be copied and distributed, after having been vised by the Senior Naval Officer in transport. Care will be exercised that no news of submarine activities is allowed to reach the troops."[22]

To attack a ship or convoy, a U-boat positioned itself ahead of and slightly on the bow. The submarine submerged and approached to the attack at a speed of six knots, while the convoy traveled at about twelve knots. The submarine captain had to estimate the target's course and speed to come up with a firing solution. The convoy's zigzagging made it difficult for U-boats to get into position and to make computations for firing torpedoes. Timing was essential for ships of the convoy; they synchronized their zigzag maneuvers and zigzag clocks were continually corrected. The senior officer present in a convoy set the zigzag time twice each day. Ships were not required to zigzag in fog or at night, except on moonlit nights when the visibility was greater than two miles. To confuse pursuing submarines, convoys changed course by a preset amount and at a preset time after total darkness. The base course was resumed, without signal, one hour later. When the wake of a torpedo was sighted, the sighting ship immediately fired a gun in the direction of the incoming torpedo to alert the rest of the convoy. Ships of the convoy turned ninety degrees from the direction of the submarine and dispersed at their best speed possible.[23]

The great German Cambria drive, which began on 21 March 1918, resulted in an urgent call for more American troops. To meet the requirement to deliver more troops across the ocean, the transports had to carry more men. Additional bunks were installed on the ships and some of the larger transports resorted to the "turn in and out" method; two soldiers were assigned to a single bunk and took turns sleeping. This method of "hot racking" increased the carrying capacity of ships by as much as 50 to 100 percent. Because of the discomfort to the troops, who needed to arrive in fighting condition, "turn in and out" was only used on the fastest ships. The fastest transports were also less likely to be attacked by submarines. The transport *Leviathan* increased the number of troops it could carry from seven thousand to fourteen thousand. To ship more troops, the army and navy also opened a second embarkation port at Hampton Roads, Virginia. On 1 April 1918 Rear Adm. Hilary P. Jones, USN, took command of the Newport News division of the transport force and Maj. Gen. Grote Hutchinson took command of terminal operations. Enough ships were initially provided to the division to transport forty thousand soldiers per month.[24]

A transport's turnaround time was another important factor in getting troops to the war zone as quickly as possible. Coaling and repair of transports when they returned to the United States was of the highest priority; crewmen and workers toiled around the clock to get the ships ready for the next voyage. When labor problems slowed the coaling of transports, the U.S. Army commandeered the coaling equipment and took over the operation. In April 1918, 117,000 American troops were shipped overseas. This number steadily increased to 306,000 in May 1918. Before May 1918, American troops were all carried on U.S. Navy transports. When the demand for forces to halt German advances became more urgent, the United States called on Britain to assist with troopships, by including its great ocean liners. The British ships, which had been used to transport Canadian troops, were ready for service. As a result, 196 British ships transported 456,854 Americans overseas. French and Italian ships were also employed in transporting American troops to Europe. From July 1918 until the signing of the armistice, American soldiers disembarked in

Europe at the rate of ten thousand a day. To protect the ships, the United States provided more than 80 percent of the convoy escorts.[25]

TROOP TRANSPORTS

To transport troops to and from Europe, the United States used five categories of ships in addition to battleships and cruisers. The categories were interned German ships, seized when war was declared; American passenger ships; U.S. Marine Corps transports; American cargo ships; and German passenger ships, allocated to return troops after the war. Thirty-three coast guard officers served aboard troop transports in all five categories. Because of their seagoing experience and maturity, six of these officers commanded transports, twelve served as executive officers, and seven were chief engineers.

Interned German Ships

German ships interned in the United States proved to be extremely valuable because the United States lacked ships suitable for carrying troops. When the ships were seized, all but a few had been sabotaged by their crews. The vessels were initially taken over by the Shipping Board. In July 1917 when repairs needed to get the ships ready for sea progressed too slowly, the work was taken over by the U.S. Navy. The overall deterioration to the hulls and machinery from sitting idle for years without any maintenance was as serious as the sabotage. The boilers suffered the most from the neglect and lack of maintenance. The idled ships were also filthy and had to be fumigated and disinfected before they could be used to transport troops. Repairing the main engines was the most important as well as the most difficult task. While sabotaging the ships, German crews used hydraulic jacks to break out large irregular pieces from engine cylinders. "But," Gleaves boasted, "they failed to take into account electric welding, to say nothing of Yankee ingenuity, perseverance and skill." Broken pieces found in the engine rooms were welded back into place. New castings were made to replace pieces thrown overboard. After the pieces and castings were assembled and welded, a special apparatus was used to machine the cylinders in place. Repair crews worked on the engines continuously, day and night, seven days a week.[26]

When repairs were completed, each cylinder and valve chest was hydrostatically tested. This improvised method of repair took only a few months and proved to be very successful. If new cylinders had to be made, the work would have taken more than a year. The U.S. Navy reported that there was not a single incident of welded repairs failing. Auxiliary machinery on the German ships was also sabotaged. Generators and pumps were smashed, steam line valves and engine throttle valves were dropped overboard, and essential machinery parts were missing. The German crews cut electrical wiring and interchanged electric leads. Making repairs was even more difficult because there were no plans or drawings for the German machinery and Germany repair parts were not available. Every replacement part had be manufactured. Missing parts had to be designed before they could be made. Regarding the sabotage, Gleaves said, "In some instances the Germans showed originality, but in the main the destruction was similar in all the ships." Because there was no dry dock in the United States large enough to handle *Leviathan*, the largest seized ship, a method was devised to use divers to clean away three years of fouling from the ship's bottom.[27]

The U.S. Navy assigned precommissioning details to the seized ships to assist with and supervise repairs. As repairs progressed, more members of the navy crews reported, to scrub, scrape, clean, and paint the ships. In addition to general maintenance and repairs, the German ships had to be modified and outfitted to serve as troop transports. Thousands of bunks, known as "standees," were installed. They were mounted on stanchions, as many as five high. The bunks were rigged so they could be triced up when not in use to provide more room. Facilities for bathing and sanitation for thousands of men were installed, along with galleys and mess decks to feed them. Sick bays were equipped with facilities to treat hundreds of patients. Lifeboats and cork life rafts in excess of the number need to accommodate embarked troops were put aboard the ships in case some could not be launched if the ship listed. The cork life rafts were elongated ovals, made in four or five different sizes. They were designed to fit one inside the other to conserve space. Deck guns, ammunition magazines, and ready boxes were also installed. Because of the shortage of coal in France and the limited number of colliers available, the decision was made that transports should be able to carry enough coal to make the round trip between America and Europe without refueling. To accomplish this, cargo holds were converted into bunkers. Work on *Leviathan*, the last seized German ship, was completed on 17 December 1917, and the ship sailed with a load of troops for Europe.[28]

Capt. (Eng.) Charles S. Root, USCG, reported aboard the Austrian liner *Martha Washington* as part of the precommissioning crew on 10 November 1917. Before the war, the ship had carried passengers between Trieste and New York. The 12,700-ton, 460-foot liner was interned at the port of Hoboken at the outset of the war. When the United States declared war on Austria, the ship was seized and turned over to the U.S. Navy. In a letter to headquarters, Root wrote,

> In November 1917, I was assigned to the USS *Martha Washington*, of the Cruiser and Transport Force as Engineer Officer and second in command, when senior department head. The ship's machinery was found [to be] badly damaged when taken over by the US Navy. The ship was made ready for sea, in seven weeks after take over, which is believed to be the record for quick fitting out. This ship never slowed down nor stopped at sea, due to accidents to the machinery, while in convoy and never failed to sail at [the] ordered time during the period of the war. She had six engagements with submarines off the French coast and carried eastward 22,311 troops.

Root served as the ship's executive officer until he was detached on 25 January 1919.[29]

Capt. Stephen S. Yeandle, USCG, was transferred from the cruiser *Albany*, where he served as navigator, on New Year's Eve 1918. He reported aboard the cruiser *Charleston* on 5 January 1919, and made five round trips between New York and Brest, returning troops to the United States. He served as first lieutenant aboard the 9,700-ton, 426-foot cruiser for seven months before he was ordered to report as executive officer aboard the 11,480-ton, 501-foot troop transport *Philippines*. After one voyage to France aboard *Philippines*—the former German ship *Bulgaria*—Yeandle was transferred to *Martha Washington* on 22 August 1919. He served as the ship's executive officer while it was on a special mission in the Mediterranean and Black Seas. *Martha Washington* returned to the United States after stopping at France to take on returning troops. Yeandle was detached from the ship on 18 November 1919.[30]

The German ship, *Prinz Eitel Friedrich*, put into Norfolk for repairs on 11 March 1915, and was interned by the United States when it failed to leave port in the time prescribed by international law. When war was declared, the 14,180-ton, 506-foot ship was seized. Renamed *De Kalb*, the ship was armed and fitted out as a navy auxiliary cruiser. Because the need to ship American soldiers overseas was great, the ship was converted to a troop transport. First Lt. James A. Alger, USCG, reported aboard *De Kalb* on 8 December 1917. Alger first served as a watch officer aboard the ship, which was manned by a crew of 534, before becoming the ship's executive officer. While Alger was assigned to the ship, eighty-six hundred troops were transported to Europe and ten thousand were returned to the United States after the armistice. Alger was detached from *De Kalb* on 23 April 1919.[31]

When Germany went to war in 1914, the passenger ship *Kronprinz Wilhelm* was commissioned in the German navy and fitted out as an auxiliary cruiser. Cruising in the Atlantic Ocean off South America, the ship sank 56,000 tons of allied shipping. A shortage of coal and an alarming amount of sickness aboard the ship forced the captain to intern the ship at a neutral port in the United States on 11 April 1915. When America declared war on Germany, the 663-foot, 23,500-ton ship was seized by the United States and renamed *Von Steuben*. The huge ship was refitted as a navy troop transport and was manned by a crew of 975 men. Originally rigged to carry twelve hundred troops, this number was later increased to twenty-nine hundred. *Von Steuben* sailed on its first transatlantic voyage on 31 October 1917. At 6:05 AM on the morning of 9 November, the ship collided with troop transport *Agamemnon*, another ship of the convoy. Both ships lost men overboard and *Von Steuben*'s bow was severely damaged. When the ship returned to the United States, 1st Lt. Howard E. Rideout, USCG, was transferred from the cruising cutter *Mohawk* and assigned to *Von Steuben* as navigator. He reported on 20 December 1917, the day the ship departed for the naval shipyard, at Balboa, Panama, to be repaired. Rideout served aboard *Von Steuben* until the end of the war; he was replaced as navigator by Capt. Lloyd T. Chalker, USCG, on 18 December 1918.[32]

In 1914 Germany fitted out the 663-foot, 23,500-ton passenger ship *Kronprinz Wilhelm* as an auxiliary cruiser. When the ship was forced to put into a U.S. port in 1915, it was interned and later seized when the United States declared war. Renamed *Von Steuben*, the vessel was refitted as a U.S. Navy troop transport. A silhouette of a destroyer was painted on the side of the ship as camouflage. *U.S. Naval Historical Center*

When pursued by a British cruiser in 1915, the German merchant steamship *Princess Alice* took shelter at the Philippines port of Cebu. The United States seized the ship when war was declared and sailed it, under charter of the Shipping Board, from Cebu to New York. Turned over to the navy at New York and converted into a troop transport, the ship was commissioned on 27 April 1917 and renamed *Princess Matoika*. With a draft of 20,500 tons and a length of 545 feet, it was one of the largest transports and could carry thirty-nine hundred troops. Capable of making 16 knots, the ship was armed with four 6-inch guns and manned by a crew of 449 men. Capt. Harold D. Hinckley, USCG, reported aboard *Princess Matoika* on 12 February 1919 as the ship's executive officer. One month later, he relieved Cdr. Theodore A. Kittinger, USN, as commanding officer. Capt. W. K. Scammell, USCG, was Hinckley's executive officer aboard the ship. Under Hinckley's command, the troop transport made seven round trips between New York and embarkation ports in France; it brought American troops home from Europe and repatriated German prisoners of war.[33]

After picking up troops in France on 15 May, Hinckley received a letter from Brig. Gen. S. D. Rockemback, USA, in charge of the port: "From information received from the Naval Port Officer and the Superintendent Army Transportation Service, it appears that the *Princess Matoika* was docked at this port at about 8:00 PM this date, received her passengers (105 officers and 3666 men), and sailed the same night on the next tide. Such efficient service merits the highest commendation and the Commanding General is pleased to be able to congratulate you and your officers and crew for the splendid efforts in supporting the policy of getting our troops home quickly." Capt. (Eng.) California C. McMillan reported aboard the 41,500-ton troop transport *America* on 28 April 1919 for duty as the engineer officer. The ship, formerly the German passenger ship *Amerika*, was the second largest of seized German vessels. Seized at Boston when war was declared, the ship was fitted out as a troop transport, capable of carrying four thousand soldiers. Its capacity was later expanded to seven thousand. McMillan served aboard *America* until 6 September 1919, when it was turned over to the Army Transportation Service.[34]

The 19,500-ton North German Lloyd Line's passenger ship *Barbarossa* took refuge in Hoboken, New Jersey, at the beginning of World War I. When the United States entered the war, the ship was seized. Renamed *Mercury*, the 544-foot ship was used to transport American troops. Capt. Raymond L. Jack, USCG, served as navigator and then executive officer aboard *Mercury* when it returned troops home after the war. *Hamburg* was another German liner that took refuge in the United States because of Britain's control of the seas. The ship was seized at New York when the United States declared war on Germany. The 545-foot liner was renamed *Powhatan* and manned with a crew of 533. The ship transported American forces to Europe. Capt. Thaddeus G. Crapster, USCG, took command of the transport after the war ended, when it was used to return soldiers to the United States. Five days after Christmas in 1918, Capt. (Temp.) Michael J. Ryan reported aboard the transport *Pocahontas* for duty as navigator. The 18,000-ton transport was formerly the German ship *Prinzess Irene*; it was seized by the United States when war was declared. After the ship was refitted, it was assigned to Cruiser and Transport Force. After

When the interned German passenger ship *Hamburg* was seized, it was renamed *Powhatan*. The 18,026-ton ship, painted with a "dazzle" camouflage scheme, was used to transport troops. Capt. Thaddeus G. Crapster, USCG, commanded *Powhatan* with a crew of 533 officers and men when the ship was used to return troops from Europe. *U.S. Naval Historical Center*

the armistice, the 16-knot ship, manned by a crew of 610, carried American troops returning from Europe. Ryan was promoted to executive officer on 2 April 1919 and served in that billet until the ship was decommissioned at Brooklyn on 7 November 1919. The German passenger ship *Rhein* took refuge at the port of Baltimore at the beginning of World War I. When the United States entered the war, the 17,875-ton ship was seized. The vessel was overhauled and fitted out at Norfolk and commissioned *Susquehanna*. Manned by a crew of 514, the ship transported troops to Europe and returned them after the war ended. Second Lt. (Temp.) John Trebes Jr. was assigned to the ship as navigator a month before it was decommissioned on 19 September 1919.[35]

Marine Corps and Charter Transports

The 8,500-ton, 466-foot *Hancock* was manned by the U.S. Navy and used to transport U.S. Marine Corps units. The ship, built in 1879, had a crew of 278 personnel and carried one thousand troops. *Hancock* had a speed of thirteen knots and was lightly armed with six 3-inch guns. The ship sailed as a cruiser transport with the first expedition bringing troops to France. *Hancock* was the flagship of Convoy Group IV, which departed 15 June 1917. After its transatlantic voyage, *Hancock* was limited to shorter runs to deliver troops and cargo to ports in the West Indies and the Gulf of Mexico. First Lt. Harold D. Hinckley, USCG, first served as gunnery officer and then as executive officer aboard the ship. The U.S. Marine Corps transport *Henderson* was commissioned on 24 May 1917 and arrived at New York on 12 June 1917. The transport sailed two days later with the first expedition to France; the ship carried fifteen hundred men and twenty-four mules. *Henderson* had a displacement of 7,750 tons and a length of 484 feet. It had a maximum speed of fourteen knots and was armed with eight 5-inch guns and two 3-inch guns. Originally outfitted to carry twenty-five hundred troops, *Henderson's* capacity was increased to thirty-four hundred to meet the need to deploy more soldiers. Capt. William H. Shea, USCG, served as executive officer aboard *Henderson* after the armistice, when it was used to bring troops home from Europe. The ship made eight trips, returning ten thousand personnel.[36]

The U.S. Navy chartered the Dutch steamship *Zeelandia* in March 1918, to meet the increased need for transporting troops overseas. The 11,500-ton, 440-foot ship was commissioned at New York on 3 April 1918 and retained its name. The fifteen-knot ship was mounted with four 6-inch guns and was manned by a crew of 322. Assigned to the Newport News division of the transport forces, *Zeelandia* made five voyages to France during the war. First Lt. James Pines was attached to the ship as a watch officer during the war. The ship had one verified encounter with a U-boat. The submarine surfaced at dusk on 31 August 1918, but was unable to attack because the convoy zigzagged and had a strong escort. *Zeelandia* was originally outfitted to carry eighteen hundred troops, but was later modified to carry three thousand soldiers.[37]

American Passenger and Cargo Ships

The Shipping Board acquired the west coast passenger steamship *Northern Pacific* for use as transport on 17 September 1917. The 9,708-ton, 526-foot ship was commissioned by the U.S. Navy. After being converted to carry troops, the transport sailed from San Francisco for New York on 7 March 1918. *Northern Pacific* was one of the fastest transports, capable of making twenty-three knots. Because of its speed, it usually crossed the Atlantic Ocean without escorts. The ship was armed with four 6-inch guns and had a complement of 371 officers and men. First Lt. William P. Kain, USCG, served as a deck watch officer aboard the ship during the war when it transported troops to France. After the armistice, Capt. (Eng.) California C. McMillan, USCG, reported aboard *Northern Pacific* as engineer officer on 12 April 1919. Two weeks later he was transferred to the transport *America* for duty as engineer officer. Capt. Frank L. Austin, USCG, reported aboard *Northern Pacific*, on 6 May 1919 while the ship was engaged in bringing American troops back to the United States. In a letter to headquarters, he reported, "I served as the executive officer of the transport *Northern Pacific*, making three round trips between Brest and New York. The log should show that we brought home about 2,000 soldiers on one trip and about 2,000 officers (officers only) on the last two trips." Austin took command of the ship after its last voyage and put the transport out of commission on 20 August 1919.[38]

The 10,910-ton, 440-foot passenger ship *Henry R. Mallory* was built for Mallory Lines in 1916. The ship was acquired by the U.S. Navy for use as a troop transport and commissioned on 17 April 1917. Capable of making fifteen knots, the ship carried two thousand troops and was armed with four 5-inch guns. Capt. Thomas M. Molloy, USCG, took command of the ship on 27 June 1919. Capt. Lucien J. Ker, USCG, was his engineer officer. Capt. (Eng.) Benjamin C. Thorn reported aboard the converted American cargo ship *Mexican* on 24 June 1919, for duty as executive officer. He served aboard the ship until its decommissioning on 2 August 1919. The War Department originally acquired the 19,550-ton, 488-foot *Mexican* on 10 December 1917 as an animal transport. The ship was refitted in December 1918 to carry returning American troops. The ship had a crew of 108 officers and men and carried twenty-five hundred troops. *Mexican* made five trips, bringing home a total of 12,386 men. Completing its last voyage on 23 July 1919, it was returned to its owners, the American Hawaiian Steamship Company, on 4 August.[39]

Another American Hawaiian Steamship Company vessel, *Texan*, was acquired by the Shipping Board on 18 March 1918. The former passenger ship was turned over to NOTS and refitted to carry general military supplies. The 18,000-ton, 484-foot ship had a speed of 13.5 knots and was minimally armed with one 5-inch gun and one 3-inch gun. The ship was used to carry cargo until 18 January 1919, when it was refitted as a transport and placed in service to return American troops from Europe. Capt. Aaron L. Gamble, USCG, reported aboard *Texan* for duty as commanding officer on 1 July 1919 at Norfolk. The ship was outfitted to carry twenty-two hundred troops. Gamble commanded the ship until it was decommissioned on 22 August 1919. Capt. (Eng.) Philip B. Eaton was relieved of command of Naval Air Station Chatham on 6 June 1919. After thirty days leave he was reassigned to sea duty as engineer officer aboard the 14,405-ton steamship *Kentuckian*. The ship was acquired by the U.S. Navy on 16 December 1918 and commissioned on 28 January 1919. The 415-foot ship was outfitted to handle cargo. It had two tall masts, one forward and one aft, rigged with cargo booms. *Kentuckian*'s bridge stood amidships on its rust-streaked hull, forward of its single tall smokestack. It carried general cargo to the remaining forces in France and brought home nineteen hundred American troops on each return trip. Completing its final cruise on 31 August 1919, *Kentuckian* was decommissioned two weeks later.[40]

German Passenger Ships Taken Over after the War

Nine former German passenger vessels were allocated to the United States by the peace conference to bring American troops home after the armistice. The ships were first inspected and then, with the exception of *Cleveland, Imperatur,* and *Santa Elana,* sailed by German crews to British ports. The ships were turned over to the U.S. Navy in Britain and then sailed to France to be fitted out as troop transports. All the German ships kept their original names, with the exception of *Cleveland. Cleveland,* which had been held at the Isle of Wight throughout the war, sailed from Cowes Roads to the shipyard at Liverpool, England, on 27 March 1919, and was renamed *Mobile* on 29 March. German crews sailed *Imperatur* and *Santa Elana* directly from Germany to Brest. After repairs and modifications were completed on the ships, they loaded troops and sailed for the United States. Seven German officers remained on each ship to assist

American crews in learning the ships. The Germans were repatriated after one trip.

The 30,400-ton, 678-foot, *Kaiserin Auguste Victoria* was placed in commission at Paullac, France, on 15 February 1919, and sailed from Brest with its first contingent of American troops on 8 April. The 17.5-knot ship arrived at New York on 19 April, and was further modified to carry more troops. When fitting out was complete, it could accommodate 5,500 troops. After being detached from the mine planter *Canandaigua* in March 1919, Capt. Philip W. Lauriat, USCG, reported to *Kaiserin Auguste Victoria* as the ship's executive officer. Capt. Clarence H. Dench, USCG, was assigned to the ship for duty at the end of June 1919, and served aboard the ship until it completed its final trip transporting returning troops to the United States on 21 August 1919. Capt. Louis L. Bennett, USCG, was detached from duty as navigator aboard the cruiser *Columbia* and transferred to *Kaiserin Auguste Victoria* while it was moored at New York. He served aboard the ship until it was decommissioned on 23 December 1919.[41]

After being fitted out as a troop transport in Britain, the 27,000-ton, 608-foot *Mobile* sailed to Brest on 6 April 1919 to embark its first contingent of troops. The ship had a complement of 573 men and accommodations for a maximum of fifty-two hundred troops. Capt. (Eng.) Harvey F. Johnson, USCG, was assigned to *Mobile* as engineer officer with the original crew; he reported on 26 March 1919. Johnson served aboard *Mobile* until the ship completed its final voyage. He was detached on 8 September 1919. While he was aboard the ship, *Mobile* returned 21,085 troops to the United States. The 585-foot German passenger ship *Graf Waldersee* was commissioned on 28 March 1919, and assigned to the Naval Overseas Transportation Service. The 25,000-ton ship sailed from Brest on it first trip to the United States on 30 March, carrying more than fifteen hundred troops. When the ship was completely outfitted, it was manned by a crew of 553 men and could carry forty-three hundred troops. Capt. Thomas M. Molloy, USCG, was detached from *Nokomis* on 8 April 1919 and assigned to duty with the initial crew aboard *Graf Waldersee*. On 19 September he was reassigned to the troop transport *Henry R. Mallory* as commanding officer. Capt. Clarence H. Dench, USCG, released from the naval hospital at Brooklyn, joined *Graf Waldersee* when it arrived in

New York, after its first crossing. In June 1919, Dench was reassigned to the troop transport *Kaiserin Auguste Victoria*.[42]

Cap Finisterre's German crew delivered the ship to Southend, England, where it was commissioned a U.S. Navy ship in April 1919. The 14,457-ton, 560-foot ship departed the next day for Brest. Manned by a crew of 450 and capable of carrying thirty-eight hundred troops, *Cap Finisterre* made three crossings to New York. On its two return trips to France, the ship transported replacement troops for the occupation army. Capt. William T. Stromberg, USCG, was assigned as navigator aboard the ship. *Cap Finisterre* completed its third and last trip to New York on 17 August 1919, and was decommissioned on 25 November 1919. The former German passenger ship *Patricia* was turned over to the United States on 26 March 1919, and commissioned by the U.S. Navy two days later. The 12,500-ton, 560-foot ship departed on its first run from Brest to New York on 30 March 1919. Capt. (Eng.) G. R. O'Connor, USCG, was assigned to engineering duty aboard the ship. *Patricia* had accommodations for twenty-nine hundred troops and was manned by a crew of 569. The 13.5-knot ship made four transatlantic crossings, returning nearly eighty-nine hundred troops to the United States. *Patricia* was decommissioned on 13 September 1919 and turned over to Great Britain.[43]

LIFE ABOARD TRANSPORTS

Initially, the U.S. Army attempted to keep the movement of troops overseas secret. No civilians were allowed in the embarkation area and, once aboard the transports, the troops were kept hidden below decks until the ships were clear of the harbor. This attempt at secrecy allowed no farewells, thus demoralizing the troops and their families. Also, the movement of thousands of troops through populated areas to huge transport ships moored at New York's busy harbor could hardly be kept secret. Maj. Gen. David C. Shanks, in charge of the troop embarkation, succeeded in getting the secrecy policy changed. Thereafter, flags flew and bands played patriotic music as the transports left for Europe. In high spirits, the troops crowded the decks and proudly waved to family members who had come to see them off. When a ship was ready to receive troops, gangways were opened. To facilitate loading, access to the embarkation area was restricted; no civilians were allowed on the piers. The young women of the Red Cross were the only exception and they were not allowed to talk to the troops. A navy officer waited on the ship at the end of each gangway. As the soldiers came aboard, they were each handed a card with printed instructions. The card concisely told the trooper where he would eat, sleep, the location of his abandon ship station, and the rules he must obey aboard the ship. The soldiers were marched aboard in a continuous line. Sailors led groups of soldiers to their berthing compartment and told them how to find the bunk indicated on their card. Each man's lifejacket was attached to his bunk. Transports had a lifeboat and life raft capacity 10 percent above the number of troops that could be carried. There was also an excess of cork and kapok life belts and lifejackets. To avoid congestion in the compartments, soldiers were instructed to immediately climb into their bunk and stay there until the compartment was completely filled. On most ships the soldiers kept their rifles and gear with them and used their own blankets or sleeping bags. Once the compartment was filled, the men learned the rules and routes for getting to washrooms, mess decks, and abandon ship stations. Using this procedure, thousands of troops were embarked and absorbed into the ship's routine in one short hour.[44]

While the troops were being oriented, the transport's executive officer met with the commanding officer of the troops and his assistants to explain their duties while aboard the ship. The U.S. Army's duties were divided into five details: sentry, guard, police, general, and mess. On *Princess Matoika*, there were thirty sentry posts that controlled troop movements about the ship. They were manned by a detail of ninety privates under the command of four officers of the guard, four sergeants of the guard, and two corporals of the guard. The guard detail required seventy-two officers, sergeants, and corporals. An officer was always on duty at each hatch and a sergeant or corporal was on duty in every troop compartment and every mess room. The police detail kept order among the troops, restricting smoking and policing and cleaning of latrines and washrooms. The general detail required 147 men, including 15 plumbers and 8 carpenters. The detail did general repair work around the ship, handled garbage and rubbish, and provided men for deck work parties. Mess detail required 150 men. In addition to butchers, bakers, and cooks, the

The 545-foot transport *Princess Matoika* was formerly the German steamship *Prinzess Alice*. Troops embarked in the transports were fed only two meals a day and ate standing up. Because of the threat of submarine attack, the men slept in their life preservers and mustered at abandoned ship stations at sunrise and sunset, the most likely times for U-boat attacks. *Mariners' Museum, Newport News, Virginia*

detail included store breakers, messmen, ushers, and vegetable peelers. Details were assigned and posts were manned; work began immediately.[45]

Because German submarines operated off the coast of the United States, the first abandon ship drill, or the "drowning drill" as the troops called it, was held before the ship cleared the harbor, and were held daily thereafter. Soldiers learned to go quickly and silently to their stations, both during the day and in the total darkness of night. Army personnel took no part in preparations for abandoning ship. Troops stood fast in their compartments, letting the navy crew get to their stations to lower boats and rafts, until they were ordered to their abandon ship stations. Army buglers were posted at the hatches to sound assembly. The abandon ship evolution was divided into four parts: stop ship and lower boats; lower rafts, when boats are clear; army disembark; and navy disembark.[46]

Troop transports were divided into forward and aft for berthing troops. Separate mess decks and latrines were provided for men berthing forward and men berthing aft. Each transport was inspected by the ship's executive officer and an army officer every day at 10:00 AM. On board transports, troops were only given two meals a day. The two meals were large, however, and contained a full day's ration. Bread was baked aboard the ships at the rate of roughly one loaf per man per day. When conditions permitted, cold sandwiches and coffee were also served late in the day. Troops did their physical exercising while waiting for their morning meal. The first relay began eating breakfast in the troop mess halls at 7:30 AM. Dinner call was sounded at 3:45 PM. Each relay of troops was given twenty minutes to eat, from the time they entered the mess deck until the time they exited. The troops used their own mess gear. They entered a door on one side, were served their food cafeteria style, and moved to tables suspended from the overhead. They ate standing up. The troops left by a door on the other side of the ship and cleaned their mess gear in troughs. No food was allowed to be taken from the mess deck. The transport's navy officers and enlisted men messed separately from the army. They ate in their own quarters, using folding mess tables and benches. They ate in one seating when possible.[47]

Sunset was the most likely time for a submarine to attack. All hands were called to quarters one half hour before sundown. Each man wore his lifejacket and carried a full canteen of water. Army personnel were restricted to certain areas of the ship: their berthing and mess compartments; latrines, showers, and washrooms; and in certain areas above decks. Troops were allowed to smoke on deck and in the mess rooms during the day. No tobacco use was allowed in the berthing area. The troops slept in stacked bunks that were three, four, or five high depending on the space available. Bunks were twenty-eight inches wide and six foot seven inches long; the men alternated sleeping head forward and head aft. The standard spacing between bunks was twenty-two inches and no mattresses were used. The navy crew slept in hammocks, which were stowed during the day. They slept and messed in the same compartment. The ships carried adequate fresh water for drinking and washing. Their tanks carried not less than five gallons per man per day for a twelve-day crossing. Transports also had sick bay accommodations for the troops. They generally had two sick bay bunks for every one hundred men aboard. Sick bays were equipped with an examining room, an operating room, and three isolation wards; there were nine isolation bunks for every thousand troops. The threat of an infectious disease aboard a troop transport was a grave concern. Hoses were rigged fore and aft, and saltwater soap was provided for the troops to bathe on deck. Barber shops were provided for ships' crews, with a chair for every 250 crew members.[48]

RECREATION

The ships had athletic and entertainment officers and recreation committees to organize programs to entertain the troops during the passages. Boxing matches were probably the most popular events. The navy transports had their own boxers in different weight categories. Navy boxers challenged competitors from the embarked army troops to three-round matches. *Princess Matoika*'s newspaper, *The Wigwam*, described one venue: "Before a capacity audience that occupied every available inch on the forward well deck, every foot of loading boom, every inch of ventilator pipe, gobs and doughboys this afternoon slashed their way through nine boxing bouts and one wrestling match, during which there was not one dull minute." Of the four interservice bouts that day, the army won two and the navy won two. Tug of war competitions were also popular, pitting army against navy and officers against enlisted men. Five-man teams from both services also competed in trap shooting from *Princess Matoika*'s fantail while the ship was under way.[49]

The ships had their own bands to entertain the troops as well as sailors. Army bands making the voyages also performed. Talented transport crew members and performers from among the embarked troops put on performances during the crossings. It was not unusual to find some exceptional talent among the thousands of men. YMCA Theatrical Workers, aboard for passage, were much appreciated. Two such performers, Hazel Morn and Clara Howard, appeared twice during a *Princess Matoika* voyage. Miss Moran was assisted by one of the ship's company in performing the sketch, "Don't Shake That Shimmy Here." The ship's paper reported, "Miss Howard, who put over several popular numbers in her own inimitable manner, also proved to the boys that she could shake the shimmy to perfection. Her clever imitation of Charlie Chaplin would make Charlie blush with shame." The 123rd Machine-gun Battalion, embarked on the transport *Siboney*, contained a number of talented actors. They presented "Mary's Ankle," a Broadway play, on the ship's quarterdeck. Presented twice, every available space was occupied for the performances, despite a drizzling rain.[50]

Moving pictures were shown below decks during the war and above decks on trips after the armistice. Educational activities were also provided for the troops and the crews. French officers aboard some of the ships gave lessons in practical French for soldiers en route to Europe. One engineer officer was such a good teacher that his class on the rudiments of practical marine engineering was well attended by enthusiastic students. The transports were also proud of the newspapers they published while the troops were embarked. Forty-five hundred copies of the *Siboney Signal* were published daily aboard the transport *Siboney*. Profits from the ship's canteen paid for the cost of materials to publish the paper. The ship's chaplain was the editor-in-chief. Transport newspapers contained navigation information about the voyage, including distances traveled and the change of time zones. News received on the ship's radio about the war and events at home were the most popular feature. Several papers contained human interest columns about happenings on the ship and reported the antics of well-known troopers or crew members. Drawings and original poems were solicited and published. Most ships had welfare workers aboard, including representative from the Youngmans Christian Association, the Knights of Columbus, and the Jewish Welfare Board. These representatives willingly helped out with the entertainment and welfare programs on the ships.[51]

Bringing the Troops Home

After the armistice, there was tremendous pressure in the United States to "get the boys home." Transport ships took on coal in the United States for the entire round trip to speed up turnarounds and get the troops home faster. The average round trip took approximately thirty-eight days. At the end of November 1919, the Transport Fleet, Atlantic Fleet had a total of thirty-eight troop transports. Another twenty-four U.S. Navy battleships and cruisers were pressed into service transporting returning troops. British, French, Italian, Dutch, Spanish, and Scandinavian ships were also used for the returning troop lift. The Italians used seven Austrian ships that were turned over to them as part of the armistice agreement. Ships flying the U.S. flag were used to transport more than 75 percent of the returning American forces. Every ship leaving a French port en route to the United States carried returnees. Ships sailed from Le Havre, Brest, St. Nazaire, Bordeaux, and Marseilles. Passengers included 132 French wives; the women had married navy personnel while they were stationed in France. The return troop lift took half the time it took to get the forces to Europe.[52]

CHAPTER IO

DUTY ON SHORE

In the early part of the war, Coast Guard officers were not requested for assignment to naval vessels, but a considerable number were assigned to naval duty on shore thereby making naval officers available for sea duty. Among the more important assignments of Coast Guard officers to naval duty were chiefs of staff, aids for information, section commanders, district naval force commanders, and commanding officers and assistants at naval reserve training camps and air stations. Several officers, mostly engineers, were assigned to duty in bureaus of the Navy Department and in navy yards. . . . In the latter part of the war, several Coast Guard officers performed important duty in conjunction with Naval Overseas Transportation Service and with Ship Routing Offices.

— CDR. CHARLES E. JOHNSTON, USCG, COAST GUARD HEADQUARTERS,
  OCTOBER 1919

NAVAL DISTRICTS

To respond to the needs of a rapidly expanding war force, the U.S. Navy adopted an organization of geographic districts. The organization provided a better means for efficiently administering the extensive and diverse work of the service by grouping activities under decentralized authority. The United States and its possessions were subdivided into districts, with navy officers "of rank and experience" in charge as commandants. The commandants supervised all naval activities within their districts. Secretary of the Navy Josephus Daniels, in his annual report, said, "In this way the department has been able, through the various commandants of districts to carry out [solutions to] problems involving patrol and defenses of the coast, mine sweeping, communications, commandeering vessels, etc., in a very efficient manner." When war was declared and the U.S. Coast Guard was transferred to the U.S. Navy, several coast guard officers were assigned to the staffs of commandants of naval districts.[1]

Sr. Capt. William E. Reynolds was in command of the U.S. Coast Guard's southern division on the Pacific coast on 6 April 1917. When the U.S. Coast Guard was transferred, he reported to the U.S. Navy for duty. Although now serving with the navy, he continued to command the southern division for the duration of the war. On 11 April Reynolds was put in command of the harbor patrols for the Twelfth Naval District. Second Lt. (Eng.) B. A. Minor was retired when war was declared. Recalled to active duty on 26 May, he was assigned to maintain the harbor patrol vessels for Reynolds. Five months later, the Twelfth Naval District commandant designated Reynolds as his chief of staff on 11 September 1917. He served in that capacity until after the war ended. Sr. Capt. Howard M. Broadbent, in command of the Pacific coast's northern division, was assigned to the Thirteenth Naval District at Bremerton, Washington, on 21 May 1917. Four months later, he was transferred to Coast Guard Headquarters as superintendent of construction and repair. After Broadbent's departure, the division commander's responsibilities were accomplished by the district engineer, Capt. (Eng.) Harry L. Boyd. Boyd carried out this duty while serving as a senior engineer with the Thirteenth Naval District.[2]

Two days before war was declared, Capt. Claude S. Cochran was transferred to the commandant of the Great Lakes naval districts—the Ninth, Tenth, and Eleventh. He was ordered to report for duty as supervisor of anchorages at the port of Chicago. Capt. (Eng.) Urban Harvey was assigned to the Great Lakes districts as supervisor of anchorages on the Saint Mary's River. Four more coast guard engineers were assigned to work for naval district commandants as machinery inspectors. First Lt.

(Eng.) H. O. Slayton—recalled from retirement—and 1st Lt. (Eng.) John E. Dorry worked for the commandant of the Fifth Naval District. Slayton reported on 16 April 1917 and Dorry on 23 November 1917. Lt. (Eng.) Kurt W. Krafft and Lt. (Eng.) Carl M. Green served as vessel inspectors for the Fourth and Seventh Naval Districts, respectively. Capt. George C. Carmine commanded the cruising cutter *Algonquin* on ocean escort duty in the war zone. He was relieved on 6 September 1918 and ordered to San Francisco. He reported to the Twelfth Naval District for duty and served there until seven months after the war ended.[3]

After war was declared, the U.S. Navy's Bureau of Operations created the Naval Overseas Transportation Service (NOTS) to ship materials and troops to Europe. First Lt. Eben Barker was assigned to the NOTS office at the Fourth Naval District in Philadelphia on 9 April 1918. After the armistice, Slayton and Dorry were transferred from the Fifth Naval District to the NOTS district supervisor at Norfolk, Virginia, to work on returning troops from Europe. Dorry continued working for NOTS even after the U.S. Coast Guard was returned to the Treasury Department. He was released by the U.S. Navy on 11 November 1919. Capt. (Eng.) John S. Baylis was transferred from the Third Naval District to the NOTS office at New York on 15 January 1919. He also worked on the sealift of troops from Europe. The Navy Department operated ship routing offices to track the movement of ships and support NOTS. The principal offices were at New York, Philadelphia, and Norfolk. Initially, the offices were directed and manned by navy line officers. Later, the navy officers were transferred to other duties and coast guard officers were assigned to take charge of the offices. Coast guard officers assigned to ship routing offices included Capt. Byron L. Reed, Capt. Detlef F. A. de Otte, Capt. James G. Ballinger, and 3d Lt. (Eng.) John N. Heiner.[4]

ENGINEERS

Six coast guard engineers were assigned to the U.S. Navy's Bureau of Steam Engineering in Washington, D.C. Lieutenants Frank E. Bagger, Francis E. Fitch, Charles H. Johnson, Charles J. Odend'hal, and Mason W. Torbet were assigned to the division of repairs; 2d Lt. (Eng.) Ellis Reed-Hill was attached to the supply division. Another four lieutenants of engineers were assigned by the bureau's division of repairs to work in machinery divisions at navy shipyards. Lt. (Eng.) Michael N. Usina was ordered to the shipyard at Portsmouth, New Hampshire, and Lt. (Eng.) Alvan H. Bixby reported to the Philadelphia Navy Yard. Lieutenants Edwin W. Davis and Sidney B. Orne were assigned to the navy yard at Charleston, South Carolina. Two officers, 1st Lt. (Eng.) Horatio N. Wood and 1st Lt. (Eng.) Albert C. Norman, were ordered to private shipyards as machinery inspectors. Wood reported to Morse's shipyard in August 1917, and Norman reported to Fletcher's shipyard two months later. Fitch was later reassigned from the Bureau of Steam Engineering's repair division in Washington to New York. At New York, he inspected repairs and alterations being made to troop transports. On 10 September 1919, Fitch was released from his duties with the U.S. Navy and returned to the U.S. Coast Guard. Third Lt. (Eng.) Paul R. Smith was originally assigned to the converted yacht *Zara* as it was being outfitted for overseas duty. When it was determined unsuitable for foreign service, Smith was transferred on 26 March 1918. He was ordered to inspection duty, reporting to the industrial manager at the New York Navy Yard.[5]

First Lt. (Eng.) Norman B. Hall, one of the U.S. Coast Guard's earliest aviation enthusiasts, was assigned to the Curtis Aeroplane and Motor Manufacturing Company at Hammondsport, New York, when war was declared. On 5 May 1917 he was ordered to duty under the U.S. Navy's contractor of aircraft superintendent at Buffalo. After four months, he was transferred to the Bureau of Steam Engineering's inspection division at New York, where he worked in the aeronautical section of the Brooklyn district. Second Lt. (Eng.) Thomas H. Yeager was also involved with aviation engineering. In August 1918 he was ordered from duty with the inspector of engineering materials at Keyport, New Jersey, to the Bureau of Steam Engineering. Yeager was assigned to temporary duty in Akron, Ohio, where he tested twin engine dirigibles. On 18 March 1919 he was detached from aviation duties and assigned as engineer officer aboard the cruiser *Huntington*.[6]

The U.S. Coast Guard's depot in South Baltimore, Maryland, was located on Arundel Cove. The U.S. Coast Guard continued to operate the facility after being transferred to the U.S. Navy. The depot worked extensively on both coast guard and navy vessels. During the war, repairs were made on eleven cutters, seventeen navy warships and patrol boats, and three navy transports. Thirty-six small boats were constructed at the yard for use by coast guard cutters and stations. In addition to work on vessels, the depot manufactured hammocks, sails, and seabags as well as various other canvas work for vessels. Signal lights, lead boxes, and cable boxes were manufactured and issued to coast guard stations. The depot also provided ordnance supplies to cutters and stations. Sr. Capt. James M. Moore, who took command of the depot on 15 July 1911, remained in charge until the war was over. Capt. Harry G. Hamlet was stationed at the depot, as captain of the yard, from November 1915 until May 1917, when he took command of a section base in the Third Naval District. Two captains of engineers, Christopher G. Porcher and Herbert M. Perham, were assigned to the depot's engineering department until after the war ended.[7]

When war was declared, 3d Lt. (Eng.) Roderick. S. Patch requested service overseas. When it did not appear he would have the opportunity for service in the war zone, Patch requested resignation so he could serve with the U.S. Army. After resigning on 7 September 1917, he accepted a commission as an officer in the army's field artillery. After ten months of training, he was sent overseas with the army's 6th Division, and later served with the 89th Division. In France, he served in the second and third phases of the Meuse-Argonne offensive. While inspecting guns at the front, he was blown from his motorcycle by the concussion of an incoming round, but only received minor injuries. He was later exposed to gas at Beauclair. Neither of the injuries caused him to leave the front. He was decorated for his service as a battery commander, ordnance officer, and, for a short while, battalion commander. Patch was recommissioned as a third lieutenant of engineers in the U.S. Coast Guard on 3 December 1919.[8]

SECTION BASES

On 15 August 1917 Capt. Hiram R. Searles reported to the U.S. Navy's section base at San Pedro, California, for duty as hull inspector for the section's vessels. Third Lt. Clement J. Todd was assigned to the San Diego section base to perform the same duty. After the cruising cutter

McCulloch sank as a result of the collision with the steamship *Governor* on 13 June 1917, the cutter's commanding officer, Capt. John C. Cantwell, reported to the commandant of the Twelfth Naval District for duty. On 3 November he was ordered to proceed to San Diego and assume command of the section base there. Two months later, Cantwell was ordered to take command of the naval reserve training center at San Diego. He commanded the training center for a year; he was then transferred to the commandant of the Fourth Naval District at Philadelphia. First Lt. Philip W. Lauriat reported to the San Francisco section base on 3 November 1917. While attached to the section base, he had the additional duty as the U.S. Coast Guard's west coast purchasing officer. Lauriat was detached from the section base nine month later and assigned to sea duty in European waters.[9]

At the port of New York, Capt. Harry G. Hamlet took command of Section Base No. 6 at Brooklyn on 1 May 1917. Capt. Gordon T. Finlay was detached from the cutter *Acushnet* on 22 May 1917 and ordered to command Section Base No. 8 at Tompkinsville, New York, nine weeks later. Finlay was reassigned to the Brooklyn Navy Yard on 14 July. After repeated requests for an assignment in the war zone, Hamlet received orders on 17 October 1918. When he arrived in France, he took command of the navy gunboat *Marietta*. Captains Staley M. Landrey and Frederick J. Haake were ordered to report to the commandant of the Fourth Naval District, headquartered at Philadelphia. Landrey was given command of the section base at Cape Henlopen, Delaware, at the entrance to the Delaware Bay. He also commanded Mine Squadron Six. A month later, Landrey was relieved and placed on sick leave. Across Delaware Bay, in New Jersey, Haake took command of the Cape May section and the section base at Sewell's Point on 7 April 1918. He continued in command of the section bases until 24 April 1919, when he was detached from all navy duties.[10]

RECRUITING

Even before the United States entered the war, the U.S. Coast Guard was experiencing difficulties in obtaining enough men to man its cutters and stations. Coast guard crewmen who were immigrants from the warring countries were leaving at the end of their enlistments or deserting to return to their homelands to fight for their countries. Prior to the war in Europe, local recruiting by cutters was adequate to meet manpower needs; once war was declared that was no longer true. All the armed forces were impacted by the shortage of suitable recruits, creating a competition for available manpower. Prior to the declaration of war, the services anticipated U.S. involvement and attempted to bring their units up to full strength. On 16 October 1916, Capt. Godfrey L. Carden was assigned as a special recruiting officer at New York City. The city was a primary source for recruit applicants. After transfer to the U.S. Navy on 6 April 1917, the U.S. Coast Guard continued its recruiting efforts. Captain Commandant Ellsworth P. Bertholf was uncertain whether the U.S. Navy would provide manpower assistance. He continued to rely on coast guard recruiting to provide the men needed to fill vacancies and meet the anticipated needs of increased wartime cutter complements. The U.S. Coast Guard opened more recruiting offices and, as in the past, cutters and stations continued to actively recruit candidates for training.[11]

First Lt. (Eng.) John I. Bryan was in command of the eighty-eight-foot harbor cutter *Gutherie* at Philadelphia on 6 April 1917. After assisting customs officials to seize the German ships *Prinz Oskar* and *Rahetia*, Bryan was transferred to the Fourth Naval District, headquartered at Philadelphia. With the consent of the naval district commandant, he recruited for the U.S. Coast Guard in the Philadelphia area. On 9 May 1917, 1st Lt. (Eng.) Lorenzo C. Farwell was assigned to assist Captain Carden with recruiting at New York. First Lt. (Eng.) Lucien J. Ker was detached from the cruising cutter *Yamacraw* before it departed for Europe. He was ordered to take charge of the U.S. Coast Guard's branch recruiting office at Baltimore on 9 August 1917. Three months later, he was reassigned to be the assistant recruiting officer at Buffalo. When the U.S. Navy began supplying personnel for coast guard units in 1918, the need for recruiting lessened and recruiters were assigned to other duties. The U.S. Navy stopped supplying personnel to man cutters and stations after the war ended, and the U.S. Coast Guard again began recruiting. Having recruiting experience, Bryan was assigned as a recruiter in the Philadelphia area. Captains Thomas S.

Klinger and Muller S. Hay were also assigned to recruiting duty in the fall of 1919. When Capt. Stanley V. Parker was relieved as command-ing officer of the naval air station at Rockaway, New York, he was ordered to report to the commandant of the naval air station at Pensacola, Florida. On 26 July 1919, he was assigned duty as a naval recruiting officer to obtain candidates interested in naval aviation duty.[12]

NAVAL TRAINING CAMPS

The U.S. Navy had 65,777 men in the service when war was declared. When the armistice was signed on 11 November 1918, navy rolls had increased to 497,030 enlisted persons and 32,474 officers; the naval fleet had grown from 197 ships to 2,002 vessels of all types. Supplying trained sailors to man the ships of the expanded fleet was a major undertaking. In addition to training crews for the more than eighteen hundred new ships, the U.S. Navy also trained officers and crews for the expanded merchant marine. Secretary of the Navy Josephus Daniels said, "This rapid expan-sion, intensive training, and ability to furnish officers and men under unprecedented demand is one of the foremost achievements of the Navy during the war."[13]

The U.S. Navy's Bureau of Navigation was assigned responsibility for recruiting, training, and assigning officers and men. Prior to the war, there were four facilities for training navy seamen, firemen and, to some extent, petty officers. The four stations, located on the east coast, Great Lakes, and west coast, could train six thousand recruits. By the end of the war, training facilities were constructed, or under construction, to accom-modate seventy-five thousand recruits. When war was declared, a navy training camp was established in each naval district. Initially, the camps were constructed and manned to train men for the National Coast Defense Reserve. They were quickly expanded, however, and training programs similar to those at the four training stations were initiated to train naval reserves. All the training stations and training camps provided recruit training for seamen and firemen, as well as training for yeomen and buglers, and preliminary training for signalmen. Specialized training for specific petty officer ratings was conducted at certain training stations and training camps. Additional billets were created aboard all naval vessels to provide follow-on underway training for the men after they left shoreside training facilities.[14]

Bumpkin Island Training Camp

Capt. Bernard H. Camden, USCG, was relieved as commanding officer of the cruising cutter *Gresham* and ordered, by the Bureau of Navigation, to take command of the naval training camp at Bumpkin Island, Massachusetts. He assumed command on 21 January 1918, and remained in command until several months after the end of the war when he was detached on 1 June 1919. The Bumpkin Island facility was also the site of one of the U.S. Navy's two mining and minesweeping schools. During the time Camden was in command of the camp, thousands of navy enlisted men were trained and sent to the fleet. The commandant of the First Naval District, Rear Adm. Spencer S. Wood, USN, commended Camden in an August 1918 letter: "He has been earnest and displayed excellent judgment which has brought his station to a high standard of efficiency." Capt. (Eng.) George W. David, USCG, who served with Camden aboard the cutter *Gresham*, was also assigned to the training camp. When the U.S. Navy obtained additional transports after the armistice to bring troops back from Europe, they needed qualified officers to command them. In May 1919, Camden was relieved of his duties at the training camp and ordered to take command of the navy transport *Antigone*. David was also transferred to *Antigone* as the ship's chief engineer.[15]

The routine for recruits reporting to various facilities for training was similar. The men completed the necessary paperwork, were given a physical examination, and received vaccinations against smallpox and typhoid fever. They were fed separately in the mess hall and then changed out of their civilian clothes, which were then packed and sent home. After showering, they drew their uniform outfit. Each recruit received $100 worth of initial outfit; it consisted of all the clothes and supplies he would need for the next several months. Because of the threat of influenza and other communicable diseases, recruits were isolated before starting their training. The new recruits were formed into companies and put into "detention," the term used for quarantining them away from the rest of the personnel in training. While in Barracks A, the detention barracks, the company commander—a chief petty officer—instructed the men in the fundamentals of discipline, regulations, and life in the U.S. Navy. During the several days of detention, the men had a daily routine of lectures and classes. Medical officers gave them lectures on health and hygiene and warned them about the dangers of venereal diseases. Chaplains provided spiritual guidance and lectured about morality. When the quarantine was over, the men packed their seabags and marched off to join the rest of the brigade for military training.[16]

The recruit's daily routine included an early breakfast, eaten before forming up on the parade ground when assembly was sounded. In company formations, they exercised at close order drill and the manual of arms until 9:00 AM. The recruits next attended hour-long classes. Lessons included seamanship, compass, signaling, characteristics of ships, and U.S. Navy customs and organization. At the waterfront, recruits were taught how to row, how to steer and keep a course, and how to handle a boat under sail. Exercise and physical training were an important part of the program. At the Newport training station, as well as at other camps, every recruit was given a course in boxing and taught how to "handle himself."[17]

Bensonhurst Training Camp

On 4 May 1917, Capt. Harry G. Hamlet, USCG, reported to Rear Adm. Nathaniel R. Usher, commandant of the Third Naval District, for duty. The district commandant assigned Hamlet to command the training camp at Bensonhurst, New York, as well as commanding Section Base No. 6. The next day Hamlet took command of the camp, which had been in operation for less than two months. To meet the need for trained sailors to man new ships being commissioned, the camp's enrollment was steadily increased until five hundred men were arriving for training each week. By 17 April 1918, 7,021 enlisted men and 355 officers had been trained at the camp. To accommodate the expanded activities at the facility, new buildings were leased by the U.S. Navy and modified for training and berthing. In addition to training full-time trainees at the camp, another two thousand men were temporarily assigned to the facility for training. The camp also trained crews for 104 submarine chasers stationed at the Pelham Bay Park naval reserve training camp.[18]

The marine basin at Brooklyn's Bath Beach was acquired by the Navy Department and added to Hamlet's Section Base No. 6 on 24 September 1917. The basin was obtained for docking, repairing, and overhauling smaller vessels operated by the Third Naval District. In the six months after operations began, 83 vessels were docked and another 232 vessels were repaired at the facility. In a 17 July 1918 letter to Rear Adm. John D. McDonald, commandant of the Third Naval District, the district's chief of staff, Capt. Louis R. de Steiguer, wrote that Hamlet

> has been in command of section Base 6 since the beginning of the war. It is still a training station, but is also the principal operating base, and has fifty-six vessels based upon it. Marine basin, which is the most important repair station for district vessels, is a part of this station. Captain Hamlet has been most successful in the training of young men and has the most fortunate disposition for this work. I know of no finer type of officer than Captain Hamlet, and the Third Naval district has been most fortunate in having his services. If a thing is possible, he will accomplish it. He has never failed us in the many difficult problems that have come up at that station, both as a section base and as an operating station.

On 16 October 1918, Hamlet's repeated request for overseas duty was finally granted. He was relieved of the command of Section Base No. 6 and ordered to France, where he took command of the gunboat USS *Marietta*.[19]

Cape May Naval Training Station

Second Lt. Paul H. Harrison, USCG, was in command of the harbor cutter *Guard* at Friday harbor in Washington State when he received orders to report to the Fourth Naval District. He reported to the district commandant at Philadelphia on 21 June 1917 and was assigned to be the first commanding officer of the naval training camp to be built at Wissahickon Barracks in Cape May, New Jersey. Ground was broken for the camp in July 1917; Harrison took command in August 1917. While the camp was under construction, Harrison had the opportunity to travel to other naval training facilities to observe their training methods and procedures. The visits were obviously beneficial because Harrison was repeatedly commended by his seniors for the quality of the training at Wissahickon. Seven thousand men were trained at the camp while Harrison was in command.[20]

The navy captain, serving as chief of staff to the commandant of the Fourth Naval District, wrote in an 11 March 1919 letter to the U.S. Navy's Bureau of Navigation:

> I have often heard that the men from Wissahickon were the best that could be obtained. Repeatedly Armed Guard [merchant ship gun crews] officers have informed us that the Guards that were trained at Wissahickon were the best they could get. . . . I am convinced that the men put through at Wissahickon will compare most favorably with those from any training camp in the world. . . . I have made numerous inspections of Wissahickon Barracks and I have never been able to find anything wrong with it. The training, the uniforms of men, their spirit was always of the very highest type and standard.

Eight months after the war ended, Harrison was transferred to the Bureau of Navigation, which had responsibility for navy training. On 10 September 1919, he was relieved of all duty with the U.S. Navy and reported to the commandant of the U.S. Coast Guard.[21]

COMMUNICATIONS

The possibility of being drawn into the war in Europe caused the United States to consider threats to its coasts. Lengthy shorelines, sparsely populated in many areas and vulnerable to enemy activity, were of great concern. On 16 February 1916, President Woodrow Wilson signed Executive Order No. 2318, creating the Interdepartmental Board on Coastal Communications. The board was tasked with examining and evaluating the various communications systems that existed along the coasts of the United States under the control of different federal agencies. It was directed to "submit recommendations as to the manner in which the different means of communications could best be coordinated, improved, and extended for the purpose of (a) saving life and property,

(b) for national defense, and (c) for administration in times of peace and war." Such a system would connect the remote coastal stations into an alerting network.[22]

The board completed its work on 13 November 1916, recommending that "means be provided as soon as practical to enable the Coast Guard to bring the present telephone system of coastal communication to a high state of efficiency, and to extend such system so as to include all Coast Guard stations not now connected, and also to include certain important light stations [lighthouses and lightships]." President Wilson approved the recommendations and the U.S. Coast Guard immediately began work on improving and expanding the communications system. The work included "changing the important grounded lines to metallic circuits; replacing iron conductors with copper wire where advantageous; installing special types of telephones, switches, and other instruments in order to obtain efficient transmission; and connecting the lines to commercial telephone systems so as to obtain flexible as well as long distance service." New lines were run to connect stations and light stations to the commercial telephone and telegraph system in their vicinity. Wires and cables were run to connect an additional twenty-three coast guard stations and sixty-seven light stations to the system. Previously, these units had no means of rapid communications.[23]

After war was declared, the Navy Department ordered that the communications system be expanded even further. This was accomplished under the direct supervision of the commodore commandant of the U.S. Coast Guard, with funding from the U.S. Navy. Before the war, the communications office at Coast Guard Headquarters consisted of one officer. With the rapid increase in the scope and importance of the communications network, a division of communications was established. First Lt. Russell R. Waesche, later promoted to temporary captain, was designated chief of the division. The staff was increased to include two commissioned assistants and a large number of warrant officers, enlisted men, and civilian employees. At the beginning of the war, there were 1,435 miles of overhead communications lines and 65 miles of submarine cable owned and maintained by the U.S. Coast Guard. By the end of the war, the system had more than twice as much cable.[24]

In addition to the expanded staff in Washington, relatively senior coast guard line officers were assigned to the staffs of commandants of naval districts to supervise and administer the communications system in the field. The officers—mostly captains—assigned to the sensitive project were given the nondescript title: aides for information. By the time the armistice was signed, the system had increased to three thousand miles of landlines and four hundred miles of marine cable. Even the manned light structures built on the offshore Florida reefs were connected by marine cable. The communications system also included coastal stations of the U.S. Weather Bureau and navy wireless stations along the coast. Most of the construction work was accomplished by the U.S. Coast Guard, with advice and assistance from American Telephone and Telegraph and associated companies. A submarine cable was laid across Delaware Bay, connecting Cape May, New Jersey, with Cape Henlopen, Delaware. A continuous telephone circuit was established along the coast from Sandy Hook, New Jersey, to Morehead City, North Carolina; it served ninety-five coast guard stations, thirteen lighthouses, fifteen navy radio stations, and six miscellaneous units.[25]

USS *Palmer*, a former menhaden fishing vessel, was taken over by the U.S. Navy after war was declared. Designated S.P. 319, it was assigned as a section boat in the Fifth Naval District with its headquarters at Norfolk. Later it was fitted out as a cable steamer by the U.S. Navy and assigned to the U.S. Coast Guard on 11 April 1918 to support and extend the communications system. *Palmer*, under the command of Chief Boatswain W. A. Hudgins, USNRF, was manned by a navy crew. The ship worked from the northern tip of Maine to Key West, Florida, maintaining underwater cables and transporting cables and supplies. The system ultimately provided telephone service for 282 coast guard stations, 44 other coast guard units and offices, 139 lighthouses, 22 radio compass naval stations, 8 navy radio stations, 8 miscellaneous naval units, 10 U.S. Weather Bureau stations, 5 army units, and 25 other miscellaneous facilities. Secretary Daniels described the coast guard communications system as a "highly important branch of the service indispensable in war or in peace." During the war, all information about the extent of the communications network was carefully censored to protect the security of the system. When the armistice was signed, *Palmer*—still under Hudgins's command—was undergoing repairs at the coast guard depot at Arundel

Cove. In 1919, *Palmer* was permanently transferred to the U.S. Coast Guard and renamed *Pequot*; it continued to support the communications system along the Atlantic and Gulf coasts.[26]

RECALLED RETIREES

Sixteen retired coast guard officers were recalled to active duty when war was declared. In anticipation of going to war, the U.S. Coast Guard sent some of the officers recall orders in March 1917. The orders became effective upon declaration of war. When the United States entered the war, the following three captains were recalled from retirement and assigned as aides for information: W. W. Joyner, Fifth Naval District; F. A. Levis, Sixth Naval District; and Johnstone H. Quinan, Seventh Naval District. They continued to serve at the naval districts until approximately six months after the end of the war. When they were released by the U.S. Navy, they returned to retired status. Three recalled officers were assigned to naval reserve training facilities. Recalled to duty, Capt. John E. Reinberg served on the staff of the commandant of the Fourth Naval District for seven months before being assigned to the naval reserve training camp at San Diego in March 1918. First Lt. (Eng.) W. L. Maxwell was recalled on 14 June 1917 and assigned to training duty at the naval reserve training station at San Pedro, California. First Lt. John Mel was recalled a month later and assigned to the same training station. Maxwell was released from active duty on 21 October 1919, and Mel was released on 2 April 1919.[27]

Two recalled officers were ordered to recruiting duties. First Lt. P. H. Brereton was sent to the branch recruiting office at Buffalo, and 1st Lt. W. A. O'Malley was assigned as the assistant recruiter in Baltimore. When 1st Lt. (Eng.) H. O. Slayton was recalled to active duty, he was first assigned to the commandant of the Fifth Naval District and then to the Naval Overseas Transportation Service. Slayton was returned to retired status on 18 August 1919. Two second lieutenants of engineers, Alexander Dennett and B. A. Minor, were assigned to duty at navy section bases. Dennett was ordered to the base at Portsmouth, New Hampshire. Minor, after being detached from duty at San Francisco, reported to the base at San Diego. Their duty at the bases involved machinery inspection and repair. First Lt. (Eng.) F. R. Falkenstein was assigned as an aide to Capt. Godfrey L. Carden, commander of the U.S. Coast Guard's rapidly expanding New York division. Capt. Kirkland W. Perry was attached to the staff of the commandant of the Third Naval District in New York after being recalled. First Lt. C. W. Zastro was assigned as the U.S. Coast Guard's purchasing officer at New York. First Lt. C. W. Cairnes was recalled on 3 May 1917 and ordered to the Bureau of Ordnance in Washington, D.C. Boatswain Nil Sjoberg was sent to the coast guard depot at South Baltimore after being recalled to active duty.[28]

First Lt. Samuel P. Edmonds retired from the U.S. Coast Guard in 1912 because of physical disability. In retirement, he occupied himself with inventing life-saving equipment. He exhibited some of his more successful inventions at the Pan American Exposition at San Francisco in 1915 and was awarded a first order medal and diploma for his work. Convinced that the kapok life preserver he invented would save lives, Edmonds offered it to the Revenue-Cutter Service in 1914. He allowed the service to manufacture the patented kapok life preservers without collecting royalties. In return, the secretary of the treasury sent Edmonds a letter stating that he "has been instrumental in devising a life preserver which, it is believed, will in times of disaster, be instrumental in saving human lives." The Edmonds lifejacket was adopted by the U.S. Coast Guard, the U.S. Navy, and the Steamboat Inspection Service before the beginning of the war. When war was declared and the need for massive troop movements by ship was recognized, the U.S. Army wanted a life preserver that could be worn by soldiers even while they were sleeping in their bunks. Competitive testing was done and Edmonds's patented designs were found to be superior to all others. When the Navy Department contracted for the manufacture of 425,000 kapok lifejackets, Edmonds volunteered to return to active duty to assist with the contract. He was recalled on 27 August 1918 by the Bureau of Construction and Repair and was ordered to report to the U.S. Navy's superintending constructor at New York. Edmonds was assigned to duty, supervising the manufacturer of his life preservers. After the war, Edmonds said a million and a half lifejackets had been manufactured for the army and navy. Even the British, French, and Italian transports were required to have Edmonds's kapok jackets aboard when they were carrying American troops.[29]

Edmonds was detached from all duties and returned to retired status on 3 July 1919. Rear Adm. D. W. Taylor, chief of the Bureau of Construction and Repair, wrote a letter to the commandant of the U.S. Coast Guard commending Edmonds. The 14 July 1919 letter said, "The Bureau desires to express its appreciation of the services of Captain S. P. Edmonds, U.S. Coast Guard, retired, while on duty under the Bureau for the period from August 27, 1918, to June 30, 1919. During this period, he was engaged chiefly on work in connection with the production and repair of life garments, a matter of great importance due to the special conditions obtaining during the war. Captain Edmonds' energy and ability, together with his expert knowledge of this particular subject, made his services of great value to the Bureau."[30]

CHAPTER II

AFTER THE ARMISTICE

Again the country is in a state of war and again the Coast Guard is serving under the Navy, but this time it seems the Navy does not want to turn us loose, does not want us to return to the Treasury Department and resume our normal functions and to that end this bill proposes the Navy absorb the Coast Guard. The officers and men are to be distributed among the several grades and ratings in the Navy; the seagoing ships are to be turned over to the Navy, and the Coast Guard, thus having been swallowed, will cease to exist.

—COMMODORE COMMANDANT ELLSWORTH P. BERTHOLF, USCG,
  CONGRESSIONAL HEARING, 6 FEBRUARY 1919

PRESIDENT WILSON RETURNS

President Woodrow Wilson returned from his mission to the Paris Peace Conference aboard the navy transport *George Washington*. While Wilson strongly favored U.S. participation in the proposed League of Nations, approval of such a proposal by the Senate was in serious doubt. When *George Washington* was slowed by stormy seas during the last two days of its crossing, the president continued to conduct the affairs of state by sending wireless messages. When a gray dawn broke on Monday, 24 February 1919, the people of Boston saw the silhouette of *George Washington* through the morning mist. The 39,435-ton gray troop transport was anchored in President Roads at the inner harbor between Long and Deer Islands. Aboard the ship, the presidential party was up early. From the deck of the transport, they could see military vessels in the harbor at dress ship, their flags flapping in the strong breeze. Civilian craft in the harbor were decked out as well. The colors of the flags and bunting were muted by a threatening sky.[1]

The committee to receive the president boarded the coast guard cruising cutter *Ossipee* at Boston's Commonwealth pier. The cutter, still wartime gray and operating under the Navy Department, had arrived at Boston four days earlier. Capt. William H. Munter, who commanded *Ossipee* during its deployment in the European war zone, backed away from the pier. When the cutter turned and headed for *George Washington*, guns at the Charlestown Navy Yard began firing a salute to the president. The sound of the guns echoed off the forts lining the harbor. The dignitaries aboard the cutter included the recently elected Massachusetts governor, Calvin Coolidge; Mayor Andrew J. Peters of Boston; Rear Adm. Spencer S. Wood, USN; and Maj. Gen. Clarence R. Edwards, USA. The presidential party was waiting when *Ossipee* came alongside *George Washington* at precisely 11:00 AM. A gangway was run out at a steep angle from a lower deck of the huge transport for the official party to disembark. Six navy submarine chasers circled the two ships to keep excursion boats and curious private craft at a safe distance.[2]

Honors were rendered aboard *Ossipee* and, with the tug of a halyard, the presidential flag was broken at the masthead when the president, followed by Mrs. Wilson, Ambassador David R. Francis, Assistant Secretary of the Navy Franklin D. Roosevelt, Mrs. Roosevelt, and three congressmen, boarded the cutter. They were followed by the remainder of the party. Two thousand returning troops, lining the rails above, cheered loudly from the upper decks when the president boarded the cutter. Just as *Ossipee* pulled away from *George Washington* and headed for Commonwealth pier, three aircraft from Naval Air Station Chatham passed overhead and every siren in Boston harbor began to wail. The wind calmed and the sun broke through the overcast while the cutter

The cruising cutter USS *Ossipee*, with President Woodrow Wilson aboard, in Boston harbor on 24 February 1919. The president and official party returned from the Paris Peace Conference aboard the transport USS *George Washington*. *Ossipee* took the president to Commonwealth pier, where a reception committee was waiting. *Mariners' Museum, Newport News, Virginia*

made its way toward the pier. President Wilson, muffled in a fur coat, stood on the cutter's open bridge waving his silk hat. Mayor Peters said, "For the first time in history, the President of the United States returns from foreign shores following the most important international conference the world has ever witnessed. In returning to the Port of Boston, the President pays us a single honor. It is our privilege and duty to do him the honor, he so richly deserves."[3]

A thousand people stood at the dock in the chilly morning air, waiting for the president. Buildings on the long concrete pier were elaborately festooned with American flags and bunting. For security purposes, only authorized people were admitted onto the pier after being screened by the Boston police. Policemen thoroughly searched the dock and surrounding area, checking for explosives, before the cutter returned. Sharpshooters were also posted on fishing boats moored nearby. The crowd began to cheer and applaud when *Ossipee* approached. After the cutter moored, a gangway was run out and President Wilson was greeted by the general reception committee waiting on the pier. Wilson waved to the crowd while he made his way to the waiting motorcade to begin his parade through the streets of Boston. The sidewalks were lined with cheering crowds; the mayor had closed the city's businesses and schools for the occasion. After delivering an address at the Mechanics' Hall, the president proceeded to South Station, where he boarded a train for Washington at 4:30 PM. When President Wilson arrived at Washington, he met with congressional leaders. He discussed the various articles of the constitution of the League of Nations and told them why he supported U.S. participation. The president faced another issue, one of less significance, upon his return to Washington. He had to decide whether to act on the joint resolution of Congress that called for the return of the U.S. Coast Guard to the Treasury Department. Secretary of the Navy Josephus Daniels and Assistant Secretary of the Navy Roosevelt strongly opposed the resolution. They wanted the personnel and resources of the U.S. Coast Guard to be permanently transferred to the U.S. Navy. Recently appointed, Secretary of the Treasury Carter B. Glass wanted the U.S. Coast Guard returned to his department immediately.[4]

POSTWAR NAVY

In January 1919, the U.S. Navy found itself in a difficult situation. It only had 2,550 officers in the regular service and, after the armistice, reserve officers were separating from the service by the thousands. Under existing law, the U.S. Navy was authorized 5,499 regular officers and pending legislation was likely to increase that number to 7,000. Capt. H. Laning, acting chief of the U.S. Navy's Bureau of Operations, said, "It is a very serious proposition with us to get officers to handle the situation. We have in the Coast Guard, the source of the best officers we can get from anyplace, except the Naval Academy. They have fitted in, in this war, in a remarkable way. We utilize them in almost every kind of position, from commanding officer down." Prior to the war, the U.S. Navy was generally unfamiliar with many of the U.S. Coast Guard's capabilities. After units and personnel of the two services had worked together during the war, the navy came to recognize the service's potential, particularly its well trained and experienced officer corps. Within a few months after the United States entered the war, the U.S. Navy was transferring coast guard officers to more responsible positions.[5]

The U.S. Navy also recognized the high caliber of the U.S. Coast Guard's enlisted men, with many of the men successfully passing examinations to receive commissions in the navy. Since there was no shortage of enlisted men in the post-war navy, however, it was the coast guard officers who were of the greatest interest. In making his appeal to have coast guard officers transferred permanently to the navy, Laning spoke of the greater good to the country. He said, "We feel that the officers who are experienced in the Coast Guard service will render the Government much more valuable service in the Navy than they can in the Coast Guard, as conducted by the Treasury Department, and naturally we are anxious to have them." The proposed transfer to the navy contained significant incentives for coast guard officers. Primarily, they would retain their higher temporary ranks and the pending expansion of the navy's officer corps offered excellent opportunities for further promotion.[6]

Proposed Legislation

On 14 December 1918 a bill was prepared and introduced by Rep. Guy E. Campbell of Pennsylvania. The bill proposed to "permanently transfer the United States Coast Guard from the Treasury Department to the Navy Department." Under the provisions of the bill, the U.S. Coast Guard would not only "cease to exist as a separate and distinct organization," it would cease to exist at all. The bill called for all personnel and materiel of the coast guard, except for harbor vessels needed to perform customs duties, to permanently become a part of the navy. All former duties and missions of the coast guard would be performed by the navy under regulations prescribed by the secretary of the navy. Protecting customs revenues and enforcing navigation laws were the only missions that would remain the responsibility of the Treasury Department. The second section of the bill required that all coast guard officers become commissioned officers in the navy. Senior captains would be commissioned as commanders and other officers would be commissioned at ranks equivalent to those held by regular permanent naval officers with the same length of total service. This provision of the bill was critical to coast guard officers, who faced reduction to their prewar ranks if returned to the Treasury Department. In his "Overseas, 1917–1919" memoir, Fletcher W. Brown said: "I went overseas as ensign [third lieutenant] with nearly nine years of service behind me. I came home a lieutenant [first lieutenant]." After returning to the United States, Brown received another advancement to captain in the U.S. Coast Guard, when his navy running mate was promoted to lieutenant commander. If the U.S. Coast Guard was returned to the Treasury Department, Brown faced a two-grade reduction to second lieutenant.[7]

The bill called for coast guard cadets, warrant officers, petty officers, and enlisted men to become regular personnel of the navy in comparable grades and ratings. The fourth section of the original bill contained an onerous provision; surfmen who were coast guard petty officers would be reduced to nonrated seamen in the navy. Surfman was, by far, the largest enlisted rating in the U.S. Coast Guard. The bill was later amended to create a petty officer rating of surfman in the navy, with coast guard surfmen transferring to the navy without loss of grade. The initial unjust provision of the bill, which negatively affected a large portion of the coast guard enlisted force, was indicative of the lesser importance given the transfer of the men. Commodore Commandant Ellsworth P. Bertholf said, "The enlisted man is entitled to consideration as well as the officer. . . . In this bill the enlisted man is given very short consideration." If the bill became law and the U.S. Coast Guard was transferred to the U.S. Navy, coast guard enlisted men would serve out their contracts. When they were discharged, they would be given the opportunity to reenlist in the navy if they were physically qualified. Physical qualification was an important provision. As enlisted men became older and closer to retirement, they were less likely to qualify physically. The requirement could be used as an excuse for eliminating older, former coast guardsmen—particularly surfmen. They did not have navy experience much less the shipboard experience that was the incentive for reenlisting older navy enlisted men. When a man was discharged under coast guard rules, his enlistment the next day was guaranteed without a physical examination. Bertholf said the bill could deprive coast guard enlisted men of their right to retire. Lt. William R. Bagger, USN, said, "That could be readily remedied in the wording of the bill." Bertholf retorted, "The whole thing could be remedied by cutting out the bill."[8]

CONGRESSIONAL HEARINGS

The first hearing on the bill was held on 13 January 1919 by the House of Representatives' Committee on Interstate and Foreign Commerce, the committee with authorization responsibility for the U.S. Coast Guard. The meeting was called to order by the committee chairman, Rep. Thetus W. Sims of Tennessee, at 10:30 AM. The hearing was requested by Congressman Campbell to present and discuss the merits of the bill. In his opening statement, Campbell said that the objective of the bill was the "efficient operation of the Coast Guard and that, placing it permanently under the Navy . . . would tend to [improve] efficiency and economy in operation." Campbell called on four officers—two coast guard and two navy—to speak in support of the bill. The two coast guard officers, Capt. Frank L. Austin and Capt. Paul H. Harrison, had been stationed together in the U.S. Coast Guard's northern division on the west coast when war was declared. Austin commanded the eighty-five-foot harbor cutter *Arcata* and Harrison commanded the sixty-eight-foot harbor cutter *Guard*. The cutters were homeported in Washington's Puget Sound. The coast guard commandant attended the hearing. Campbell called Austin to speak first. Austin had served as navigator aboard the navy cruiser *Columbia* during the war. He opened his remarks by pointing out that the bill was prepared in accordance with the desires of three separate branches of public service, "Officers in the Coast Guard, the Navy, and prominent civilians, interested in government reorganization." His failure to include the interests of coast guard enlisted men in his opening statement tended to prejudice his case. Congressmen, particularly those from coastal districts, were more likely to be concerned about the interests of coast guard surfmen within their congressional districts, because they were a more stable constituency with large numbers of local contacts. The votes of coast guard officers, who were more transient, were less certain.[9]

Austin stated that coast guard officers were obviously interested in retaining their rank, but they favored the bill more because it would give them the opportunity to perform more responsible duties on naval vessels and throughout the navy. During the war, coast guard officers had successfully commanded large naval ships and units. They were reluctant to return to the prewar duties they performed under the Treasury Department. Austin said that coast guard officers of considerable experience would be required to perform duties similar to those performed by junior officers, chief petty officers, or petty officers in the navy, because of the slowness of promotion in the U.S. Coast Guard. He said the situation would be "not only humiliating to those officers but result in a dead loss to the Government." Austin estimated that 70 percent of the coast guard officer corps favored transferring to the Navy.[10]

The acting chief of naval operations, Adm. J. S. McKean, said it was his personal view and the view of the U.S. Navy that the U.S. Coast Guard should have been a part of the navy some time ago. He said, "We are convinced of our theoretical ideas by the practical experience gained during the war. . . . For efficiency in war, and I believe efficiency in peace, and I am quite certain for economy, the Coast Guard should be absorbed by the Navy. . . . It is a military organization and fundamentally does not belong in the Treasury Department." As for the coast guard missions, the admiral said the navy could fully accomplish them and had accomplished the missions for the past nearly two years. And, he said, the missions could be done without the additional expense of maintaining two organizations. McKean may have displayed a lack of political acumen when he pointed out that the savings resulting from the transfer would come from closing coast guard facilities such as the U.S. Coast Guard Academy at New London, Connecticut; the depot at South Baltimore, Maryland; and the storehouse and coaling station at Woods Hole, Massachusetts. Closing these facilities would result in the loss of jobs and curtailment of funding in the congressional districts. Secretary of the Navy Josephus Daniels did not attend the hearing and discretely withheld his endorsement of the bill, which would take away funding, functions, and resources from another department of the government. Campbell pointed out that Secretary Daniels was friendly to the bill, but he did not care to interfere at this time, although he might later come out in its support.[11]

While not a member of the committee, Rep. Joseph Walsh of Massachusetts was actively interested in the outcome of the hearing. He had introduced Joint Resolution 382, which directed the "United States

Coast Guard to resume its operations under the Treasury Department."
After Austin finished his statement, Walsh asked, "You want the Coast
Guard service, that has existed for over 125 years, entirely disrupted
because you claim you could abolish certain storehouses, combine acad-
emies, and give officers who have been temporarily promoted, under the
law passed by Congress, their permanent promotions and give them better advantages and wider opportunities?" Campbell looked at Walsh and
said, "We are not abandoning a service with century old traditions. It is
only about three years old, now. It has no tradition as at present consti-
tuted. . . . And [Secretary of the Treasury] Alexander Hamilton, soon after
the Revenue-Cutter Service was created, recommended it be put under
the Navy." Walsh responded, "Well, if Alexander Hamilton, with all his
wisdom and greatness and power, could not convince Congress it was the
proper thing to do, I should think it would be hard to convince Congress,
today." "Well," Campbell explained, "He did not happen to be in the
majority, at that time." Walsh retorted, "With all due respect for the officers of the Coast Guard who are urging the passage of this act, they may
not be in the majority!"[12]

Campbell called on Capt. Paul H. Harrison, USCG, commanding officer of the naval training station at Cape May, New Jersey, to speak.
Harrison stated his support for consolidating all maritime marine functions of the government under one executive department—the Navy
Department. Harrison reported that a half million dollars could be saved
annually by transferring the coast guard to the navy. He said very few of
the U.S. Coast Guard's fourteen duties were specifically delegated to the
Treasury Department. Most of the duties were assigned by various government departments, such as Commerce and Justice Departments.
Harrison claimed that only four of the fourteen missions were considered
to be essential: (1) assistance to vessels in distress and the saving of life and
property at sea; (2) destruction or removal of wrecks, derelicts, or other
dangers to navigation; (3) protection of game and seal and other fisheries
in Alaska; and (4) service as a part of the navy in time of war. He pointed
out that without the last duty, there would be no reason for the coast guard
to be a military service. Of the four primary duties, or cornerstones, as
Harrison described them, the navy was required by law to accomplish the
first two duties and the secretary of commerce was specifically authorized

to call on naval vessels to accomplish the third duty. The fourth duty was the navy's primary mission. The objective of Harrison's statement was to show that the navy not only had the resources to carry out the primary duties being performed by the coast guard, but also had the authority. He said the incidental duty to transport customs officers to merchant ships could easily be accomplished by the customs service with harbor vessels turned over to them by the coast guard as stated in the bill. Harrison said it was clearly not a duty requiring military personnel.[13]

Proponents of the bill described how capital investment funds would be saved, because the coast guard would not have to build new cutters as planned. Navy vessels, particularly the new minesweepers built during the war, were of the appropriate size and seaworthiness for accomplishing missions formerly carried out by the coast guard. In particular, the minesweepers would be excellent for rescue work. The use of these vessels and others obtained by the navy during the hostilities would represent an immediate savings of several million dollars.[14]

From the different terminology used by coast guard officers, navy officers, and congressmen in discussing the "transfer," there appeared to be different views as to the degree to which the coast guard would continue to exist as an entity. In Austin's statement, he said that the coast guard would "be incorporated in and operate under the Navy," and Harrison said, "I believe the place for the Coast Guard is in the Navy." Comments from the coast guard officer corps indicated that they envisioned a distinct coast guard operating within the navy, possibly with an arrangement similar to the U.S. Marine Corps. Such a perception was unrealistic, however, as the services were too similar in form and function, and they had just undergone a high degree of integration during the war. Regardless of the different perceptions, the wording of the proposed legislation was very specific on the matter, stating that the U.S. Coast Guard "shall cease to exist as a separate and distinct organization." This was consistent with the position of Congressman Campbell and the naval officers. They saw the transfer as an absorption, with all vestiges of the coast guard disappearing. Of the bill, Congressman John Esch of Wisconsin said it would cause the coast guard to pass out of existence.[15]

Carter B. Glass, formerly a congressman from Virginia, succeeded William G. McAdoo as secretary of the treasury on 15 December 1918.

Glass strongly opposed the proposed legislation and wanted the U.S. Coast Guard returned to his department. In a letter to the committee, he wrote, "The Treasury Department has need now for the Coast Guard, . . . it is no longer needed by the Navy for the actual prosecution of the war. . . . These reasons cause me to urge early legislation to permit the Coast Guard to return to its prewar status under the Treasury Department without waiting for a formal proclamation of peace." Permanently removing an agency, like the coast guard, from a department—particularly a department with the seniority of the Treasury Department—was extremely difficult, especially when the department secretary strongly opposed such action. Glass spent eight terms in congress as a representative from Virginia before becoming secretary of the treasury, and he was not without friends. For such a proposed transfer to take place, the benefits to the government would have to be substantial and compelling. Secretary of the Navy Daniels realized that the best opportunity for a successful transfer would be while the coast guard was still a part of the navy.[16]

In Congress, a transfer within the departmental structure of the government had a significant impact on the congressional committee system. If the coast guard was transferred to the navy, authority over matters involving the coast guard would shift from the Committee on Interstate and Foreign Commerce to the Naval Affairs Committee. Members of the Interstate and Foreign Commerce Committee would have to give up their authority over an agency of the government with which they had a long relationship. Before that could take place, opposition to the proposal by any member of the committee would be given careful consideration. Again, the justification would have to be overwhelming. The navy's argument for transferring the coast guard was based on improved efficiency and economy. Congressman Esch said the coast guard was already efficient and if transferred to the navy its cutters would cost more to operate. To support his argument, he cited a study done in connection with proposed 1913 legislation. The study compared the operating and maintenance costs of five vessels of the Revenue-Cutter Service and five similar vessels of the U.S. Navy for the years 1909, 1910, and 1911. In the three years, the navy's operating and maintenance costs averaged 56 percent more per year. When statements and discussion were finished, the chairman of the committee said he would send the joint resolution, calling for the return of the U.S.

Coast Guard to the Treasury Department, and the bill under discussion to the treasury and navy secretaries. After the secretaries reported back on the matter, the committee would be reconvened to confer further. At 1:20 PM, the committee adjourned, subject to the call of the chairman.[17]

SECOND HEARING

The second hearing on the bill was called to order at 8:00 PM on the evening of 6 February 1919. Congressman Dan V. Stephens of Nebraska called the committee to order. Two letters from the secretary of the navy were the first order of business. Secretary Daniels's first letter stated his support for the bill proposing to transfer the U.S. Coast Guard to the U.S. Navy. In the letter, he said, "In the opinion of the department, the enactment of legislation such as that proposed in this bill would be most desirable. . . . To maintain the Coast Guard as a separate service to be returned to the jurisdiction of the Treasury Department at the conclusion of war or other national emergency would simply be to disarrange a large amount of the organization which has been perfected for the proper operation of the Coast Guard as a part of the Navy. . . . The department is strongly in favor of the enactment of this bill into law, and to this end it respectfully urges its favorable consideration." His second letter was in opposition to Joint Resolution 382, calling for the immediate return of the U.S. Coast Guard to the Treasury Department. Daniels said, "The Navy Department does not favor the passage of any such resolution, there being no necessity for it at this time. Coast Guard vessels are operating under the Navy Department in accordance with law, which will extend such operation until the termination of the existing emergency."[18]

Daniel's motivation for permanently transferring the coast guard to the navy went beyond the need to fill officer vacancies. After leaving the Navy Department, he wrote a book about his experiences as secretary. His book, entitled *Our Navy at War*, contained a chapter about the coast guard. In it Daniels said,

At the close of the war, I strongly recommended to the President and Congress that the Coast Guard be continued permanently as a part of the Navy. . . . The professional ability of the Coast Guard officers is evidenced by the fact that twenty-four commanded combatant ships operating in European waters, five vessels of the patrol force in the Caribbean Sea, and twenty-four combatant craft attached to naval districts. Five Coast Guard officers commanded training camps, six performed aviation duty, two being in command of air stations, one of these in France. The Navy Department, naturally enough, assigned to command of combatant ships only officers whose experience and ability warranted such detail and only those officers in whom the Department had implicit confidence.[19]

After the letters were entered into the record, the coast guard commandant was the first person to speak. In a prepared statement, Bertholf recounted how the coast guard had served under the navy during several previous wars, after which it returned to its normal duties with the Treasury Department. But this time the navy wants to absorb the coast guard, he said, and, "The officers and men are to be distributed among the several grades and ratings in the Navy; the seagoing ships are to be turned over to the Navy, and the Coast Guard, thus having been swallowed, will cease to exist." Bertholf pointed out that proposals for the U.S. Navy to take over the Revenue-Cutter Service had been brought before Congress repeatedly. The first attempt was made in 1796. The next effort to combine the services took place in 1821, when navy officers were detailed to duty aboard cutters. The arrangement was discontinued by Secretary of the Treasury Louis McLane eleven years later. In the 7 January 1832 order, McLane had said that "experience [has] shown that the employment of officers of the Navy in the Revenue-Cutter Service is liable to objection. It is deemed proper to discontinue the practice and in the future to keep the two services distinct and separate." Propositions to combine the services were subsequently brought before Congress in 1840, 1841, 1842, 1843, 1846, 1859, 1882, 1883, 1884, and 1892. Each proposal was rejected after congressional consideration.[20]

Bertholf next addressed the navy's argument for the takeover based on improving efficiency, economy, and administration. He said the coast guard was already efficient and there was never any doubt about the navy's regard for its efficiency. Bertholf cited the secretary of the navy's 1918 annual report: "The entire personnel of the Coast Guard is performing with great efficiency the various naval duties assigned to them, and in addition, have carried out as occasion has arisen their peace-time duties of humanitarian nature." He quoted Admiral McKean, who had told the committee, "Their's is a very efficient organization. We have used Coast Guard men for all sorts of duties with the fleet. We have used them in the districts. We have used them for patrol work, and in all these duties they have done well. They are a fine crowd." He referred to Captain Laning's statement, that "they [coast guardsmen] have fit in this war in a remarkably splendid way. We have utilized them in every kind of position from that of commanding officer down. In the same way, the men are very excellent men." With regard to McKean's argument that the coast guard should be in the navy in peacetime, so as to be better prepared for war, Bertholf contended that the coast guard's primary peacetime functions were the activities of peace. He posited that the coast guard was a military service because of the emergency nature of its work and that military training, drills, and discipline maintained its ships and personnel in a state of readiness to perform its emergent duties. Because of the training and experience gained during emergency operations, the coast guard was a valuable asset to the navy in time of war. Bertholf stated, "But, to be an asset of the Navy in war is not the sole reason for the Coast Guard. That is simply a by-product of the Coast Guard, and it is certainly not logical to destroy an organization simply because of the value of its by-product."[21]

If the coast guard's peacetime operations prepared it for service with the navy in time of war, Bertholf argued, there would be nothing to be gained by permanently transferring the service to the navy.

On the contrary, there is much to be lost. In assuming our war-time duties under the Navy Department, every officer and man, in addition to his desire to do his duty, was filled with the desire to make a showing for the Coast Guard and uphold the record of the past. He was proud of his service and wished that his service might be proud of him. The traditions of the Coast Guard—and with all due respect to Mr. Campbell, these traditions have grown out of achievements during 128 years of useful service both in peace and war. . . . The traditions of the Coast Guard are very fine, and this pride of service and desire to live up to its traditions is a very vital force which cannot be overestimated.

Bertholf attacked Campbell's economic argument, saying that while facilities such as the academy, depot, and storehouses would be discontinued, the functions they performed would still have to be done by the navy, at an additional expense. The officers and men who manned the facilities would not be eliminated, but would be transferred elsewhere in the navy. He said any savings realized from the transfer would be offset by the higher pay of coast guard officers, who would be incorporated into the navy at their advanced ranks. That would represent $160,000 per year. The increased pay for warrant officers would be another $320,000. Pay for enlisted men would stay essentially the same. The $440,000 savings projected by the navy would be more than offset by the cost of the higher salaries alone. The figure would be increased further by more costly operation and maintenance of cutters under the navy, as well as the additional funding required to accomplish coast guard peacetime missions.[22]

Bertholf spoke of the expanding U.S. merchant marine and the U.S. Coast Guard's long history of providing services to merchantmen. He said, "These traditions are not to be thoughtlessly squandered by allowing the identity of the [coast guard] ships and men to be lost by deliberately scattering the service through the vast Naval establishment." He feared the next generation of officers would neither know nor care about the work once performed by the coast guard. At the time the hearing was held, the coast guard still had the statutory responsibility to respond to distresses at sea. "And yet," said Bertholf, "Coast Guard headquarters has no directive control over its vessels, at this time." He said cutters should be systematically patrolling the Atlantic coast at that time of the year, ready to aid vessels in distress during the inclement winter weather. He pointed out that cutters were no longer required for active war operations, but were needed to carry out coast guard peacetime missions. He said 50 percent of coast guard officers were still attached to naval units, having been replaced on cutters by naval reservists, and that some cutters only had one or two coast guard officers left aboard. In a final plea, Bertholf urged, "If the Coast Guard is to be maintained and the Coast Guard is worthwhile, it should be maintained properly and allowed to resume its normal system, a system that has stood the test of a great many years, and been found efficient whenever that question has been raised." To allow a service, such as the U.S. Coast Guard with all its tradition and reputation for seagoing efficiency, to pass out of existence, Bertholf said, "seems to be almost a ridiculous proposition."[23]

Following his statement, the commandant was questioned by

Congressman Campbell. Campbell attempted to pressure Bertholf by referring to his obligation to be loyal and conform with the views of his commander: "As a Coast Guard officer, aren't you subject to the orders of the Secretary of the Navy at the present time?" When Bertholf said he was, Campbell quoted the secretary of the navy's letter, in which he wrote that the Navy Department endorsed the bill and "strongly urges its favorable consideration." Bertholf looked at Campbell and said, "If you are asking me if I agree with the Secretary of the Navy, I do not agree." Rep. Walter R. Stiness of Rhode Island spoke up and said that he did not think the commandant should have to answer a question that would put him in opposition to the secretary of the navy. Bertholf thanked Stiness for giving him the opportunity not to answer, but said he would. He told Campbell and the committee that Secretary Daniels was aware of his opposition to the bill. He said, "The secretary has never intimated to me that I should remain quiet in this matter." Campbell then asked Bertholf if he was aware that his superior, Chief of Naval Operations McKean, supported the bill. Campbell continued, "Do you think it would be wise for Congress to be guided by his opinion, or by your own, regarding the Navy and what is best and most efficient in regard to the Coast Guard? Which would you ask Congress to be guided by, Admiral McKean's opinion or your own?" Bertholf replied, "My own. I have spent 35 years in the Coast Guard and he hasn't spent a day." He then added, "I wouldn't be here, Mr. Campbell, if I didn't have the courage of my convictions."[24]

Bertholf completed his response to Campbell:

Of course I could not and would not oppose any proposition which appeared to be for the best interest of the Government. But here is a service that is admitted by the Navy to be composed of efficient officers and men. It has earned that reputation during 128 years of useful service. It has traditions; it has ships; it has officers; and it has men. It is now proposed to distribute the personnel through the various grades of the Navy and put the Service out of business—out of existence. Why? We are told, in order that they might better prepare for war. What war? War only covers a small part of any man's existence. It is only 5 percent, possibly. If we sacrifice the Coast Guard during 95 percent of its existence to prepare for the work of war, which takes up about 5 percent of the time, what is to be gained, from the Government's point of view.[25]

When the committee finished questioning Bertholf, Campbell called on Sr. Capt. John C. Cantwell, USCG, to speak in favor of the proposed transfer. Cantwell was one of the U.S. Coast Guard's most senior officers; he had thirty-seven years of commissioned service, with twenty-five of those years spent at sea. Cantwell said, "I believe that the principal benefit would be the consolidation, under one department of the Government, two services which are almost exactly similar in organization, discipline, education, and duties." He said the transfer would be beneficial for junior naval officers who would learn to handle smaller vessels and it would enlarge the field of operations for young coast guard officers. Cantwell said he opposed the earlier Cleveland Commission's attempt to combine the two services because he personally resented a statement made by the secretary of the navy at that time. The secretary had said "he was willing and believed it would be desirable to take over the enlisted force and ships of the Revenue-Cutter Service, but that he did not believe the officers were of such caliber as could to be entrusted with the manifold and delicate duties performed by Naval Officers." Cantwell said the situation was different now, because officers of the two services had worked together during the past war and appreciated each other's capabilities. When Capt. Francis S. Van Boskerck, USCG, was called before the committee, he said American taxpayers funded the U.S. Coast Guard and they were entitled to have it operate to the fullest degree of its efficiency. He proposed that such efficiency would be possible under the Navy Department with its resources rather than under the Treasury Department, which provided limited funding.[26]

Congressman Walsh made a statement to the committee in opposition to the coast guard transfer to the navy. His congressional district contained several coast guard stations on Cape Cod, Massachusetts. He said the committee had primarily heard from officers who hold commissions and wear the gold braid, but they should not forget the men who are performing arduous duty. Walsh had sent out letters to the men at the stations, asking what they thought about being transferred to the navy. Of the seventy replies he already received, sixty-eight favored returning to the Treasury Department. He said, "There are one hundred and sixty odd men, along that coast, and I expect to hear from most of them." Walsh said he understood and could appreciate why coast guard officers wanted to stay with the navy, but their potential advancement and economic benefit "is no sufficient reason, I submit, for combining these two services." Walsh said he was surprised that as many as 30 percent of coast guard officers did not favor the transfer given the potential for higher salaries in the navy. He described the warrant officers and enlisted men at the rescue stations as not being warlike men. He said that the Navy Department knew nothing of the needs of the life-saving stations and a transfer would result in inefficient conduct and management for many years. Congressman Stiness said his congressional district in Rhode Island also had coast guard stations and that his constituents had the greatest confidence in the capability of the stations as they were presently operated.

Congressman Campbell quoted from two letters submitted anonymously by coast guard captains. One described the poor material condition of coast guard cutters when war was declared, saying they were not ready for immediate service. The second letter's author, who purported to speak for a number of officers, said, "After our details of real responsibility in the Navy during the war are we, as is threatened, to be relegated to the back waters of petty duties such as performed in the Navy, largely by warrant and petty officers, and this at a time when the Navy needs trained officers?" In concluding his letter, the officer wrote he was not looking for personal gain, but only "to do what I can to prevent the utter demoralization of an old and honorable service which will occur if we return to the Treasury." Obviously, this officer, and the officers he represented, did not see the proposed merger as the end to the U.S. Coast Guard.[27]

Cambell said, "In my opinion, the need for this service ceased to exist on the date of the organization of the Navy in 1798." The fact that there were so many attempts to abolish the service as a separate organization was proof that its existence was always questionable. He said, "The Navy needs these officers, the Treasury Department does not. Where is the logic in keeping them tied down to insignificant duties, where their abilities are not used to capacity, and where their energies and enthusiasm wither away and die from disuse." Campbell concluded his remarks by saying he was convinced the proposed transfer would result in improved efficiency and economy and that it would benefit the Treasury Department and relieve it of the administration of a military service with which it was "very slightly connected." He said the only substantial objection to the transfer was based on the grounds of sentiment against violating "an old tradition and the dismemberment of an old institution. Sentiment is a fine thing when it is constructive, but this sentiment is destructive—it impedes the wheels of progress and it costs the country considerable good money furnished by the tax payers."[28]

Return to Treasury Department

Three weeks after the second hearing, Congressman Walsh's Joint Resolution 382, directing the U.S. Coast Guard to resume its operations under the Treasury Department, was approved by the House Interstate and Foreign Commerce Committee. No action was taken on the approved resolution by President Wilson before he returned to the Paris Peace Conference in France in early March 1919. Bertholf retired as commandant of the U.S. Coast Guard on 30 June 1919 before the issue was resolved. Secretary Glass continued his vigorous efforts to have the U.S. Coast Guard returned to the Treasury Department. Secretaries Daniels and Glass jointly decided not to appoint a new coast guard commandant to replace Bertholf until the issue of transfer was resolved. Capt. Daniel P. Foley served as acting commandant in the interim. When President Wilson returned from Europe, he began making preparations for a national tour to promote U.S. participation in the League of Nations. Before the president left on his tour, Secretary Glass met with him and convinced him to act on the pending joint resolution. On 28 August 1919, Wilson issued Executive Order No. 3160, which returned the U.S. Coast Guard to the Treasury Department.[29]

During the hearings, those in favor of the transfer repeatedly said that the reason the coast guard was originally created—to enforce customs laws and control smuggling—no longer existed and there was no need for a seagoing force to carry out such an obsolete mission. Campbell said the need for seagoing enforcement vessels was "based on conditions which may have existed 50 or 100 years ago, but which do not exist today" and that "the smuggling that is now done is so insignificant in amount that it does not warrant the Government maintaining an expensive equipment to prevent it."[30] Congressman Esch was prophetic when he raised an issue during the hearing. He asked, "In view of the fact that national prohibition is about upon us, do you think there will be increased necessity for Coast Guard service to prevent unlawful importation of certain products?" After the U.S. Coast Guard's return to the Treasury Department, the service experienced difficult times. Reductions in pay caused dissatisfaction among officers and enlisted men. Officers resigned and men did not reenlist, leaving the service well below its authorized strength. Another bill, proposing the transfer of the U.S. Coast Guard to the U.S. Navy, was again brought before the committee and hearings were held in May 1920. It was also rejected. After that, domestic developments changed the situation for the U.S. Coast Guard. Once the service was fully tasked with enforcing the provisions of the National Prohibition Act, it underwent a period of unprecedented expansion. Twice as many men, more cutters, and aviation facilities were needed to stop the flood of alcohol being smuggled into the United States by sea. The separate existence and need for the U.S. Coast Guard was no longer questioned.[31]

APPENDIX A

Coast Guard Cutters Transferred to the Navy

CRUISING CUTTERS TRANSFERRED TO THE NAVY

Name	Assignment	Displacement (Tons)	Length (Feet)	Guns	Crew
USS *Acushnet*	2d and 3d Naval Districts	800	152	two 3-pdr.	75
USS *Algonquin*	Squadron 1, Patrol Force, Gibraltar	1,181	206	four 4-in. Y-guns	106
USS *Androscoggin*	1st Naval District	1,605	210	four 3-in. Y-guns	107
USS *Apache*	5th and 6th Naval Districts	708	185	three 3-pdr.	—
USS *Bear*	12th Naval District	1,700	198	three 6-pdr.	—
USS *Comanche*	8th Naval District	670	171	two 3-pdr.	76
USS *Gresham*	1st and 5th Naval Districts	1,090	205	four 3-in. Y-guns	103

continued on next page

CRUSING CUTTERS TRANSFERED TO THE NAVY (*continued*)

Name	Assignment	Displacement (Tons)	Length (Feet)	Guns	Crew
USS *Itasca*	3d, 4th, and 6th Naval Districts	980	190	four 3-in. Y-guns	104
USS *Manning*	Squadron 1, Patrol Force, Gibraltar	1,155	205	four 4-in. Y-guns	109
USS *McCulloch*	11th Naval District	1,432	219	four 6-pdr.	130
USS *Mohawk*	3d Naval District	1,148	206	four 6-pdr.	105
USS *Morrill*	4th, 9th, 10th, and 11th Naval Districts	420	145	two 3-pdr.	60
USS *Onondaga*	Coast Guard Headquarters (Academy)	1,192	206	four 6-pdr.	106
USS *Ossipee*	Squadron 1, Patrol Force, Gibraltar	908	166	four 4-in. Y-guns	87
USS *Pamlico*	5th Naval District	451	158	two 3-pdr.	48
USS *Seminole*	5th and 6th Naval Districts	860	188	four 6-pdr.	97

USS Seneca	Squadron 1, Patrol Force, Gibraltar	1,445	four 4-in. Y-guns	204	119
USS Snohomish	2d and 13th Naval Districts	879	two 3-pdr.	152	73
USS Tallapoosa	5th and 7th Naval Districts, and First Patrol Squadron	912	two 6-pdr.	166	78
USS Tampa	Squadron 1, Patrol Force, Gibraltar	1,181	four 4-in. Y-guns	190	115
USS Tuscarora	2d, 9th, 10th, and 11th Naval Districts	739	two 3-pdr.	178	94
USS Unalga	12th Naval District	1,181	three 6-pdr.	190	106
USS Yamacraw	Squadron 1, Patrol Force, Gibraltar	1,082	four 4-in. Y-guns	192	106

Note: Wartime crew complements were 45 percent larger on average than peacetime complements. All vessels serving with the U.S. Navy, including U.S. Coast Guard cutters, were designated "USS."

Harbor Cutters Transferred to the Navy

Name	Assignment	Displacement (Tons)	Length (Feet)	Gun	Crew
USS Alert	8th Naval District	33	61	—	—
USS Arcata	13th Naval District	138	85	—	12
USS Calumet	3d Naval District	170	94	—	—
USS Carolina	5th Naval District	—	57	—	—
USS Coquet*	3d Naval District				
USS Davey	8th Naval District	182	92 ft. 6in.	—	14
USS Emma Kate Ross**	3d Naval District	350	104	one 6-pdr.	—
USS Golden Gate	12th Naval District	240	110	—	22
USS Guard	13th Naval District	52	67 ft. 7in.	—	10
USS Guide	3d Naval District	41	70	—	7
USS Gutherie	4th Naval District	149	88	—	—
USS Hartley	12th Naval District	64	64 ft. 6 in.	—	—
USS Hudson	3d Naval District	179	96 ft. 6 in.	one 1-pdr.	—
USS Mackinac	3d, 9th, 10th, and 11th Naval Districts	241	110	—	11
USS Magotby***	5th Naval District	83	100	—	—
USS Manbattan	3d Naval District	145	102	—	—

USS *Patrol*	3d Naval District	23	68 ft. 9 in.	9
USS *Penrose*	8th Naval District	41	67	—
USS *Richard Caswell**	3d Naval District	—	—	—
USS *Scout*	13th Naval District	40	61 ft. 6 in.	6
USS *Tioga*	5th Naval District	131	82	11
USS *Tybee*	4th Naval District	45	63	5
USS *Winnisimmet*	1st Naval District	182	96 ft. 6 in.	11
USS *Wissahickon*	3d Naval District	194	96 ft. 6 in.	11

*Transferred to Coast Guard from the Army Engineer Department.

**Transferred to Coast Guard from the port of New York.

***Transferred to Coast Guard from the Public Health Service.

Sources: U.S. Treasury Department, Coast Guard, *Register of the Officers, Vessels, and Stations of the United States Coast Guard, 1917* (Washington, D.C.: U.S. Government Printing Office, 1917); James L. Mooney, ed., *Dictionary of American Naval Fighting Ships*, 8 vols. (Washington, D.C.: Navy Historical Center, 1959–1991); U.S. Navy Department, *Supplement to the Monthly Navy List, Showing the United States Naval Forces Operating in European Waters, Corrected to September 1st 1918* (London: Harrison and Sons, 1918); U.S. Treasury Department, Coast Guard, Assistant Commandant, *Record of the Movements, Vessels of the United States Coast Guard: 1790–December 31, 1933* (Washington, D.C.: U.S. Coast Guard Headquarters, 1934); Donald L. Canney, *U.S. Coast Guard and Revenue Cutters, 1790–1935* (Annapolis: Naval Institute Press, 1995).

APPENDIX B

Navy Ships Commanded by Coast Guard Officers

Name	Type	Assignment	Displacement (Tons)	Length (Feet)	Guns	Crew
USS *Albatross*	Bureau of Fisheries	American Patrol Detachment, Gulf of Mexico and Caribbean	638	234	one 3-in.	110
USS *Aloha*	Yacht	3d Naval District and Inspector of Districts	659	218	two 4-in., two 3-in.	86
USS *Aphrodite*	Yacht	Squadron 3, Patrol Force, Rochefort, France, Base 20	1,500	302	four 3-in.	132
USS *Arcturus*	Yacht	Squadron 2, Patrol Force, Gibraltar, Base 9	456	177 ft. 6 in.	two 3-in.	67

USS *Bella*	Supply Ship	Naval Aviation Service, Brest, France, Base 7	2,500	235	two 3-in.	51
USS *Castine*	Gunboat	Squadron 2, Patrol Force, Gibraltar, Base 9	1,177	204	eight 4-in., four 6-pdr.	154
USS *Corona*	Yacht	Squadron 3, Patrol Force, Brest, France, Base 7	—	172	two 3-in.	63
USS *Cytherea*	Yacht	Squadron 2, Patrol Force, Gibraltar, Base 9	1,000	215	three 3-in.	113
USS *Dorothea*	Gunboat	Mexican Waters and Cuban Officer Training Ship	—	—	—	—
USS *Druid*	Yacht	Barracks Ship, Gibraltar, Base 9	—	217	three 3-in.	113
USS *Eagle*	Yacht	American Patrol Detachment, Gulf of Mexico and Caribbean	434	155 ft. 6 in.	two 6-pdr.	67
USS *Emeline*	Yacht	Squadron 3, Patrol Force, Brest, France, Base 7	407	196	two 3-in., one Y-gun	72
USS *Explorer*	U.S. Coast and Geodetic Survey	13th Naval District, Alaska	450	135	two 6-pdr.	49

continued on next page

Navy Ships Commanded by Coast Guard Officers (*continued*)

Name	Type	Assignment	Displacement (Tons)	Length (Feet)	Guns	Crew
USS *Forward* (ex-*Patterson*)	U.S. Coast and Geodetic Survey	13th Naval District, Alaska, and 12th Naval District	719	163	two 6-pdr.	49
USS *Galatea*	Yacht	Special Duty, Azores, Portugal, Base 13	367	192	three 3-in.	57
USS *Granite State*	Receiving Ship	3d Naval District Flagship	—	—	—	—
USS *Halcyon*	Bureau of Fisheries	1st Naval District	275	—	—	—
USS *Lady Anne*	Yacht	6th Naval District	27	65	one 1-pdr.	10
USS *Lydonia*	Yacht	Squadron 2, Patrol Force, Gibraltar, Base 9	497	181	four 3-in.	—
USS *Maggie*	Barracks Ship	5th Naval District	606	164	—	—
USS *Marietta*	Gunboat	Special Duty, Brest, France, Base 7	1,000	189 ft. 7 in.	six 4-in., one 3-in., four 6-pdr.	140
USS *May*	Yacht	Squadron 3, Patrol Force, Rochefort, France, Base 20	1,100	239	one 4-in., two 3-in.	77

Ship	Type	Assignment				
USS *Niagra*	Escort	Cruiser and Transport Force and West Indies	2,690	282	four 4-in.	195
USS *Nokomis*	Yacht	Squadron 2, Patrol Force, Brest, France, Base 7	1,265	243	four 3-in.	191
USS *Noma*	Yacht	Squadron 3, Patrol Force, Rochefort, France, Base 20	1,250	262 ft. 6 in.	four 3-in.	—
USS *Paducah*	Gunboat	Squadron 1, Patrol Force, Gibraltar, Base 9	1,084	200 ft. 5 in.	four 4-in.	184
USS *Rambler*	Yacht	Squadron 3, Patrol Force, Brest, France, Base 7	288	177	two 3-in.	—
USS *Surveyor*	U.S. Coast and Geodetic Survey	Squadron 2, Patrol Force, Gibraltar, Base 9	1,143	186	two 3-in.	85
USS *Venetia*	Yacht	Squadron 5, Patrol Force, Gibraltar, Base 9	589	226	four 3-in.	69
USS *Wanderer*	Yacht	Squadron 3, Patrol Force, Brest, France, Base 7	362	197	two 3-in.	56
USS *Xarifa*	Yacht	3d Naval District	378	192	two 3-pdr.	71
USS *Yacona*	Yacht	3d Naval District	527	211	two 3-in.	67
USS *Zara*	Yacht	3d Naval District	184	152	two 6-pdr.	62

Sources: U.S. Navy Department, *Supplement to the Monthly Navy List, Showing the United States Naval Forces Operating in European Waters, Corrected to September 1st 1918* (London: Harrison and Sons, 1918); James L. Mooney, ed., *Dictionary of American Naval Fighting Ships*, 8 vols. (Washington, D.C.: Navy Historical Center, 1959–1991).

APPENDIX C

Navy Ships with Coast Guard Officers Assigned

Name	Type	Assignment	Displacement (Tons)	Length (Feet)	Guns	Crew	Officer Billets*
USS *Albany*	Light Cruiser	Cruiser Force, Atlantic Fleet	3,769	354	three 18-in., six 6-in., four 4.7-in.	365	Gun, Nav, WO
USS *Birmingham*	Light Cruiser	Squadron 1, Patrol Force, Gibraltar, Base 9	3,750	423	two 21-in., two 5-in., six 3-in.	359	Ch Eng, WO, EWO
USS *Black Hawk*	Flagship Tender	ComMine Forces, Inverness, Scotland, Base 8	5,690	420	four 5-in., one 3-in.	471	Ch Eng
USS *Buffalo*	Flagship Tender	Gibraltar, Base 9	6,530	406	two 5-in., four 4-in.	350	Nav
USS *Canandaigua*	Minelayer	Squadron 1,	6,080	380	one 5-in.,	368	WO

Ship	Type	Force			Armament		
		Mine Force, Inverness, Scotland, Base 18			two 3-in.		
USS *Canonicus*	Minelayer	Squadron 1, Mine Force, Inverness, Scotland, Base 18	6,300	405	one 5-in., two 3-in.	368	WO
USS *Charleston*	Cruiser	Caribbean Patrol Force, Cruiser and Transport Force	9,700	426	three 18-in., fourteen 6-in.	673	XO, EWO
USS *Chattanooga*	Cruiser	Caribbean Patrol Force, Cruiser and Transport Force	3,200	309	ten 5-in., eight 6-pdr.	339	WO
USS *Cleveland*	Cruiser	Squadron 5, Patrol Force	3,200	308	ten 5-in.	339	WO
USS *Columbia*	Cruiser Flagship	Squadron 5, Patrol Force	7,375	413	four 18-in., one 8-in., two 6-in., eight 4-in.	475	Nav
USS *Denver*	Cruiser	Cruiser and Transport Force	3,200	309	ten 5-inch	339	XO

continued on next page

Navy Ships Coast Guard Officers Assigned (*continued*)

Name	Type	Assignment	Displacement (Tons)	Length (Feet)	Guns	Crew	Officer Billets*
USS *Des Moines*	Cruiser	Cruiser and Transport Force	3,200	308	ten 5-inch	339	WO
USS *Dixie*	Destroyer Tender	Flotilla 2, Destroyer Force, Queenstown, Ireland, Base 6	6,114	392	ten 3-in.	224	WO
USS *Galveston*	Cruiser	Squadron 2, Cruiser Force, Atlantic Fleet	3,200	308	ten 5-in., eight 6-pdr., two 1-pdr.	339	EWO
USS *Huntington*	Armored Cruiser	Cruiser and Transport Force	13,860	506	two 18-in., four 8-in., fourteen 6-in.	829	Ch Eng, Aviators
USS *Machias*	Gunboat	Gibraltar, Base 9	1,177	204	eight 4-in., four 6-pdr., four 1-pdr.	154	Ch Eng
USS *Minneapolis*	Cruiser	Cruiser and Transport Force	7,375	413	four 18-in., one 8-in., two 6-in., eight 4-in.	477	Nav, WO

Ship	Type	Force			Armament		
USS *New Orleans*	Cruiser	Cruiser and Transport Force	3,769	354	three 18-in., six 6-in., four 4.7-in., ten 6-pdr., eight 1-pdr.	366	WO
USS *Petrel*	Gunboat	American Patrol Detachment, Boston	867	188	four 4-in., two 3-pdr.	138	Ch Eng, WO
USS *Roanoke*	Mine Planter	Squadron 1, Mine Force, Inverness, Scotland, Base 18	6,620	379	one 5-in.,. two 3-in	493	WO
USS *San Diego*	Armored Cruiser Flagship	Cruiser and Transport Force	13,680	504	two 18-in., four 8-in., fourteen 6-in., eighteen 3-in.	829	WO

continued on next page

NAVY SHIPS COAST GUARD OFFICERS ASSIGNED (*continued*)

Name	Type	Assignment	Displacement (Tons)	Length (Feet)	Guns	Crew	Officer Billets*
USS *San Francisco*	Mine Planter	Squadron 1, Mine Force, Inverness, Scotland, Base 18	4,391	325	twelve 6-in., four 6-pdr., four 3-pdr.	384	Nav
USS *St. Louis*	Cruiser	Cruiser Force Atlantic	9,700	426	fourteen 6-in., eighteen 3-in., twelve 3-pdr., eight 1-pdr.	673	Nav
USS *Utowana*	Yacht	Squadron 3, Patrol Force, Brest, France, Base 7	414	169	—	32	Ch Eng

*Ch Eng, chief engineer; EWO, engineering watch officer; Gun, gunnery officer; Nav, navigator; WO, watch officer; XO, executive officer.

Sources: U.S. Navy Department, *Supplement to the Monthly Navy List, Showing the United States Naval Forces Operating in European Waters, Corrected to September 1st 1918* (London: Harrison and Sons, 1918); James L. Mooney, ed., *Dictionary of American Naval Fighting Ships*, 8 vols. (Washington, D.C.: Navy Historical Center, 1959–1991); U.S. Treasury Department, Coast Guard, Assistant Commandant, *Record of the Movements, Vessels of the United States Coast Guard: 1790–December 31, 1933* (Washington, D.C.: U.S. Coast Guard Headquarters, 1934).

APPENDIX D

Coast Guard Officers Serving in Troop Transports

TROOP TRANSPORTS COMMANDED BY COAST GUARD OFFICERS

Name	Former Name (Nationality)	Troop Capacity	Displacement (Tons)	Length (Feet)	Guns	Crew	Officer Billets*
USS Antigone	Neckar (Germany)	3,500	17,024	518	four 5-in.	585	CO, XO, Ch Eng, Nav, EWO
USS Henry R. Mallory	Same (United States)	2,000	10,910	440	four 5-in.	—	CO, Ch Eng
USS Northern Pacific	Same (United States)	2,800	9,708	526	four 6-in., two 1-pdr.	371	CO, XO, Nav, WO, EWO
USS Powhatan	Hamburg (Germany)	3,100	18,026	545	four 6-in., two 1-pdr	533	CO
USS Princess Matoika	Prinzess Alice (Germany)	3,900	20,500	545	four 6-in.	449	CO, XO
USS Texan	Same (United States)	2,200	18,000	484	one 5-in., one 3-in.	—	CO

continued on next page

Troop Transports Commanded by Coast Guard Officers

Name	Former Name (Nationality)	Troop Capacity	Displacement (Tons)	Length (Feet)	Guns	Crew	Officer Billets*
USS America	Amerika (Germany)	7,000	41,500	—	—	—	Ch Eng
USS Cap Finisterre	Same (Germany)	3,800	14,457	560	None	450	Nav
USS De Kalb	Prinz Eitel Friedrich (Germany)	1,600	14,180	506	eight 5-in., six 3-in.	534	XO
USS Graf Waldersee	Same (Germany)	4,300	25,000	585	None	553	2 Officers
USS Hancock	Same (United States)	1,000	8,500	466	six 3-in.	278	XO, Gun
USS Henderson	Same (United States)	2,500	7,750	484	eight 5-in., two 3-in., twelve 1-pdr.	233	XO
USS Imperator	Same (Germany)	9,800	60,000	906	None	—	1 Officer
USS Kaiserin Auguste Victoria	Same (Germany)	5,500	30,400	678	None	—	XO, Ch Eng, Nav
USS Kentuckian	Same (United States)	1,900	14,405	415	None	—	Ch Eng
USS Martha Washington	Same (Austrian)	3,400	12,700	460	four 5-in., two 1-pdr.	949	XO, Ch Eng

Ship	Former name (origin)			Armament		Billet
USS Mercury	Barbarossa (Germany)	3,200	544	four 6-in., two 1-pdr.	494	XO, Nav
USS Mexican	Same (United States)	2,500	488	one 6-in.	108	XO
USS Mobile	Cleveland (Germany)	5,200	608	None	573	Ch Eng
USS Patricia	Same (Germany)	2,900	560	None	569	EWO
USS Philippines	Bulgaria (Germany)	4,000	501	—	470	XO
USS Pocahontas	Prinzess Irene (Germany)	2,900	564	four 6-in., two 3-in., two 1-pdr.	610	XO
USS Susquehanna	Rhein (Germany)	3,300	520	four 6-in., two 1-pdr.	514	XO, Nav
USS Von Steuben	Kronprinz Wilhelm (Germany)	2,900	663	eight 5-in., four 3-in., two 3-in.	975	Nav
USS Zeelandia	Same (Germany)	3,000	440	four 6-in., two 1-pdr.	322	WO

*Ch Eng, chief engineer; CO, commanding officer; EWO, engineering watch officer; Gun, gunnery officer; Nav, navigator; WO, watch officer; XO, executive officer.

Sources: U.S. Treasury Department, Coast Guard, *Register of the Officers, Vessels, and Stations of the United States Coast Guard, 1917* (Washington, D.C.: U.S. Government Printing Office, 1917); James L. Mooney, ed., *Dictionary of American Naval Fighting Ships*, 8 vols. (Washington, D.C.: Navy Historical Center, 1959–1991); U.S. Treasury Department, Coast Guard, Assistant Commandant, *Record of the Movements, Vessels of the United States Coast Guard: 1790–December 31, 1933* (Washington, D.C.: U.S. Coast Guard Headquarters, 1934); Albert Gleaves, *History of the Transport Force: Adventures and Experiences of United States Transports and Cruisers in the World War* (New York: George H. Doran, 1921).

APPENDIX E

Coast Guard Stations Transferred to the Navy

Coast Guard District	Coastal Area Covered before the Outbreak of War	Number of Stations	Coast Guard Superintendent Headquarters	Naval District Assignment at Outbreak of War	Coastal Area Covered by the Naval District	Number of Stations	Naval District Head-quarters
First	Maine, New Hampshire, and Massachusetts to Plum Island	18	Portsmouth, N.H.	First	Eastport, Maine, to Chatham, Mass.	38	Boston, Mass.
Second	Plum Island to Woods Hole, Mass.	23	Provincetown, Mass.				
Third	Woods Hole, Mass., to Thames River, Conn., and Nantucket, Martha's Vineyard, and Fishers Islands	16	Wakefield, R.I.	Second	Chatham, Mass., to New London, Conn.	19	Narragansett Bay, R.I.

Fourth	Coast of Long Island, N.Y.	31	Bay Shore, N.Y.
Fifth	Coast of New Jersey	33	Asbury Park, N.J.
Sixth	Coast between Delaware and Chesapeake Bays	19	Lewes, Del.
Seventh	Cape Henry, Va., to New River, N.C.	31	Elizabeth City, N.C.
Eighth	Coast of North Carolina south of New River, N.C., and South Carolina, Georgia, and Florida	12	Jacksonville, Fla.

Third	New London, Conn., to Barnegat, N.J.	47	New York, N.Y.
Fourth	Barnegat, N.J., to Assateague Inlet, Va.	37	Philadelphia, Penn.
Fifth	Assateague Inlet, Va., to New River Inlet, N.C.	37	Norfolk, Va.
Sixth	New River Inlet, N.C., to St. Johns River, Fla.	3	Charleston, S.C.

continued on next page

Coast Guard Stations Transferred to the Navy (*continued*)

Coast Guard District	Coastal Area Covered before the Outbreak of War	Number of Stations	Coast Guard Superintendent Headquarters	Naval District Assignment at Outbreak of War	Coastal Area Covered by the Naval District	Number of Stations	Naval District Headquarters
Ninth	Alabama, Mississippi, Louisiana, and Texas	7	Galveston, Tex.	Seventh	St. Johns River, Fla., to Tampa, Fla.	8	Key West, Fla.
				Eighth	Tampa, Fla., to Rio Grande, Tex.	8	New Orleans, La.
Tenth	Coasts of Lakes Ontario, Erie, and Huron, to Hammond Bay	20	Buffalo, N.Y.	Ninth, Tenth, and Eleventh	Great Lakes	62	Great Lakes, Ill.

District	No.	Headquarters	Area	District	No.	Headquarters	Area
Eleventh	21	Grand Haven, Mich.	West of Lake Huron and East Coast of Lake Michigan, with Beaver and Mackinac Islands and Louisville, Ky.				
Twelfth	22	Green Bay, Wis.	Lake Michigan	Twelfth	7	San Francisco, Calif.	Southern border Pacific coast to latitude 42°N
Thirteenth	19	San Francisco, Calif.	Coasts of California, Oregon, and Washington, and a station at Nome, Alaska	Thirteenth	11	Puget Sound, Wash.	Latitude 42°N to northern border Pacific coast

Source: U.S. Treasury Department, Coast Guard, *Annual Report of the United States Coast Guard for the Fiscal Year Ended June 30, 1917* (Washington, D.C.: U.S. Government Printing Office, 1917); U.S. Treasury Department, Coast Guard, *Mobilization of the U.S. Coast Guard When Required to Operate as a Part of the Navy. Confidential Order No. 2* (Washington, D.C.: U.S. Government Printing Office, 1917).

APPENDIX F

Medals Awarded to Coast Guardsmen
for Meritorious Service during World War I

THE DISTINGUISHED SERVICE MEDAL
Capt. C. Satterlee
Acting Machinist W. L. Boyce

THE GOLD LIFE-SAVING MEDAL
Capt. H. G. Hamlet
Acting Asst. Master-at-Arms J. C. Osborn
Keeper J. A. Midgett
No. 1 Surfman Z. S. Midgett
Surfman A. V. Midgett
Surfman C. E. Midgett
Surfman L. S. Midgett
Surfman P. L. O'Neal

U.S. NAVY CROSS
Sr. Capt. G. C. Carmine
Sr. Capt. A. J. Henderson
Sr. Capt. W. V. E. Jacobs
Capt. J. G. Berry
Capt. F. C. Billard
Capt. B. M. Chiswell
Capt. W. H. Munter
Capt. R. Ridgely Jr.

Capt. W. J. Wheeler
Capt. (Temp.) C. F. Howell
Capt. (Temp.) J. J. Hutson
Capt. (Temp.) R. L. Jack
Capt. (Temp.) T. M. Molloy
Capt. (Temp.) L. C. Mueller
Capt. (Temp.) L. Reinburg
Capt. (Temp.) P. F. Roach*
Capt. (Temp.) E. G. Rose
Capt. (Temp.) E. F. Stone
1st Lt. F. W. Brown
1st Lt. J. E. Stika
3d Lt. F. J. Birkett
Keeper W. S. Bennett
Keeper J. G. Hearon
Acting Master-at-Arms F. M. Noble
Acting Asst. Master-at-Arms D. E. Grimshaw
Acting Asst. Master-at-Arms J. C. Osborn
Acting Asst. Master-at-Arms A. Zuleger*
Gunner's Mate 2d Class P. L. Marvelle, USN*
Acting Gunner C. L. Wright
Machinist 1st Class M. J. Ryan
Coxswain C. S. Newbury*
Coxswain J. A. Pederson
Acting Coxswain H. J. Ryan
Bugler W. F. Cavaston
Signal Quartermaster A. V. Horton
Electrician 2d Class M. C. Mason
Oiler 2d Class G. W. Christy
Water Tender W. H. Best*
Water Tender R. H. Tingard*
Acting Water Tender M. M. Ovesen*
Cook R. Elam*
Seaman R. J. Gorman
Seaman A. Orhelein
Seaman W. H. Prime*
Seaman M. Stellenwerf*
Seaman W. V. Walsh

Ordinary Seaman C. F. Bennett
Ordinary Seaman J. Grimes
Boy 1st Class J. J. Nevins*

SPECIAL LETTERS OF COMMENDATION (UNITED STATES)
Sr. Capt. J. G. Ballinger
Sr. Capt. F. J. Haake
Capt. H. G. Hamlet
Capt. P. H. Harrison
Capt. (Temp.) J. S. Baylis
Capt. (Temp.) H. G. Hemingway
Capt. (Temp.) C. E. Sugden
Capt. (Temp.) G. E. Wilcox
1st Lt. C. M. Green
Gunner J. DeCosta

GOLD MEDAL FOR GALLANTRY AND HUMANITY IN SAVING LIFE AT SEA (GREAT BRITAIN)
Keeper J. A. Midgett
No. 1 Surfman Z. S. Midgett
Surfman A. V. Midgett
Surfman C. E. Midgett
Surfman L. S. Midgett
Surfman P. L. O'Neal

WAR CROSS AND GOLD MEDAL (ITALY)
Capt. R. Ridgely Jr.

CHEVALIER OF THE LEGION OF HONOR (FRANCE)
Capt. (Temp.) Charles E. Sugden
1st Lt. (Temp.) E. G. Rose

MILITARY ORDER OF THE AVIS (PORTUGAL)
2d Lt. C. H. Dench

COMMANDER OF THE MILITARY ORDER OF THE AVIS (PORTUGAL)
Capt. J. G. Berry

*Awarded posthumously.

NOTES

Chapter 1. Transfer to the Navy

1. "Depicts Suffering of *Healdton* Crew," *New York Times*, 27 March 1917, 4; "7 Americans Lost on *Healdton*," *New York Times*, 24 March 1917, 1.
2. "7 Americans Lost on *Healdton*," 1; "Depicts Suffering of *Healdton* Crew," 4.
3. "Depicts Suffering of *Healdton* Crew," 4.
4. "Text of President Wilson's Address," *New York Times*, 4 February 1917, 1; Barbara W. Tuchman, *The Zimmermann Telegram* (1958; reprint, New York: Ballantine Books, 1994), 149.
5. "*Housatonic* Captain Made Protest in Vain," *New York Times*, 6 February 1917, 1–2; "Captain Says U-35 Sank *Housatonic*," *New York Times*, 21 February 1917, 2.
6. Albert Gleaves, *History of the Transport Force: Adventures and Experiences of United States Transports and Cruisers in the World War* (New York: George H. Doran, 1921), 137.
7. Ibid.
8. "Captain Says U-35 Sank *Housatonic*," 2.
9. Tuchman, *The Zimmermann Telegram*, 146; U.S. President (Wilson), "War Message to Congress," 2 April 1917.
10. "President's Proclamation of a State of War, and Regulations Governing Alien Enemies," *New York Times*, 7 April 1917, 1; "Navy and Reserves Ordered Mobilized," *New York Times*, 7 April 1917, 6.
11. U.S. Congress, "Act to Create the Coast Guard," *Congressional Record*, 63d Cong., 3d sess., 1915, vol. 2, pt. 2.
12. "Navy and Reserves Ordered Mobilized," 6; U.S. Treasury Department, Coast Guard, *Mobilization of the U.S. Coast Guard When Required to Operate as a Part of the Navy* (Washington, D.C.: U.S. Government Printing Office, 1917), 2.
13. U.S. Treasury Department, Coast Guard, *Mobilization of the U.S. Coast Guard*, 5–6.
14. U.S. Treasury Department, Coast Guard, *Annual Report of the United States*

Coast Guard for the Fiscal Year Ended June 30, 1917 (Washington, D.C.: U.S. Government Printing Office, 1917), 34 (hereafter cited as Coast Guard 1917 Annual Report).

15. U.S. Treasury Department, Coast Guard, Headquarters, Commander Richard O. Crisp and Commander Charles E. Johnston, "A History of the Coast Guard in the World War" (unpublished manuscript, Washington, D.C., 1922), 25 (hereafter cited as Crisp and Johnston, "History").

16. Ibid.; U.S. Treasury Department, Coast Guard, *Mobilization of the U.S. Coast Guard*, 5–6; Coast Guard 1917 Annual Report, 39–40.

17. U.S. Navy Department, Secretary, *Annual Report of the Secretary of the Navy, 1918* (Washington, D.C.: U.S. Government Printing Office, 1918), 347–50 (hereafter cited as Navy 1918 Annual Report); U.S. Treasury Department, Coast Guard, USS *Tampa*, Ship's Log, 4 July 1917 (hereafter cited as USS *Tampa*).

18. Coast Guard 1917 Annual Report, 59.

19. Ibid., 50; U.S. Treasury Department, Coast Guard, *Register of the Officers, Vessels, and Stations of the United States Coast Guard, 1917* (Washington, D.C.: U.S. Government Printing Office, 1917), 60–61 (hereafter cited as Coast Guard 1917 Register).

20. Coast Guard 1917 Annual Report, 49.

21. Ibid., 50, 58.

22. Ibid., 51–57.

23. Coast Guard 1917 Register, 77–79; Coast Guard 1917 Annual Report, 39–40, 58; Navy 1918 Annual Report, 1616; Josephus Daniels, *Our Navy at War* (New York: George H. Doran, 1922), 338; Byron Farwell, *Over There: The United States in Great War, 1917–1918* (New York: W. W. Norton, 1999), 70; Crisp and Johnston, "History," 27–28.

24. Stephen H. Evans, *The United States Coast Guard, 1790–1915: A Definitive History* (Annapolis: U.S. Naval Institute, 1949), 6; Coast Guard 1917 Annual Report, 58.

25. Coast Guard 1917 Register, 77–79.

26. Fletcher W. Brown, "Overseas, 1917–1918," booklet, personal monograph, n.p., n.d., 19; Crisp and Johnston, "History," 19, 21.

27. Coast Guard 1917 Annual Report, 58; Crisp and Johnston, "History," 26–27.

28. Crisp and Johnston, "History," 34; Coast Guard 1917 Annual Report, 59.

29. Crisp and Johnston, "History," 34.

30. Coast Guard 1917 Annual Report, 59; U.S. Treasury Department, Coast Guard, *Mobilization of the U.S. Coast Guard*, 4.

31. Crisp and Johnston, "History," 40; Navy 1918 Annual Report, 1618.

32. Ellsworth P. Bertholf, Statement before U.S. Congress, House, Committee

on Interstate and Foreign Commerce, Coast Guard Service Hearings on H.R. 13392 [to permanently transfer Coast Guard from Treasury Department to Navy Department] and H.J.R. 382 [directing Coast Guard to resume operations under Treasury Department], 6 February 1919, 70.

33. Crisp and Johnston, "History," 28; Hamilton Cochran, "Hunting the Hun with the Coast Guard by an American Sailor," June 1919, File No. MVF-675, Accession No. 1764, U.S. Coast Guard Museum, New London, Conn., 2.

34. Crisp and Johnston, "History," 200–201.

35. Ibid.; Navy 1918 Annual Report, 1617.

36. Coast Guard 1917 Annual Report, 48.

37. Ibid.

Chapter 2. Cutters to the War Zone

1. William J. Wheeler, "Reminiscences of World War Convoy Work," *U.S. Naval Institute Proceedings* (May 1929): 390; Crisp and Johnston, "History," 96.

2. During World War I, cutters recorded times in log and record entries using a twelve-hour clock.

3. Glen Perry, *Watchmen of the Sea* (New York: Charles Scribner's Sons, 1938), 194–95; Wheeler, "Reminiscences of World War Convoy Work," 390; Crisp and Johnston, "History," 97; U.S. Treasury Department, Coast Guard, *Operations of the Coast Guard in Time of War* (Washington, D.C.: U.S. Coast Guard, 1940), 5 (hereafter cited as *Operations of the Coast Guard*).

4. Crisp and Johnston, "History," 97; Wheeler, "Reminiscences of World War Convoy Work," 390.

5. Crisp and Johnston, "History," 97.

6. Wheeler, "Reminiscences of World War Convoy Work," 390; Brown, "Overseas," 18; "Ten Americans Perish Trying to Save Ship," *New York Times*, 22 September 1918, 5; U.S. Treasury Department, Coast Guard, USS *Seneca*, Ship's Log, September 1918 (hereafter cited as USS *Seneca*).

7. "Ten Americans Perish Trying to Save Ship," 5; Archibald Hurd and H. H. Bashford, *The Heroic Record of the British Navy: A Short History of the Naval War 1914–1918* (Garden City, N.Y.: Doubleday, Page and Company, 1919), 266; Crisp and Johnston, "History," 97.

8. *Operations of the Coast Guard*, 6.

9. Ibid.

10. Ibid.; "Ten Americans Perish Trying to Save Ship," 5.

11. Hurd and Bashford, *The Heroic Record of the British Navy*, 266; Wheeler, "Reminiscences of World War Convoy Work," 391.

12. *Operations of the Coast Guard*, 7; Perry, *Watchmen of the Sea*, 204.

13. *Operations of the Coast Guard*, 7–8; Perry, *Watchmen of the Sea*, 206; Wheeler, "Reminiscences of World War Convoy Work," 391.

14. Hurd and Bashford, *The Heroic Record of the British Navy*, 268–69; *Operations of the Coast Guard*, 8.

15. Brown, "Overseas," 18; *Operations of the Coast Guard*, 8–9; U.S. National Archives, Record Group 26, Entry 306, U.S. Treasury Department, Coast Guard, *Citations and Commendations*, volume 1 of 1, canvas bound ledger book, June 1918 (hereafter cited as *Citations and Commendations*).

16. Navy 1918 Annual Report, 351–52, 356–61, 2657; U.S. National Archives, Record Group 26, Entry 279, NC-31, Box 9, "Historical Notes, World War I"; U.S. Treasury Department, Coast Guard, *Naval Orientation* (Washington, D.C.: Bureau of Naval Personnel, 11 August 1947), 7.

17. Coast Guard 1917 Annual Report, 60–61; Donald L. Canney, *U.S. Coast Guard and Revenue Cutters, 1790–1935* (Annapolis: Naval Institute Press, 1995), 56; James L. Mooney, ed., *Dictionary of American Naval Fighting Ships* (Washington, D.C.: Navy Historical Center, 1959–1991), 1:29, 4:223.

18. Russell R. Waesche, "Armament and Gunnery in the Coast Guard," *U.S. Naval Institute Proceedings* (May 1929): 381–84.

19. Crisp and Johnston, "History," 43, 61.

20. Cochran, "Hunting the Hun," 3, 44.

21. Crisp and Johnston, "History," 61–62.

22. Ibid., 76.

23. Brown, "Overseas," 10.

24. USS *Seneca*, Ship's Log, 8 April 1917.

25. Coast Guard 1917 Annual Report, 62–63.

26. Crisp and Johnston, "History," 90.

27. Coast Guard 1917 Annual Report, 64; USS *Tampa*, Ship's Log, 20 March 1917.

28. USS *Tampa*, Ship's Log, 4 and 30 July 1917.

29. Crisp and Johnston, "History," 140; Coast Guard 1917 Register, 60–61.

30. Crisp and Johnston, "History," 90; Wheeler, "Reminiscences of World War Convoy Work," 385.

31. U.S. Treasury Department, Coast Guard, Captain Commandant E. P. Bertholf, Letter to Eastern Division Commander, File No. 311, E1, 46, 3 August 1917.

32. USS *Tampa*, Ship's Log, 30 July, 4, 6, and 8 August 1917.

33. Ibid., 11 August 1917.

34. Ibid., 7, 10, 15, 16, 18, 19, and 22 September 1917.

35. Crisp and Johnston, "History," 62, 76, 90.

36. Cochran, "Hunting the Hun," 3–4.

37. Crisp and Johnston, "History," 43–44, 5.

38. USS *Tampa*, Ship's Log, 22 September, 3, 6, 14, 17, 21, and 27 October 1917.

Chapter 3. Convoy Escort Duty

1. U.S. National Archives, Record Group 26, Entry 279, NC-31, Box 12, "The new Cutter *Tampa* was launched on April 16, 1921"; U.S. National Archives, Record Group 26, Entry 279, NC-31, Box 9, "Historical Notes, World War I."

2. U.S. National Archives, Record Group 26, Entry 279, NC-31, Box 12, "The new Cutter *Tampa* was launched on April 16, 1921."

3. "Veteran's Day Ceremony Honors WWI *Tampa* Crew, Purple Hearts Awarded Posthumously," *The Reservist* (December 1999): 7; author's observations at the ceremony.

4. Crisp and Johnston, "History," 122, 158; Wheeler, "Reminiscences of World War Convoy Work," 392; U.S. Treasury Department, Coast Guard, Commodore Commandant, "Coast Guard Cutter *Tampa* movements," letter, 30 June 1919, File 601; Mooney, *Dictionary of American Naval Fighting Ships*, 7:30.

5. Coast Guard 1917 Annual Report, 64; *Operations of the Coast Guard*, 4.

6. Navy 1918 Annual Report, 347.

7. U.S. National Archives, Record Group 26, Entry 279, NC-31, Box 9, "Historical Notes, World War I"; *Operations of the Coast Guard*, 4; U.S. Navy Department, Coast Guard, Captain Commandant, Letter to Mrs. Bertha L. Earp, "Loss of the Coast Guard Cutter *Tampa*," Washington, D.C., 8 October 1918.

8. Wheeler, "Reminiscences of World War Convoy Work," 385; Crisp and Johnston, "History," 63, 77, 90.

9. Crisp and Johnston, "History," 62, 90; Brown, "Overseas," 10.

10. Crisp and Johnston, "History," 44, 114; Cochran, "Hunting the Hun," 6.

11. William Bridgewater, ed., *The Columbia Viking Desk Encyclopedia* (New York: Viking Press, 1953), 482; Cochran, "Hunting the Hun," 5.

12. Cochran, "Hunting the Hun," 6.

13. Wheeler, "Reminiscences of World War Convoy Work," 387.

14. Frederick R. Foulkes, Letter to Father, 10 April 1918, File No. MVF-675, Accession No. 1764, U.S. Coast Guard Museum, New London, Conn.

15. Crisp and Johnston, "History," 90; Wheeler, "Reminiscences of World War Convoy Work," 385–86.
16. Wheeler, "Reminiscences of World War Convoy Work," 387.
17. Ibid., 385–86.
18. Ibid.
19. Cochran, "Hunting the Hun," 8–9.
20. Wheeler, "Reminiscences of World War Convoy Work," 387.
21. Ibid.; Crisp and Johnston, "History," 64; Harry L. Whitney, Donald L. Pratt, and William M. O'Connor, eds., "A Brief Retrospective Summary of Our Work Experiences in the World War Aboard the USS *Algonquin*, CG, 1917–1919," 1919, File No. MVF 675, Accession No. 1764, U.S. Coast Guard Museum, New London, Conn.
22. Wheeler, "Reminiscences of World War Convoy Work," 387; Whitney et al., "A Brief Retrospective Summary."
23. USS *Tampa*, Ship's Log, 21 November 1917.
24. Crisp and Johnston, "History," 95–96.
25. Wheeler, "Reminiscences of World War Convoy Work," 387; Crisp and Johnston, "History," 118.
26. Frederick R. Foulkes, Letter to Father, 10 April 1918.
27. Cochran, "Hunting the Hun," 26.
28. Frederick R. Foulkes, Letter to Father, 10 April 1918.
29. Cochran, "Hunting the Hun," 13.
30. Brown, "Overseas," 13; Wheeler, "Reminiscences of World War Convoy Work," 388, 389; Maurice Pendergast, ed., *Jane's Fighting Ships, 1918* (London: Sampson Low, Marston and Company, Ltd., 1918), 9.
31. Brown, "Overseas," 13–15; Daniels, *Our Navy at War*, 336; Wheeler, "Reminiscences of World War Convoy Work," 388–89.
32. Brown, "Overseas," 15–16; Wheeler, "Reminiscences of World War Convoy Work," 388–89; Crisp and Johnston, "History," 91–92.
33. Brown, "Overseas," 15–16; Wheeler, "Reminiscences of World War Convoy Work," 388–89; USS *Seneca*, Ship's Log, 25 April 1918.
34. Crisp and Johnston, "History," 63; Cochran, "Hunting the Hun," 7; USS *Seneca*, Ship's Log, 28 June 1918.
35. Crisp and Johnston, "History," 114–16; Cochran, "Hunting the Hun," 18.
36. Brown, "Overseas," 10.
37. Ibid., 11–12; Wheeler, "Reminiscences of World War Convoy Work," 388.
38. Cochran, "Hunting the Hun," 9.
39. Ibid., 27; James M. Earp, Letter to brother Arthur, 8 September 1918, letter given to author by Earp's nephew, Charles A. Earp, 11 December 2001.
40. Cochran, "Hunting the Hun," 18, 25.

41. Ibid., 23.

42. Ibid., 10–13.

43. Crisp and Johnston, "History," 94–95.

44. Wheeler, "Reminiscences of World War Convoy Work," 388; U.S. Treasury Department, Coast Guard, *Naval Orientation*, 7.

Chapter 4. Home Waters

1. Irv V. Beall, "Epic Cruise of the USS *Morrill*," *Sparks Journal* (n.d.): 24; Crisp and Johnston, "History," 159.

2. Beall, "Epic Cruise of the USS *Morrill*," 24; Crisp and Johnston, "History," 159.

3. Beall, "Epic Cruise of the USS *Morrill*," 25.

4. Ibid., 26; "*Halifax* Wrecked: More Than One Thousand Killed in this City, Many Thousands Are Injured and Homeless," *Halifax Herald*, 7 December 1917, 1.

5. Felix Riesenberg, *Standard Seamanship for the Merchant Marine* (New York: D. Van Nostrand, n.d.), 614–15; Beall, "Epic Cruise of the USS *Morrill*," 26.

6. Beall, "Epic Cruise of the USS *Morrill*," 26.

7. Ibid., 26–27.

8. Ibid.

9. Ibid.; Crisp and Johnston, "History," 258.

10. Crisp and Johnston, "History," 259.

11. Ibid., 260–61.

12. Ibid., 261.

13. Beall, 27–30.

14. Crisp and Johnston, "History," 66–67; Coast Guard 1917 Register, 60.

15. Crisp and Johnston, "History," 47–48, 56, 110; Coast Guard 1917 Annual Report, 61; Mooney, *Dictionary of American Naval Fighting Ships*, 3:157; Coast Guard 1917 Register, 60.

16. Bettilou B. Hand, "World War I Service of Her Father, John J. Bitting," letter to author, 17 September 2001.

17. Crisp and Johnston, "History," 45, 47–48, 85–86, 131, 139; Coast Guard 1917 Register, 60, 62–63; Canney, *U.S. Coast Guard and Revenue Cutters*, 60, 64.

18. Crisp and Johnston, "History," 107–8.

19. Ibid., 53, 58–59, 131, 139; Canney, *U.S. Coast Guard and Revenue Cutters*, 54; David R. Ponstein, interview by author about USCG WWI service of grandfather Francis P. Smith, Ponstein's grandfather, 31 July 2001; U.S. Treasury

Department, Coast Guard, "Service Record of Francis Patrick Smith, April 4, 1918 to April 7, 1919, Excerpts," author received copy from grandson David R. Ponstein, 22 July 2001; Coast Guard 1917 Annual Report, 61.

20. Crisp and Johnston, "History," 48–49, 56, 85–86; Coast Guard 1917 Annual Report, 60; Coast Guard 1917 Register, 60–61.

21. Crisp and Johnston, "History," 138; Mooney, *Dictionary of American Naval Fighting Ships*, 7:375.

22. Crisp and Johnston, "History," 46, 54, 57, 83; "German Ships Seized by the Government," *New York Times*, 7 April 1917, 2; Canney, *U.S. Coast Guard and Revenue Cutters*, 64; Mooney, *Dictionary of American Naval Fighting Ships*, 2:243; Coast Guard 1917 Register, 61–63, 67.

23. Crisp and Johnston, "History," 55, 57; Mooney, *Dictionary of American Naval Fighting Ships*, 3:116.

24. Crisp and Johnston, "History," 50, 56, 59, 84; Coast Guard 1917 Register, 62–63.

25. Crisp and Johnston, "History," 49, 56, 58, 88, 243–44; Beall, "Epic Cruise of the USS *Morrill*," 30; Canney, *U.S. Coast Guard and Revenue Cutters*, 53.

26. Crisp and Johnston, "History," 45, 47–48.

27. Ibid., 72, 75, 200.

28. Ibid., 86–88; "14 Seized Steamers Receive New Names," *New York Times*, 5 June 1917, 17; "German Ships Seized by the Government," 2.

29. Crisp and Johnston, "History," 102, 104; Canney, *U.S. Coast Guard and Revenue Cutters*, 66; Pendergast, *Jane's Fighting Ships*, 165a.

30. Crisp and Johnston, "History," 109–10, 131, 135, 137.

31. Ibid., 50–51, 60; Evans, *The United States Coast Guard*, 109; Coast Guard 1917 Annual Report, 39; Navy 1918 Annual Report, 351; Canney, *U.S. Coast Guard and Revenue Cutters*, 55; Robert E. Johnson, *Guardians of the Sea: History of the United States Coast Guard 1915 to the Present* (Annapolis: Naval Institute Press, 1987), 46–47.

32. Crisp and Johnston, "History," 49, 56, 86, 130–31; Coast Guard 1917 Register, 60–61.

33. Crisp and Johnston, "History," 49, 56, 81, 86.

34. Ibid., 47–48.

35. Ibid., 87, 298–99.

36. Ibid., 72–73, 87, 131.

37. Ibid., 177, 194–95; Mooney, *Dictionary of American Naval Fighting Ships*, 3:205, 8:501, 558; U.S. Treasury Department, Coast Guard, Assistant Commandant, *Record of the Movements, Vessels of the United States Coast Guard, 1790–December 31, 1933* (Washington, D.C.: U.S. Coast Guard Headquarters, 1934), 563.

38. Crisp and Johnston, "History," 169, 171; Mooney, *Dictionary of American Naval Fighting Ships*, 2:290, 316, 4:192; *Record of the Movements*, 565.

39. Crisp and Johnston, "History," 160–61, 169, 171–72; Mooney, *Dictionary of American Naval Fighting Ships*, 1:22, 35.

40. Crisp and Johnston, "History," 174, 185; Mooney, *Dictionary of American Naval Fighting Ships*, 2:380, 436; "Roosevelt Would Ostracize Slackers," *New York Times*, 18 June 1917, 7; Coast Guard 1917 Register, 14.

41. Crisp and Johnston, "History," 180–81; Mooney, *Dictionary of American Naval Fighting Ships*, 5:82, 277; *Record of the Movements*, 578–79; Navy 1918 Annual Report, 354.

42. Crisp and Johnston, "History," 408; Mooney, *Dictionary of American Naval Fighting Ships*, 1:21–22, 5:66–67; *Record of the Movements*, 381; "Centennial Issue: Class Listings," *The Bulletin* (New London, Conn.: U.S. Coast Guard Academy Alumni Association, 1976), 84.

43. Mooney, *Dictionary of American Naval Fighting Ships*, 2:129, 4:370–71; *Record of the Movements*, 536, 538, 546, 550, 560, 577, 582; U.S. Treasury Department, Coast Guard, *Annual Report of the United States Coast Guard for the Fiscal Year Ended June 30, 1918* (Washington, D.C.: U.S. Government Printing Office, 1918), 16 (hereafter cited as Coast Guard 1918 Annual Report).

44. Mooney, *Dictionary of American Naval Fighting Ships*, 6:13–14; *Record of the Movements*, 574; "Sunk after Explosion," *New York Times*, 20 July 1918, 4; "*San Diego* Loss Still Unexplained," *New York Times*, 21 July 1918, 7; Gleaves, *History of the Transport Force*.

CHAPTER 5. ON NAVY SHIPS IN THE WAR ZONE

1. Information for USS *Marietta* narrative was taken from U.S. Navy Department, Naval Forces in France, Commanding Officer, USS *Marietta*, "Report of Convoy," 29 April 1919, 1–4; Mooney, *Dictionary of American Naval Fighting Ships*, 4:238–39; Crisp and Johnston, "History," 262–63, 363–64; *Operations of the Coast Guard*, 13; U.S. Navy Department, Crew of the USS *James*, Letter to Lt. Cdr. H. G. Hamlet, Commanding Officer, USS *Marietta*, U.S. Naval Base, Brest, France, 7 May 1919; *Citations and Commendations*; Lawrence Wainwright, *A Brief History of the U.S. Naval Forces in France from 11 November 1918 to 1 October 1919* (Brest, France: USS *Bridgeport*, 1919), 74–76.

2. Mooney, *Dictionary of American Naval Fighting Ships*, 4:101.

3. Crisp and Johnston, "History," 490.

4. U.S. Navy Department, *Supplement to the Monthly Navy List, Showing the United States Naval Forces Operating in European Waters, Corrected to September 1st 1918* (London: Harrison and Sons, 1918), 68 (hereafter cited

as *Monthly Navy List*); Mooney, *Dictionary of American Naval Fighting Ships*, 2:50, 3:237; Crisp and Johnston, "History," 165–66, 350.

5. Crisp and Johnston, "History," 371; Mooney, *Dictionary of American Naval Fighting Ships*, 5:198–99; *Monthly Navy List*, 69–70.

6. *Monthly Navy List*, 5, 68; Mooney, *Dictionary of American Naval Fighting Ships*, 1:56, 7:479–80; Crisp and Johnston, "History," 163.

7. Milton R. Daniels Jr., Telephone conversation with author, 25 February 2001; Crisp and Johnston, "History," 166; *Monthly Navy List*, 6, 69; Mooney, *Dictionary of American Naval Fighting Ships*, 2:227, 4:180.

8. Crisp and Johnston, "History," 167–68; Daniels, Telephone conversation.

9. *Record of the Movements*, 537; Crisp and Johnston, "History," 168, 352; Milton R. Daniels Jr., Letter to author, 27 February 2001.

10. Mooney, *Dictionary of American Naval Fighting Ships*, 4:167–68; Crisp and Johnston, "History," 178, 358; *Monthly Navy List*, 70.

11. Crisp and Johnston, "History," 171–72; Mooney, *Dictionary of American Naval Fighting Ships*, 2:301; *Monthly Navy List*, 69.

12. Crisp and Johnston, "History," 353–54.

13. Ibid., 406.

14. Ibid., 407.

15. Ibid.

16. *Record of the Movements*, 549, 571, 578; Mooney, *Dictionary of American Naval Fighting Ships*, 1:125.

17. Crisp and Johnston, "History," 190–91, 375; Mooney, *Dictionary of American Naval Fighting Ships*, 6:684; *Monthly Navy List*, 71; *Record of the Movements*, 578.

18. Crisp and Johnston, "History," 175.

19. Ibid., 176–77.

20. Ibid.

21. Ibid., 187, 189; Mooney, *Dictionary of American Naval Fighting Ships*, 6:24.

22. Crisp and Johnston, "History," 188–89; H. Wickliffe Rose, *Brittany Patrol: The Story of the Suicide Fleet* (New York: W. W. Norton, 1937), 213–14; U.S. Treasury Department, Coast Guard, *United States Coast Guard Roll of Honor, April 6 1917–November 30, 1918* (Washington, D.C.: U.S. Government Printing Office, 1919), 20.

23. Crisp and Johnston, "History," 162, 349; Mooney, *Dictionary of American Naval Fighting Ships*, 1:52; *Monthly Navy List*, 51.

24. Crisp and Johnston, "History," 172–73; Mooney, *Dictionary of American Naval Fighting Ships*, 2:347; *Monthly Navy List*, 39.

25. Crisp and Johnston, "History," 174; Henry Braid Wilson, *An Account of the Operations of the American Navy in France During the War with Germany* (written aboard USS *Pennsylvania*: n.p., n.d.), 66–67.

26. Crisp and Johnston, "History," 355.

27. Ibid., 179, 365; *Monthly Navy List*, 51; Wilson, *Account of the Operations*, 31; Daniels, *Our Navy at War*, 70, 139, 140; Mooney, *Dictionary of American Naval Fighting Ships*, 4:281.

28. Mooney, *Dictionary of American Naval Fighting Ships*, 5:102; *Monthly Navy List*, 41; Crisp and Johnston, "History," 164, 182, 367; Wilson, *Account of the Operations*, 58.

29. *Monthly Navy List*, 51; Mooney, *Dictionary of American Naval Fighting Ships*, 5:102–3; Crisp and Johnston, "History," 368–69; *Record of the Movements*, 573.

30. *Record of the Movements*, 538, 540; Mooney, *Dictionary of American Naval Fighting Ships*, 7:429, 8:91; Crisp and Johnston, "History," 193, 377; *Monthly Navy List*, 43–44.

31. Daniels, *Our Navy at War*, 127, 137, 139, 144.

32. Mooney, *Dictionary of American Naval Fighting Ships*, 2:23, 26, 6:118; *Record of the Movements*, 564, 584; Crisp and Johnston, "History," 405; *Monthly Navy List*, 83–84.

33. Mooney, *Dictionary of American Naval Fighting Ships*, 1:128, 6:290–91; *Record of the Movements*, 576; *Monthly Navy List*, 82.

34. Crisp and Johnston, "History," 164; Mooney, *Dictionary of American Naval Fighting Ships*, 1:113; *Record of the Movements*, 571; *Monthly Navy List*, 37.

35. Mooney, *Dictionary of American Naval Fighting Ships*, 1:171, 2:281–82; *Record of the Movements*, 536–38, 576; *Monthly Navy List*, 25, 67–68.

Chapter 6. Aviation

1. "U-boat Gives No Warning," *New York Times*, 22 July 1918, 1; Joseph D. Buckley, *Wings Over Cape Cod: A History of the Chatham Naval Air Station, 1917–1922* (Orleans, Mass.: Lower Cape Publishing, 2000), 27.

2. "U-boat Gives No Warning," 6; Pendergast, *Jane's Fighting Ships*, 110; Lowell Thomas, *Raiders of the Deep* (Garden City, N.Y.: Garden City Publishing, 1932).

3. Crisp and Johnston, "History," 264; Pendergast, *Jane's Fighting Ships*, 110.

4. Crisp and Johnston, "History," 265.

5. Adrian O. Van Wyen, *Naval Aviation in World War I* (Washington, D.C.: Chief of Naval Operations, Government Printing Office, 1969), 77; Buckley, *Wings Over Cape Cod*, 29, 31.

6. Crisp and Johnston, "History," 222–23.

7. Ibid., 223.

8. Ibid., 225; Van Wyen, *Naval Aviation in World War I*, 77; Robert J. O'Leary, "Victory Denied: The Battle of Chatham," *The Bulletin* (New London,

Conn.: U.S. Coast Guard Academy Alumni Association, October 1998), 24; Buckley, *Wings Over Cape Cod*, 31; Thomas, *Raiders of the Deep.*

9. "Navy Without Information," *New York Times*, 23 July 1918, 1; "Investigate Aerial Bombs," *New York Times*, 24 July 1918, 6.

10. U.S. National Archives, Record Group 26, Entry 283, Box 4, U.S. Treasury Department, Coast Guard, Public Relations, "The United States Coast Guard Aviation and the War," 1946, 1.

11. Arthur Pearcy, *A History of U.S. Coast Guard Aviation* (Annapolis: Naval Institute Press, 1989), 5.

12. E. P. Bertholf, letter to E. F. Stone, "Duties in Connection With Aviation," 29 March 1916, Stone File, Coast Guard Historian's Office, Washington, D.C.

13. Pearcy, *A History of U.S. Coast Guard Aviation*, 6.

14. Robert H. Rankin and Norman N. Rubin, "The Story of Coast Guard Aviation," *U.S. Naval Institute Proceedings* (June 1959): 89; *U.S. Coast Guard Aviation* (Paducah, Ky.: Turner Publishing, 1997), 10; U.S. National Archives, Record Group 26, Entry 283, Box 4, U.S. Treasury Department, Coast Guard, Public Relations, "The United States Coast Guard Aviation and the War," 1946, 2.

15. Van Wyen, *Naval Aviation in World War I*, 6, 7.

16. *Flying Officers of the USN* (Atglen, Pa.: Schiffer Military History, 1997), 30; "First Coast Guard Aviation Group, Naval Air Sta., Pensacola, Fla., Mar. 22, 1917," photograph, Elmer F. Stone File, Coast Guard Historian's Office, Washington, D.C.; *U.S. Coast Guard Aviation*, 13.

17. E. A. Coffin, letter to Paul N. Wells, 6 December 1953, Coast Guard Historian's Office, Washington, D.C.

18. Ibid.; U.S. Defense Department, U.S. Navy, "United States Naval Hall of Honor Enshrinement Ceremony," program (Pensacola, Fla.: U.S. Naval Aviation Museum, May 12, 1983), 21; Van Wyen, *Naval Aviation in World War I*, 45.

19. Mooney, *Dictionary of American Naval Fighting Ships*, 4:402.

20. *Record of the Movements*, 551; U.S. Treasury Department, Coast Guard, *Register of the Officers, Vessels, and Stations of the United States Coast Guard, January 1, 1918* (Washington, D.C.: Government Printing Office, 1918), 22 (hereafter cited as Coast Guard 1918 Register); "Effort To Fly Overseas," *New York Times*, 11 May 1919, 4:1; Ashley D. Pace Jr. "Interview by Captain Pat Wendt and Bill Broughton, Jr. concerning his uncle, Coast Guard aviator Elmer Stone," n.d., Stone File, U.S. Coast Guard Historian's Office, Washington, D.C. (hereafter cited as Pace Interview).

21. Pace Interview; U.S. Navy Department, Secretary, *Annual Report of the*

Secretary of the Navy, 1919. (Washington, D.C.: U.S. Government Printing Office, 1919), 218–21 (hereafter cited as Navy 1919 Annual Report); Coast Guard 1918 Register, 22; "Official Log of the Flight," *New York Times,* 18 May 1919, 1; "Schedule of NC-4's Eventful Flight From Rockaway to the Portuguese Capitol," *New York Times,* 28 May 1919, 2; Pearcy, *A History of U.S. Coast Guard Aviation,* 160; U.S. Navy Department, Secretary (Acting), Franklin D. Roosevelt. Letter to First Lieutenant Elmer F. Stone, USCG, "Commendation," Washington, D.C., 23 August 1919.

22. "Centennial Issue: Register of Graduates," *The Bulletin* (New London, Conn.: U.S. Coast Guard Academy Alumni Association, 1976), 84.
23. Van Wyen, *Naval Aviation in World War I,* 61, 76–77; Wilson, *Account of the Operations,* 141–43.
24. Van Wyen, *Naval Aviation in World War I,* 76; Mooney, *Dictionary of American Naval Fighting Ships,* 8:92.
25. Van Wyen, *Naval Aviation in World War I,* 45, 76.
26. Ibid., 81; *Citations and Commendations; U.S. Coast Guard Aviation,* 11.
27. Van Wyen, *Naval Aviation in World War I,* 45; Crisp and Johnston, "History," 227.
28. Crisp and Johnston, "History," 227; Van Wyen, *Naval Aviation in World War I,* 44, 88.
29. Van Wyen, p. 81; *Record of the Movements,* 547.
30. *Sunday Boston Herald,* 1 June 1919; Crisp and Johnston, "History," 221.
31. *U.S. Coast Guard Aviation,* 11.

CHAPTER 7. COASTAL STATIONS

1. U.S. Treasury Department, Coast Guard, Station No. 179, "Report of Assistance, August 16, 1918, in Case of British Steamship *Mirlo.*" Washington, D.C.: U.S. Coast Guard Historian's Office, Midgett File, 1918 (hereafter cited as "Report of Assistance").
2. Midgett (Daughter of John A. Midgett), "Life Saving Stations," manuscript, Midgett File, U.S. Coast Guard Historian's Office, Washington, D.C., 2 (hereafter cited as "Life Saving Stations").
3. "Report of Assistance," 1.
4. Ibid.
5. Ibid.
6. Ibid.; "Life Saving Stations," 3.
7. David Stick, *Graveyard of the Atlantic* (Chapel Hill, N.C.: University of North Carolina Press, 1952); "Gasoline Cargo Exploded," *New York Times,* 18 August 1918, 6.

8. Awards for SS *Mirlo* rescue, in *Citations and Commendations;* Crisp and Johnston, "History," 276.

9. Johnson, *Guardians of the Sea,* 44.

10. Robert F. Bennett, *Sand Pounders* (Washington, D.C.: U.S. Coast Guard Historian's Office, 1998), 182.

11. Coast Guard 1917 Annual Report, 51–57.

12. Ibid., 248–49; Navy 1918 Annual Report, 125.

13. Bennett, *Sand Pounders,* 8.

14. U.S. Treasury Department, Coast Guard, *Instructions for Coast Guard Stations, 1921* (Washington, D.C.: U.S. Government Printing Office, 1921), 32–33; Coast Guard 1917 Annual Report, 67–72.

15. Coast Guard 1917 Annual Report, 67–68; Bennett, *Sand Pounders,* 140.

16. U.S. Treasury Department, Coast Guard, *Instructions for Coast Guard Stations,* 17; Coast Guard 1917 Annual Report, 72.

17. U.S. Treasury Department, Coast Guard, *Instructions for Coast Guard Stations,* 17.

18. Coast Guard 1917 Annual Report, 72–73.

19. Ibid.

20. U.S. Treasury Department, Coast Guard, *Instructions for Coast Guard Stations,* 37, 38; Dennis L. Noble, *That Others Might Live: The U.S. Life Saving Service, 1878–1915* (Annapolis: Naval Institute Press, 1994), 126.

21. Buckley, *Wings Over Cape Cod,* 44–47; Coast Guard 1917 Annual Report, 51.

22. P. R. Egner, *The Log of the USS* Northern Pacific *During the Great War. A True Story of the Adventures of the USS* Northern Pacific *During the War* (New York: Brooklyn Eagle Press, 1919), 98; "Transport Ashore Off Fire Island, 3,000 Aboard Safe," *New York Times,* 2 January 1919, 1–2.

23. "Transport Ashore," 1; Egner, *Log of the USS* Northern Pacific, 99.

24. Egner, *Log of the USS* Northern Pacific, 99; "Navy Boats Land 2,100 More from *Northern Pacific,*" *New York Times,* 4 January 1919, 1–2, 5.

25. Coast Guard 1917 Annual Report, 54; "Virginia Beach Station, Answer Sheets, Buildings No. 1 through No. 5," 20 March 1916, Collection of the Old Coast Guard Station Museum, Virginia Beach, Va.

26. *The Old Coast Guard Station: A Brief History* (Virginia Beach, Va.: Old Coast Guard Station Museum Staff, 1 December 2000).

27. "Virginia Beach Station, Answer Sheets."

28. "Virginia Beach Station Crew List 1910–1929," Collection of the Old Coast Guard Station Museum, Virginia Beach, Va.

29. Navy 1918 Annual Report, 127; Daniels, *Our Navy at War,* 339.

30. Stick, *Graveyard of the Atlantic,* 200; John B. McMaster, *The United States in the World War: 1918–1920* (New York: D. Appleton-Century, 1940), 16.

31. Stick, *Graveyard of the Atlantic*, 202–3.

32. Ibid.; McMaster, *United States in the World War*, 19; U.S. National Archives, Record Group 26, Entry 279, NC-31, Box 9, "Historical Notes, World War I," 4–5.

Chapter 8. Port Security

1. "Day of Explosions and Fire Finishes Shell Plant Ruin," *New York Times*, 5 October 1918, 18; "Begin Shell Plant Rebuilding Today," *New York Times*, 7 October 1918, 1; "Great Munitions Plant Blown Up," *New York Times*, 5 October 1918, 8.

2. Crisp and Johnston, "History," 285–86.

3. Ibid., 288; Navy 1918 Annual Report, 366.

4. Crisp and Johnston, "History," 290–91.

5. Ibid., 287.

6. Ibid., 287–90; Navy 1918 Annual Report, 366.

7. Crisp and Johnston, "History," 290.

8. Ibid., 291; "Day of Explosions," 1, 18.

9. "Great Munitions Plant Blown Up," 8; Crisp and Johnston, "History," 191, 192; Robert M. Browning Jr., *Captains of the Port* (Washington, D.C.: U.S. Coast Guard Historian, 1993), 4.

10. Crisp and Johnston, "History," 105–6.

11. Ibid., 294.

12. Ibid., 293; "Begin Shellplant Rebuilding Today," 8; "Day of Explosions," 18.

13. Crisp and Johnston, "History," 289; Navy 1918 Annual Report, 361; Browning, *Captains of the Port*, 4; "Day of Explosions," 18; "Begin Shellplant Rebuilding Today," 1.

14. Crisp and Johnston, "History," 295.

15. Ibid., 209; K. R. Kaplan and James L. Hunt, *This Is the Coast Guard* (Cambridge, Md.: Maritime Press, 1972), 45; "Espionage Bill Is Signed," *New York Times*, 16 June 1917, 10; Browning, *Captains of the Port*, 3.

16. Crisp and Johnston, "History," 210.

17. Ibid., 36.

18. "New Post for Coast Guard Captain," *New York Times*, 16 December 1917, 5; Crisp and Johnston, "History," 39–40; Navy 1918 Annual Report, 125; Johnson, *Guardians of the Sea*, 49–50.

19. Navy 1918 Annual Report, 125, 1618; Coast Guard 1918 Annual Report, 10.

20. Coast Guard 1917 Annual Report, 50, 65; Crisp and Johnston, "History," 60, 62–63, 65, 82; Canney, *U.S. Coast Guard and Revenue Cutters*, 64.

21. Crisp and Johnston, "History," 58; Pendergast, *Jane's Fighting Ships*, 167a; Coast Guard 1917 Annual Report, 66.

22. Pendergast, *Jane's Fighting Ships*, 166a; Coast Guard 1917 Annual Report, 64; Crisp and Johnston, "History," 52, 55; Canney, *U.S. Coast Guard and Revenue Cutters*, 72.

23. Crisp and Johnston, "History," 52–54, 75.

24. Ibid., 105–6.

25. *Record of the Movements*, 557.

26. Ibid., 553; Florence Kern and Barbara Voulgaris, *Traditions: 200 Years of History* (Washington, D.C.: U.S. Coast Guard Public Affairs, n.d.), 6; Crisp and Johnston, "History," 57.

CHAPTER 9. SEIZED GERMAN SHIPS AND TROOP TRANSPORTS

1. Crisp and Johnston, "History," 252–53.

2. Ibid., 254; Coast Guard 1918 Register, 6, 32.

3. "German Officers Held," *New York Times*, 10 April 1917, 4.

4. Crisp and Johnston, "History," 255.

5. Ibid., 256.

6. Ibid., 256–57; "German Officers Held," 4.

7. Crisp and Johnston, "History," 209a.

8. Ibid., 60, 66, 139, 209a–b; Coast Guard 1917 Register, 60–61; "Crews Dispossessed Early this Morning on Port Collector's Orders," *New York Times*, 6 April 1917, 1; "27 Ships Taken Here," *New York Times*, 7 April 1917, 1; "War-Bound German Ships Here Seized," *New York Times*, 7 April 1917, 2.

9. Crisp and Johnston, "History," 43, 48, 57, 84; Coast Guard 1917 Register, 62–63; "27 Ships Taken Here," 1; "War-Bound German Ships Here Seized," 2.

10. Crisp and Johnston, "History," 53–54, 85, 107; Coast Guard 1917 Register, 60–63; "27 Ships Taken Here," 1; Canney, *U.S. Coast Guard and Revenue Cutters*, 59.

11. Crisp and Johnston, "History," 53–54, 83–84, 107, 113; Canney, *U.S. Coast Guard and Revenue Cutters*, 54, 69; "27 Ships Taken Here," 1; Coast Guard 1917 Register, 62–63.

12. William J. Wilgus, *Transporting the AEF in Western Europe, 1917–1919* (New York: Columbia University Press, 1931), 483; Navy 1918 Annual Report, 26; Mooney, *Dictionary of American Naval Fighting Ships*, 3:231–32, 295; Gleaves, *History of the Transport Force*, 246; Leonard P. Ayres, *The War with Germany: A Statistical Summary* (Washington, D.C.: U.S. Government Printing Office, 1919), 43.

13. Gleaves, *History of the Transport Force*, 32–33.

14. Ibid., 34–36, 38, 41, 48, 62.

15. Ibid., 36–37.

16. Ibid., 44–48, 62.

17. Ibid., 26.

18. Lewis P. Clephane, *History of the Naval Overseas Transportation Service in World War I* (Washington, D.C.: U.S. Government Printing Office, 1969), xvii, 61–62.

19. Gleaves, *History of the Transport Force*, 30–31, 63; Clephane, *History of the Naval Overseas Transportation Service*, 61.

20. Clephane, *History of the Naval Overseas Transportation Service*, vii; Gleaves, *History of the Transport Force*, 88.

21. Gleaves, *History of the Transport Force*, 64, 87; U.S. Navy Department, Atlantic Fleet, Commander Cruiser Force and Transport Force, Rear Admiral Albert Gleaves, "Orders for Ships in Convoy: Cruiser Force and Transport Force, 1918" (Washington, D.C.: Navy Historical Center, 1918), 1–3 (hereafter cited as "Orders for Ships"); David C. Shanks, *As They Passed Through the Port* (Washington, D.C.: Cary Publishing, 1927), 144.

22. "Orders for Ships," 3.

23. Ibid., 3–5, 7.

24. Gleaves, *History of the Transport Force*, 87.

25. Ibid., 88–89; Shanks, *As They Passed Through the Port*, 153.

26. Gleaves, *History of the Transport Force*, 70–71.

27. Ibid.

28. Ibid., 69–70; Clephane, *History of the Naval Overseas Transportation Service*, 72.

29. Crisp and Johnston, "History," 408; Mooney, *Dictionary of American Naval Fighting Ships*, 4:252–53; Gleaves, *History of the Transport Force*, 258; Coast Guard 1917 Register, 32; *Record of the Movements*, 580.

30. Mooney, *Dictionary of American Naval Fighting Ships*, 2:82, 5:289; Crisp and Johnston, "History," 408.

31. Mooney, *Dictionary of American Naval Fighting Ships*, 2:254; *Record of the Movements*, 568; Coast Guard 1917 Register, 10.

32. *Record of the Movements*, 580; Coast Guard 1917 Register, 10; Crisp and Johnston, "History," 405.

33. Mooney, *Dictionary of American Naval Fighting Ships*, 5:382; U.S. Navy Department, USS *Princess Matoika*, *The Wigwam* (ship's monthly periodical), vol. 2, no. 1, May 1919, 2.

34. *Record of the Movements*, 578; Gleaves, *History of the Transport Force*, 246.

35. *Record of the Movements*, 538–40, 584; Mooney, *Dictionary of American Naval Fighting Ships*, 4:330, 5:333, 365–66, 7:686.

36. Mooney, *Dictionary of American Naval Fighting Ships*, 3:231–32, 295; Gleaves, *History of the Transport Force*, 41, 246; *Record of the Movements*, 537; Crisp and Johnston, "History," 405.

37. Mooney, *Dictionary of American Naval Fighting Ships*, 8:561–62; Gleaves, *History of the Transport Force*, 250; *Record of the Movements*, 540; Crisp and Johnston, "History," 405.

38. Mooney, *Dictionary of American Naval Fighting Ships*, 5:112; Crisp and Johnston, "History," 406; *Record of the Movements*, 578.

39. Mooney, *Dictionary of American Naval Fighting Ships*, 4:306, 334; Gleaves, *History of the Transport Force*, 248, 257–58; *Record of the Movements*, 564, 578, 583.

40. Mooney, *Dictionary of American Naval Fighting Ships*, 3:625–26, 7:113; Gleaves, *History of the Transport Force*, 256, 260; *Record of the Movements*, 553, 262; Crisp and Johnston, "History," 505.

41. *Record of the Movements*, 537, 557, 572; Mooney, *Dictionary of American Naval Fighting Ships*, 3:584; Crisp and Johnston, "History," 504; Wainwright, *Brief History*, 77–80.

42. Mooney, *Dictionary of American Naval Fighting Ships*, 3:127–28, 4:401; Gleaves, *History of the Transport Force*, 262–63; *Record of the Movements*, 572, 575–76, 578; Crisp and Johnston, "History," 504.

43. Mooney, *Dictionary of American Naval Fighting Ships*, 2:27–28, 5:227; Gleaves, *History of the Transport Force*, 262–63; *Record of the Movements*, 535; Crisp and Johnston, "History," 405.

44. Gleaves, *History of the Transport Force*, 180–81; Shanks, *As They Passed Through the Port*, 22, 138, 140, 143.

45. U.S. Navy Department, USS *Princess Matoika*, "Instructions for Army Officers," Wartime, n.d.; Gleaves, *History of the Transport Force*, 182.

46. Gleaves, *History of the Transport Force*, 182–83; U.S. Navy Department, USS *Princess Matoika*, "Instructions for Officers," Wartime, n.d.

47. U.S. Navy Department, Bureau of Construction and Repair, *General Specifications for Fitting Out Troop Transports* (Washington, D.C.: U.S. Government Printing Office, February 1919), 20; Gleaves, *History of the Transport Force*, 187.

48. U.S. Navy Department, Bureau of Construction and Repair, *General Specifications for Fitting Out Troop Transports*, 4, 6, 13–14, 29; U.S. Navy Department, USS *Princess Matoika*, "Instructions for Army Officers," Wartime, n.d.

49. U.S. Navy Department, USS *Princess Matoika*, *The Wigwam* (ship's monthly periodical), vol. 2, no. 1, May 1919, 4–5.

50. Ibid.; U.S. Navy Department, USS *Princess Matoika, The Wigwam* (ship's monthly periodical), vol. 2, no. 4, August 1919, 4, 8; Egner, *Log of the USS* Northern Pacific; U.S. Navy Department, USS *Siboney. Historical Souvenir of the USS* Siboney: *April 8, 1918–August 1, 1919* (Washington, D.C.: Navy Historical Library, Special Collection, n.d.), 22.

51. U.S. Navy Department, USS *Siboney. Historical Souvenir,* 43–46.

52. Wilgus, *Transporting the AEF in Western Europe,* 283, 490, 514–15; Wainwright, *Brief History,* 85–86, 89.

CHAPTER 10. DUTY ON SHORE

1. Navy 1918 Annual Report, 20–21.

2. *Record of the Movements,* 551, 555; Crisp and Johnston, "History," 210a, 211.

3. *Record of the Movements,* 570, 574.

4. Ibid., 545, 556–57; Crisp and Johnston, "History," 218.

5. Navy 1918 Annual Report, 524, 537–38, 544–45, 548–50, 554–56, 558, 565, 570–75; *Record of the Movements,* 544, 545, 548–50, 556, 565, 571–75, 582, 585.

6. *Record of the Movements,* 548, 585; Navy 1918 Annual Report, 537.

7. Navy 1918 Annual Report, 1619; *Record of the Movements,* 550–51; Crisp and Johnston, "History," 302.

8. *Record of the Movements,* 565; Crisp and Johnston, "History," 299.

9. *Record of the Movements,* 552, 559, 564, 581.

10. Ibid., 548, 562, 564, 573.

11. Crisp and Johnston, "History," 216.

12. Ibid., 217; *Record of the Movements,* 546, 551, 558, 564.

13. Navy 1918 Annual Report, 66, 72.

14. Ibid., 78–79.

15. Crisp and Johnston, "History," 230–31; Coast Guard 1918 Register, 32; Navy 1918 Annual Report, 83.

16. U.S. Navy Department, Recruiting Bureau, "Newport Naval Training Station," pamphlet (New York: U.S. Navy Recruiting Bureau Press, 1918).

17. Ibid.

18. Crisp and Johnston, "History," 231–32.

19. Ibid., 232–33.

20. Ibid., 237.

21. Ibid., 237–38; *Record of the Movements,* 562.

22. Coast Guard 1917 Annual Report, 35.

23. Ibid.; Crisp and Johnston, "History," 247.

24. Crisp and Johnston, "History," 36, 207, 247; Navy 1918 Annual Report, 1617; Navy 1919 Annual Report, 2654; E. M. Webster, "Coast Guard Communications," *U.S. Naval Institute Proceedings* (May 1929): 438–39.

25. Crisp and Johnston, "History," 36, 207, 247, 301; Navy 1918 Annual Report, 1617; Navy 1919 Annual Report, 2654; *Record of the Movements*, 555, 557; Webster, "Coast Guard Communications," 438–39.

26. Crisp and Johnston, "History," 183–84, 372; Navy 1918 Annual Report, 1617; Navy 1919 Annual Report, 2654.

27. *Record of the Movements*, 555–57; Crisp and Johnston, "History," 301.

28. *Record of the Movements*, 555–57; Crisp and Johnston, "History," 301, 302.

29. Crisp and Johnston, "History," 305; *Record of the Movements*, 554.

30. Crisp and Johnston, "History," 306–7.

CHAPTER 11. AFTER THE ARMISTICE

1. "Doubt If Wilson Seeks Senate Vote," *New York Times*, 22 February 1919, 2; "President Cheered from Pier to Hotel," *New York Times*, 25 February 1919, 1.

2. "President Cheered," 2.

3. "President to Talk in General Terms at Boston Meeting," *New York Times*, 24 February 1919, 1.

4. "President Cheered," 1.

5. U.S. Congress, House, Committee on Interstate and Foreign Commerce, *Coast Guard Service Hearings on H.R. 13392 [to permanently transfer Coast Guard from Treasury Department to Navy Department] and H.J.R. 382 [directing Coast Guard to resume operations under Treasury Department]*, 13 January 1919, 44 (hereafter cited as U.S. Congress Hearings on H.R. 13392).

6. Ibid.

7. Ibid., 3; Brown, "Overseas," 19.

8. U.S. Congress Hearings on H.R. 13392, 13 January 1919, 52–53.

9. Frank L. Austin Statement, U.S. Congress Hearings on H.R. 13392, 13 January 1919, 5.

10. U.S. Congress Hearings on H.R. 13392, 13 January 1919, 6–7.

11. Ibid., 8–9; J. S. McKean Statement, U.S. Congress Hearings on H.R. 13392, 13 January 1919, 5.

12. U.S. Congress Hearings on H.R. 13392, 13 January 1919, 6, 25.

13. Paul H. Harrison Statement, U.S. Congress Hearings on H.R. 13392, 13 January 1919, 27–28.

14. U.S. Congress Hearings on H.R. 13392, 13 January 1919, 29.

15. Ibid., 5, 12, 27.

16. "Glass Takes Oath as Treasury Head," *New York Times*, 17 December 1918, 2; U.S. Congress Hearings on H.R. 13392, 13 January 1919, 26.

17. U.S. Congress Hearings on H.R. 13392, 13 January 1919, 17–18, 57.

18. U.S. Congress Hearings on H.R. 13392, 6 February 1919, 58–59.

19. Daniels, *Our Navy at War*.

20. U.S. Congress Hearings on H.R. 13392, 6 February 1919, 59.

21. Ellsworth P. Bertholf Statement, U.S. Congress Hearings on H.R. 13392, 6 February 1919, 60–62.

22. Ibid., 62–66, 88.

23. Ibid., 68, 70–71.

24. Ibid., 76–77.

25. Ibid., 83–84.

26. John C. Cantwell Statement, U.S. Congress Hearings on H.R. 13392, 6 February 1919, 93–94, 99–102; Francis S. Van Boskerck Statement, U.S. Congress Hearings on H.R. 13392, 6 February 1919, 104.

27. U.S. Congress Hearings on H.R. 13392, 6 February 1919, 121–22.

28. Guy E. Campbell Letter to Chairman of Committee on Interstate and Foreign Commerce, House of Representatives, 7 February 1919, in U.S. Congress Hearings on H.R. 13392, 6 February 1919, 113; U.S. Congress Hearings on H.R. 13392, 6 February 1919, 124.

29. "Will Press Legislation," *New York Times*, 26 February 1919, 2.

30. Guy E. Campbell Letter to Chairman of Committee on Interstate and Foreign Commerce, House of Representatives, 7 February 1919.

31. U.S. Congress, House, Committee on Interstate and Foreign Commerce, *Coast Guard Service Hearings on H.R. 5516 [to permanently transfer Coast Guard from Treasury Department to Navy Department]*, 27–28 May 1920.

BIBLIOGRAPHY

PRIMARY SOURCES

U.S. Government Records

U.S. Congress. "Act to Create the Coast Guard." *Congressional Record.* 63d Cong., 3d sess., 1915. Vol. 2, pt. 2.

———. House. Committee on Interstate and Foreign Commerce. *Coast Guard Service Hearings on H.R. 13392 [to permanently transfer Coast Guard from Treasury Department to Navy Department] and H.J.R. 382 [directing Coast Guard to resume operations under Treasury Department].* 65th Cong., 3d sess., 13 January and 6 February 1919.

———. *Coast Guard Service Hearings on H.R. 5516 [to permanently transfer Coast Guard from Treasury Department to Navy Department],* 66th Cong., 2d sess., 27–28 May 1920.

———. *Report to Accompany H.R. 9747 [to provide temporary increased rank for officers of Coast Guard while operating as a part of Navy during period of present war].* 65th Cong., 1st sess., 1918, House Doc. 514, Serial 7308.

———. *Report to Accompany H.J.R. 382 [to resume operations under Treasury Department].* 65th Cong., 3d sess., 1919, House Doc. 514, Serial 7308.

U.S. Defense Department. U.S. Navy. "United States Naval Hall of Honor Enshrinement Ceremony." Program. Pensacola, Fla.: U.S. Naval Aviation Museum, 12 May 1983.

———. *U.S. Naval History Sources in the United States.* Washington, D.C.: Naval History Division, 1979.

———. *U.S. Naval History Sources in the Washington Area and Suggested Research Subjects.* Washington, D.C.: U.S. Government Printing Office, 1970.

U.S. National Archives. Record Group 26. Entry 248. U.S. Treasury Department, Coast Guard. *Life Saving Medals 1 June 1903–16 November 1926,* volume 2 of 3.

———. Entry 279. NC-31. Box 9. "Historical Notes, World War I."

———. Entry 279. NC-31. Box 12. "The new Cutter *Tampa* was launched on April 16, 1921."

———. Entry 283. Box 4. U.S. Treasury Department, Coast Guard, Public Relations. "The United States Coast Guard Aviation and the War," 1946, 1.

———. Entry 306. U.S. Treasury Department, Coast Guard. *Citations and Commendations*, volume 1 of 1, canvas bound ledger book, June 1918.

U.S. Navy Department. Aeronautic Station Pensacola, Commandant. "Orders as Naval Aviator." Letter to Third Lieutenant E. F. Stone, USCG File No. 41f237, 10 April 1917.

———. Atlantic Fleet. Commander Cruiser Force and Transport Force, Rear Admiral Albert Gleaves. "Orders for Ships in Convoy: Cruiser Force and Transport Force, 1918." USS *Huntington*, Flagship, 1 January 1918. Washington, D.C.: Navy Historical Center, 1918.

———. Bureau of Construction and Repair. *General Specifications for Fitting Out Troop Transports*. Washington, D.C.: U.S. Government Printing Office, February 1919.

———. Cape May Training Camp. *The Naval Reserve: The Enlisted Man's Paper*, Cape May, N.J., 1918.

———. Coast Guard. Captain Commandant. Letter to Mrs. Bertha L. Earp, "Loss of the Coast Guard Cutter *Tampa*." Washington, D.C., 8 October 1918.

———. Commander Patrol Squadrons Based at Gibraltar. Letter, "First Lieutenant of Engineers M. R. Daniels, USCG, Orders." USS *Buffalo*, Flagship, Ref. 474f1, 29 August 1918.

———. Crew of the USS *James*. Letter to Lt. Cdr. H. G. Hamlet, Commanding Officer, USS *Marietta*, U.S. Naval Base, Brest, France, 7 May 1919.

———. Naval Forces in France. Commanding Officer, USS *Marietta*. "Report of Convoy," 29 April 1919.

———. Recruiting Bureau. "Newport Naval Training Station." Pamphlet. New York: U.S. Navy Recruiting Bureau Press, 1918.

———. Secretary. *Annual Report of the Secretary of the Navy, 1918*. Washington, D.C.: U.S. Government Printing Office, 1918.

———. Secretary. *Annual Report of the Secretary of the Navy, 1919*. Washington, D.C.: U.S. Government Printing Office, 1919.

———. Secretary (Acting) Franklin D. Roosevelt Letter to First Lieutenant Elmer F. Stone, USCG, "Commendation," Washington, D.C., 23 August 1919.

———. *Supplement to the Monthly Navy List, Showing the United States Naval Forces Operating in European Waters, Corrected to September 1st 1918*. London: Harrison and Sons, 1918.

———. USS *Princess Matoika*. "Instructions for Army Officers," Wartime, n.d.

———. USS *Princess Matoika*. *The Wigwam* (ship's monthly periodical), vol. 2, no. 1, May 1919.

———. USS *Princess Matoika. The Wigwam* (ship's monthly periodical), vol. 2, no. 4, August 1919.

———. USS *Siboney. Historical Souvenir of the USS* Siboney: *April 8, 1918–August 1, 1919.* Washington, D.C.: Navy Historical Library, Special Collection, n.d.

U.S. President (Wilson). Executive Order No. 2587 [authorizing Coast Guard to operate as part of Navy, subject to orders of secretary of Navy], 1917.

———. Executive Order No. 3160 [authorizing transfer of operation of Coast Guard from Navy Department to Treasury Department], 1919.

———. "War Message to Congress," 2 April 1917.

U.S. Transportation Department. Coast Guard. Public Information Division. *United States Coast Guard Annotated Bibliography.* Washington, D.C.: U.S. Government Printing Office, 1972.

———. *United States Coast Guard Annotated Bibliography.* Washington, D.C.: U.S. Government Printing Office, 1982.

U.S. Treasury Department. Coast Guard. *Annual Report of the United States Coast Guard, 1915.* Washington, D.C.: U.S. Government Printing Office, 1915.

———. *Annual Report of the United States Coast Guard for the Fiscal Year Ended June 30, 1917.* Washington, D.C.: U.S. Government Printing Office, 1917.

———. *Annual Report of the United States Coast Guard for the Fiscal Year Ended June 30, 1918.* Washington, D.C.: U.S. Government Printing Office, 1918.

———. Assistant Commandant. *Record of the Movements, Vessels of the United States Coast Guard, 1790–December 31, 1933.* Washington, D.C.: U.S. Coast Guard Headquarters, 1934.

———. Auxiliary Training Unit. *The United States Coast Guard: Its History Vessels and Doctrine.* Washington, D.C.: CGA Press, n.d.

———. Captain Commandant Bertholf. Letter to Eastern Division Commander, File No. 311, E1, 46, 3 August 1917.

———. Captain Commandant Bertholf. Letter to Secretary of Treasury, Subj. Class 631, "Cooperation with the Navy: Plans and orders, etc.," 20 March 1915.

———. "Coast Guard Aviation and the Present War." 2 February 1942.

———. Commodore Commandant. "Coast Guard Cutter *Tampa* movements," letter, 30 June 1919, File 601.

———. *Deeds of Valor from the Annals of the United States Coast Guard.* Washington, D.C.: U.S. Government Printing Office, 1943.

———. Headquarters. Commander Richard O. Crisp and Commander Charles E. Johnston. "A History of the Coast Guard in the World War." Unpublished manuscript. Washington, D.C., 1922.

———. Headquarters. Statistical Division. *Captain of the Port.* Washington, D.C.: Statistical Division, U.S. Coast Guard, 1943.

————. *Instructions for Coast Guard Stations, 1921.* Washington, D.C.: U.S. Government Printing Office, 1921.

————. *Mobilization of the U.S. Coast Guard When Required to Operate as a Part of the Navy. Confidential Order No. 2.* Washington, D.C.: U.S. Government Printing Office, 1917.

————. *Naval Orientation.* Washington, D.C.: Bureau of Naval Personnel, 11 August 1947.

————. *Operations of the Coast Guard in Time of War.* Washington, D.C.: U.S. Coast Guard, 1940.

————. *Register of the Officers, Vessels, and Stations of the United States Coast Guard, August 1, 1915.* Washington, D.C.: U.S. Government Printing Office, 1915.

————. *Register of the Officers, Vessels, and Stations of the United States Coast Guard, 1917.* Washington, D.C.: U.S. Government Printing Office, 1917.

————. *Register of the Officers, Vessels, and Stations of the United States Coast Guard, January 1, 1918.* Washington, D.C.: U.S. Government Printing Office, 1918.

————. "Service Record of Francis Patrick Smith, April 4, 1918 to April 7, 1919, Excerpts." Author received copy from grandson David R. Ponstein, 22 July 2001.

————. Station No. 179. "Report of Assistance, August 16, 1918, in Case of British Steamship *Mirlo*." Washington, D.C.: U.S. Coast Guard Historian's Office, Midgett File, 1918.

————. *United States Coast Guard.* Washington, D.C.: U.S. Government Printing Office, 1926.

————. *United States Coast Guard, 1919.* Washington, D.C.: U.S. Government Printing Office, 1919.

————. *United States Coast Guard Roll of Honor, April 6, 1917–November 30, 1918.* Washington, D.C.: U.S. Government Printing Office, 1919.

————. USS *Algonquin* Ship's Logs. 1917–19.

————. USS *Manning* Ship's Logs. 1917–19.

————. USS *Ossipee* Ship's Logs. 1917–19.

————. USS *Seneca* Ship's Logs. 1917–19.

————. USS *Tampa* Ship's Logs. 1917–19.

————. USS *Yamacraw* Ship's Logs. 1917–19.

Unpublished Material

Bertholf, E. P. Letter to E. F. Stone, "Duties in Connection With Aviation," 29 March 1916, Stone File, Coast Guard Historian's Office, Washington, D.C.

Cochran, Hamilton. "Hunting the Hun with the Coast Guard by an American Sailor," 1917–19, File No. MVF-675, Accession No. 1764, U.S. Coast Guard Museum, New London, Conn.

Coffin, E. A. Letter to Paul N. Wells, 6 December 1953, Coast Guard
    Historian's Office, Washington, D.C.

Daniels, Milton R., Jr. Letter to author, 27 February 2001.

———. Telephone conversation with author, 25 February 2001.

Earp, James M. Letter to brother Arthur, 8 September 1918, letter given to
    author by Earp's nephew, Charles A. Earp, 11 December 2001.

"First Coast Guard Aviation Group, Naval Air Sta., Pensacola, Fla., Mar. 22,
    1917," photograph, Elmer F. Stone File, Coast Guard Historian's Office,
    Washington, D.C.

Foulkes, Frederick R. Letters to family, 1917–18, File No. MVF-675, Accession
    No. 1764, U.S. Coast Guard Museum, New London, Conn.

Hand, Bettilou B. "World War I Service of Her Father, John J. Bitting," letter to
    author, 17 September 2001.

Midgett (Daughter of John A. Midgett). "Life Saving Stations," manuscript,
    Midgett File, U.S. Coast Guard Historian's Office, Washington, D.C.

Pace, Ashley D., Jr. "Interview by Captain Pat Wendt and Bill Broughton, Jr.
    concerning his uncle, Coast Guard aviator Elmer Stone," n.d., Stone File,
    U.S. Coast Guard Historian's Office, Washington, D.C.

Ponstein, David R. Interview by author about USCG World War I service of
    Francis P. Smith, Ponstein's grandfather, 31 July 2001.

"Virginia Beach Station, Answer Sheets, Buildings No. 1 through No. 5." 20
    March 1916, Collection of the Old Coast Guard Station Museum, Virginia
    Beach, Va.

"Virginia Beach Station Crew List 1910–1929." Collection of the Old Coast
    Guard Station Museum, Virginia Beach, Va.

Whitney, Harry L., Donald L. Pratt, and William M O'Connor, eds. "A Brief
    Retrospective Summary of Our Work Experiences in the World War Aboard
    the USS *Algonquin*, CG, 1917–1919," 1919, File No. MVF 675, Accession No.
    1764, U.S. Coast Guard Museum, New London, Conn.

SECONDARY SOURCES

Alden, John D. "The Yacht That Was a Destroyer." U.S. Naval Institute
    Proceedings (December 1967): 156–59.

Allard, Dean C., and Betty Bern, *U.S. Naval History Sources in the Washington Area and
    Suggested Research Subjects*. Washington, D.C.: Naval History Division, Office of
    Chief of Naval Operations, U.S. Navy Department, 1970.

Ayres, Leonard P. *The War with Germany: A Statistical Summary*. Washington,
    D.C.: U.S. Government Printing Office, 1919.

Beall, Irv V. "Epic Cruise of the USS *Morrill*." *Sparks Journal* (n.d.): 24–30.

"Begin Shell Plant Rebuilding Today." *New York Times*, 7 October 1918, 1.

Bell, Kensil. *Always Ready.* New York: Dodd, Mead and Company, 1943.

Bennett, Robert F. *The Lifesaving Service at Sandy Hook Station, 1854–1915.* Washington, D.C.: Public Affairs Division, United States Coast Guard, 1976.

———. *Sand Pounders.* Washington, D.C.: U.S. Coast Guard Historian's Office, 1998.

———. *Surfboats, Rockets, and Carronades.* Washington, D.C.: Department of Transportation, 1976.

Bloomfield, Howard V. L. *The Compact History of the United States Coast Guard.* New York: Hawthorn Books, 1966.

Breckel, H. F. "The Suicide Flotilla." U.S. Naval Institute *Proceedings* (June 1921): 661–70.

Bridgewater, William, ed., *The Columbia Viking Desk Encyclopedia.* New York: Viking Press, 1953.

Brief Sketch of the Naval History of the United States Coast Guard with Citations of Various Statutes Defining Its Military Status from 1790 to 1933. Washington, D.C.: Byron and Adams, 1922.

Brown, Fletcher W. "Overseas: 1917–1918." Booklet. Personal monograph, n.p., n.d.

Browning, Robert M., Jr. *Captains of the Port.* Washington, D.C.: U.S. Coast Guard Historian, 1993.

Buckley, Joseph D. *Wings Over Cape Cod: A History of the Chatham Naval Air Station, 1917–1922.* Orleans, Mass.: Lower Cape Publishing, 2000.

Canney, Donald L. *U.S. Coast Guard and Revenue Cutters, 1790–1935.* Annapolis: Naval Institute Press, 1995.

Capron, Walter C. *The U.S. Coast Guard.* New York: Franklin Watts, 1965.

"Captain Says U-35 Sank *Housatonic.*" *New York Times,* 21 February 1917, 2.

"Centennial Issue: Class Listings." *The Bulletin.* New London, Conn.: U.S. Coast Guard Academy Alumni Association, 1976.

"Centennial Issue: Register of Graduates." *The Bulletin.* New London, Conn.: U.S. Coast Guard Academy Alumni Association, 1976.

Chewning, Alpheus J. *The Approaching Storm: U-boats off the Virginia Coast During World War II.* Lively, Va.: Brandylane, 1994.

Clephane, Lewis P. *History of the Naval Overseas Transportation Service in World War I.* Washington, D.C.: U.S. Government Printing Office, 1969.

"Crews Dispossessed Early this Morning on Port Collector's Orders." *New York Times,* 6 April 1917, 1.

Crump, Irving. *Our United States Coast Guard Academy.* New York: Dodd Mead and Company, 1961.

Daniels, Josephus. *Our Navy at War.* New York: George H. Doran, 1922.

———. "The United States Navy in the World War." *North Carolina Historical Review* (January 1927): 115–26.

"Day of Explosions and Fire Finishes Shell Plant Ruin." *New York Times*, 5 October 1918, 1.

"Depicts Suffering of *Healdton* Crew." *New York Times*, 27 March 1917, 4.

"Doubt If Wilson Seeks Senate Vote." *New York Times*, 22 February 1919, 2.

Edmison, Mary W., Martha L Crawley, and Dean C. Allard, *U.S. Naval History Sources in the United States*. Washington, D.C.: Naval History Division, U.S. Department of the Navy, U.S. Government Printing Office, 1979.

"Effort To Fly Overseas." *New York Times*, 11 May 1919, 4:1.

Egner, P. R. *The Log of the USS* Northern Pacific *During the Great War. A True Story of the Adventures of the USS* Northern Pacific *During the War*. New York: Brooklyn Eagle Press, 1919.

Enser, A. G. S. *A Subject Bibliography of the First World War: Books in English 1914–1978*. London: Andre Deutsch, 1979.

Erickson, Frank A. "The Transatlantic Flight." *U.S. Coast Guard Academy Alumni Bulletin* (May/June 1977): 18–23.

"Espionage Bill Is Signed." *New York Times*, 16 June 1917, 10.

"Establishment of a Coast Guard." *New York Times*, 31 January 1915.

Evans, Stephen H. *The United States Coast Guard, 1790–1915: A Definitive History*. Annapolis: U.S. Naval Institute, 1949.

Farwell, Byron. *Over There: The United States in Great War, 1917–1918*. New York: W. W. Norton, 1999.

Flying Officers of the USN. Atglen, Pa.: Schiffer Military History, 1997.

Foner, Eric, and John A Garraty, eds., *The Reader's Companion to American History*, Boston: Houghton Mifflin, 1991.

"14 Seized Steamers Receive New Names." *New York Times*, 5 June 1917, 17.

"Gasoline Cargo Exploded." *New York Times*, 18 August 1918, 6.

"German Officers Held." *New York Times*, 10 April 1917, 4.

"German Ships Seized by the Government." *New York Times*, 7 April 1917, 2.

"Glass Takes Oath as Treasury Head," *New York Times*, 17 December 1918, 2.

Gleaves, Albert. *History of the Transport Force: Adventures and Experiences of United States Transports and Cruisers in the World War*. New York: George H. Doran, 1921.

"Great Munitions Plant Blown Up." *New York Times*, 5 October 1918, 1.

Grossnick, Roy A. *United States Naval Aviation 1910–1995*. Washington, D.C.: U.S. Government Printing Office, 1998.

"*Halifax* Wrecked: More Than One Thousand Killed in this City, Many Thousands Are Injured and Homeless." *Halifax Herald*, 7 December 1917, 1.

Halpern, Paul G. *A Naval History of World War I*. Annapolis: Naval Institute Press, 1994.

"*Housatonic* Captain Made Protest in Vain." *New York Times*, 6 February 1917, 1–2.

Hurd, Archibald, and H. H. Bashford, *The Heroic Record of the British Navy: A Short History of the Naval War 1914–1918*. Garden City, N.Y.: Doubleday, Page and Company, 1919.

Ingraham, Reg. *The First Fleet: The Story of the U. S. Coast Guard at War*. Cornwall, N.Y.: Cornwall Press, 1944.

"Investigate Aerial Bombs." *New York Times*, 24 July 1918, 6.

Johnson, Robert E. *Guardians of the Sea: History of the United States Coast Guard 1915 to the Present*. Annapolis: Naval Institute Press, 1987.

Kaplan, K. R., and James L. Hunt, *This Is the Coast Guard*. Cambridge, Md.: Maritime Press, 1972.

Kauffman, Reginald W. *Our Navy at Work: The Yankee Fleet in French Waters*. Indianapolis: Bobbs-Merrill, 1918.

Kern, Florence, and Barbara Voulgaris, *Traditions: 200 Years of History*. Washington, D.C.: U.S. Coast Guard Public Affairs, n.d.

Kerr, Evor Samuel, Jr. *The United States Coast Guard: Its Ships Duties, Stations*. New York: Robert W. Kelly, 1935.

Lawrence, Perry. *Our Navy in the War*. New York: Charles Scribner's Sons, 1922.

Layman, R. D. *Naval Aviation in the First World War*. Annapolis: Naval Institute Press, 1996.

Maxam, Oliver M. "The Life Saving Stations of the Coast Guard." U.S. Naval Institute *Proceedings* (May 1929): 374–80.

McMaster, John B. *The United States in the World War: 1918–1920*. New York: D. Appleton-Century, 1940.

Metson, Graham, ed. *The Halifax Explosion: December 6, 1917*. New York: McGraw-Hill Ryerson, 1978.

Minnoch, Jim. "Blast in Halifax." *Camaraderie: The Journal of the United States Branch, The Western Front Association* (July 2001): 7–11.

———. "U-boat Ace Forever." *Camaraderie: The Journal of the United States Branch, The Western Front Association* (March 2001): 4–7.

Mitchell, Thornton W., and Arthur Dyer, *List of Logs of United States Coast Guard Vessels in the National Archives, 1790–1941*. Washington, D.C.: National Archives, compiled by Treasury Department, Division of Archives, 1944.

Mooney, James L., ed. *Dictionary of American Naval Fighting Ships*, 8 vols. Washington, D.C.: Navy Historical Center, 1959–1991.

"Naval War Notes." U.S. Naval Institute *Proceedings* (October 1918): 2667.

"Navy and Reserves Ordered Mobilized." *New York Times*, 7 April 1917, 6.

"Navy Boats Land 2,100 More from *Northern Pacific*." *New York Times*, 4 January 1919, 1, 5.

"Navy Without Information." *New York Times*, 23 July 1918, 1.

"New Post for Coast Guard Captain." *New York Times*, 16 December 1917, 5.

Noble, Dennis L. *That Others Might Live: The U.S. Life Saving Service, 1878–1915.* Annapolis: Naval Institute Press, 1994.

"Official Log of the Flight." *New York Times,* 18 May 1919, 1.

The Old Coast Guard Station: A Brief History. Virginia Beach, Va.: Old Coast Guard Station Museum Staff, 1 December 2000.

O'Leary, Robert J. "Victory Denied: The Battle of Chatham." *The Bulletin.* New London, Conn.: U.S. Coast Guard Academy Alumni Association, October 1998, 23–24.

Paine, Ralph D. *The Corsair in the War Zone.* Boston: Houghton Mifflin, 1920.

Pearcy, Arthur. *A History of U.S. Coast Guard Aviation.* Annapolis: Naval Institute Press, 1989.

———. *U.S. Coast Guard Aircraft Since 1916.* Annapolis: Naval Institute Press, 1992.

Pendergast, Maurice, ed. *Jane's Fighting Ships, 1918.* London: Sampson Low, Marston and Company, Ltd., 1918.

Perry, Glen. *Watchmen of the Sea.* New York: Charles Scribner's Sons, 1938.

"President Cheered from Pier to Hotel." *New York Times,* 25 February 1919, 1.

"President to Talk in General Terms at Boston Meeting." *New York Times,* 24 February 1919, 1.

"President's Proclamation of a State of War, and Regulations Governing Alien Enemies." *New York Times,* 7 April 1917, 1.

Rankin, Robert H., and Norman N. Rubin. "The Story of Coast Guard Aviation." U.S. Naval Institute *Proceedings* (June 1959): 86–89.

Raquet, Edward C. "United States Submarine Chasers at Gibraltar, November 1918." U.S. Naval Institute *Proceedings* (December 1936): 1703–11.

Reisinger, Harold C. "The Flying Lifeboats of the Coast Guard." U.S. Naval Institute *Proceedings* (January 1933): 81–88.

Riesenberg, Felix. *Standard Seamanship for the Merchant Marine.* New York: D. Van Nostrand, n.d.

Romig, Donald K. *History of the USS Great Northern During the War: The Fastest Navy Troop Transport.* Brooklyn, N.Y.: Eagle Press, 1919.

"Roosevelt Would Ostracize Slackers." *New York Times,* 18 June 1917, 7.

Rose, H. Wickliffe. *Brittany Patrol: The Story of the Suicide Fleet.* New York: W. W. Norton, 1937.

Rose, H. Wickliffe, and Felix Riesenberg, *Standard Seamanship for the Merchant Marine.* New York: D. Van Nostrand, n.d.

"*San Diego* Loss Still Unexplained." *New York Times,* 21 July 1918, 7.

"Schedule of NC-4's Eventful Flight From Rockaway to the Portuguese Capitol." *New York Times,* 28 May 1919, 2.

Scheina, Robert L. "A History of Coast Guard Aviation." *Commandant's Bulletin* 21-86. 10 October 1986.

"Seven American Ships Sunk, Costing 36 Lives, Since Feb. 1." *New York Times*, 23 March 1917, 1.

"7 Americans Lost on *Healdton*." *New York Times*, 24 March 1917, 1.

Shanks, David C. *As They Passed Through the Port*. Washington, D.C.: Cary Publishing, 1927.

Smith, Darrell H., and Fred W. Powell. *The Coast Guard: Its History, Activities and Organization*. Service Monographs of the U.S. Government, no. 51. Washington, D.C.: Brookings Institute, 1929.

Smith, Myron J. *World War I in the Air: A Bibliography and Chronology*. Metuchen, N.J.: Scarecrow Press, 1977.

Stick, David. *Graveyard of the Atlantic*. Chapel Hill, N.C.: University of North Carolina Press, 1952.

"Stood at Wheel When Shell Hit His Arm." *New York Times*, 22 July 1918, 6.

"Sunk after Explosion." *New York Times*, 20 July 1918, 4.

Taussig, Joseph K. "Destroyer Experience During the Great War." U.S. Naval Institute *Proceedings* (December 1922): 2015–40; (January–March 1923): 39–69, 221–48, 383–408.

"Ten Americans Perish Trying to Save Ship." *New York Times*, 22 September 1918, 5.

"Text of President Wilson's Address." *New York Times*, 4 February 1917, 1.

Thomas, Lowell. *Raiders of the Deep*. Garden City, N.Y.: Garden City Publishing Co., 1932.

"Torpedo Set Fire to Tanker; 10 Dead." *New York Times*, 18 August 1918, 6.

Traditions of Gallantry: Graduates of the U.S. Coast Guard. New London, Conn.: U.S. Coast Guard Academy Alumni Association, 1992.

"Transport Ashore Off Fire Island, 3,000 Aboard Safe." *New York Times*, 2 January 1919, 1–2.

Tuchman, Barbara W. *The Guns of August*. 1962. Reprint. New York: Ballantine Books, 1990.

———. *The Zimmermann Telegram*. 1958. Reprint. New York: Ballantine Books, 1994.

"27 Ships Taken Here." *New York Times*, 7 April 1917, 1–2.

Tyler, Fielding L. *Stand By Your Oars: A History of the Seatack/Virginia Beach Life-Saving/Coast Guard Station*. Virginia Beach, Va.: Virginia Beach Maritime Museum, September 1999.

"U-boat Gives No Warning." *New York Times*, 22 July 1918, 1.

U.S. Coast Guard Aviation. Paducah, Ky.: Turner Publishing, 1997.

"USS *Tampa* Sunk, Crew of 118 Lost." *New York Times*, 4 October 1918, 1.

Van Boskerck, F. S. "The United States Coast Guard: Its Military Necessities." U.S. Naval Institute *Proceedings* (April 1919): 623–36.

Van Wyen, Adrian O. *Naval Aviation in World War I*. Washington, D.C.: Chief of

Naval Operations, U.S. Government Printing Office, 1969.

"Veteran's Day Ceremony Honors WWI *Tampa* Crew, Purple Hearts Awarded Posthumously." *The Reservist* (December 1999): 7.

Waesche, Russell R. "Armament and Gunnery in the Coast Guard." U.S. Naval Institute *Proceedings* (May 1929): 381–84.

Wainwright, Lawrence. *A Brief History of the U.S. Naval Forces in France from 11 November 1918 to 1 October 1919.* Brest, France: USS *Bridgeport,* 1919.

"War-Bound German Ships Here Seized." *New York Times,* 7 April 1917, 2.

Webster, E. M. "Coast Guard Communications." U.S. Naval Institute *Proceedings* (May 1929): 438–39.

Wechter, Nell Wise. *The Mighty Midgetts of Chicamacomico.* Nanto, N.C.: Times Printing, 1974.

Wells, H. G. *The Outline of History.* Garden City, N.Y.: Garden City Books, 1956.

Wheeler, William J. "Reminiscences of World War Convoy Work." U.S. Naval Institute *Proceedings* (May 1929): 385–92.

Wilgus, William J. *Transporting the AEF in Western Europe, 1917–1919.* New York: Columbia University Press, 1931.

"Will Press Legislation." *New York Times,* 26 February 1919, 2.

Wilson, Henry Braid. *An Account of the Operations of the American Navy in France During the War with Germany.* Written aboard USS *Pennsylvania:* n.p., n.d.

Woodward, David R., and Maddox, Robert F. *America and World War I: A Selected Annotated Bibliography of English-Language Sources.* New York: Garland, 1985.

INDEX

Stika, Joseph E., 172, 175–78

Stiness, Walter R., 252, 254

St. Luc, 115

Stone, Elmer F.: and coast guard,
　137–39; flight training, 140–43;
　Huntington aviation detachment,
　143–44; transatlantic flight, 144–46

Stromberg, William T., 96, 213

submarine chasers, 44

submarines, German: attack position,
　100; attacks on troop ships,
　124–25; countermeasures and
　detection, 195–96, 199; damaged
　U-boat interned at Spanish port,
　122; in French waters, 147–48; in
　Mediterranean Sea, 116–17; mine
　planting, 105, 124; night attacks,
　66; surfaced attacks, 64; unre-
　stricted warfare, 3, 4, 6

Sugden, Charles E.: aviation training,
　140–42; at Air Station, Ile Tudy,
　France, 146, 148–49

superintendents, district, 10, 156

Supervisor of the Harbor, Brest,
　France, 179

surfboat, Beebe-McLellan, 152–53,
　165, 167

surfmen, 155, 156, 158–61, 242

Surveyor, 117, 119–20

Swanburg, Charles, 197

T. A. Gillespie and Company,
　Morgan City, N.J., explosions and
　fire, 170–78

Takana, 176, 185

Tallapoosa, 14, 35, 38, 86, 95, 192

Tampa: description and crew, 11, 43;
　duties, 14, 38, 39; deployed over-
　seas, 39–41, 44; sinking, 47–50;

accomplishments, 49; convoy duty,
　50, 51, 58, 59, 67; coastal patrol, 83

Tampa (new cutter), 45

Tangier, Morocco, 58, 78, 117

Tapley, J. H., 134–35

Taranto, Italy, 127

Teresa, 107–8

Texan, 210–11

Thomas, R. G., 139

Thorn, Benjamin C., 210

Todd, Clement J., 224

Tompkinsville, N.Y., 37

Torbet, Mason W., 222

towing, 92–95

training, 95–97

Training Station, Cape May, 245

transatlantic flight, 144–46

Tras Os Montes, 136–38

Trebes, John, Jr., 129, 208

troop transports: accommodations,
　meals, and duties, 214–17; depar-
　ture, 213–14; foreign, 201, 218–19;
　recreation, 217–18; submarine
　attacks, 125. *See also individual ships*

Turkey, surrender of, 117

Turner, John B., 131

Tuscarora, 85, 95, 96, 98

Tuttle, Joseph D., 163

Tybee, 89, 192

U-20, 6

U-53, 4–6

U-91, 48

U-117, 154

U-140, 167–69

U-156, 134–37

Uberroth, Preston H., 95

U-boat. *See* submarines, German

Ulke, Henry, 84

ABOUT THE AUTHOR

Alex Larzelere is a retired coast guard captain who served on seven cutters, five of which he commanded. His assignments included duty as the first coast guard aide to the president, two commands ashore, congressional affairs, chief of search and rescue and chief of staff for the Seventh Coast Guard District in Miami. Larzelere graduated from the Coast Guard Academy, the Naval War College, where he was a distinguished graduate, and the National War College. He also holds a master's degree in international affairs from George Washington University. While a senior fellow at the National Defense University, he wrote *The 1980 Cuban Boatlift*, which appeared in 1988. The American Library Association selected it as a Notable Document. His book, *The Coast Guard at War: Vietnam 1965–1975*, appeared in 1997 and details his experiences as a patrol boat skipper in Southeast Asia. Among other awards, Larzelere has received the Legion of Merit from President Richard M. Nixon and the Bronze Star with Combat V. He lives with his wife Rita in Alexandria, Virginia.